This book comes with access to more content online.

Quiz yourself, track your progress,
and score high on test day!

Register your book or ebook at
www.dummies.com/go/getaccess.

Select your product, and then follow the prompts
to validate your purchase.

You'll receive an email with your PIN and instructions.

GED® Test 2022/2023

5th Edition with Online Practice

by Tim Collins, PhD

A Wiley Brand

GED® Test 2022/2023 For Dummies®, 5th Edition with Online Practice

Published by: **John Wiley & Sons, Inc.**, 111 River Street, Hoboken, NJ 07030-5774, www.wiley.com

Copyright © 2022 by John Wiley & Sons, Inc., Hoboken, New Jersey

Published simultaneously in Canada

No part of this publication may be reproduced, stored in a retrieval system or transmitted in any form or by any means, electronic, mechanical, photocopying, recording, scanning or otherwise, except as permitted under Sections 107 or 108 of the 1976 United States Copyright Act, without the prior written permission of the Publisher. Requests to the Publisher for permission should be addressed to the Permissions Department, John Wiley & Sons, Inc., 111 River Street, Hoboken, NJ 07030, (201) 748-6011, fax (201) 748-6008, or online at http://www.wiley.com/go/permissions.

Trademarks: Wiley, For Dummies, the Dummies Man logo, Dummies.com, Making Everything Easier, and related trade dress are trademarks or registered trademarks of John Wiley & Sons, Inc., and may not be used without written permission. The GED® and GED® Testing Service brands are administered by GED Testing Service LLC under license from American Council on Education. All other trademarks are the property of their respective owners. John Wiley & Sons, Inc., is not associated with any product or vendor mentioned in this book. All other trademarks are the property of their respective owners. John Wiley & Sons, Inc., is not associated with any product or vendor mentioned in this book.

For general information on our other products and services, please contact our Customer Care Department within the U.S. at 877-762-2974, outside the U.S. at 317-572-3993, or fax 317-572-4002. For technical support, please visit https://hub.wiley.com/community/support/dummies.

Wiley publishes in a variety of print and electronic formats and by print-on-demand. Some material included with standard print versions of this book may not be included in e-books or in print-on-demand. If this book refers to media such as a CD or DVD that is not included in the version you purchased, you may download this material at http://booksupport.wiley.com. For more information about Wiley products, visit www.wiley.com.

Library of Congress Control Number: 2021950171

ISBN 978-1-119-67723-9 (pbk); ISBN 978-1-119-67722-2 (ebk); ISBN 978-1-119-67724-6 (ebk)

SKY10031987_121521

Contents at a Glance

Table of Contents

PART 2: MINDING YOUR PS AND QS: THE REASONING THROUGH LANGUAGE ARTS TEST 57

Introduction

Perhaps you've applied for a job and have been turned down because you don't have a high-school diploma or a GED. Or maybe you were up for a promotion at work, but when your boss found out that you didn't finish high school, she said you weren't eligible for the new job. Maybe you've always wanted to go to college but couldn't even apply because the college of your choice requires a high-school diploma or GED for admission. Or perhaps your kids are just about to graduate from high school, and you're motivated to finish, too. Perhaps you just want to set a good example for them.

Whatever your reasons for wanting to earn a high-school diploma — whether we've mentioned them here or not — this book is for you. It helps you to prepare for the computer-based GED test — which, if you pass, offers you the equivalent of a high-school diploma without attending all the classes.

About This Book

If you want a high-school diploma, you can always go back and finish high school the old-fashioned way. Of course, it may take you a few years, and you may have to quit your job to do it. Plus, you'd have to sit in a class with teenagers for six or so hours a day (and probably be treated like one, too). You could also try night school, but at one or two courses a year, that could take forever.

For most people, that situation doesn't sound too appealing. *GED Test For Dummies,* 5th Edition, presents a different solution: Earn a high-school diploma and do so in the shortest time possible, without ever having to share a classroom with other people. If you don't mind preparing yourself for a series of challenging test sections that determine whether you've mastered key skills, you can get a GED diploma that's the equivalent of a high-school education — and you can do so in much less than four years.

If taking the GED test to earn your diploma sounds like a great idea to you, this book is a necessary study tool. It's a fun-filled and friendly instruction manual for succeeding on the all-computerized GED test. Use this book as your first stop. It isn't a subject-matter preparation book — that is, it doesn't take you through the basics of math and then progress into algebra, geometry, and so on. It does, however, prepare you for the GED test by giving you detailed information about each section, two full-length practice tests for each section, a complete online test, and plenty of easy-to-understand answers and explanations for the test questions. After taking the practice tests and going through the answers and explanations, you can determine which subject areas you need to work on.

Just as important, we walk you through how to take and pass the test using a computer. Although people needing special accommodations may still have access to the old paper-and-pencil test format, for most, it's now offered only on a computer. Having basic computer knowledge is very important. Some of the question formats have changed as well, so knowing how to use the computer mouse and keyboard to answer them is also important.

A Few Assumptions

When we wrote this book, we made a few assumptions about you, dear reader. Here's who we think you are:

>> You're serious about earning your GED as quickly as you can.

>> You've made earning a GED a priority in your life because you want to advance in the workplace or move on to college.

>> You're willing to give up some activities so you have the time to prepare, always keeping in mind your other responsibilities, too.

>> You meet your state's requirements regarding age, residency, and the length of time since leaving school that make you eligible to take the GED test. (You can find these on the GED Testing Service's website, ged.com.)

>> You have sufficient English language skills to handle the test (or sufficient Spanish language skills if you take the test in Spanish).

>> You want a fun and friendly guide that helps you achieve your goal.

If any of these descriptions sounds like you, welcome aboard. We've prepared an enjoyable tour of the GED test.

Icons Used in This Book

Icons — little pictures you see in the margins of this book — highlight bits of text that you want to pay special attention to. Here's what each one means:

TIP

Whenever we want to tell you a special trick or technique that can help you succeed on the GED test, we mark it with this icon. Keep an eye out for this guy.

REMEMBER

This icon points out information you want to burn into your brain. Think of the text with this icon as the sort of stuff you'd tear out and put on a bulletin board or your refrigerator.

WARNING

Take this icon seriously! Although the world won't end if you don't heed the advice next to this icon, the warnings are important to your success in preparing to take the GED test.

EXAMPLE

We use this icon to flag example questions that are much like what you can expect on the actual GED test. So if you just want to get familiar with the types of questions on the test, this icon is your guide.

Beyond the Book

For some helpful advice to prepare for and succeed on the GED, check out the online Cheat Sheet. Just go to www.dummies.com and type in "GED Test For Dummies Cheat Sheet" in the search box.

In addition to all of the tips, study aids, and practice that this book provides, you can go online and work through three full-length practice tests. All you have to do is register by following these simple steps:

1. **Register your book or ebook at Dummies.com to get your PIN. Go to** www.dummies.com/go/getaccess.

2. **Select your product from the dropdown list on that page.**

3. **Follow the prompts to validate your product, and then check your email for a confirmation message that includes your PIN and instructions for logging in.**

If you do not receive this email within two hours, please check your spam folder before contacting us through our Technical Support website at http://support.wiley.com or by phone at 877-762-2974.

Now you're ready to go! You can come back to the practice material as often as you want. Simply log on with the username and password you created during your initial login. No need to enter the access code a second time.

Your registration is good for one year from the day you activate your PIN.

Where to Go from Here

Some people like to read books from beginning to end. Others prefer to read only the specific information they need to know now.

Chapter 1 starts off with an overview of the GED test and how to register for the exam. For those less comfortable with computers, Chapter 2 provides a lot more detail about the computerized GED test and what computer basics you need to know. If you want an overview of the different types of questions and how you can prepare for those subjects, check out Chapter 3. Chapter 4 gives you plenty of hands-on material to help you leading up to and the morning of test day, including what to do right before the test starts.

The chapters in Parts 2, 3, 4, and 5 go into detail about each of the test sections, starting with Reasoning through Language Arts, then Social Studies, Science, and finally Mathematical Reasoning. In each of those parts, you can find an introduction to the specific test section, along with question types and solving strategies, and some practice questions. When you're ready to dive into full-length practice tests that mimic the real GED test, check out Parts 6 and 7 and then check your answers with the detailed answer explanations we provide for each test section. (Just be sure to wait until *after* you take the practice test to look at the answers!)

1

Getting Started with the GED Test

Discover how the GED test and its various sections are organized and what to expect on the test.

Get familiar with each test section's specific focus and manner of dealing with the content.

Explore the format of the computerized GED test, including how the questions are presented and how you're expected to answer them.

Prepare for the actual test day, and find out what you should or shouldn't do on the day(s) before, the day of, and during the exam.

Chapter **1**

A Quick Glance at the GED Test

The GED test offers people without a high school diploma the opportunity to earn the equivalent of an American high school diploma without the need for full-time attendance in either day or night school. The GED test is a recognized standard that makes securing a job or starting college easier.

The recently revised test is in line with current Grade 12 standards in the United States and meets the College and Career Readiness Standards for Adult Education. The GED test also covers the Common Core Standards, used by 41 states. These standards are based on the actual expectations stated by employers and postsecondary institutions.

The GED test measures whether you understand what high school seniors across the country have studied before they graduate. Employers seek better-educated employees. Colleges want to make sure students are qualified. When you pass the GED test, you earn a high school equivalency diploma that can open many doors for you — perhaps doors that you don't even know exist at this point.

You may wonder why you should even bother taking the GED test and getting your GED diploma. One reason is that people with high school diplomas earn more and spend less time unemployed than people without diplomas. In a recent year, unemployment for people without a high school diploma was 5.9 percent. That dropped to 3.7 percent for individuals with a diploma or a GED certificate. Incomes were about 25 percent higher for high school or GED graduates than people without diplomas. In addition, your GED can qualify you for even more education. Earnings increase and unemployment decreases at each level of education from associate's degree on up. Even with just some college, you can earn more, on average.

Ready to get started? This chapter gives you the basics of the GED test: how the test is administered, what the test sections look like, how to schedule the test (and whether you're eligible), and how the scores are calculated (so you know what you need to pass).

What to Expect: The Testing Format

There are two options for taking the GED. You can take the GED at a testing center or online at home. (The GED Testing Service calls the at-home version the "online-proctored" GED.) Either way, a computer administers the GED test. That means that all the questions appear on a computer screen, and you enter all your answers into a computer. You read, calculate, evaluate, analyze, and write everything on the computer, including rough math calculations or outlining your essay. Instead of paper, the test centers provide you with an erasable tablet, or you use an onscreen whiteboard.

If you know how to use a computer and are comfortable with a keyboard and a mouse, you're ahead of the game. If not, practice your keyboarding. Also, practice reading from a computer screen because reading from a screen is very different from reading printed materials. At the very least, you need to get more comfortable with computers, even if that means taking a short course at a local learning emporium. In the case of the GED test, the more familiar you are with computers, the more comfortable you'll feel taking the test.

If you have a special need, you are also covered. The GED offers accommodations so that all test-takers have a fair chance. You can indicate that you need accommodations when you open your account on ged.com, or later, by updating your profile.

TIP

Throughout this book, you see references to the GED Testing Service's website, ged.com. It's a great repository of information, learning aids, and online practice tests. It's also where you sign up to take the test. If you don't have an account there, now is a good time to open one. Just go to ged.com, select Sign Up, and follow the prompts.

The GED test provides speedy, detailed feedback on your performance. When you pass (yes, I said *when* and not *if*, because I believe in you), the GED Testing Service provides both a diploma and a detailed transcript of your scores, similar to what high school graduates receive. These are now available in your online account at ged.com within a day of completing the test. You can then send your transcript and diploma to an employer or college. Doing so allows employers and colleges access to a detailed outline of your scores, achievement, and demonstrated skills and abilities. This outline is also a useful tool for you to review your progress. It highlights those areas where you did well and areas where you need further work. If you want to (or have to) retake the test, your score report will provide a detailed guide to what you should work on to improve your scores. Requests for additional copies of transcripts are handled online and also are available within a day.

Reviewing the Test Sections

The GED test includes the following four sections (also referred to as tests), each of which you can take separately:

>> Reasoning through Language Arts

>> Social Studies

>> Science

>> Mathematical Reasoning

REMEMBER

You can take each of the four test sections separately, at different times, and in any order you want. You can also take some of them online at home and others at a testing center. This flexibility is one of the benefits of doing the test by computer. Because everyone is working individually on the various test sections rather than as a group, the computer-based test eliminates the need for the whole group of test-takers to work in tandem. For example, you may be working on the Mathematical Reasoning test, while your neighbor is working on the Social Studies test. Just don't look around at all your neighbors to verify this because proctors may think you're doing more than satisfying your curiosity.

The following sections offer a closer look into what the test sections cover and what you can expect.

Because the GED tests are always evolving, be sure to check out the latest and greatest about the GED program at ged.com.

Reasoning through Language Arts test

The Reasoning through Language Arts (RLA) test is one long test that covers all the literacy components of the GED test. You have 150 minutes overall. However, the test is divided into three sections: first, you have 35 minutes of reading comprehension questions, then 45 minutes for the Extended Response (essay), followed by a 10-minute break, and then another 60 minutes for grammar and language questions. Remember that the time for the Extended Response can't be used to work on the other questions in the test, nor can you use leftover time from the other sections on the Extended Response.

Here's what you can expect on the RLA test:

>> The reading component asks you to demonstrate a critical understanding of various passages.

>> The Extended Response item, also known as "the essay," examines your skills in organizing your thoughts and writing clearly. Your response will be based on one or two source text selections, drawing key elements from that material to prepare your essay.

The essay is evaluated both on your interpretation of the source texts and the quality of your writing. You type on the computer, using a tool that resembles a word processor. It has neither a spell-checker nor a grammar-checker. How well you use spelling and grammar as you write is also part of your evaluation. You'll have an erasable tablet and/or an onscreen whiteboard on which to write notes or an outline before writing your essay on the computer.

>> The grammar and language component asks you to correct errors in various kinds of texts. This includes demonstrating a command of proper grammar, punctuation, and spelling.

>> The scores from all three components will be combined into one single score for the RLA test.

The question-answer part of this test consists mainly of various types of multiple-choice questions and drop-down menu questions with four answer choices. You'll also see drag-and-drop questions. For details on the different question types, see Chapters 2 and 3.

The questions are based on source texts, which are materials presented to you for your response. Some of this source material is nonfiction, from science and social studies content as well as from the workplace. Only 25 percent is based on literature. Here's a breakdown of the materials.

>> **Workplace and community materials:** These include work-related letters, memos, and instructions that you may see on the job. They also include letters and documents from companies and community organizations, such as banks, hospitals, libraries, credit unions, and local governments.

>> **U.S. founding documents and documents that present part of the Great American Conversation:** These may include extracts from the Bill of Rights, the Constitution, and other historical documents. They also may include opinion pieces on relevant issues in American history and civics.

>> **Informational works:** These include documents that present information (often dry and boring information), such as the instructional manual that tells you how to set the clock on your DVD player. They also include materials that you may find in history, social studies, or science books.

>> **Literature:** These include extracts from novels and short stories.

TIP

See Chapter 3 for a more detailed overview of the RLA test. Chapters 6 and 7 give the lowdown on both the reading comprehension questions and the grammar and language questions. I devote two whole chapters (Chapters 8 and 9) to helping you with the essay. For practice, see Chapters 19 and 27 for two complete Reasoning through Language Arts tests, with answers and explanations in Chapters 20 and 28. I also provide a third, complete online-only test. Check out Chapter 2 for the format of the questions as they appear on the computer.

Social Studies test

The Social Studies test is scheduled for 70 minutes for the 50 questions. On this test, you will see standard multiple-choice questions, as well as fill-in-the-blank questions, drag-and-drop questions, and drop-down menu questions. A few questions may ask you to calculate an answer. In this case, a calculator icon will appear on your test screen, or you can bring your TI-30XS MultiView calculator if you test at a test center. In Chapter 3, you can see examples of these questions.

The questions are based on various kinds of source texts. About half of the questions are based on one source text, such as a graph or short reading, with one question. Other questions have a single source text as the basis for several questions. In either case, you'll need to analyze and evaluate the content presented to you as part of the question. A few questions may ask you to compare and contrast information from two different sources. The test questions evaluate your ability to use reasoning and analysis skills. The information for the source materials comes from primary and secondary sources, both text and visual. That means you need to be able to "read" and interpret tables, maps, and graphs as well as standard text materials.

The content of the Social Studies test is drawn from the following four basic areas.

>> **Civics and government:** The largest part (about 50 percent of the test) focuses on civics and government. The civics and government questions examine the development of democracy, from ancient times to present day. Other topics include how civilizations change over time and respond to crises.

>> **American history:** American history makes up 20 percent of the test. It covers all topics from the pilgrims and early settlement to the Revolution, the Civil War, World Wars I and II, the Vietnam War, and current history — all of which involve the United States in one way or another.

>> **Economics:** Economics make up about 15 percent of the test. The economics portion examines basic theories, such as supply and demand, the role of government policies in the economy, and macro- and microeconomic theory.

>> **Geography and the world:** This area also makes up 15 percent of the test. The areas with which you need to become familiar are very topical: sustainability and environmental issues, population issues, and rural and urban settlement. Other topics include cultural diversity and migration.

A good way to prepare for this test is to read as much as possible. As you prepare for the test, read articles about civics, history, economics, and geography from reliable online sources. Even reading solid news coverage can help you develop the strong reading skills you need. See Chapters 10, 11, and 12 for detailed coverage on how to prepare for the Social Studies test. Chapters 21 and 29 give you two complete Social Studies tests, with complete answers and explanations in Chapters 22 and 30. I also provide a third, complete online-only test. See Chapter 2 for the format of the questions as they appear on the computer.

Science test

The Science test is scheduled for 90 minutes. My advice for the Science test is the same as for the Reasoning through Language Arts test: read as much as you can, especially science material. Whenever you don't understand a word or concept, look it up in a dictionary or online. The questions in the Science test assume a high school level of science vocabulary.

You don't have to be a nuclear physicist to answer the questions, but you should be familiar with the vocabulary normally understood by someone completing high school. If you work at improving your scientific vocabulary, you should have little trouble with the Science test. (*Note:* That same advice applies to all the GED test's sections. Improve your vocabulary in each subject, and you'll perform better.)

The Science test concentrates on two main themes:

>> Human health and living systems

>> Energy and related systems

In addition, the content of the test focuses on the following areas.

>> **Physical science:** About 40 percent of the test focuses on physics and chemistry, including topics such as conservation, transformation, and flow of energy; work, motion, and forces; and chemical properties and reactions related to living systems.

>> **Life science:** Another 40 percent of the Science test deals with life science, including biology and, more specifically, human body and health, relationship between life functions and energy intake, ecosystems, structure and function of life, and molecular basis for heredity and evolution.

>> **Earth and space science:** This area makes up the remaining 20 percent of this test and includes astronomy — interaction between Earth's systems and living things, Earth and its system components and interactions, and structure and organization of the cosmos.

Go ahead and type one of the three areas of content into your favorite search engine to find material to read. You'll find links to articles and material from all different levels. Filter your choices by the level you want and need — for example, use keywords such as "scientific theories," "scientific discoveries," "scientific method," "human health," "living systems," "energy," "the universe," "organisms," and "geochemical systems" — and don't get discouraged if you can't understand technical material that one scientist wrote that only about three other scientists in the world can understand.

The questions on the Science test are in multiple-choice, fill-in-the-blank, drag-and-drop, and drop-down menu formats. As on the Social Studies test, you will read passages and interpret graphs, tables, and other visual materials. A few questions may ask you to calculate an answer. For these questions, a calculator icon will appear on your test screen or you can use your own TI-30XS MultiView calculator if you test at a test center.

See Chapters 13, 14, and 15 for detailed coverage on how to prepare for the Science test. Chapters 23 and 31 give you two complete Science tests, with complete answers and explanations in Chapters 24 and 32. I also provide a third, complete online-only test. See Chapter 2 for the format of the questions as they appear on the computer.

Mathematical Reasoning test

The Mathematical Reasoning (Math) test checks that you have the same knowledge and understanding of mathematics as a typical high school graduate. Because the GED is designed to prepare you for both postsecondary education and employment, it has an emphasis on both workplace-related mathematics and academic mathematics. About 45 percent of the test is about quantitative problem solving, and the rest is about algebra.

The Math test consists of different question formats to be completed in 115 minutes. Because the GED test is administered on the computer, the questions take advantage of the power of the computer. Some questions will simply pose a problem for you to solve. Other questions will refer to various kinds of stimulus materials, including graphs, tables, menus, price lists, and much more. Check out Chapters 2 and 3 for more information and a sneak peek at what the questions look like onscreen.

The following are the types of questions that you'll encounter in the Math test.

>> **Multiple-choice:** Most of the questions in the Math test are multiple-choice with four answer choices.

>> **Drop-down:** This type of question is a form of multiple-choice in that you get a series of possible answers, one of which is correct. The only difference is that you see all the options at once within the text where it's to be used. For examples, see Chapters 2 and 3.

>> **Drag-and-drop:** This question type asks you to arrange information in a certain way by clicking and dragging it on your screen. For example, you may be asked to order a list of positive and negative fractions, decimals, and numbers in order from lowest to highest.

>> **Fill-in-the-blank:** In these questions, you have to provide an answer. The fill-in-the-blank questions are straightforward: You're asked for a very specific answer, either a number or one or two words, and you type the answer into the space provided.

Some questions may be stand-alone with only one question for each stimulus. Others may have multiple questions based on a single stimulus. Each stimulus, no matter how many questions are based on it, may include text, graphs, tables, or some other representation of numeric, geometrical, or algebraic materials. Practice reading mathematical materials and become familiar with the vocabulary of mathematics. As on the Social Studies and Science tests, you will have available an onscreen calculator, or you can bring your own TI-30XS MultiView calculator. On the Math test, you are allowed to use your calculator on all but the first five questions. However, some questions can be answered more quickly using mental math or simple calculations on the whiteboard.

See Chapters 16, 17, and 18 for detailed coverage of the Math test. Chapters 25 and 33 give you two complete Math tests, with complete answers and explanations in Chapters 26 and 34. I also provide a third, complete online-only test. See Chapter 2 for the format of the questions as they appear on the computer.

It's a Date: Scheduling the Test

You book your appointment through the GED Testing Service's website, ged.com, based on available testing dates. Because a computer administers the test, you will schedule an individual appointment. Your test starts when you start and ends when the allotted time ends. If you sign up to take the test online at home, your computer and your home (or other location where you take the test) have to meet special requirements outlined when you sign up. The ged.com website will walk you through these requirements. If you sign up to take the test at a testing center, you will take the test in a computer lab, often containing no more than 15 seats; testing facilities may be located in many communities in your state.

At the time of publication of this edition of *GED For Dummies*, 5th Edition, some states — Indiana, Iowa, Louisiana, Maine, Missouri, Montana, New Hampshire, New York, Tennessee, and West Virginia — don't offer the test. You can take the test in a neighboring state that allows non-residents to test. Just select the state you'd like to test in when you set up your online account. This information changes periodically, so be sure to check ged.com/state-information-online-testing for the latest information. And remember: nearly all employers and higher education schools nationally accept your passing score.

The following sections answer some questions you may have before you schedule your test date, including whether you're eligible to take the test, when you can take the test, and how to sign up to take the test.

Determining whether you're eligible

Before you schedule your test date, make sure you meet the requirements to take the GED test. You're eligible to apply to take the GED test only if

>> **You're not currently enrolled in a high school.** If you're currently enrolled in a high school, you're expected to complete your diploma there. The purpose of the GED test is to give people who aren't in high school a chance to get an equivalent high school diploma.

>> **You're not a high school graduate.** If you're a high school graduate, you should have a diploma, which means you don't need to take the GED test. However, you can use the GED to upgrade or update your skills and to prove that you're ready for further education and training.

>> **You meet state requirements regarding age, residency, and the length of time since leaving high school.** When you open your online account at ged.com, the software will screen you to ensure you meet your state's requirements.

Knowing when you can take the test

You can take the GED test when you're eligible and prepared. You can then apply to take the GED test as soon as you want. Pick a day (or days) that works for you. If you want to take the test online at home, you must pass the GED Ready® practice test before you can sign up. Even if you are taking the test at a test center, this short online test can help you determine whether you are likely to be successful. This can help you avoid wasting time and money on retests. And if you don't pass, the detailed feedback will help you find your strengths and areas for improvement.

ARE SPECIAL ACCOMMODATIONS AVAILABLE?

If you have a special need, it can be accommodated. Remember, though, that if you request an accommodation, you will need to provide acceptable documentation.

The GED Testing Service makes every effort to ensure that all qualified people have access to the tests. If you have a disability, you may not be able to register for the tests and take them the same week, but, with some advanced planning, you can probably take the tests when you're ready. Here's what you need to do:

- Review the information and instructions at https://ged.com/about_test/accommodations/.
- At least a month before you want to take the test, go to ged.com and open an online account, or log into an existing account.
- Follow the instructions to request an accommodation. The software will walk you through the steps to request an accommodation and submit the proper documentation.
- You will need documentation of your special need from an appropriate professional. The software will give the exact requirements and instructions you can show the professional so they can provide the correct documentation.
- Complete all the proper forms and submit them with a medical or professional diagnosis.
- Start planning early so that you're able to take the tests when you're ready.

The GED Testing Service defines specific disabilities, such as the following, for which it may make special accommodations:

- Learning and cognitive disorders (LCD)
- Attention deficit/hyperactivity disorder (ADHD)
- Psychological and psychiatric disorders (EPP)
- Physical disabilities and chronic health conditions (PCH)

REMEMBER

Taking all four sections of the GED test together takes about seven hours. However, the test is designed so that you can take each section when you're ready. In fact, you can take the test sections one at a time, in evenings or on weekends, depending on the individual testing center. You can also take some of the tests at a testing center, and others at home. If you pass one test section, that section of the GED test is considered done, no matter how you do on the other sections. If you fail one section, you can retake that section of the test. At the time of the publication of this book, there are limits on the frequency at which you can retake the test online at home. That's why the GED Ready practice test is required — if you pass it, you will likely pass the real test.

Because the test starts when you're ready and finishes when you have used up the allocated time, you can take it alone and don't have to depend on other people. This offers great flexibility in scheduling the test, especially when testing online at home. When you sign up for the test, you can search for times and locations that suit you.

If you need special arrangements to accommodate your situation, the GED Testing Service will help arrange the test for you at a convenient time and location.

Taking the GED Test When English Is Your Second Language

The good news is that English doesn't have to be your first language for you to take the GED test. In the United States, the GED test is offered in English and Spanish. A French version is available in Canada.

TIP

If English (or Spanish) isn't your first language, you must decide whether you can read and write English or Spanish as well as or better than 40 percent of high school graduates. If so, then you can prepare for and take the test without additional language preparation. If you don't read or write English or Spanish well enough to pass, then you need to take additional classes to improve your language skills until you think you're ready. Your local community college or adult education center is the best place to get started. Your account at ged.com can also help you find local programs that will suit your needs.

GETTING MORE INFORMATION ABOUT THE GED TEST

There are plenty of resources for getting more information about the GED. The first place to start is the GED Testing Service's website, ged.com. In addition to the information offered there, you will find many other ways to get additional information. There are links to several blogs where you can submit questions directly to GED staff. You can also communicate via online chat or send an email to help@ged.com. And if you need to talk to a real person, you can call their toll-free number, 1-877-EXAM-GED (1-877-392-6433).

What You Have to Score to Pass the GED Test

To pass, you need to score a minimum of 145 on each section of the test, and you must pass each section of the test to earn your GED diploma. If you achieve a passing score, congratulate yourself: You've scored better than at least 40 percent of today's high school graduates, and you're now a graduate of the largest virtual school in the country. And if your scores range between 165 and 174, you've reached the GED College Ready level. This means you may be able to start your college studies right away, without any additional college-readiness classes. This can save you time and money. If your scores are even higher, between 175 and 200, you've reached the lofty GED College Ready + Credit level. Depending on the policies of your institution, you can qualify for college credit in each of the GED subject areas.

TIP

If you score at the College-Ready or College Ready + Credit level, shop around at various colleges and universities. Some institutions may be more willing than others to waive requirements or grant credit. For example, you can start at a community college that grants credit. Then those credits will be on your transcript if you later go on to a four-year college.

There is more good news. Scores from the computer-based and online tests do not expire, so if you passed some sections years ago, you do not need to take them again. And if you took a test between 2014 and 2016 and scored below 150 but above 145, you will now get credit for passing that section of the test. (The passing score was lowered from 150 to 145 at that time.) Your transcript should have been adjusted automatically, so check your transcript at ged.com; there may be good news waiting for you. The following sections address a few more points you may want to know about how the GED test is scored and what you can do if you score poorly on some or all of the test sections.

Identifying how scores are determined

Correct answers may be worth one, two, or more points, depending on the question and the level of difficulty. The Extended Response (also known as the essay) is scored separately. However, the Extended Response is only one part of the Reasoning through Language Arts test. On each test section, you must accumulate a minimum of 145 points.

TIP

Because you don't lose points for incorrect answers, make sure you answer all the questions on each test. After all, a guessed answer can get you a point. Leaving an answer blank, on the other hand, gives you only a zero. Refer to Chapter 4 for some hints to help you narrow down your choices.

Knowing what to do if you score poorly on one or more tests

If you discover that your score is less than 145 on any test section, start planning to retake the test(s) — and make sure you leave plenty of time for additional studying and preparing.

TIP

As soon as possible after seeing your results, check out the rules for retaking that section of the test at ged.com. Remember, you need to retake only those sections of the test that you didn't pass. Any sections you pass are completed and count toward your diploma. Furthermore, the detailed feedback you receive on your results will help you discover areas that need more work before retaking a section of the test. That information can help you determine the sections of this book to review or whether you want to sign up for a class. You can find nearby adult education centers on ged.com.

No matter what score you receive on your first round of the section, don't be afraid to retake any section that you didn't pass. After you've taken it once, you know what you need to work on, and you know exactly what to expect on test day. Just take a deep breath, and get ready to prepare some more before you take your next test.

Chapter **2**

The Ins and Outs of the Computerized GED Test

The GED test is offered only on a computer, either at a testing center or online at home using the online-proctored test. Either way, the test format looks quite different from the old paper tests you may have taken. No longer do you have to fill in little circles or use a pencil or scratchpad. Now everything is paperless; even the scratchpad of previous years has been upgraded to an erasable tablet or online whiteboard. Now you enter all your answers into the computer. You use the keyboard to type your essay, or the mouse to select your answer choices.

This chapter provides what you need to know for using the computer to take the GED test and explains the different formats of questions on the GED test. I even throw in a few sample questions to ensure that you understand this important information. Demonstrating how to take a test on a computer with a printed book isn't easy, but this chapter includes several screenshots of question formats and other images you need to understand to be successful. All you have to do is read and digest it. I can't promise you a banquet of information, but this chapter is at least a satisfying meal to help you prepare for the next big step on your road to the future.

Familiarizing Yourself with the Computer

When taking the computerized GED test, you have two important tools to allow you to answer questions: the keyboard and the mouse. The following sections examine each of them in greater depth and explain exactly how you use them to complete the GED test. Make sure you understand the mechanics and use of the keyboard and mouse beforehand so you don't end up wasting valuable time trying to figure all of this stuff out on test day when you should be answering the questions.

REMEMBER

Because bundling the book with a computer would make it very expensive, I developed a different way for you to interact with the GED test questions in this book. I present questions in a format somewhat similar to the computer screen for that type of question's format, and you mark your choice directly in the book or on an answer sheet. Then, you get to check your answer and read the answer explanation. Make sure you read the explanations even if you got the answer right because they provide additional information that may help with other questions. That type of presentation may not be the most technologically savvy, but it does prepare you for the types of questions you'll encounter in the various sections of the GED test. For the practice tests in Parts 6 and 7, I provide an answer sheet, and I give you the correct answers and detailed explanations for each test in a separate chapter. After that, you can take the included online test. That will give you the closest possible match to the actual test.

Typing on the keyboard

You need to have at least some familiarity with a computer's keyboard. If you constantly make typing errors or aren't familiar with the keyboard, you may be in trouble. The good news is that you don't have to be a keyboarding whiz. In fact, the behind-the-scenes GED people have shown through their research that even people with minimal keyboarding skills still have adequate time to complete the test.

On the GED test, you'll use the keyboard to type your answers in the essay (Extended Response) segment in the Reasoning through Language Arts test and in the short answer segment of the Science test. Although you may be familiar with typing by using one or two fingers on your smartphone or tablet, with the screen often predicting and suggesting (correctly spelled) words that you need, the word processor on the GED test for the Extended Response has a bare minimum of features. It accepts keyboard entries, cuts, pastes, copies, and lets you redo and undo changes, but no more. It doesn't have a grammar-checker or a spell-checker, so be careful with your keyboarding because spelling and grammatical errors are just that — errors.

TIP

The GED test uses the standard English keyboard (see Figure 2-1), so if you're not familiar with it, take time to acquaint yourself with it before you take the GED test. If you're used to other language keyboards, you will find that the English keyboard has some letters and punctuation that appear in different places. Before test day, practice using the English keyboard so that the differences in the keyboard don't throw you off the day of the test. You won't have time to figure out the keyboard while the clock is ticking.

FIGURE 2-1:
An example
of a
standard
English
keyboard.

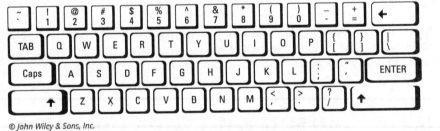

© John Wiley & Sons, Inc.

EXAMPLE

To complete the test in the required time, you should have

(A) comfortable running shoes.

(B) minimal keyboarding skills.

(C) really strong thumbs.

(D) lots of coffee at your desk.

Choice (B) is the correct answer. In preliminary testing, the GED test-makers and bigwigs found that test-takers with minimal keyboarding skills were able to complete the test in the time allotted. That doesn't mean that working on your keyboarding skills is a waste of time. The better these skills are, the faster you can type in answers, and the more time you'll have for the difficult questions.

You may want to wear comfortable running shoes, as Choice (A) suggests, but that in itself won't help you finish the test in the allotted time, although it may make you more comfortable sitting for all those hours. Choice (C) would be useful if you submitted your answers by texting, but on the computerized GED test, you have to use a traditional keyboard, which requires the use of your fingers and knowing which keys are where. Choice (D) may present you with a new set of problems. Computers and liquids don't go well together, and in most cases, the test centers don't let you take liquids into the test room. If you test online at home, you are only allowed to have a glass of water on your desk — in a clear glass. No iced tea is allowed!

REMEMBER

You don't need to become a perfect typist, but you should at least be comfortable pecking away with a couple of fingers. If you want to improve your typing skills, search online in your favorite search engine using the keywords "free typing tutor." Any number of free programs can teach you basic typing skills. (Just know that some software may be free to try for a short period of time or may be loaded with ads.)

EXAMPLE

When looking at the keyboard, you have to remember that

(A) all keyboards are the same.

(B) keyboards from different countries have some letters in different locations.

(C) you should always use the space bar with your little finger.

(D) touch typists don't have to worry about where the keys are located.

Choice (B) is correct. Keyboards from different countries have letters and punctuation in different locations and could present problems to touch typists who have memorized the location of each letter so they don't have to look at the keyboard. Choices (A), (C), and (D) are wrong.

Clicking and dragging with the mouse

Most questions on the GED test require no more than the ability to use the mouse to move the cursor on your screen to point to a selection for your answer and then click on that selection, which is very basic. If you're unfamiliar with computers, take time to become familiar with the mouse, including the clickable buttons and the scroll wheel. If the mouse has a scroll wheel, you can use it to move up or down through text or images. When you hold down the left button on the mouse, it highlights text as you drag the cursor across the screen, or you can "drag and drop" questions on the screen. If test online at home using a laptop, that computer may have a trackpad mouse (a small panel at the bottom of the screen that you touch with one finger to move the pointer onscreen and click in the left or right corner). Use the instructions that come with your laptop to get familiar with a trackpad mouse. If you're more comfortable with a traditional mouse, you can buy a wired or wireless one for a few dollars online. Make sure it's compatible with your specific laptop.

On the GED test, you'll use the mouse to answer the four main question types: multiple-choice, fill-in-the-blank, drop-down menu, and drag and drop. You'll use both the mouse and the keyboard to answer the Extended Response item on the RLA test. Refer to Chapter 1 for more basics about these types of questions. Here, I simply explain how to use your computer to answer them.

EXAMPLE

On the new series of GED tests, you indicate your choice of answer by

(A) using a pencil.

(B) tapping the screen.

(C) clicking the mouse.

(D) yelling it out.

The correct answer is Choice (C). For most questions, the mouse is your best friend because you use it to indicate the correct answer. The present test computers don't have a touch screen. Tapping on them will only leave fingerprints, so Choice (B) is wrong. If you're going to use a pencil to indicate your answer (Choice A), you're taking the wrong version of the GED test or you'll look silly trying to mark on the computer screen with a pencil. If you chose Choice (D), you'll, at a minimum, be ejected from the test site for being a nuisance and a possible cheater.

Fill-in-the-blanks are another type of question you'll encounter on the GED test. They're simply statements with a blank box in the text somewhere. To complete the sentence, you need to enter the word(s), name, or number. The statement will be preceded by directions setting up the text, so you'll know what is expected. Here's an example.

Type the appropriate word in the box.

The fill-in-the-blank question simply consists of a statement and a sentence with a ☐ into which you type the appropriate text.

EXAMPLE

The correct answer is *box*.

You must type the precise word or number required. Spelling mistakes, misplaced decimals, and even wrong capitalization count as errors.

REMEMBER

GETTING MORE HELP WITH YOUR COMPUTER SKILLS

Some websites offer free training on basic computer skills, but you need a computer to use them. Your local library should have free computer access if you don't have your own computer. Many libraries and community agencies offer free computer classes that are worth checking out. If you're a bit computer savvy, type "basic computer skills training + free" into a search engine and follow the links until you find one that suits you. Be aware that free or limited-time trial software can be full of advertising.

Take your time at home or in the library developing your skills and working through the practice tests. Test day isn't the time to figure out how to use the computer.

Try this question: A good place to get help using a computer is

(A) your local school.

(B) the Internet.

(C) libraries.

(D) all of the above.

The correct answer is Choice (D). Any place that offers instruction in using a computer is a good place to go for help.

Recognizing What the Questions Look Like on the Computer Screen

As you take the computerized GED test, you'll encounter four main types of questions to answer: multiple-choice, fill-in-the-blank, drop-down menu, and drag and drop.

The following sections show you what the different questions look like on the screen in the different test sections and explain how to answer these questions.

Reasoning through Language Arts test

The Reasoning through Language Arts (RLA) test puts several skills to work, including reading and comprehension, grammar and spelling, and writing skills. Most of the content for answering literature and comprehension questions is in the source text itself, but for grammar and spelling, you need to know the answers from your studying.

Multiple-choice questions

Like in all the four test sections, the multiple-choice question is the most popular. The basic multiple-choice question, as shown in Figure 2-2, looks very similar to what you may expect. It's presented in split-screen form, with the source text on the left and the question and answer choices on the right. If the source text extends beyond one screen, you use the scroll bar on the right side of the left screen. When you're ready to answer, use the mouse to click on the appropriate answer, and then click on Next to continue.

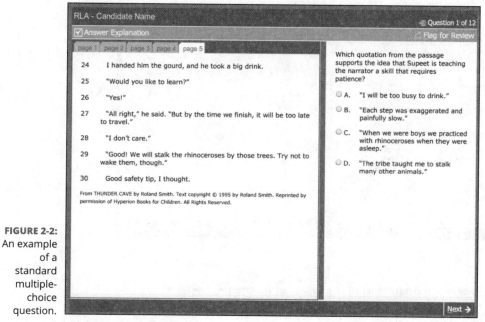

FIGURE 2-2: An example of a standard multiple-choice question.

© 2014 GED Testing Service LLC

If a scroll bar accompanies the source text on the left side of the screen, some of the text isn't visible unless you scroll down. If that scroll bar is on the answer side, some of the answer choices may not be visible without scrolling. This is important to remember because you may miss some important text when trying to answer the question. To use the scroll bar, click on it with your cursor and then move your mouse up or down. When the text you want is visible, release the button.

EXAMPLE

The scroll bar in some questions will help you

(A) find scrolls.

(B) see the onscreen whiteboard.

(C) go on to the next question.

(D) view more text above or below what is currently on the screen.

Choice (D) is correct. The scroll bar tells you more text is available and helps you view it. It doesn't help you do anything else — not see the onscreen whiteboard, go to the next question, or find scrolls.

Sometimes the source text consists of several screen pages (see Figure 2-3). The tabs at the top of the page are your clue. They actually look like tabs on file folders. Each one opens a different page in the source text when you click on the tab. Remember that you must read all the text to be able to answer the question. Notice, too, that the question side of the screen doesn't change as you go through the tabs. Otherwise, it works the same way: read, decide on an answer, click on the matching choice, and then click on Next to continue.

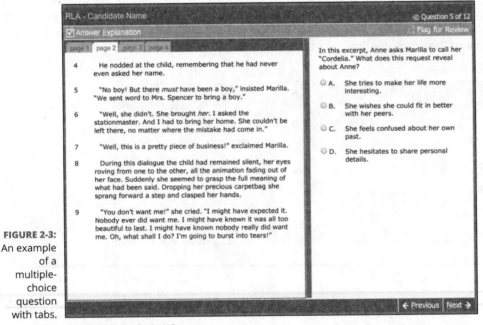

FIGURE 2-3: An example of a multiple-choice question with tabs.

© 2014 GED Testing Service LLC

EXAMPLE

Tabs are a very important part of the passages on the test because

(A) they give you something to do while you think about your answer.

(B) they allow you to advance to the next page of text.

(C) they allow you to move down the page of text.

(D) it's the brand name of a diet cola from yesteryear.

Choice (B) is the correct answer. If you have to advance through a passage, the tabs give you the mechanism to do so. If you choose not to use the tabs, you'll be able to read only one page of the passage. Because the answer to the question is dependent on all the material, it puts you at a major disadvantage.

Most of the questions on the test will be some form of multiple-choice, presented in the same manner as the preceding two examples.

Drag-and-drop questions

The RLA test also uses other question formats suited to computer testing. The drag-and-drop question (see Figure 2-4) is one variation. The source text, an excerpt from *Anne of Green Gables*, is on the left side of the screen.

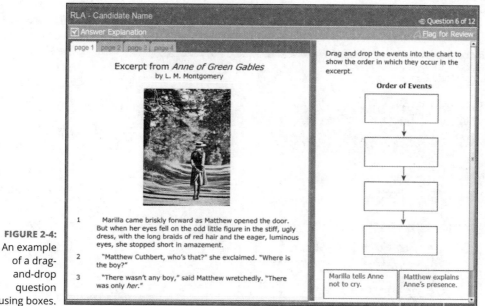

FIGURE 2-4: An example of a drag-and-drop question using boxes.

© 2014 GED Testing Service LLC

This source text covers more than one page, accessible via the tabs at the top of the screen. On the answer side, the scroll bar indicates that the content continues on, and you must scroll down to see it all (see Figure 2-5). When you scroll down, you can see the content you missed on the initial screen.

After you finish reading the content under all four tabs, drag the choices on the right into the boxes. You click on the answer choice, and without letting go of the mouse button, you drag the choice up to the correct box. Let go of the mouse button, and the choice drops into the box. If you've moved it properly, it will stay where you dropped it.

Figure 2-6 shows another sample drag-and-drop question. This question uses the same four-page source text and asks you to select characteristics that apply to Anne. The key is that you can select only three of the five listed words. That isn't stated in the question but is obvious from the drag-and-drop targets, which include only three oval spaces. You have to read the text carefully to find the correct choices. When you decide which words apply, drag each word to one of the ovals and leave it there. Click on Next to continue.

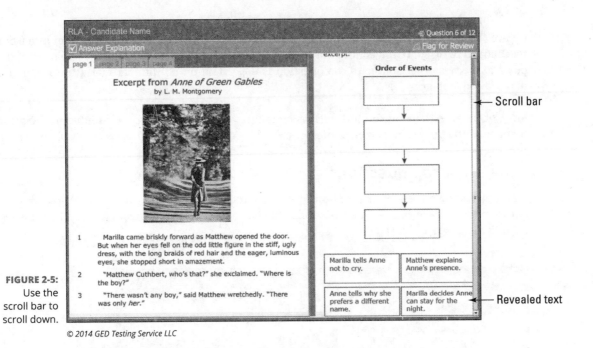

FIGURE 2-5: Use the scroll bar to scroll down.

© 2014 GED Testing Service LLC

FIGURE 2-6: Another drag-and-drop example.

© 2014 GED Testing Service LLC

In this book, you clearly can't drag and drop on the practice tests, so for questions in this format, you indicate your answer by writing letters. Here is an example.

EXAMPLE

Answering a drag-and-drop question on the computer requires you to [   ] (choose three letters)

(A) use your mouse.

(B) type directly into a box.

(C) click on and move an answer choice.

(D) select more than one answer choice.

Choices (A), (C), and (D) are correct. Choice (B) is incorrect because you type an answer into a box in a fill-in-the-blank question.

Drop-down menu questions

You'll also encounter other more technologically enhanced questions. Grammar and language questions ask you to choose the correct answer choice to complete a sentence correctly. In Figure 2-7, the source text contains drop-down menus. In one line of the text, you see a blank space and the word *Select. . .* with an arrow next to it. When you click on that line, a number of variations appear. You pick the best choice as your answer. Figure 2-8 shows what you see when you click on the Select line.

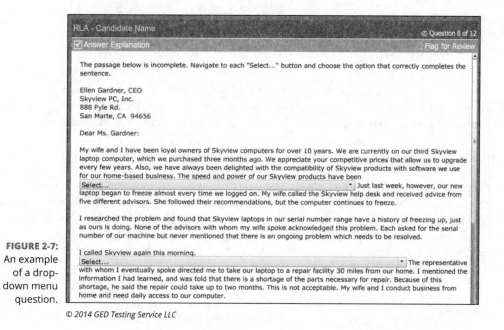

FIGURE 2-7: An example of a drop-down menu question.

© 2014 GED Testing Service LLC

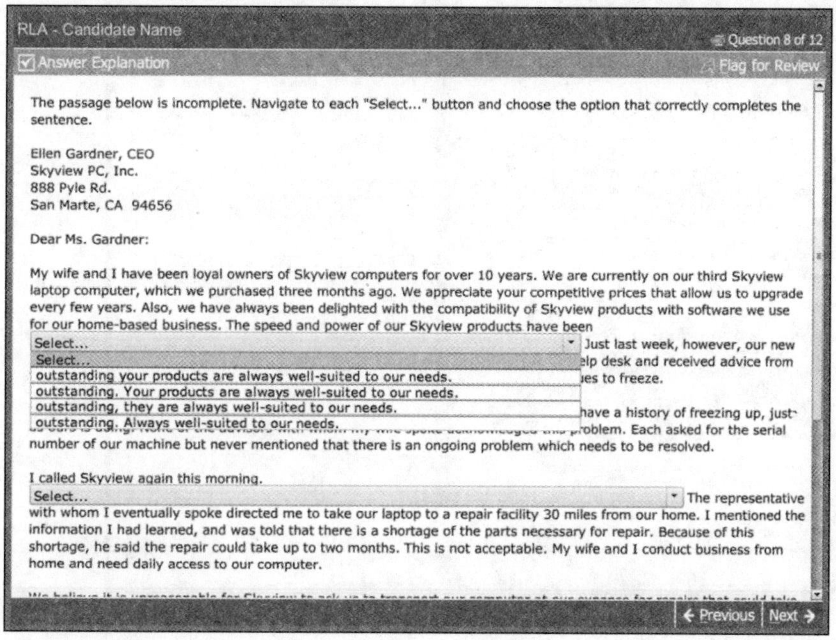

FIGURE 2-8: Click on Select, and a variety of answer choices appear in that line.

© 2014 GED Testing Service LLC

From the context of the letter, you have to select the sentence that fits best and shows both correct grammar and spelling. Move the mouse to the proper choice and let go. The selected wording will appear in the space. You can now read the entire text to review and decide whether you indeed selected the appropriate choice. Figure 2-9 is a close-up of one question where the drop-down menu asks you to choose only a single correct word.

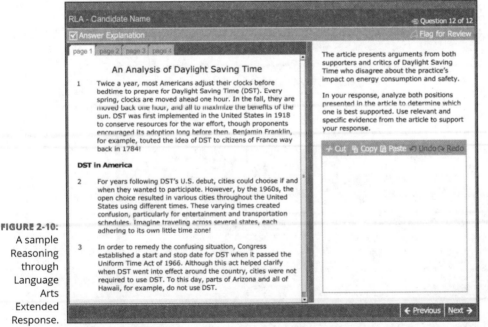

FIGURE 2-9:
Another
example of
a drop-down
menu
question.

We would like to give Skyview the opportunity to remedy this situation. We firmly believe that Skyview needs to stand behind its products. If our laptop has a problem which makes it unusable, Skyview should immediately replace it with one that works, with as little inconvenience to Select... ▾ as possible.

Select...
We look forward to hearing from you about how it to resolve this issue.
us
Sincerely yours, him
both
James Hendricks

← Previous | Next →

TIP

For the purposes of this book, the drop-down menu questions look a lot like multiple-choice questions. I include a list of answer choices for you to choose from, labeled with A, B, C, and D. Just know that on GED test, you'll have to click on Select to view the answer choices.

The Extended Response

In the Extended Response of the RLA test, you get 45 minutes to write an essay. Figure 2-10 shows an example. Note that the source material is longer than one screen. The tabs on the top of the left side indicate that this text is spread out over four pages. Be sure to read all four pages. If you take the test at a testing center, you'll have an erasable tablet. Use it to make notes as you read and then to organize your ideas. If you test online at home, you will have an online whiteboard for taking notes and organizing your ideas. Either way, nothing you write on the boards will be seen by anyone but you. Only the answer that you enter in the answer window counts.

RLA - Candidate Name ⩧ Question 12 of 12

☑ Answer Explanation ⌁ Flag for Review

page 1 | page 2 | page 3 | page 4

An Analysis of Daylight Saving Time

1   Twice a year, most Americans adjust their clocks before bedtime to prepare for Daylight Saving Time (DST). Every spring, clocks are moved ahead one hour. In the fall, they are moved back one hour, and all to maximize the benefits of the sun. DST was first implemented in the United States in 1918 to conserve resources for the war effort, though proponents encouraged its adoption long before then. Benjamin Franklin, for example, touted the idea of DST to citizens of France way back in 1784!

DST in America

2   For years following DST's U.S. debut, cities could choose if and when they wanted to participate. However, by the 1960s, the open choice resulted in various cities throughout the United States using different times. These varying times created confusion, particularly for entertainment and transportation schedules. Imagine traveling across several states, each adhering to its own little time zone!

3   In order to remedy the confusing situation, Congress established a start and stop date for DST when it passed the Uniform Time Act of 1966. Although this act helped clarify when DST went into effect around the country, cities were not required to use DST. To this day, parts of Arizona and all of Hawaii, for example, do not use DST.

The article presents arguments from both supporters and critics of Daylight Saving Time who disagree about the practice's impact on energy consumption and safety.

In your response, analyze both positions presented in the article to determine which one is best supported. Use relevant and specific evidence from the article to support your response.

✂ Cut ⎘ Copy ⧉ Paste ↺ Undo ↻ Redo

← Previous | Next →

FIGURE 2-10:
A sample
Reasoning
through
Language
Arts
Extended
Response.

The answer window is a very limited, mini word processor. In Figure 2-10, you can see that it allows you only to cut, paste, copy, redo, and undo. As this is a writing test, it doesn't have either a grammar-checker or a spell-checker. Your brain, with its experience and knowledge, supplies those. To copy, cut, paste, or save, you move the mouse cursor to the area of the screen with the symbols for performing these tasks, and then you click on a mouse button to activate the feature (or you can use the standard keyboard shortcuts for copy, cut, and paste). You use these features if you want to quote something in your essay, to delete unwanted words or phrases, or to move something to another part of your essay.

TIP

Take a stab at writing a full-length essay in Chapter 9, in the practice tests in Chapters 19 and 27, and in the included online test. Time the test so you're taking it under the same conditions as the real GED test.

Social Studies test

In the Social Studies test, you encounter types of multiple-choice questions similar to those in the Reasoning through Language Arts test. The following sections give you a brief guide to the kinds of questions to expect.

Multiple-choice questions

Most questions on the Social Studies test are a variation of multiple-choice questions. You're probably most familiar with this simplest version (see Figure 2-11).

Social Studies - Candidate Name — Question 2 of 16
✓ Answer Explanation — Flag for Review

This excerpt is from a speech by Thomas Jefferson.

> Friends & Fellow Citizens,
>
> . . . A rising nation, spread over a wide and fruitful land . . . engaged in commerce with nations who feel power and forget right . . . when I . . . see the honour, the happiness, and the hopes of this beloved country . . . I shrink from the contemplation and humble myself before the magnitude of the undertaking . . . . I shall find resources of wisdom, of virtue, and of zeal, on which to rely under all difficulties . . . . I look with encouragement for that guidance and support which may enable us to steer with safety the vessel in which we are all embarked amidst the conflicting elements of a troubled world . . . .
>
> I repair then, fellow citizens, to the post you have assigned me. . . . [M]y future solicitude will be, to retain the good opinion of those who have bestowed it in advance . . . and to be instrumental to the happiness and freedom of all.
> This excerpt is taken from the public domain.

Based on the excerpt, which event was Jefferson attending when he made this speech?

○ A. the signing of the Declaration of Independence

○ B. his first inauguration as President of the United States

○ C. the purchase of the Louisiana Territory from France

○ D. his founding of the University of Virginia

← Previous | Next →

FIGURE 2-11: An example of a Social Studies multiple-choice question.

To answer this question, you click on the correct choice, and then click on Next to continue. (To answer this type of question in the book, you simply mark your choice of answer on an answer sheet.)

You'll also find the multiple-choice and other questions presented as a split-screen, as in Figure 2-12. In this example, the text exceeds one page but only by a little. A scroll bar on the text side lets you scroll down to see the rest.

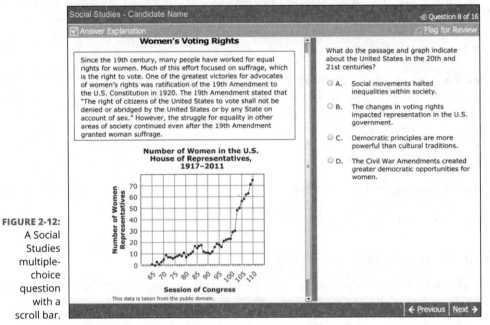

FIGURE 2-12: A Social Studies multiple-choice question with a scroll bar.

Other types of Social Studies questions

The other questions on the Social Studies test are just like the ones I discuss earlier in this chapter. They include questions with source text (the materials you need to read to answer the question) spread over several pages (as in Figure 2-13). The tabs on the top left of the screen indicate more pages of text. Each page is one tab.

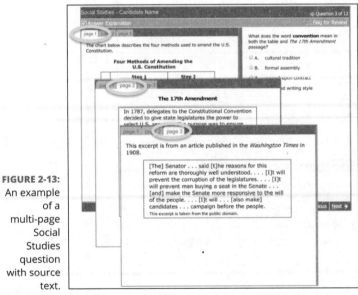

FIGURE 2-13: An example of a multi-page Social Studies question with source text.

You'll also encounter fill-in-the-blank questions (as in Figure 2-14). On this type of question, you use the material presented in the passage to fill in the box. As in other subject areas, you need a specific word or number for the blank. You must be accurate; spelling mistakes are scored as an error. In this book, you write the answer on the answer sheet.

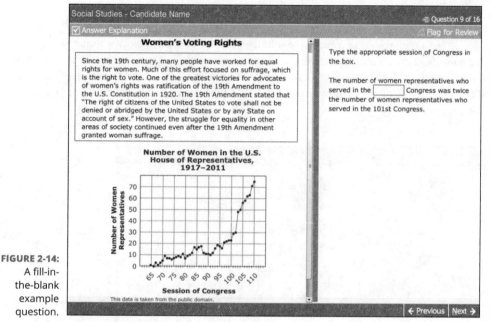

FIGURE 2-14: A fill-in-the-blank example question.

© 2014 GED Testing Service LLC

The Social Studies test also includes drop-down menu questions and drag-and-drop questions. You answer these the same way as on the Reasoning through Language Arts test (refer to the earlier sections, "Drag-and-drop questions" and "Drop-down menu questions," for more information). Figure 2-15 is an example of a Social Studies drag-and-drop question.

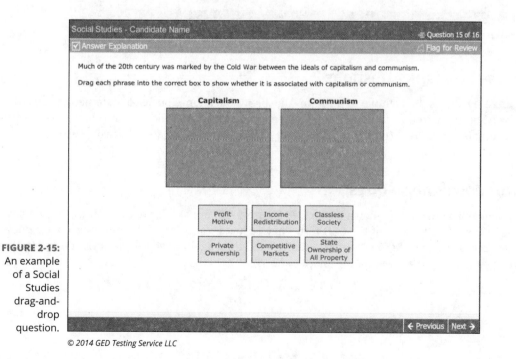

FIGURE 2-15: An example of a Social Studies drag-and-drop question.

© 2014 GED Testing Service LLC

Science test

When you take the Science test, you have to answer a variety of the same types of questions as in the other tests. The following sections focus on the slight differences you may see on the computer screen in the different types of questions.

Multiple-choice questions

Figure 2-16 shows an example of a multiple-choice Science question. Notice that the passage is longer than one page on the computer screen. Tabs on the side can move the text up and down. Moving it down reveals the other possible answers. Always be aware of the screen size limitation, and advance pages or scroll up or down to ensure that you have all the information you need to answer the questions.

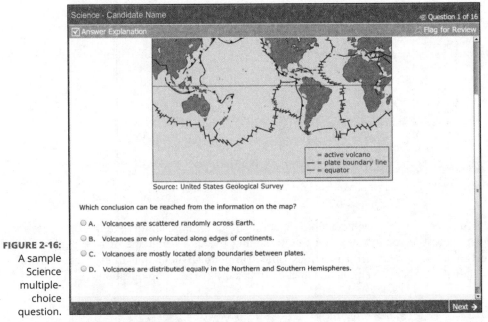

FIGURE 2-16: A sample Science multiple-choice question.

© 2014 GED Testing Service LLC

Fill-in-the-blank questions

Figure 2-17 shows an example of a fill-in-the-blank question. You see a statement or question followed by a box. You're expected to type the appropriate word(s) or number(s) into that box. In the example in Figure 2-17, the percent sign after each box indicates that you need to enter a number.

Drop-down menu questions

Questions involving a drop-down menu (see Figure 2-18) are similar to drop-down menu questions in the other sections of the GED test. They're just a variation of the multiple-choice questions. You use the mouse to expand the choices and then again to select the correct one. (In this book, you mark your answer on the answer sheet.)

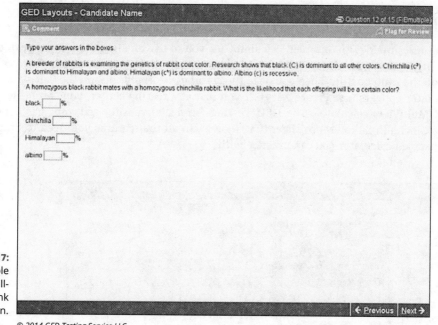

FIGURE 2-17:
A sample Science fill-in-the-blank question.

© 2014 GED Testing Service LLC

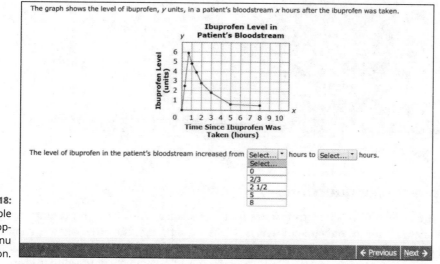

FIGURE 2-18:
An example of a drop-down menu question.

© 2014 GED Testing Service LLC

Drag-and-drop questions

The general format of these types of questions is similar throughout all the sections of the GED test (refer to Figures 2-4 and 2-15 for examples of this question type). On the computer, you'll see spaces and a list of possible answers to use in filling the spaces. Using the mouse, you can drag the word, numbers, or phrases to their appropriate location to create an answer. (In this book, write the answers on the answer sheet provided. Always check your answers after completing each test section to make sure you understand the material.)

Mathematical Reasoning test

Here are some of the specific test formats you'll encounter in the Mathematical Reasoning (Math) test.

Calculator

The Math test provides an onscreen calculator for you to use on all but the first five questions of the test (if you don't see the calculator tab on the screen, then you have to do the math in your head or on the whiteboard). When you need the calculator, simply click on the Calculator link, and the calculator appears (see Figure 2-19). If you test at a testing center, you can bring your own TI-30XS MultiView calculator. The GED Testing Service's website, ged.com, has a number of resources, including a reference sheet that shows you all the features you need to know and an actual onscreen calculator you can practice with.

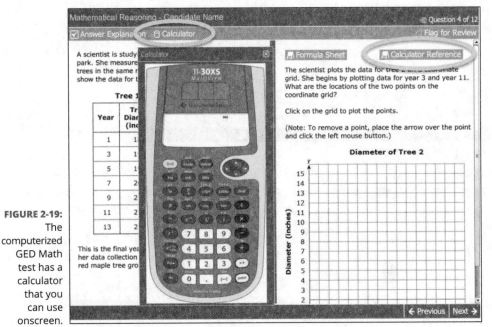

FIGURE 2-19:
The computerized GED Math test has a calculator that you can use onscreen.

© 2014 GED Testing Service LLC

Multiple-choice questions

Most of the questions in the Math test are multiple-choice. The question presents you with four possible answer choices, only one of which is correct, although the other answer choices may be close or incorporate common errors. Carefully read the question and answer choices. Answer the question using the information provided. The only exception is the list of formulas given when you click on the Formula button. You can use any of these formulas where appropriate. Figure 2-20 shows a basic example of a multiple-choice question.

On the computer, you use the mouse to select the answer. (In practice tests in this book, you mark your answer on an answer sheet. Always check your answer with the explanation.)

Sometimes multiple-choice questions appear in a split-screen with the question on the left-hand side and the possible answers on the right-hand side (see Figure 2-21). In either case, after you decide on the correct answer, you click on the appropriate answer choice with your mouse.

This particular question has some interesting buttons integrated into the format: a button to call up the calculator, one to open the formula sheet, and one for the calculator reference sheet.

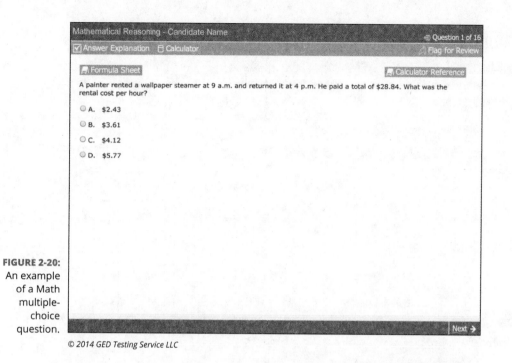

FIGURE 2-20:
An example
of a Math
multiple-
choice
question.

© 2014 GED Testing Service LLC

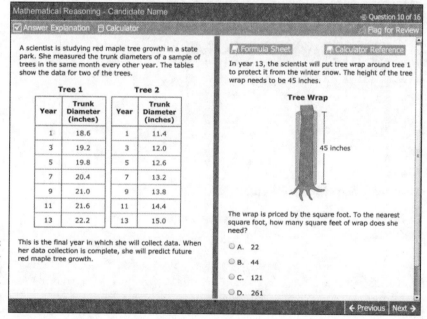

FIGURE 2-21:
A split-
screen
multiple-
choice
question.

© 2014 GED Testing Service LLC

REMEMBER

Getting familiar with the calculator reference sheet before the test can save you time during the test. But if you forget something, you can use the online calculator reference sheet to refresh your memory. Good to know if you get nervous and start to fumble with the calculator!

Fill-in-the-blank questions

These questions require that you type a numeric answer or an equation in a box provided, using the keyboard. Check out Figure 2-22. You may have to use the symbols on the keyboard or click on the Æ Symbol tab for additional symbols that you may need (see Figure 2-23).

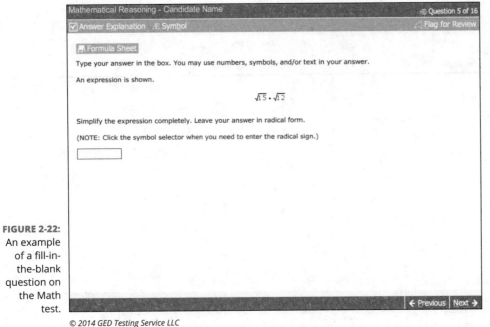

FIGURE 2-22:
An example
of a fill-in-
the-blank
question on
the Math
test.

© 2014 GED Testing Service LLC

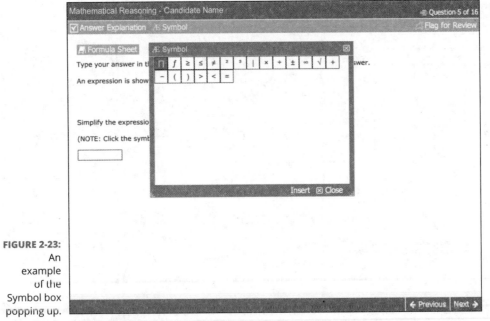

FIGURE 2-23:
An
example
of the
Symbol box
popping up.

© 2014 GED Testing Service LLC

After reading the question carefully, you use the keyboard and the Symbol box to type your answer in the box. To insert a symbol, place your cursor in the correct place in the answer box. Then, click on the Æ Symbol Tab. The Symbol box will open. In the Symbol box, click on the symbol you want and then click the Insert button in the lower-right corner of the Symbol box. The symbol will appear next to your cursor. To make the Symbol box go away, press the Close button in the lower-right corner.

Other types of questions

The Mathematical Reasoning test also has drop-down menu and drag-and-drop questions just like the other three sections of the test.

Flag for Review button

The Flag for Review button is a very useful feature on all four tests. This button allows you to mark questions for review later. You can select an answer and then press Flag for Review, or simply press Flag for Review without selecting an answer. At the end of the test, or at any time, you can go to the Review screen, which shows all the questions that are flagged or skipped. This way, you can return to these questions quickly at any time. When you complete the test, you will also be taken to this screen (as long as there is time remaining). You can continue to check your answers or complete unanswered questions until time runs out.

TIP

There is not any extra penalty for guessing on the GED, so do not leave any questions unanswered. Throughout this book, you will learn several strategies for improving your odds when guessing. But if you simply don't know, or are running out of time, you have nothing to lose by selecting an answer at random for every unanswered question. Use the Review screen to help you find and answer all unanswered questions in the last few minutes of the test.

Chapter **3**

The GED Test's Four Sections and You

I t's time to start your preparation for the GED test with a look at what to expect on the four sections that comprise the GED exam — Reasoning through Language Arts, Social Studies, Science, and Mathematical Reasoning. You can take them all at once in one really long and tough day or individually whenever you feel sufficiently prepared. *Remember:* You don't have to do all the test sections on the same day. And after you pass a test section, you're finished with that section forever. You'll earn your GED diploma whenever you've completed and passed all four test sections. In this chapter, I break down what you can expect on each section and help you prepare for answering the different question types. See Chapter 2 for examples of all the different question types and how they appear both on the actual GED test and in the practice tests in this book.

Examining the Reasoning through Language Arts Test

The Reasoning through Language Arts (RLA) test consists of a short reading comprehension test, the Extended Response section (the essay), a break, and a grammar and language section.

In this section, I offer some example questions for each part of the RLA test, which show you how the questions work and what's expected of you to answer them. You'll first answer a series of reading comprehension questions, mainly multiple-choice (35 minutes). However, you'll also see questions in the form of fill-in-the-blanks, drag-and-drop questions, and drop-down menu questions. In each case, you will need to look for the answer in the text presented to you. To find the answer, you may simply have to refer to the text, or you may have to draw conclusions from what you've read and choose the best answer from either the choices presented or from your understanding of the passage. After that, you will have 45 minutes to complete the Extended

Response, followed by a 10-minute break. And, finally, you'll have the 60-minute grammar and language section, which consists entirely of drop-down menu questions. The total time is 150 minutes.

The reading section

On this part of the RLA test, you're given text to read, followed by a set of questions about that text, designed to test your ability to read and comprehend. Some questions will simply ask about content; other questions will require analysis. The information you need to answer will be right in the text you read. Some questions will ask you to draw conclusions based on the information in the text, which are the "why" or "how do you know" questions.

TIP

Here are two bits of collective wisdom: First, before taking the RLA test, read, read, and read some more. And, secondly, when taking the RLA test, read carefully; the answer is in the text. The best guarantee that you'll do well on this section is to become a fluent and analytical reader. Read editorials, analyze how the writers make their point, and provide supportive evidence of their points. Read newspaper stories to extract the bare-bones key points that make the story. Read and think about how the writer creates a mood, image, or point of view. Although you don't have to master any specific content before taking the reading portion of the RLA test, the more you read, the better equipped you'll be to deal with this.

I go into detail about the types of questions to expect on the RLA test and how to answer them in the following sections.

Multiple-choice questions

Most of the questions on the RLA test are some form of multiple-choice question, where you choose from four answers. (Refer to Chapter 2 for how multiple-choice questions appear in this test section on the computer screen when you're taking the actual GED test.)

Multiple-choice questions give you the correct answer but make it harder by adding three wrong answers. For this reason, it's helpful to read the questions and answer choices first and then the text, looking for related material. Go back to the answer choices and eliminate the obviously wrong ones as you progress. Eventually, you'll be left with one or two choices from which to pick your answer.

REMEMBER

Pick the most correct, most complete answer from the choices offered. You may find, based on your previous knowledge, that none of the choices are complete. However, you need to go with the materials in the text, so use the answer choice closest to what's in the text. The best advice for completing the reading portion of the RLA test is to

(A) read, read, and read some more.

(B) memorize every poem ever written by Shakespeare.

(C) read the short versions of any famous books you can find.

(D) relax, because reading is easy.

The correct answer is Choice (A). You don't have to know any specific content for this test, but you need to be able to read quickly and accurately and understand what you've read. The only way to do that is to practice and practice and practice some more.

Here are a couple of examples of multiple-choice questions like those you'll see on the GED test.

People have a natural metabolic "set point" that is predetermined at birth and influences just how slim or heavy they will be. That is why it is difficult for the obese to lose weight beyond a particular point and for the slim to gain and retain weight for long. Some studies now suggest that the chemicals in clothing and upholstery flame-retardants interfere with that set point when they are absorbed into the body. This may affect a child in the womb and even after birth, which is one reason some jurisdictions are banning flame-retardants from children's clothing. California is even considering banning them from upholstery, another common application.

EXAMPLE

Why are chemicals in upholstery potentially harmful?

(A) They can cause a disability.

(B) They interfere with the natural metabolic set point.

(C) California is considering banning them.

(D) They are ineffective in preventing fires.

The correct answer is Choice (B), which is clearly stated in the text. Choice (A) may be true, but it isn't supported by the text. Choice (C) is irrelevant to the question, and choice (D) is wrong. Other reasons to place a ban on flame-retardants should be considered, but you're not asked about them, so stick with the options offered.

EXAMPLE

Why is anyone concerned about the metabolic set point?

(A) The set point determines how much people will weigh. Anything that interferes with that is dangerous.

(B) Most people want to be slim.

(C) People don't want chemicals in their bodies.

(D) People are against the misuse of chemicals in the environment.

The correct answer is Choice (A). The text states that these chemicals interfere with the set point, and that is dangerous, causing obesity or drastic underweight. Choices (B), (C), and (D) are all possibly true but aren't supported by the text.

Drag-and-drop questions

The RLA test also uses the drag-and-drop question type. This type of question requires you to drag and drop information from one location on the screen to another. Usually, the purpose is for you to reorder something from least important to most, to place events into a sequence, or simply to select a series of answer choices that answer the question. For example, you may be asked to pick two or three words that describe a person or event in the text, from a choice of four or five options. Doing so is relatively simple: You just click on the answer choice you want to move with your mouse, and then, while holding down the mouse button, you drag the answer choice to the new location. When you reach the new location, let go of the mouse button and drop the answer choice. If you've moved it properly, it will stay where you dropped it. Check out Chapter 2 to see how a drag-and-drop question looks on the actual GED test. Answering a drag-and-drop question requires you to

(A) do some heavy lifting.

(B) type an answer into a box.

(C) click on and move an answer choice.

(D) play a lot of computer games.

Choice (C) is correct. Choice (A) refers more to a job in the real world and not taking a test. Choice (B) applies to fill-in-the-blank or Extended Response questions. Choice (D) is one way to waste time that could be better spent preparing for the test. Although playing games on your computer is a good way to practice using the mouse, this answer choice doesn't answer the specific question based on the material in this section.

Here are a couple types of drag-and-drop questions that you may encounter on the GED test.

> Bradley was determined to get the job. Although he wanted to go to the movies with Keesha, he also needed to work, and the job interview looked promising. He loved his job at the mill, but it was not enough to provide him with the income he needed. Of course, the hours were great, but the hourly rate was not. He could have left early, grabbed some lunch, gone to the interview, and still had his date with Keesha, but that would have created problems with his boss at the mill. Bradley made the only choice he could. He finished his day at the mill and then went to the job interview. Keesha waited by the phone but never heard from him.

EXAMPLE

Put the names and phrases in order of their importance to Bradley in the boxes with the most important on top and the least important at the bottom.

(A) Keesha

(B) job at the mill

(C) job interview

(D) lunch

Based on the text, the best order is Choice (B), *job at the mill*; Choice (C), *job interview*; Choice (A), *Keesha*; and then Choice (D), *lunch*.

EXAMPLE

Which two of these terms best apply to Bradley? Indicate your answers in the box.

(A) friendly

(B) a good boyfriend

(C) hardworking

(D) determined

You know you need to choose two answers because the instructions state this and because there are two boxes to fill. The correct answers are *hardworking* and *determined*. The text states that "Bradley was determined to get the job." He is also hardworking. He didn't leave his current job early to go to the interview. He left his girlfriend in the lurch, not even calling her about the change in plans, so he is certainly not the best of boyfriends. He may be friendly, but that idea is not developed in the text, and so is not the answer.

In the RLA practice tests in Chapters 19 and 27, when you see a question in this format, you see the content of the boxes as words or phrases preceded by capital letters. You can then enter the letters into boxes on the answer sheet to indicate your choices.

Fill-in-the-blank questions

You're likely familiar with the fill-in-the-blank question type. It requires you to find a word, phrase, or number in the source text that answers a question and then type that text or number in a space. On the GED test, the blank that you need to fill in looks like an empty box. Just click in that box and type in your answer. For the fill-in-the-blank questions in this book, you can write your answer directly in the box or on the answer sheet for the practice tests. Refer to the source text in the previous section to answer this question.

Bradley's girlfriend is named ⬚.

There is nothing fancy about fill-in-the-blank questions; they simply require good reading skills.

The grammar and language section

The grammar and language section of the RLA test evaluates your ability to use correct spelling and grammar to write clearly and succinctly. It tests your ability in various ways. Some questions ask you to select the correct alternative to a misspelled or grammatically incorrect sentence. Others ask you to provide a better wording for a sentence. The text will vary from business letters to extracts from textbooks. They can be based on instruction manuals for a phone, a newspaper story, an email, or a contract.

To study and prepare for these types of questions, try the following tips:

>> Review your spelling and grammar skills.

>> Use the local library to find high-school grammar texts or look for free grammar and spelling quizzes online. Some online quizzes correct your answers immediately, giving you excellent feedback on what you know and what needs improvement. For a good review of grammar, check out www.grammar-monster.com.

>> After you take the practice tests in Chapters 19 and 27, you may see some areas where you need to improve. Fortunately, the *For Dummies* series has just the thing for you: *English Grammar For Dummies,* 2nd Edition, by Geraldine Woods (John Wiley & Sons). As you work on your grammar and writing skills, periodically redo the practice tests to see how much you have improved.

Question types

All the questions in the grammar and language section use the same format: the drop-down menu question. In these questions, you select the correct answer from a number of choices. Like multiple-choice, the drop-down menu includes four answer choices.

Drop-down menu questions consist of a sentence with a box on the line containing a down arrow and the word *Select.* When you click on Select, several choices appear. You click on the best choice, and the sentence appears with your selection. *Note:* In this book, you won't see a drop-down menu, but just a list of answer choices. See Chapter 2 for details on how this question format appears onscreen in the actual test.

EXAMPLE

When we got there, we discovered Select... ▼ car was missing.

(A) their

(B) they're

(C) there

(D) they are

The correct answer is Choice (A), *their.* The words in Choices (A), (B), and (C) are *homonyms* — words that sound alike but have different meanings. Choice (A), *their,* shows possession, as in "their book"; Choice (B), *they're,* is a contraction of *they are;* and Choice (C), *there,* is a location. Choice (D) is the full form of *they're,* and so is also incorrect.

EXAMPLE

We Select... ▼ like to thank you for your kind words.

(A) wood

(B) would

(C) would have

(D) would have had

The correct answer is Choice (B). The auxiliary verb *would* is used here to indicate politeness. Choice (A) is another example of a homonym. There is no reason to use the forms in Choices (C) and (D).

The Extended Response

After you finish the first part of the RLA test (the 35-minute Reading Comprehension question-and-answer section), you start on the Extended Response — where you write an essay by analyzing arguments presented in two pieces of sample text. You get 45 minutes to work through this part of the RLA test, and you can't tack on extra time from the previous section. So if you find that you have time left on the first part, go back and review some of the questions where you had difficulties before starting the Extended Response. And remember, after the Extended Response, you have a ten-minute break and then an hour of grammar and language questions.

For the Extended Response section, you must write an essay, with a clear thesis statement, an introductory paragraph, two or three paragraphs of supporting arguments, and a concluding paragraph. You'll have an erasable tablet or an onscreen whiteboard on which to make notes and organize your ideas. You won't use or have access to paper, pencils, or dictionaries. When you are ready to write, you can type your essay into a window on the computer that functions like a basic word processor. The word processor doesn't have a grammar-checker or spell-checker. You're expected to know how to write properly.

The topic you're given to write on is based on given source material: two documents with different or opposing opinions. You're expected to analyze the source material and write an appropriate analytical response. You must show that you can read and understand the source material, do a critical analysis, and prepare a reasoned response based on content drawn from the source texts.

In your essay, you analyze both positions and then give your opinion or explain your viewpoint on which position is better supported by the evidence. Remember to back up your points with specific facts from the source material. When you write this essay, make sure it's a series of interconnected paragraphs on a single topic. Not only should the entire essay begin with an introduction and end with a conclusion, but each paragraph should also have an introductory sentence and a concluding sentence.

WARNING

Write only on the assigned topic. To make sure you understand what the topic is about, read it several times. Essays that are off topic don't receive scores. If you don't get sufficient points on the Extended Response, you likely won't accumulate enough points on the other portions of the RLA test to pass.

Your essay is evaluated on the following criteria:

>> Your argument is based specifically on the source material.

>> You use the evidence from the source material to support your argument.

>> You use valid arguments and separate the supported claims in the material from the unsupported or false claims.

>> Your flow of ideas is logical and well organized.

>> You correctly and appropriately use style, structure, vocabulary, and grammar.

Take a look at these examples of possible Extended Response source materials:

"I will give up my muscle car when the world runs out of oil, not before. . .."

"We need to find alternatives to gasoline-powered vehicles. Climate change is a real threat, and burning fossil fuels contributes to that problem. . .."

These two opinions are the beginnings of two arguments, taking obviously different positions.

You start by determining which argument you see as stronger. Then, you make a list of information that may go into your essay to back up your argument. Trim out any information that doesn't pertain to the topic. If one side or the other uses unsubstantiated opinions as evidence, you can use that evidence to argue that it's a weaker argument.

When you start writing your essay, start with a good, strong introductory sentence that will catch a reader's attention. When you're satisfied with your introductory sentence, review your list of information. Follow that introductory sentence with a couple of sentences outlining, without explanation, your key points. Now turn each key point into a paragraph, paying attention to the flow between paragraphs to show that one relates to the previous one. When you have all these paragraphs, it's time for a conclusion. The easiest way to write a good conclusion is to restate your evidence briefly and state that this indeed proves your point. Don't just rewrite your information, but summarize it in a memorable way. This may be difficult the first time, but with practice, it can become second nature.

The main criteria used to evaluate your essay are ideas and organization, but spelling, grammar, and punctuation count, too. Still, you don't want to get hung up on these details as you write. Focus on strong ideas and clear logic while writing. Then, when you are finished writing, check your essay for spelling, grammar, and punctuation.

If you have time, you can test how well your essay works and stays on topic. Read the introduction, the first and last sentence of every paragraph, and then the conclusion. They should all have the same basic points and flow together nicely. If something seems out of place, you need to go back and review.

TIP

To prepare for this part of the test, in the months and weeks leading up to your test date, read newspapers and news magazines, especially opinion pieces. Analyze how arguments are presented and how the writers try to form and sway your opinion. Examine how well they present their data and how they use relevant and irrelevant data to persuade the reader. Then try your hand with the Extended Response questions in Chapter 9, the two complete GED practice tests in Chapters 19 and 27, and the complete, included online practice test.

Handling the Social Studies Test

For the Social Studies test, you have 70 minutes to answer 50 questions. The questions use the same formats as the RLA test questions: multiple-choice, fill-in-the-blank, drag-and-drop, and drop-down menu questions (see the earlier sections on Reasoning through Language Arts for details). You may also have some questions that require use of the calculator. (For these questions, the calculator icon appears at the top of the computer screen.) The questions on the Social Studies test deal with the following subject areas:

>> Civics and government (50 percent)

>> American history (20 percent)

>> Economics (15 percent)

>> Geography and the world (15 percent)

The questions in this test are based on written texts (source texts) and visual materials — pictures, tables, graphs, photographs, political cartoons, diagrams, or maps. These textual and visual materials come from a variety of sources, such as government documents, academic texts, work-related documents, and atlases.

You can do only a limited amount of studying for this test. The information to answer each question is in the text or graphic that comes with the question. You need to analyze the material and draw conclusions based on what's presented. However, you can prepare by reading books that offer you a basic outline of American history and by learning about how government functions. Read the newspapers to follow current events and the business section for economics. You don't need to go into great depth or memorize pages of dates and names, but you should have an idea of the general flow of history. You also need to know how government — from federal to local — works.

A second skill you need to master for this test is reading and extracting information from maps, graphs, and tables. On the Social Studies test, you may see a map with different shadings, and you have to determine what the shadings mean and what the difference is between a light gray and a dark gray area on the map. They're not just decoration. If you look carefully at all the text and boxes with information on the map or chart, you'll see that everything has a meaning. So find some maps online, or get an atlas, and practice reading maps.

You may see the following types of questions on the Social Studies test.

The following question is based on this table.

The Five Longest Rivers in the World

River	*Location*	*Length in Miles*
Nile	Africa	4,160
Amazon	South America	4,083
Yangtze	China	3,915
Mississippi/Missouri/Red Rock	United States	3,741
Huang	China	3,395

EXAMPLE

According to the table, the length of the fourth-longest river in the world is [ ] miles.

(A) 4,160

(B) 4,083

(C) 3,741

(D) 3,395

The correct answer is Choice (C). The table shows that the Mississippi/Missouri/Red Rock River is 3,741 miles long.

The following question is based on this excerpt from the diary of Christopher Columbus.

> Monday, 6 August. The rudder of the caravel *Pinta* became loose, being broken or unshipped. It was believed that this happened by the contrivance of Gomez Rascon and Christopher Quintero, who were on board the caravel, because they disliked the voyage. The Admiral says he had found them in an unfavorable disposition before setting out. He was in much anxiety at not being able to afford any assistance in this case, but says that it somewhat quieted his apprehensions to know that Martín Alonzo Pinzón, Captain of the *Pinta*, was a man of courage and capacity. Made progress, day and night, of twenty-nine leagues.

EXAMPLE

Why would Rascon and Quintero have loosened the rudder?

(A) They were trying to repair the rudder.

(B) The Admiral found them in an unfavorable disposition.

(C) The captain was very competent.

(D) They did not want to be on the voyage.

The correct answer is Choice (D). This answer is the only one supported by the text. The others may be related to statements in the passage, but they don't answer the question.

EXAMPLE

The expedition traveled [ ] leagues that day.

The correct answer is 29. This number is stated directly in the last sentence of the excerpt.

Knowing How to Grapple with the Science Test

When you take the Science test, you have to answer the same variety of question formats, including multiple-choice, fill-in-the-blank, drop-down menu, and drag-and-drop questions, in 90 minutes. The questions deal with the following topics:

>> Life science (40 percent)

>> Physical science, including chemistry and physics (40 percent)

>> Earth and space science (20 percent)

REMEMBER

Most of the information you need to answer the questions on the Science test is given to you in the passages and other graphic material, such as tables, graphs, illustrations, diagrams, and photos. To get a high score, though, you're expected to have picked up a basic knowledge of science. However, even if you correctly answer only the questions based entirely on the information presented, you should get a score high enough to pass. As on the Social Studies test, some questions may ask you to calculate a numeric answer. For these questions, the calculator icon will appear.

Although you're not expected to be an expert on the various topics in the Science test, you are expected to understand the vocabulary. To accomplish this, read as widely as you can in science books. If you run across words you don't understand, write them down with a definition or explanation. Doing so will provide a vocabulary list for you to review before the test.

You must read and understand the source material in the Science test to be able to select the best choice for an answer. Practice reading quickly and accurately. Because you have a time limit, practice skimming passages to look for key words. The less time you spend on the passages, the more time you'll have to answer the questions, and the more time you'll have at the end of the test to review your answers and attempt questions that you found difficult the first time you read them. Attempt to answer every question. You may get a point for your answer if you try it, but you can't get a point for a question you've skipped. If you completely run out of time, answer remaining questions with random guesses.

Here are some sample questions similar to those that may be in the Science test.

The following questions are based on this excerpt from a press release.

> A key feature of the Delta 4's operation is the use of a common booster core, or CBC, a rocket stage that measures some 150 feet long and 16 feet wide. By combining one or more CBCs with various upper stages or strap-on solid rocket boosters, the Delta 4 can handle an extreme range of satellite applications for military, civilian, and commercial customers.

EXAMPLE

The CBC in this context is

(A) an upper stage rocket booster.

(B) a common booster core.

(C) a cooperative boosters corps.

(D) a common ballistic cavalier.

The correct answer is Choice (B). After all, it's the only answer choice mentioned in the passage. Skimming the passage for CBC would give you an idea of where to look for a full explanation of the abbreviation.

EXAMPLE

How can the Delta 4 handle a wide range of applications?

(A) developing a Delta 5

(B) continuing research

(C) using the CBC as the base of a rocket ship

(D) creating a common core booster

The correct answer is Choice (C). The passage says that "By combining one or more CBCs with various upper stages or strap-on solid rocket boosters. . .," so Choice (C) comes closest to answering the question.

Conquering the Mathematical Reasoning Test

The Mathematical Reasoning test covers the following four major areas:

>> Algebra, equations, and patterns

>> Data analysis, statistics, and probability

» Measurement and geometry

» Number operations

More specifically, about 45 percent of the questions focus on quantitative problem-solving and the other approximately 55 percent focuses on algebraic problem-solving. You have 115 minutes to answer 50 questions.

The Mathematical Reasoning (Math) test has many of the same types of questions as the other sections (multiple-choice, fill-in-the-blank, and so on). Check out Chapter 2 for how these questions look on the computer screen when you take the GED.

Mathematics is mathematics. That may sound simple, but it isn't. To succeed on the Math test, you should have a good grasp of the basic operations: addition, subtraction, multiplication, and division. You should be able to perform these operations quickly and accurately and, in the case of simple numbers, perform them mentally. The more automatic and accurate your responses are, the less time you'll need for each question, and the greater your chances are of finishing the test on time with a few minutes to spare to check any questions you may have skipped or answers you want to double-check.

The other skill you should try to master is reading and solving "story problems." These questions ask you to read a short situation and then figure out how to answer the question. The question may be about how much fabric is needed to make a tablecloth, what food you can order at a fast food restaurant for under $7, or how many cups of a certain ingredient are needed if you triple the recipe. You need to understand the situation as described and use the information you have to answer the question. These questions also contain extra information, and part of your job is to figure out which information is important and which you can safely ignore as you figure out your answer.

You can use a calculator on all but the first five questions on the GED Math test. If you take the test online at home, you can access the onscreen calculator by clicking the calculator icon in the toolbar. If you test at a testing center, you can use the onscreen calculator or use your own TI-30XS MultiView calculator.

Consider the following questions (one traditional multiple-choice question and two questions that use different formats that you'll encounter on the computer) that are similar to what you may see on the Math test.

EXAMPLE

A right-angle triangle has a hypotenuse of 5 feet and one side that is 36 inches long. What is the length of the other side in feet?

(A) 3 ft.

(B) 48 ft.

(C) 6 ft.

(D) 4 ft.

The correct answer is Choice (D). The tricky part of this question is that you need to know that you have to apply the Pythagorean Theorem to answer this question. Using the Pythagorean Theorem (a formula that's given to you on the formula sheet that is available during the test), you know that $a^2 + b^2 = c^2$, where c is the hypotenuse and a and b are the other two sides. Because you know the hypotenuse and one side, turn the equation around so that it reads $a^2 = c^2 - b^2$.

TIP

You can open the formula sheet on the computer when needed. But keep in mind that the less you need to open it, the more time you have to answer questions.

To get c^2, you square the hypotenuse: $(5)(5) = 25$.

The side is given in inches — to convert inches to feet, divide by 12: $36/12 = 3$. To get b^2, square this side: $(3)(3) = 9$.

Now solve the equation for a: $a^2 = 25 - 9$ or $a^2 = 16$. Take the square root of both sides, and you get $a = 4$.

The Math test presents real-life situations in the questions. So if you find yourself answering 37 feet to a question about the height of a room or $3.00 for an annual salary, recheck your answer because you're probably wrong.

The following question asks you to fill in the blank.

Barb is counting the number of boxes in a warehouse. In the first storage area, she finds 24 boxes. The second area contains 30 boxes. The third area contains 28 boxes. If the warehouse has 6 storage areas where it stores boxes and the areas have an average of 28 boxes, the total number of boxes in the last 3 areas is [   ].

The correct answer is 86. If the warehouse has 6 storage areas and it has an average of 28 boxes in each, it has $(6)(28) = 168$ boxes in the warehouse. The first 3 areas have $24 + 30 + 28 = 82$ boxes in them. The last 3 areas must have $168 - 82 = 86$ boxes in them.

A rectangle has one corner on the origin. The base goes from the origin to the point (3,0). The right side goes from (3,0) to (3,4). Where does the missing point go on the graph? [   ]

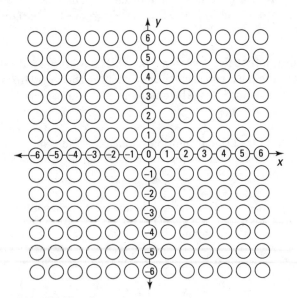

The correct answer is to (0,4). If you draw the three points given on the graph, you see that a fourth point at (0,4) creates the rectangle. Write that answer in the box.

IN THIS CHAPTER

» Getting ready in the weeks before, the night before, and the day of the test

» Relying on practice tests

» Figuring out what to expect on test day

» Nailing down important test-taking strategies

» Staying calm and relaxed while you take the test

Chapter **4**

Succeeding on the GED Test

You may never have taken a standardized test before. Or if you have, you may wake up sweating in the middle of the night from nightmares about your past experiences. Whether you've experienced the joys or sorrows of standardized tests, in order to succeed on the GED test, you must know how to perform well on this type of test, which consists mostly of multiple-choice questions.

The good news is, you've come to the right spot to find out more about this type of test. This chapter offers some important pointers on how to prepare on the days and nights before the test, what to do on the morning of the test, and what to do during the test to be successful. You also discover some important test-taking strategies to help you feel confident.

Leading Up to Test Time

Doing well on the GED test involves more than walking into the test site and answering the questions. You need to be prepared for the challenges in the test. To ensure that you're ready to tackle the test head-on, make sure you do the following leading up to the test:

» **Get enough sleep.** I'm sorry if I sound like your parents, but it's true — you shouldn't take tests when you're approaching exhaustion. Plan your time so you can get a good night's sleep for several days before the test, and avoid excess caffeine. If you prepare ahead of time, you'll be ready, and sleep will come easier.

» **Eat a good breakfast.** A healthy breakfast fuels your mind and body. You have to spend several hours taking the test, and you definitely don't want to falter during that time. Eat some protein and whole grains, and avoid sugars (donuts, jelly, fruit) because they can cause you to tire easily. You don't want your empty stomach fighting with your full brain.

- » **Take some deep breaths.** During your trip to the testing site, prepare yourself mentally for the test. Clear your head of all distractions, practice deep breathing, and imagine yourself acing the test. Don't panic.

- » **Start at the beginning, not the end.** Remember that the day of the test is the end of a long journey of preparation and not the beginning. It takes time to build mental muscles.

- » **Be on time.** Make sure you know what time the test begins and the exact location of your test site. Arrive early. If necessary, take a practice run to make sure you have enough time to get from your home or workplace to the testing center. You don't need the added pressure of worrying about whether you can make it to the test on time. In fact, this added pressure can create industrial-strength panic in the calmest of people.

Traffic congestion happens whether you test at a test center or are driving home from the supermarket to take the test. No one can plan for it, but you can leave extra time to make sure it doesn't ruin your day. If you test at a test center, plan your route and practice it. Then leave extra time in case a meteor crashes into the street and a crowd gathers around it, stalling your progress. Even though the GED test is now administered on a computer and not everyone has to start at the same time, you still need to be punctual. Examiners won't show you a lot of consideration if you show up too late to complete the test or tests because you didn't check the times. They have even less sympathy if you show up on the wrong date.

If you test online at home, double-check your computer, Internet connection, and room arrangement the night before. Make sure everyone in your house knows that they cannot disturb you during the test. Specifically, they cannot enter the room during the test. If you have children and are using childcare or a babysitter during the test, double-check those arrangements, too.

You can check in for the test as early as 30 minutes before your appointment time if you test online at home, and you can start as soon as a proctor is available. Checking in early can help you finish on time if you have other activities planned after the test.

Using Practice Tests to Your Advantage

Taking practice GED tests is important for a few reasons, including the following:

- » **They give you an indication of how well you know the material.** One or two tests won't give you a definite answer, because you need to do four or five tests to cover all possible topics, but they do give you an indication of where you stand.

- » **They confirm whether you know how to use the computer to answer the questions.** Until you try, you simply won't know for sure.

- » **They familiarize you with the test format.** You can read about test questions, but you can't actually understand them until you've worked through several.

- » **They can ease your stress.** A successful run-through on a practice test allows you to feel more comfortable and confident in your own abilities to take the GED test successfully and alleviate your overall anxiety.

TIP

You can find a practice test of each section in Parts 6 and 7, as well as a complete online practice test. The practice tests are an important part of any preparation program. They're the feedback mechanism that you may normally get from a private tutor. As long as you check your answers after the practice test and read the answer explanations, you can benefit from taking practice tests. If possible, take as many practice tests as you can before taking the actual GED test. You can find more practice tests at `https://ged.com/study/free_online_ged_test/`. Use your favorite Internet search engine to find more examples of online practice tests. The GED Testing Service also offers the GED Ready practice test, which is your best indicator of whether you are ready to take the test (and is required before you sign up to test at home).

Finding Out What to Take to the GED Test

Passing the GED can bring you many benefits, so you need to treat it seriously and come prepared. Make sure you bring the following items with you on test day.

>> **You:** The most important thing to bring to the GED test is obviously you. If you enroll to take the test, you have to show up; otherwise, you'll receive a big fat zero and lose your testing fee. If something unfortunate happens after you enroll, go to your online account and see if you can reschedule. You may need to call the GED Testing Service or use their online chat to reschedule.

>> **Correct identification:** Before you can start the test, the test proctors — online and in person — want to make sure you're really you. Bring a government-issued photo ID — a driver's license, a state ID card, a passport, and a matrícula consular are all fine. Have your ID in a place where you can easily reach it. And, when asked to identify yourself, don't pull out a mirror and say, "Yep, that's me."

>> **Registration confirmation:** The registration confirmation is your proof that you did register. If you're taking the test in an area where everybody knows you and everything you do, you may not need the confirmation, but I suggest you take it anyway. It's light and doesn't take up much room in your pocket or purse.

>> **Other miscellaneous items:** In the instructions you receive after you register for the test, you get a list of what you need to bring with you. Besides yourself and the items I listed previously, other items you want to bring or wear include the following:

- **Comfortable clothes and shoes.** When you're taking the test, you want to be as relaxed as possible. Uncomfortable clothes and shoes may distract you from doing your best. You're taking the GED test, not modeling the most recent fashions.

- **A bottle of water and a healthful snack.** Check whether you can bring these with you into the room at the testing center. If you test online at home, you are only allowed to have some water, in a clear glass, on the desk with you. But you can eat a quick snack in the 10-minute break between tests if you take more than one test.

- **Reading glasses.** If you need glasses to read a computer monitor, don't forget to bring them to the test. Bring a spare pair, if you have one. You can't do the test if you can't read the screen.

The rules about what enters the testing room are strict. Don't take any chances. If something isn't on the list of acceptable items and isn't normal clothing, leave it at home. Laptops, cellphones, and other electronic devices will most likely be banned from the testing area. However, you may bring a handheld Texas Instruments TI-30XS MultiView calculator to the testing center, which you may use whenever the calculator icon appears on the screen. But you aren't required to BYOC (bring your own calculator). A calculator icon appears on the screen whenever one is necessary to answer a question. All you have to do is click on the calculator icon, and you have a fully functioning calculator onscreen. However, for many people, a real calculator saves time on the test.

Leave other electronics at home, locked in your car, or in a locker at the testing center. The last place on earth to discuss whether you can bring something into the test site is at the door on test day.

REMEMBER

Whatever you do, be sure not to bring the following with you to the testing room at the GED testing center, and make sure they are out of reach (or out of the room) if you test at home:

>> Books

>> Notes or scratch paper

>> Tablets

>> Cellphones

>> Smartwatches

>> Anything valuable, like a laptop computer that you don't feel comfortable leaving outside the room while you take the test

Making Sure You're Comfortable Before the Test Begins

At a test center, you usually take the GED test in an examination room with at least one official (sometimes called a *proctor* or *examiner*) who's in charge of the test. At home, you have to take the online test in a room that meets the GED Testing Service's requirements under the observation of an online proctor using a webcam. In either case, the test is the same.

TIP

As soon as you sit down to take the GED test, take a few moments before the test actually starts to relax and get comfortable. You're going to be in that chair for quite some time, so hunker down and keep these few tips in mind before you begin:

>> **Make sure that the screen is at a comfortable height.** If necessary, adjust your chair to a height that suits you. Unlike a pencil-and-paper test, you'll be working with a monitor, keyboard, and mouse. Although you can shift the keyboard around and maybe change the angle of the monitor, generally you're stuck in that position for the duration of the test. If you need to make any adjustments, make them before you start. You want to feel as physically comfortable as possible. If you are left-handed, you may need to rearrange the keyboard and mouse. After the test starts, you can also adjust the size of the font (the type) onscreen. Choosing the right size for you can make reading easier.

>> **Use the bathroom before you start.** This may sound like a silly suggestion, but it all goes to being comfortable. You don't need distractions. Even if bathroom breaks are permitted during the test, you don't want to take away time from the test. Remember, you cannot leave the room for any reason if you test online at home.

The proctor reads the test instructions to you and lets you log into the computer to start the test. Listen carefully to these instructions so you know how much time you have to take the test as well as any other important information. Only the Reasoning through Language Arts test has a ten-minute break built into the time. The other tests are 70, 90, or 115 minutes without a break. (Refer to the next section for details about the timing of each test.)

Discovering Important Test-Taking Strategies

You can increase your score by mastering a few smart test-taking strategies. To help you do so, I give you some tips in these sections on

>> Using your time wisely

>> Addressing and answering questions

>> Using intelligent guessing

>> Leaving time for review

Watching the clock: Using your time wisely

When you start the GED test, you may feel pressed for time and have the urge to rush through the questions. I strongly advise that you don't. You have sufficient time to do the test at a reasonable pace. You have only a certain amount of time for each section in the GED exam, so time management is an important part of succeeding on the test. You need to plan ahead and use your time wisely.

REMEMBER

You must complete each section in one sitting, except for the Reasoning through Language Arts test. There, you get a ten-minute break after the Extended Response (also known as the essay).

During the test, the computer keeps you constantly aware of the time with a clock in the upper-right corner. Pay attention to the clock. When the test begins, check that time, and be sure to monitor how much time you have left as you work your way through the test. Table 4-1 shows you how much time you have for each test section.

TABLE 4-1 **Time for Each GED Test Section**

Test Section	Time Limit (in Minutes)
Reasoning through Language Arts	95 (split into two sections, 35 and 60)
Reasoning through Language Arts, Extended Response	45
Social Studies	70
Science	90
Mathematical Reasoning	115

TIP

As you start, the opening screen will tell you the number of questions you have to answer. Quickly divide the time by the number of questions. Doing so can give you a rough idea of how much time to spend on each question. For example, on the Mathematical Reasoning test, suppose that you see you have 50 questions to answer. You have 115 minutes to complete the test. Divide the time by the number of questions to find out how much time you have for each one: 115/50 = 2.3 minutes or 2 minutes and 18 seconds per question. As you progress, repeat the calculation to see how you're doing.

Remember that you can answer the questions in any order, except for the RLA Extended Response. Do the easiest questions first. If you come to a question that will take a long time to answer (such as a complicated math question), skip it. If you get stuck on a question, leave it and come back to it later if you have time. If you are unsure of an answer, use the Flag for Review button to mark it so you can return to it later if you have time. The Review Screen will help you quickly find and return to flagged and skipped questions later in the test. In the meantime, you can keep to that schedule and answer as many questions as possible.

As you can see from Table 4-1, if you don't monitor the time for each question, you won't have time to answer all the questions on the test. Keep in mind the following general time-management tips to help you complete each exam on time:

>> **Measure the time you have to answer each question without spending more time on timing than answering.** Group questions together; for example, use the information in Table 4-1 to calculate how much time you have for each question on each test. Multiply the answer by 5 to give you a time slot for any five test questions. Then try to make sure that you answer each group of five questions within the time you've calculated. Doing so helps you complete all the questions and leaves you several minutes for review.

>> **Keep calm and don't panic.** The time you spend panicking could be better spent answering questions.

>> **Practice using the sample tests in this book and the online-only test.** The more you practice timed sample test questions, the easier managing a timed test becomes. You can get used to doing something in a limited amount of time if you practice. Refer to the earlier section, "Using Practice Tests to Your Advantage," for more information.

When time is up, immediately stop and breathe a sigh of relief. When the test ends, the examiner will give you a log-off procedure. Listen for instructions on what to do or where to go next.

Addressing and answering questions

When you start the test, you want to have a game plan in place for how to answer the questions. Keep the following tips in mind to help you address each question:

>> **Whenever you read a question, ask yourself, "What am I being asked?"** Doing so helps you stay focused on what you need to find out to answer the question. Then try to answer it.

>> **Try to eliminate some answers.** Even if you don't really know the answer, the process of elimination can help. When you're offered four answer choices, some will be obviously wrong. Eliminate those choices, and you have already improved your odds of guessing a correct answer.

>> **Don't overthink.** Because all the questions are straightforward, don't look for trick questions. The questions ask for an answer based on the information given.

>> **Find the best answer and quickly verify that it answers the question.** If it does, click on that choice, and move on. If it doesn't, leave it and come back to it after you answer all the other questions, if you have time. *Remember:* You need to pick the *most* correct answer from the choices offered. It may not be the perfect answer, but it is what is required.

Guess for success: Using intelligent guessing

The multiple-choice questions, regardless of the onscreen format, provide you with four possible answers. You get between one and three points for every correct answer. Nothing is subtracted for incorrect answers. That means you can guess on the questions you don't know for sure without fear that you'll lose points. Make educated guesses by eliminating as many obviously wrong choices as possible and choosing from just one or two remaining choices.

When the question gives you four possible answers and you randomly choose one, you have a 25 percent chance of guessing the correct answer without even reading the question. Of course, I don't recommend using this method during the test.

If you know that one of the answers is definitely wrong, you now have just three answers to choose from, giving you a 33 percent (1 in 3) chance of choosing the correct answer. If you know that two of the answers are wrong, you leave yourself only two possible answers to choose from, giving you a 50 percent (1 in 2) chance of guessing right — much better than 25 percent! Removing one or two choices you know are wrong makes choosing the correct answer much more likely.

Try to spot the wrong choices by following these tips:

>> **Make sure the answer choice really answers the question.** Wrong choices usually don't answer the question — that is, they may sound good, but they answer a different question than the one the test asks.

>> **When two answer choices seem very close, consider both of them carefully because they both can't be right — but they both *can* be wrong.** Some answer choices may be very close, and all seem correct, but there's a fine line between completely correct and nearly correct. Be careful. These answer choices are sometimes given to see whether you really understand the material.

>> **Look for opposite answers in the hopes that you can eliminate one.** If two answers contradict each other, both can't be right, but both can be wrong.

>> **Trust your instincts.** Some wrong choices may just strike you as wrong when you first read them. If you spend time preparing for the test, you probably know more than you think.

Leaving time for review

Having a few minutes at the end of a test to check your work is a great way to set your mind at ease. As soon as you answer the last question, the test will take you to the Review screen, which will show you a list of all the questions, and whether you skipped or flagged any questions. This way, you can quickly review any questions that may be troubling and go back and answer any ones you skipped earlier. Keep the following tips in mind as you review your answers:

>> **Figure out how much time you have per remaining question, and try to answer each question in a little less than that time.** The extra seconds you don't use the first time through the test add up to time at the end of the test for review. Some questions require more thought and decision-making than others. Use your extra seconds to answer those questions.

>> **Don't change a lot of answers at the last minute.** Second-guessing yourself can lead to trouble. Often, second-guessing leads you to changing correct answers to incorrect ones. Numerous studies show that when a test-taker changes an answer selection, the new selection is usually incorrect. If you have prepared well and worked numerous sample questions, then you're likely to get the correct answers the first time. Ignoring all your preparation and knowledge to play a hunch isn't a good idea, either at the racetrack or on a test.

>> **If you cannot answer all the questions in the time remaining, answer them randomly.** There is no guessing penalty on the GED, so don't leave any questions unanswered. The one or two points you pick up from answering all the questions may be the points you need to pass.

>> **On the Extended Response section, use any remaining time to reread and review your final essay.** You may have written a good essay, but you always need to check for typos and grammar mistakes. The essay is evaluated for style, content, and proper English. That includes spelling and grammar.

Keeping Your Head in the Game

To succeed in taking the GED test, you need to be prepared. In addition to studying the content and skills needed for the four test sections, you also want to be mentally prepared. Although you may be nervous, you can't let your nerves get the best of you. Stay calm and take a deep breath. Here are a few pointers to help you stay focused on the task at hand:

» **Take time to relax.** Passing the GED test is an important milestone in life. Make sure you leave a bit of time to relax, both while you prepare for the test sections and just before you take them. Relaxing has a place in preparing as long as it doesn't become your main activity.

» **Make sure you know the rules of the room before you begin.** If you have questions about using the bathroom during the test or what to do if you finish early, ask the proctor before you begin. If you don't want to ask these questions in public, call the GED office in your area before test day, and ask your questions over the telephone. For general GED questions, call 877-392-6433 or check out ged.com. This site has many pages, but the FAQ page is always a good place to start.

» **Keep your eyes on your monitor.** Everybody knows not to look at other people's work during the test, but, to be on the safe side, don't stretch, roll your eyes, or do anything else that may be mistaken for looking at another test. At a test center, most of the tests will be different on the various computers, so looking around is futile, but doing so can get you into a lot of trouble. You should also keep your eyes on the screen if you test online at home. Everything you need to take the test is on the screen in front of you. Looking around the room or looking away from the screen repeatedly could be considered suspicious behavior.

» **Stay calm.** Your nerves can use up a lot of energy needed for the test. Concentrate on the job at hand. You can always be nervous or panicky some other time.

Because taking standardized tests probably isn't a usual situation for you, you may feel nervous. This is perfectly normal. Just try to focus on answering one question at a time, and push any other thoughts to the back of your mind. Sometimes taking a few deep breaths can clear your mind; just don't spend a lot of time focusing on your breathing. After all, your main job is to pass the GED test.

2

Minding Your Ps and Qs: The Reasoning through Language Arts Test

Find out everything you ever wanted to know about the Reasoning through Language Arts test.

Understand the types of materials you're expected to read and answer questions.

Recognize how the test and questions are formatted and what the Extended Response item is like.

Discover some strategies to help you do your best on this test and put them to practice on some sample test questions.

Chapter 5

Preparing for the Reasoning through Language Arts Test

The Reasoning through Language Arts (RLA) test evaluates your ability to do the following:

» Apply skills in reading comprehension.

» Apply concepts in grammar and language to correct errors in writing. *Grammar* is *the* basic structure of language — you know: subjects, verbs, sentences, fragments, and all that. *Language* includes vocabulary, usage, punctuation, capitalization, and other features of written English.

» Apply writing skills to create a logical and effective extended response (essay).

Most of what you're tested on the RLA test is stuff you've picked up over the years, either in school or just by speaking, reading, and observing. However, to help you prepare better for this test, I give you some more skill-building tips in this chapter.

The RLA test is divided into three sections. You start off with a 35-minute question-and-answer Reading Comprehension section, and then you spend 45 minutes writing the Extended Response (the essay). After a 10-minute break, you finish with Grammar and Language, a 60-minute question-and-answer section that presents more questions. The overall time is 150 minutes for all three components, including the 10-minute break.

In this chapter, I provide all you need to know to prepare for the Reading Comprehension and Grammar and Language components. From reading everything you can, to improving your grammar and spelling, to increasing your reading speed and comprehension, this chapter equips you with what you need so you can sit down at the computer the day of the test, ready to ace those components.

The RLA test also has an extended response item — often called "the essay." It's a short essay you write in 45 minutes. Not to worry: In Chapters 8 and 9, I give you a complete overview and tips on how to succeed! And I give you plenty of writing practice, including ideas on how to evaluate and improve your writing, in the practice tests!

Grasping What's on the Grammar and Language Component

To pass this component of the RLA test, you need to demonstrate that you have a command of the conventions of standard English. You need to know the appropriate vocabulary to use and avoid slang. You need to be able to spell, identify incorrect grammar, and eliminate basic errors, including such common errors as run-on sentences and sentence fragments.

To help you succeed, I provide insightful information in the following sections about what skills this part of the test covers, what you can do to brush up on those skills, and the general question format for this component. With this information in hand, you can be confident in your ability to tackle any type of grammar and language question on test day.

Looking at the skills the Grammar and Language component covers

The Grammar and Language component of the RLA test evaluates you on the following types of skills. Note that unlike the other GED test sections, this component of the RLA test expects that you *know* or at least *are familiar with* the rules of grammar. Just looking at the passages provided won't do you much good if you don't understand the basics of these rules already.

>> **Mechanics:** You don't have to become a professional writer to pass this test, but you should know or review basic mechanics. Check out *English Grammar For Dummies,* 2nd Edition, by Geraldine Woods (John Wiley & Sons, Inc.), to review what you should know or may have forgotten. The mechanics of writing include the following.

- **Capitalization:** You have to recognize which words start with a capital letter and which words don't. All sentences start with a capital letter, but so do titles, like *Miss, President,* and *Senator,* when they're followed by a person's name. Names of cities, states, and countries are also capitalized.

- **Punctuation:** This area of writing mechanics includes everyone's personal favorite: commas. (Actually, most people hate commas because they aren't sure how to use them, but the basic rules are simple.) The more you read, the better you get at punctuation. If you're reading and don't understand why punctuation is or isn't used, check with your grammar guidebook or the Internet.

The comma is the most misused punctuation mark in English. Always think carefully before you add or remove a comma.

- **Spelling:** You don't have to spot a lot of misspelled words, but you do have to know how to spell contractions and possessives and understand the different spellings of *homonyms* — words that sound the same but have different spellings and meanings, like *their* and *there.*

- **Contractions:** This area of writing mechanics has nothing to do with those painful moments before childbirth! Instead, *contractions* are formed when the English language shortens and combines two words by leaving out one or more letters. For example, when you say or write *can't,* you're using a shortened form of *cannot.*

  TIP

  The important thing to remember about contractions is that the *apostrophe* (that's a single quotation mark) takes the place of the letter or letters that are left out. That's why we write *can't.* The apostrophe takes the place of *n* and *o.*

- **Possessives:** Do you know people who are possessive? They're all about ownership, right? So is the grammar form of possessives. *Possessives* are words that show ownership or possession, usually by adding an apostrophe and an *s* to a person's or object's name. If Marcia owns a car, that car is *Marcia's* car. The word *Marcia's* is a possessive. Make sure you know the difference between singular and plural possessives. For example: "The girl**'s** coat is torn." *(Girl* is singular, so the apostrophe goes before the *s.)* "The girl**s'** coats are torn." *(Girls* is plural, so the apostrophe goes after the *s.)* When working with plural possessives, form the plural first and then add the apostrophe.

  TIP

  Some plural nouns, such as *women,* do not end in *s,* so the plural possessive is formed with *'s:* "The women**'s** coats are torn."

» **Grammar:** Grammar focuses on the basic rules for forming correct sentences. As with mechanics, *English Grammar For Dummies* can help you with commonly tested items such as the following.

- **Complete and incomplete sentences:** These include run-on sentences, sentence fragments, and improperly joined sentences. For example, "The quick red fox jumped over the lazy brown dog the dog kept on sleeping," runs two sentences together. Fix the error with a comma and *but:* "The quick red fox jumped over the lazy brown dog, **but** the dog kept on sleeping."

- **Proper agreement:** In written English, the subject and the verb of a sentence should agree. For example, "Matilda and her sister is watching TV and knitting" is incorrect. To correct this sentence, change *is* to *are* to agree with the subject of the sentence, *Matilda and her sister,* which is plural.

- **Correct word order:** Words should be in the correct order. For example, "She bought some orange, ugly, fake flowers," should be changed to, "She bought some ugly, fake, orange flowers."

  TIP

  Extensive reading before the test can give you a good idea of how good sentences are structured and put together. The advice here is to read, read, and read some more.

» **Usage:** This broad category covers a lot of topics. English has a wide variety of rules, and these questions test your knowledge and understanding of those rules. Verbs have tenses that must be consistent. Pronouns must refer back to nouns properly. If the last two sentences sound like Greek to you, make sure you review usage rules. They also cover vocabulary and acceptable standard English usage. People have become very comfortable with short forms used in texting, but "LOL" or "C U L8R" aren't acceptable in standard writing.

Having a firm grasp of these writing conventions can help you get a more accurate picture of the types of questions you'll encounter on this part of the test.

Understanding the format of the Grammar and Language component

The Grammar and Language component consists of passages each accompanied by a set of drop-down menu questions. (For more information this question type, see Chapter 2. You can find more examples in Chapter 6 and plenty of practice in Chapter 7.) Your task is to read, revise, and edit documents that may include how-to information, informational texts, and workplace materials. Don't worry — since all the questions use the drop-down menu format, you don't have to come up with the answers all on your own. You just have to find each answer among the four choices. And the best part: Preparing for this component helps you build the grammar and other language skills needed for the Extended Response.

TIP

To do your best on Grammar and Language part of the RLA test, read the passage completely before you answer the questions.

Rocking the Reading Comprehension Component

In today's society, being able to comprehend, analyze, and apply something you've read is the strongest predictor of career and college readiness and an important skill set to have. In the following sections, you explore the four aspects of good reading skills: comprehension, analysis, command of evidence, and synthesis.

Looking at the skills the Reading component covers

The questions on the RLA reading portion of the test focus on the following skills, which you're expected to be able to use as you read both fiction and nonfiction passages.

>> **Comprehension:** Questions that test your *comprehension* skills assess your ability to do close reading — that is, to read a source of information thoughtfully so that you have a precise understanding of what you've read and can restate the information in your own words. Items may also ask you to show understanding by ordering events in a passage or to rephrase what you read without losing the meaning of the passage. In addition, items can ask you to show how the details support the main idea. Other items ask you to determine the meaning of specific words in context and grasp how a writer's use of a particular word or phrase affects the meaning of a sentence, a paragraph, or the entire passage.

>> **Analysis:** Questions that test your *analysis* skills assess your ability to draw conclusions, understand consequences, and make inferences about the passage. To answer these questions, make sure your answers are based only on the information in the passage and not on outside knowledge or the online article you read last week. Items may ask you to explain how parts of the passage (such as paragraphs, sentences, and examples) work together to accomplish the writer's purpose. Other items may ask you to show how transitional words and phrases (such as *however* and *for example)* signal relationships among ideas in the passage. Other items may ask you to analyze the writer's purposes in writing the passage — to convince, to share knowledge with the reader, or even to amuse the reader!

>> **Command of evidence:** These questions assess your ability to identify and evaluate evidence. You need to understand the passage writer's point of view in order to assess the strength and weakness of their position. Some questions will ask you to identify the evidence the author uses for support. Other times, you will have to identify among the options additional supporting evidence. Other questions will ask you whether the author's evidence offers valid support for a position, or merely an opinion or belief unsupported by reasons, examples, or facts.

>> **Synthesis:** Questions that test your *synthesis* skills assess your ability to take information in one form and in one location and put it together with information in another context. Here, you get a chance to make connections between two related passages and compare and contrast them. You may be asked to compare and contrast the tone, point of view, style, effectiveness, or purposes of the passages — and saying that the purpose of a passage is to confuse and confound test-takers isn't the answer!

REMEMBER

Some reading questions may ask you to use information in the source text passages combined with information presented in the questions. So make sure you use all the information that you have available. And don't forget to use the tabs and scroll bars to reveal the complete passage and question — you never know where an answer may come from. For complete information on the tabs and scroll bars, check Chapter 2.

Understanding the format of the Reading component

The RLA Reading component measures your ability to understand and interpret fiction and nonfiction passages. It's plain and simple — no tricks involved. You don't have to do any math to figure out the answers to the questions. You just have to read, understand, and use the material presented to you to answer the corresponding questions.

The passages in this test are similar to the works a high-school student would come across in English class. To help you feel more comfortable with the RLA Reading component, I'm here to give you a better idea of what this test looks like on paper.

The reading passages are presented on the left side of a split screen, with the question on the right. Each passage will be between 450 and 900 words. The passages in this test may come from workplace (on-the-job) materials or from academic reading materials. Seventy-five percent of the source texts will be from informational texts — nonfiction documents. The remaining 25 percent will be drawn from literary texts, generally short stories and novels. With each source text, you have to answer four to eight questions. Some items will present you with two passages. These items will ask you to compare and contrast, integrate information, and draw conclusions.

TIP

Text passages are text passages. Although the next section describes what types of passages appear on the RLA test to help you prepare, don't worry so much about what type of passage you're reading. Instead, focus on understanding the information that the passage presents to you.

Identifying the types of passages and how to prepare for them

To help you get comfortable with answering the questions on the Reading Comprehension portion of the RLA test, you need to have an idea of the kinds of passages that appear on the test. The good news is that in this section, I focus on the two main types of passages you'll see: nonfiction and literary. I also give you some practical advice that you can use as you prepare for this portion of the test.

Most of the passages (75 percent of them) come from nonfiction or informational texts. This means the more informational reading you do every day — newspapers, magazine articles, workplace reports, manuals, reviews, webpages, instructions, recipes — the better prepared you are for the RLA Reading test.

Nonfiction passages

Nonfiction passages may come from many different sources. Here's a list of some of the kinds of passages you may see, and of course, answer questions about.

- » **Nonfiction prose:** *Nonfiction prose* is prose that covers a lot of ground — and all the ground is real. Nonfiction prose is material that the author doesn't create in their own mind — it's based on fact or reality. In fact, this book is classified as nonfiction prose, and so are the newspaper articles you read every day. The next time you read a textbook, a newspaper, or a magazine, tell yourself, "I'm reading nonfiction prose." Just don't say it out loud in a coffee shop or in your break room at work — or people may start to look at you in strange ways!

- » **Workplace and community documents:** You run across these types of passages in job- and community-related areas of life. The following are some examples.

  - • **Corporate statements:** Companies and organizations issue rules for employee behavior, goals for the corporation, and even statements about corporate rules on environmental stewardship. These tell the world the company's goals and basic rules of behavior. The goal statement for your study group may be as follows: "We're all going to pass the GED test on our first attempt."

  - • **Historic documents, legal documents, and letters:** Historic documents could include extracts from the Constitution, Declaration of Independence, or other government documents. These documents are obviously older materials, with a somewhat different writing style from what you may see in a modern document. Legal documents and letters may include leases, purchase contracts, and notices from your bank. If you aren't familiar with these kinds of documents, collect some examples from banks or libraries and review them. If you can explain these types of documents to a friend, then you understand them.

  - • **Manuals:** Every time you invest in a major purchase, you get a user's manual that tells you how to use the item. Some manuals are short and straightforward; others are long and complicated. Some manuals may be printed, but often they are only available online.

  - • **Textbook selections:** Passages may be drawn from social studies or science textbooks, in order to assess your ability to read and understand academic content. But don't worry — this content is no different from what is covered in other parts of the GED test!

The Reading Comprehension component can seem daunting, but it can have a big payoff on other parts of the GED. Because both the Science and Social Studies tests involve reading nonfiction prose, your preparation for the Reading Comprehension component can help you with those tests.

Literary passages

The RLA Reading component includes passages from various kinds of prose fiction. *Prose fiction* refers to novels and short stories. As you may already know, *fiction* is writing that comes straight from the mind of the author (in other words, it's made up; it's not about something that really happened). The only way to become familiar with prose fiction is to read as much fiction as you can. After you read a book or a story, try to talk about it with other people who have read it.

REMEMBER

Regardless of what type of passage the questions in the Reading component are based on, your challenge is the same: reading comprehension. You need to answer questions, using the skills outlined in the earlier section, "Looking at the skills the Reading component covers": comprehension, analysis, command of evidence, and synthesis.

Preparing for the RLA Test with Tactics That Work

The RLA test requires a number of skills, from knowing proper spelling, usage, and punctuation to reading quickly and accurately, and familiarizing yourself with the format of the test. You can master all of these skills with practice. The following sections give some advice on how to do that.

Developing skills to read well

To succeed on the RLA test, you can prepare in advance by improving your reading skills. Here are some of the best ways you can prepare:

TIP

>> **Read as often as you can.** This strategy is the best one and is by far the simplest, because reading exposes you to correct grammar. What you read makes a difference. Reading catalogs may increase your product knowledge and improve your research skills, but reading literature is preferable because it introduces you to so many rules of grammar. Reading fiction exposes you to interesting words and sentences. It shows you how paragraphs tie into one another and how each paragraph has a topic and generally sticks to it. Reading historical fiction can give you some insight into what led up to today and can also help you with the Social Studies test (see Chapters 10 through 12 for more on the Social Studies test).

Reading nonfiction — from instructions to business letters, from press releases to history books and historical documents — is also extremely important. Nonfiction generally uses a formal style, the kind expected of you when you write an essay for the Extended Response item. Older documents can be a special problem, because the writing style is very different from what's common today. Getting familiar with such documents will help you to get better results and even help with your Social Studies test.

Read everything you can get your hands on — even cereal boxes — and identify what kind of reading you're doing. Read about topics that interest you, which can include subjects as varied as new cars, sports reporting, healthcare news, or money-saving tips. Reading aloud to your children at bedtime also counts! Ask yourself questions about your reading and see how much of it you can remember.

>> **Develop your reading speed.** Reading is wonderful, but reading quickly is even better — it gets you through the test with time to spare. Check out *Speed Reading For Dummies,* by Richard Sutz with Peter Weverka (John Wiley & Sons, Inc.), or do a quick Internet search to find plenty of material that can help you read faster. Whatever method you use, try to improve your reading rate without hurting your overall reading comprehension.

>> **Read carefully.** When you read, read carefully and think about what you're reading. This is called *active reading:* your brain is working as hard as your eyes are. If reading novels, stories, or historical documents is unfamiliar to you, read these items even more carefully and thoughtfully. The more carefully you read any material, the easier it'll be for you to get the right answers on the test.

- » **Ask questions.** Ask yourself questions about what you just read. Could you take a newspaper article and reduce the content to four bulleted points and still summarize the article accurately? Do you understand the main ideas well enough to explain them to a stranger? (Note that I don't advise going up to strangers to explain things to them in person. Pretend you're going to explain it to a stranger and do all the talking in your head. If you want to explain what you read to someone in person, ask your friends and family to lend you an ear — or two.)

  Ask for help if you don't understand something you read. You may want to form a study group and work with other people. If you're taking a test-preparation course, ask the instructor for help when you need it. If you have family, friends, or coworkers who can help, ask them.

- » **Use a dictionary.** Not many people understand every word they read, so use a dictionary. There are many good free or inexpensive dictionary apps for your computer or smart phone. Looking up unfamiliar words increases your vocabulary, which, in turn, makes passages on the Reasoning through Language Arts test easier to understand. If you have a thesaurus, use it, too. Often, knowing a synonym for the word you don't know is helpful. Plus, it improves your Scrabble game!

- » **Use new words.** A new word doesn't usually become part of your vocabulary until you put it to use in your everyday language. When you come across a new word, make sure you know its meaning and try to use it in a sentence. Then try to work it into conversation for a day or two. After a while, this challenge can make each day more exciting. If you don't know what you don't know, then you can find lists of important words online, such as "the 100 most commonly misspelled or misunderstood words" or "words important to pass the GED." These can be a good start to increasing your vocabulary.

REMEMBER

All the information you need to answer the reading questions is given in the passages or in the text of the questions that accompany the passages. You're not expected to recognize a passage and answer questions about what comes before it or what comes after it in the context of the entire work. The passages are complete in themselves, so just focus on what you read.

Improving your mastery of grammar and language skills

To prepare yourself for the Grammar and Language section, you can get a leg up by reviewing rules of grammar, punctuation, and spelling. Here are some ways to get started:

- » **Master the rules of basic grammar.** On this test, you don't have to define a gerund and give an example of one, but you do have to know about verb tenses, subject-verb agreement, pronoun-antecedent agreement, possessives, and the like. As your knowledge of grammar and punctuation improves, have a bit of fun by correcting what you read in small-town newspapers and low-budget novels — both sometimes have poor editing.

- » **Practice grammar and proper English in everyday speaking and writing.** As you review the rules of grammar, practice them every day as you talk to your friends, family, and coworkers, write on the job, or send emails. Although correct grammar usually "sounds" right to your ears, sometimes it doesn't because you and the people you talk to have become used to using incorrect grammar. If you see a rule that seems different from the way you usually speak or write, put it on a flashcard and practice it as you go through your day. Before long, you'll train your ears so that correct grammar sounds right.

TIP

Correcting other people's grammar out loud or in writing doesn't make you popular, but correcting it in your head can help you succeed on this test. Also, listen for and avoid slang or regional expressions. *Y'all* may be a great favorite in the South, but it wouldn't work well on your GED essay.

>> **Understand punctuation.** Know how to use commas, semicolons, colons, and other forms of punctuation. To find out more about punctuation and when and why to use its different forms, check out a grammatical reference book like *English Grammar For Dummies,* 2nd Edition, by Geraldine Woods (John Wiley & Sons, Inc.).

>> **Practice writing.** Write as much and as often as you can, and then review your writing for errors. Look for and correct mistakes in punctuation, grammar, and spelling. If you can't find any, ask someone who knows grammar and punctuation for help.

>> **Keep a journal or blog.** Journals and blogs are just notebooks (physical or virtual) in which you write a bit about your life every day. They both provide good practice for personal writing. Blogging or responding to blogs gives you practice in public writing because others see what you write. Whether you use a personal journal or a public blog, though, keep in mind that the writing is the important part. If public writing encourages you to write more and more often, do it. If not, consider the private writing of a journal or diary.

>> **Improve your spelling.** As you practice writing, keep a good dictionary at hand. If you're not sure of the spelling of any word, look it up. I hear you. How do you look up the spelling of a word if you can't spell it? Try sounding out the word phonetically and look in an online dictionary or dictionary app on your phone. Type in the word and select the word that looks familiar and correct. If that doesn't work, ask someone for help. Add the word to a spelling list and practice spelling those words. In addition, get a list of common *homonyms* — words that sound the same but are spelled differently and have different meanings — and review them every day. (You need to know, for example, the difference between *their, there,* and *they're* and *to, two,* and *too.*) Many dictionaries contain a list of homonyms, or search for a list of common homonyms online.

>> **Keep in mind that these questions all use the drop-down menu format.** Among the various answer choices, the test questions give you the correct answer. Of course, they also tell you three other answers that are incorrect, but all you have to do is find the correct one! As you practice for the test, tune your ears so the correct answer sounds right, which, believe it or not, makes finding the correct answer easier on the test.

Learning about the format and content of each test section

Get as much experience as you can with the test content and format. Here are some ways to do that:

>> **Practice and prepare.** In addition to this chapter, you can read Chapters 6 and 7 for more information and preliminary practice for the Reading Comprehension and Language and Grammar components. And don't forget the Extended Response! Complete coverage and some preliminary practice are in Chapters 8 and 9.

>> **Take practice tests.** When you feel ready, take the Reasoning through Language Arts Practice Tests in Chapters 19 and 27. Do the questions and check your answers. Look at the detailed answer explanations that I provide in Chapters 20 and 28. Don't move on to the next answer until you understand the preceding one. Then take the online test that comes with this book. It will give you the best indication of whether you are ready for the actual test. If you want more practice tests, the GED Testing Service offers free sample tests; check them out at www.gedtestingservice.com/educators/freepracticetest. You can look for additional test-prep books at your local bookstore or library. You can also find some abbreviated tests on the Internet. Type in "GED test questions" or "GED test questions + free" into your favorite search engine and check out some of the results.

As you take practice tests, remember to keep it real! Stick to the time limits, and match the testing situation as much as possible. When you take the online practice test offered on the Dummies site, set your work area up as described in Chapter 4. When you go online or to the test center for the real test, you'll feel more at ease because you prepared in a realistic setting.

TIP

When you feel you are ready to take the real test, take the GED Ready RLA test (available on the ged.com website). You must receive a "green" GED Ready score in order to take the online-proctored test at home. A "green" score also means you are ready for the in-person test, but this score is not required to test at a test center. If you don't score high enough, you can use the detailed feedback you get to focus your review.

Chapter 6

RLA Question Types and Solving Strategies

The 150-minute Reasoning through Language Arts (RLA) test evaluates your ability to write clear and effective English and to read, analyze, and accurately assess and respond to the content of written passages. I go into detail about the RLA test particulars in Chapter 5. In this chapter, I help you navigate through the different question types on the Reading Comprehension and Grammar and Language components and how to answer them. And you can find a complete treatment of the Extended Response component in Chapters 8 and 9. You really have your bases covered!

Tackling Grammar and Language Questions

All the questions on the Grammar and Language component use the drop-down menu format, which makes it easier. You just have to the find the answer from four choices!

On the actual GED test, you click the drop-down arrow in the onscreen button and select the best choice for a word, phrase, or sentence from the options provided to complete the sentence correctly; that choice then appears in the sentence.

The following questions give you examples of the items you will encounter on the actual test. I couldn't simulate the look and feel of the drop-down menu in the print book, so I ask that you use your imagination and check out Chapter 2 for an example of how this question type appears on the actual GED test.

Along with the questions, all based on the following business letter, I give you some advice on the best ways to approach and answer these questions.

BETA Café Equipment, Inc.
700 Millway Avenue, Unit 6
Concord, MA 12345

John Charles
Executive Director
American Specialty Coffee Association
425 Pacific Drive, Suite 301
San Diego, CA 92102

Dear Mr. Charles:

Thank you for [Select... ▾] which serves the rapidly expanding specialty coffee industry. BETA Café Equipment, Inc., [Select... ▾] this year to provide an affordable source of reconditioned Italian espresso/cappuccino machines for new businesses entering the industry.

During our first year of operation, BETA plans to repair and recondition 500 machines for use in restaurants and cafés. This will generate revenue of more than $1,000,000 and create 14 good-paying jobs.

BETA [Select... ▾] will be shipped to our centralized repair and reconditioning depot. After total rebuilding, equipment will be forwarded to regional sales offices to be sold to local restaurants and cafés at a much lower price than comparable new equipment. Entrepreneurs wishing to start new specialty coffee businesses particularly should be interested in our products.

To learn more about BETA, please consult our website or give us a call. Any assistance you can provide in sharing this information with your membership will be very much appreciated.

Yours truly,

Edwin Dale, President

TIP

The drop-down questions on the writing component of the RLA test provide four answer choices, one of which is correct. If you aren't sure which one is correct, guessing is better than skipping the question and leaving it blank. This is because you don't get any points for not answering a question, and wrong answers don't count against you.

EXAMPLE

Thank you for [Select... ▾] which serves the rapidly expanding specialty coffee industry.

(A) your interest in our company,

(B) you're interest in our company,

(C) your interest in our company

(D) yours interest in our company,

This question assesses your understanding of a common comma rule and the homonyms *your* and *you're*, and another related word, *yours*. The possessive *your* — Choice (A) — is the answer. The letter is thanking the reader for their interest in the company. Choice (B) is a contraction for *you are*, which does not make sense in the sentence. Choice (C) tests your knowledge of comma rules. While Choice (C) uses *your* correctly, there is no reason to omit the comma, because a comma is needed to mark this relative clause. Choice (D) has the necessary comma, but a possessive word such as *yours* is not followed by a noun, so this choice is also incorrect.

REMEMBER

An old topic from grammar class can help you with the comma rule here. A relative clause is introduced with *which*, *that*, or *who*. These clauses give information about another word in the sentence. Here's an example: "The apartment **that I rented** has two bathrooms." The clause **that I rented** adds a necessary piece of information, so it doesn't need commas. Contrast this with, "The landlord, **who is an old friend,** gave me a discount." This time, the clause adds extra information, so it needs commas before and after it.

In the following example question, you're asked to pick the best form of the verb for one part of the sentence.

EXAMPLE

BETA Café Equipment, Inc., [Select... ▼] this year to provide an affordable source of reconditioned Italian espresso/cappuccino machines for new businesses entering the industry.

(A) were formed

(B) had formed

(C) was formed

(D) is formed

Look at the answer choices one by one. Choice (A), *were formed*, is the plural form of the simple past tense. The action happened once in the past, so the simple past tense is correct. However, the subject, BETA Café Equipment, is singular, so the plural verb form is incorrect, making Choice (A) wrong. Choice (B) uses the past perfect tense in the active voice. You don't need to worry about the name, but do remember this: In the active voice, the subject is doing the action; in the passive voice, the action is being done to the subject. Because someone was forming the company (and the company is the subject of the sentence), the voice must be passive. Therefore, Choice (B) is also wrong. Choice (C) uses the singular form of the simple past tense, *was*, which agrees with the singular subject, BETA Café Equipment. You have already determined that the simple past tense is the correct tense, so Choice (C) is correct. However, it always pays to read all the choices. Choice (D) is incorrect because it's in the present tense. The action happened in the past, so using the present tense doesn't work.

TIP

A good way to answer questions like this is to read the sentence and substitute the choices one at a time; you can often pick out the right answer just because it "sounds" right.

The next example shows another technique for finding the answer: the process of elimination.

EXAMPLE

BETA [Select... ▼] will be shipped to our centralized repair and reconditioning depot.

(A) will have purchased used equipment, which

(B) will purchase used equipment, which

(C) had purchased used equipment, which

(D) will purchase used equipment which

This question shows how you can often find the answer by eliminating the obviously incorrect choices. Looking at the answer choices here, Choice (A) simply makes no sense, because it uses the future perfect tense. That implies actions completed in the future, but this event is yet to happen. So, you can eliminate that choice right away. Choice (D) can be eliminated because you must have a comma in front of *which* because it starts a relative clause that adds extra information. (See the note earlier in this chapter about these clauses.) That leaves Choices (B) and (C). Because all the action in the passage is yet to happen, the purchase can't have been completed in the past, so the tense in Choice (C) is wrong. By process of elimination, you have determined that Choice (B) is the answer. Choice (B) is correct because it uses the simple future tense, which is appropriate for an action that will happen.

TIP

Even if you cannot eliminate all the wrong choices, the process of elimination can still help you. In this example, even if you cannot eliminate Choice (C), you have still eliminated two other choices, (A) and (D), effectively improving your odds. Even if you have to guess, your chance of choosing the right answer is fifty-fifty.

Choosing Wisely in the Reading Component

The RLA test Reading Comprehension component consists of excerpts from fiction and nonfiction prose. You're presented with a reading passage (or in some cases, two related reading passages) followed by a series of multiple-choice and drag-and-drop questions. In this section, I give you clues to help you answer each of these.

TIP

When working through the Reading component of the real GED test, read the questions first so you get an idea of what you need to look for in the passage as you read it. Read the questions carefully — they aren't trick questions, but they do require you to be a good reader. Then, read the passage. Remember to keep it simple! Your only task in reading is to find the answers to the questions you just read — nothing more! If you encounter a word that you don't recognize, look at the surrounding text, which can often give you clues about the mystery word's meaning. If you can understand the idea without knowing the word, you can skip the word. That will help you keep moving and save time!

Dealing with multiple-choice Reading questions

Most of the questions on the Reading component are multiple choice. In this section, I walk you through a few sample questions based on this short newspaper article.

(1) The constitutional mechanism that the United States uses to elect the president and vice president is called the Electoral College. This group of presidential electors forms every four years in order to elect the president and vice president. The number of electors in each state is equal to the number of senators and representatives in its congressional delegation. Holders of federal offices are barred from being electors. There are currently 538 electors, and a majority of 270 or more electoral votes is required to elect the president and vice president. The Constitution has a contingent process if no candidate receives a majority. In that case, the United States House of Representatives holds an election to elect the president, and the United States Senate holds another election to select the vice president.

(2) On election day in November, the states each hold a statewide or districtwide popular vote to choose electors based upon how they have pledged to vote for president and vice president. Every state except two uses a winner-take-all approach to choose electors. Maine and Nebraska choose one elector per congressional district and two electors for the ticket with the highest statewide vote. The electors meet and vote in their state capitals in December, and in January, the votes are counted in a special joint session of Congress. The inauguration takes place in January.

EXAMPLE

How many electors are needed to elect the president and vice president of the United States?

(A) 2

(B) 4

(C) 270

(D) 538

This question is a perfect example of when reading the questions first, before you read the passage, can really benefit you. If you know that you're looking for a specific number, you have the answer as soon as you find it in the passage. On the other hand, if you read the passage first and then have to go back and look for the number, you will lose valuable time. The correct answer in this case is 270, Choice (C), which you can find in the third-to-last sentence of the first paragraph.

EXAMPLE

The president and vice president are typically elected by a majority of electors

(A) in a direct, nationwide popular vote on election day.

(B) at a meeting of the electors in Washington, D.C.

(C) in popular votes held in each state or district on election day.

(D) in the House of Representatives for the president and the Senate for the vice president.

If you read the article carefully, you will see that states choose the electors via a popular vote in each state or district. So Choice (C) is the correct answer. Therefore, Choice (A) is incorrect. Choice (B) is contradicted by the information in the passage: the electors meet in their state capitals. Choice (D) describes a contingency process used only if the Electoral College fails to choose a president and vice-president, so it is incorrect.

Dealing with drag-and-drop Reading questions

Some items on the Reading component are called drag-and-drop items. This item type is essentially another multiple-choice question (because you get to select from a list of possible answers and don't have to come up with the answer all on your own). The difference is that you have to sort the choices in a particular order, select which words apply and which ones don't, or show which answers are details that support the main idea. Here's an example of a sorting drag-and-drop question.

EXAMPLE

Look at the following series of events. According to the passage, in which order did they happen? Drag the sentences (or write the letters, in this case) into the boxes in the appropriate order.

(A) The Electoral College votes are counted in a special session of Congress.

(B) Electors meet and make their choices in each state.

(C) States and districts hold popular elections.

(D) The president takes office in a ceremony at the Capitol.

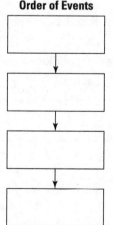

Order of Events

The answer to this question is right in the passage. You just have to sort the events into the order in which they happen every four years. The correct order is Choice (C), (B), (A), then (D). First, the popular votes are held on election day, Choice (C). Then, the electors meet in their states in December, Choice (B). After that, the Senate and House meet together in a special joint session in early January to count the votes, Choice (A). Finally, the president is inaugurated later in January, Choice (D).

TIP

Answering drag-and-drop questions on test day requires quick and accurate use of the computer mouse. You can get practice with these questions in the online test included in this book and on the GED website.

Dealing with questions with multiple passage sets

Sometimes the GED Reading component will give you two passages related to the same topic. This generally happens with nonfiction prose passages. Your task will be to integrate information in the two passages, compare and contrast information, or evaluate which passage is more logical or has stronger evidence to support it. For example, the passage about the Electoral College might be accompanied by the relevant excerpt from the Constitution, as in this example.

EXAMPLE

Twelfth Amendment to the Constitution of the United States (1804)

(1) The Electors shall meet in their respective states, and vote by ballot for President and Vice-President, one of whom, at least, shall not be an inhabitant of the same state with themselves; they shall name in their ballots the person voted for as President, and in distinct ballots the person voted for as Vice-President, and they shall make distinct lists of all persons voted for as President, and all persons voted for as Vice-President and of the number of votes for each, which lists they shall sign and certify, and transmit sealed to the seat of the government of the United States, directed to the President of the Senate;

(2) The President of the Senate shall, in the presence of the Senate and House of Representatives, open all the certificates and the votes shall then be counted;

(3) The person having the greatest number of votes for President, shall be the President, if such number be a majority of the whole number of Electors appointed; and if no person have such majority, then from the persons having the highest numbers not exceeding three on the list of those voted for as President, the House of Representatives shall choose immediately, by ballot, the President. But in choosing the President, the votes shall be taken by states, the representation from each state having one vote; a quorum for this purpose shall consist of a member or members from two-thirds of the states, and a majority of all the states shall be necessary to a choice.

Which of the following can be concluded by comparing the passage and the excerpt from the Constitution?

(A) The Electoral College gives too much power to states with small populations.

(B) The Electoral College should be replaced with a direct, popular election.

(C) The process for electing the president and vice president changed early in American history.

(D) Few Americans really understand the workings of the Electoral College.

The answer to this question is right in the title of the excerpt. The amendment came into effect in 1804, which is early in the history of the Constitution. Therefore, Choice (C) is correct. By reading the question and the answer choices before reading the excerpt, you would have been able to answer this question as soon as you came to the title of the reading. Option (A) may be true but is not a conclusion you can draw by comparing information in the two passages. Option (B) is an opinion not discussed in either passage, and so is incorrect. I hope that Option (D) is not true, but that cannot be concluded from information in the passages.

TIP

Reading two passages can take a lot of time. If you feel pressed for time on test day, you can skip questions based on two passages or flag them for later by pressing the Flag for Review button in the upper right corner of your screen. That way, you may be able to read and answer more questions. But don't leave any questions unanswered. At the end of the test, use the Review Screen to find and answer all the questions you skipped or flagged — even if you guess. A guess gives you at least a one-in-four chance of getting a point. If you guess on four questions, you will likely get at least one point, and that may be the point you need to get a passing score!

REMEMBER

The GED Reading component will frequently have at least one passage that is based on U.S. history or a fundamental document. So your preparation for the Reading component can help you on the Social Studies test, and vice versa!

Chapter 7

Working through Some Practice RLA Questions

This chapter provides sample Reasoning through Language Arts (RLA) questions for both the Reading Comprehension and Grammar and Language components of the RLA test. A sample Extended Response item is provided in Chapter 9 to help you prepare for taking that component of the GED test.

You can record your answers directly in this book, or on a sheet of paper if you think you'll want to try these practice questions again at a later date. Mark only one answer for each question, unless otherwise indicated.

At the end of each section, I provide detailed answer explanations for you. Check your answers. Take your time as you move through the explanations. Read them carefully, because they can help you understand why you missed the answers you did and confirm or clarify what you got right.

Remember, this is just preliminary practice. I want you to get used to answering different types of RLA questions. Use the complete practice tests in Chapters 20 and 27, and the included online practice test, to time your work and replicate the real test-taking experience. Then use the included online-only practice test as a final check. That way, you will be more than ready for the GED Ready test, on the GED Testing Service's website. Remember, you have to get a rating of Green to take the online-proctored GED test. It's not required if you test at a testing center, but getting a Green is the best indicator you are ready to pass. If you do not score high enough, you can use feedback from the test to focus your review.

RLA Grammar and Language Practice Questions

The questions in the Grammar and Language component of the RLA test are doubly important because understanding and using correct grammar adds to your overall score on the RLA test and also counts toward your score on the Extended Response item. One of the important things about proper grammar is that it sounds and reads well. These questions give you an opportunity to develop your ear and eye for proper sentences.

For the questions in this section, pay special attention to the mechanics of writing, spelling, and grammar. Work carefully, but don't spend too much time on any one question. Be sure you answer every question. You can find the answers for these items later in this section.

The questions

Questions 1–10 refer to the following executive summary.

Dry-Cleaning and Laundering Industry Adjustment Committee Report on the Local Labor Market Partnership Project

Executive Summary

Over the past two years, the Dry-Cleaning and Laundering Industry Adjustment Committee has worked hard to become a cohesive Select... ▾ on assessing and addressing the human resource implications associated with changes in the fabricare industry. As of August, the Committee has an active membership of Select... ▾ 15 individuals involved in all aspects of the project. The Committee has taken responsibility for undertaking actions that will benefit this large, highly fragmented Select... ▾ great difficulty speaking with one voice.

During the initial period that the Committee was in Select... ▾ work focused on reaching out to and building a relationship with key individuals within the industry. One of its first steps Select... ▾ was to undertake a Needs Assessment Survey within the industry.

During the first year, the Committee explored ways of meeting the needs identified in the Needs Assessment Select... ▾ raising the profile of the industry and offering on-site training programs, particularly in the areas of spotting and pressing. A great deal of feasibility work Select... ▾ yet each possible training solution proved to be extremely difficult and costly to implement.

As the Committee moved into its second Select... ▾ officially established a joint project with the National Fabricare Association to achieve goals in three priority areas: mentorship, training, and profile building.

During this Select... ▾ effort and vision has gone into achieving the goals established by the Industry Adjustment Committee and the Association. The new priority areas have provided an opportunity for the industry to take these Select... ▾

- Introduce technology
- Build capacity and knowledge
- Enhance skills
- Build partnerships and networks

1. Over the past two years, the Dry-Cleaning and Laundering Industry Adjustment Committee has worked hard to become a cohesive Select... ▾ on assessing and addressing the human resource implications associated with changes in the fabricare industry.

(A) group and one which has focused

(B) group. One which has focused

(C) group, and one which has focused

(D) group focused

2. As of August, the Committee has an active membership of [Select... ▼] 15 individuals involved in all aspects of the project.

   (A) most over

   (B) moreover

   (C) over than

   (D) more than

3. The Committee has taken responsibility for undertaking actions that will benefit this large, highly fragmented [Select... ▼] great difficulty speaking with one voice.

   (A) industry which has

   (B) industry, which have

   (C) industry, who has

   (D) industry, which has

4. During the initial period that the Committee was in [Select... ▼] work focused on reaching out to and building a relationship with key individuals within the industry.

   (A) existence, it's

   (B) existence, its

   (C) existence its

   (D) existence; its

5. One of its first steps [Select... ▼] to undertake a Needs Assessment Survey within the industry.

   (A) was

   (B) had been

   (C) were

   (D) would have been

6. During the first year, the Committee explored ways of meeting the needs identified in the Needs Assessment [Select... ▼] raising the profile of the industry and offering on-site training programs, particularly in the areas of spotting and pressing.

   (A) Survey and they included,

   (B) Survey. These needs included

   (C) Survey, and they included

   (D) Survey they included

7. A great deal of feasibility work [Select... ▼] yet each possible training solution proved to be extremely difficult and costly to implement.

   (A) were undertaken during this phase

   (B) was undertook during this phase

   (C) was undertaken, during this phase

   (D) was undertaken during this phase,

8. As the Committee moved into its second [Select... ▼] officially established a joint project with the National Fabricare Association to achieve goals in three priority areas: mentorship, training, and profile building.

   (A) year: it

   (B) year it

   (C) year; it

   (D) year, it

9. During this [Select... ▼] effort and vision has gone into achieving the goals established by the Industry Adjustment Committee and the Association.

   (A) passed year, many

   (B) past year, much

   (C) past year much

   (D) passed year, much

10. The new priority areas have provided an opportunity for the industry to take these [Select... ▼]

   - Introduce technology
   - Build capacity and knowledge
   - Enhance skills
   - Build partnerships and networks

   (A) actions

   (B) actions;

   (C) actions,

   (D) actions:

Questions 11–20 refer to the following description of an adult education class at a local community college.

Adult Learning 265: Prior Learning Assessment and Recognition

This course is based on a Prior Learning Assessment and Recognition (PLAR) [Select... ▼] on successful completion of the GED test. [Select... ▼] candidates are guided through the creation of a portfolio, which can be evaluated by a college for admission or advanced standing. This is an opportunity for adults, who have learned in non-formal as well as formal venues, to document and assess [Select... ▼] prior learning. The course is [Select... ▼]. It is not meant for every applicant.

[Select... ▼] should be directed to remedial programs before beginning such a rigorous course. [Select... ▼] in a pre-test may be advised to arrange immediately to take one or more of the GED tests. This course is meant for candidates who will gain from [Select... ▼] do not require extensive teaching.

This course is designed to help adult learners gain credit for [Select... ▼] prior learning in preparation for post-secondary study. Students will learn methods for documenting prior knowledge, [Select... ▼] reacquainted with educational environments. Through the use of assessment tools and [Select... ▼] will gain a realistic understanding of their levels of competence, personal strengths, weaknesses, and learning styles.

11. This course is based on a Prior Learning Assessment and Recognition (PLAR) [Select... ▼] on successful completion of the GED test.

    (A) model, and focuses

    (B) model and focuses

    (C) model it focuses

    (D) model, it focuses

12. [Select... ▼] candidates are guided through the creation of a portfolio, which can be evaluated by a college for admission or advanced standing.

    (A) In addition,

    (B) However,

    (C) Nevertheless,

    (D) In contrast,

13. This is an opportunity for adults, who have learned in non-formal as well as formal venues, to document and assess [Select... ▼] prior learning.

    (A) their

    (B) there

    (C) they're

    (D) themselves

14. The course is [Select... ▼].

    (A) intents and concentrated

    (B) intents and concentrate

    (C) intense and concentrate

    (D) intense and concentrated

15. [Select... ▼] should be directed to remedial programs before beginning such a rigorous course.

    (A) Candidates who score low in the pre-test,

    (B) Candidates, who score low in the pre-test

    (C) Candidates who score low in the pre-test

    (D) Candidates, who score low in the pre-test;

16. [Select... ▼] in a pre-test may be advised to arrange immediately to take one or more of the GED tests.

    (A) Extremely those who score well

    (B) Those who score well extremely

    (C) Those who score extremely well

    (D) Those extremely who score well

17. This course is meant for candidates who will gain from [Select... ▾] do not require extensive teaching.

   (A) review and remediation. But

   (B) review, and remediation but

   (C) review, and remediation but,

   (D) review and remediation but

18. This course is designed to help adult learners gain credit for [Select... ▾] prior learning in preparation for post-secondary study.

   (A) their

   (B) his or her

   (C) our

   (D) my

19. Students will learn methods for documenting prior knowledge, [Select... ▾] reacquainted with educational environments.

   (A) will develop academic skills while becoming

   (B) will develop academic skills, and becoming

   (C) will develop academic skills, and will become

   (D) develop academic skills, and will become

20. Through the use of assessment tools and [Select... ▾] will gain a realistic understanding of their levels of competence, personal strengths, weaknesses, and learning styles.

   (A) counseling; students

   (B) counseling. Students

   (C) counseling students

   (D) counseling, students

Questions 21–25 are based on the following business letter.

CanLearn Study Tours, Inc.
2500 River Road
Troy, MI 48083

Dr. Dale Worth, Ph.D., Registrar
BEST Institute of Technology
75 Ingram Drive
Concord, MA 01742

Dear Dr. Worth:

Our rapidly changing economic climate has created [Select... ▾] before known. It has been said that only those organizations [Select... ▾] can maintain loyalty and commitment among their employees, members, and customers will continue to survive and prosper in this age of continuous learning and globalization.

Since 1974, CanLearn Study Tours, Inc., [Select... ▾] with universities, colleges, school districts, volunteer organizations, and businesses to address the unique learning needs of their staff and clientele. These have included educational travel programs that [Select... ▾] artistic and cultural interests, historic and archeological themes, environmental and wellness experiences, and different kinds of music. All our tours [Select... ▾] professional development activities that build international understanding and boost creativity.

We would appreciate the opportunity to share our experiences in educational travel and discuss the ways we may be of service to your organization.

Yours sincerely,

Todd Croft, MA, President
CanLearn Study Tours, Inc.

21. Our rapidly changing economic climate has created [Select... ▾] before known.

    (A) both challenges and opportunities never

    (B) both challenges never

    (C) challenges and opportunities both never

    (D) both challenges and opportunities ever

22. It has been said that only those organizations [Select... ▾] can maintain loyalty and commitment among their employees, members, and customers will continue to survive and prosper in this age of continuous learning and globalization.

    (A) who

    (B) whom

    (C) that

    (D) what

23. Since 1974, CanLearn Study Tours, Inc., [Select... ▾] with universities, colleges, school districts, volunteer organizations, and businesses to address the unique learning needs of their staff and clientele.

    (A) have been working

    (B) has been working

    (C) will be working

    (D) would be working

24. These have included educational travel programs that [Select... ▾] artistic and cultural interests, historic and archeological themes, environmental and wellness experiences, and different kinds of music.

    (A) explore,

    (B) explore

    (C) explore:

    (D) explore;

25. All our tours [Select... ▾] professional development activities that build international understanding and boost creativity.

    (A) incorporates

    (B) incorporated

    (C) had incorporated

    (D) incorporate

The answers

1. **D. group focused.** With this choice, you create a concise sentence and avoid the overly wordy and awkward sentence in Choice (A). Options (B) and (C) introduce new errors.

2. **D. more than.** Choice (D) uses *more than* correctly to refer to quantities. The other choices introduce additional errors.

3. **D. industry, which has.** Choice (D) is correct because a comma is needed to indicate that this relative clause contains non-essential information. Therefore, Choice (A) is incorrect. Choice (B) introduces a subject-verb agreement error. *Industry* is the word that *which* refers to, so a singular verb is required. Option (C) uses an incorrect pronoun; *which* is required because it refers to a thing, *industry*, not a person.

4. **B. existence, its.** Choice (B) is correct because the possessive form of *it*, *its*, is needed here, not the contraction for *it is: it's* (Choice A). There is no reason to remove the comma (Choice C) or replace it with a semicolon (Choice D).

5. **D. was.** In this sentence, the subject of the verb is the singular subject *One*, so the singular form of the verb, *was*, is needed.

TIP

Are you thinking that I made a mistake in the preceding sentence? Well, I didn't. The noun that is closest to the verb is not always the subject. The prepositional phrase *of its first steps* doesn't determine how the noun and verb agree. *One*, a singular noun, is subject of the sentence and, therefore, needs *was*, not *were*.

6. **B. Survey. These needs included.** This option creates two concise sentences instead of one long, rambling one, as in the other options.

TIP

When answering Grammar and Language questions or writing your essay, keep in mind that sentences shouldn't be so long that you have to take multiple breaths just to read them aloud. Short sentences are easier to read and understand and are less likely to need all sorts of pesky punctuation.

7. **D. was undertaken during this phase,** A comma after *phase* is required because this a compound sentence joined by the conjunction *yet*. A compound sentence needs a comma before the conjunction. Therefore, the remaining options, which omit this punctuation, are incorrect. In addition, there is no reason to use *were* instead of *was* (Choice A) or to change *undertaken* to *undertook* (Choice B). Choice (C) adds an extra comma that is not needed.

TECHNICAL STUFF

A *compound sentence* contains two independent clauses or thoughts. The clauses are joined by a comma and a conjunction such as *and, but,* or *yet*.

8. **D. year, it.** This choice is correct because a comma is needed to separate the introductory clause starting with *As* from the rest of the sentence. Replacing the comma with another punctuation mark (Choices A and C) or removing it (Choice B) are both incorrect.

9. **B. past year, much.** Choice (B) is correct because it avoids the homonym spelling error (*passed/past*) in Choices (A) and (D). There is no reason to use *many* instead of *much*, which is another reason Choice (A) is incorrect. A comma is needed after *year*, so Choice (C) is incorrect.

Homonyms are two or more words that sound alike or are spelled alike but have different meanings. The word *passed* is a verb and means "went by," as in "she passed the other car," or "completed a test successfully," as in "he passed the GED." The word *past* is a noun and means "in times gone by, in a prior time," as in, "In the past, there were no computers." The GED Grammar and Language component frequently tests your ability to use the correct homonym, so keep an eye out for them. Writing the wrong homonym in your essay can also contribute to a lower score.

10. **D. actions:** The clause needs a colon at the end to introduce the list that follows (Choice D). Therefore, the other choices are incorrect.

11. **B. model and focuses.** Option (B) is correct because *and* joins two verbs (*is based* and *focuses*), not two clauses, and so does not need a comma. Therefore, Option (A) is incorrect. Option (C) creates a run-on sentence. Option (D) creates a comma splice.

Two independent clauses should be joined by a comma and a conjunction, such as *and* or *but*. When you join two clauses with just a comma, it's called a *comma splice*. When you join them without a conjunction and a comma, it's called a *run-on sentence*. Look at these examples.

Correct: This course is based on a Prior Learning Assessment and Recognition (PLAR) model, **and** it focuses on successful completion of the GED test.

Run-On: This course is based on a Prior Learning Assessment and Recognition (PLAR) model it focuses on successful completion of the GED test.

Comma Splice: This course is based on a Prior Learning Assessment and Recognition (PLAR) model, it focuses on successful completion of the GED test.

12. **A. In addition,** This sentence adds an idea to the previous one, so the best transitional phrase is in Choice (A). When one of these phrases is at the beginning of a sentence, it's followed by a comma.

Not sure about commas? Check out *English Grammar For Dummies*, 2nd Edition, by Geraldine Woods (Wiley), for the lowdown on this tricky punctuation mark.

13. **A. their.** *Their* is possessive (showing belonging) and is the correct choice in this sentence.

The homonyms *there, their,* and *they're* probably trip up more people than any other homonyms, and these tricky words are frequently tested on the GED RLA test. Before test day, be sure you know the difference!

14. **D. intense and concentrated.** *Intense* and *concentrated* are synonyms used in this sentence for emphasis, but in Choices (A) and (B), *intense* is replaced with a close homonym, *intents*. *Intents* means, "plans or purposes." *Concentrated* is an adjective, so it is used correctly in Choices (A) and (D). There is no reason to use *concentrate*, as in Choices (B) and (C), which is a verb (*to concentrate*) or a noun (as in *orange juice concentrate*). Only Choice (D) uses both correct words.

15. **C. Candidates who score low in the pre-test.** The clause *who score low in the pre-test* is an *essential relative clause*, which means it refers to a specific noun — *candidates*, in this case — and specifies something about the noun that the sentence needs in order to make sense to readers. Essential relative clauses aren't separated by commas because they're an integral part of the sentence.

TECHNICAL STUFF

Contrast the *essential* relative clause with the *non-essential* relative clause, which adds information about the noun that isn't essential to the meaning of the sentence. If you remove a non-essential clause from the sentence, you can still fully understand the meaning of the sentence. Non-essential relative clauses require commas to separate them from the sentence. For example, consider the following sentence: "The teacher, who had bright red hair, reviewed the grammar rule with the class." The information between the commas (who had bright red hair) isn't essential to the meaning of the sentence.

16. **C. Those who score extremely well.** *Those who score extremely well* is the best order of the words. *Extremely*, an adverb, is best placed before the word it modifies, which is *well*.

17. **D. review and remediation but.** Commas are not needed in this series of nouns joined by *and* and *but*. Therefore, Options (B) and (C) are incorrect. Option (A) creates a sentence fragment.

TECHNICAL STUFF

A *sentence fragment* is a group of words with an initial capital letter and a final period but that is not a complete sentence. A fragment lacks a subject or a verb. You can avoid a fragment by giving it a complete subject or a complete verb, or by joining it to another sentence using correct conjunction (such as *and* or *but*), punctuation, and capitalization.

18. **A. their.** This item assesses your ability to choose pronouns that agree with their antecedent — the noun they refer to. In this case, the antecedent is *adult learners*, so *their*, Choice (A), is correct.

19. **C. will develop academic skills, and will become.** Choice (C) puts the three things students will do (learn methods, develop skills, and become reacquainted) in the same grammatical form, verb phrases. This is called *parallel structure*.

TECHNICAL STUFF

Parallel structure makes writing clear and easy to follow because similar ideas are expressed in the same grammatical form. Parallel structure is frequently tested on the GED. Here are some examples of different kinds of parallel structure:

The GED has tests on math, language arts, social studies, and science. (nouns)

They studied academic content, reviewed test-taking skills, and learned computer skills. (verb phrases)

The students studied in the library, the teachers worked in their classrooms, and the administrators sat in their offices. (clauses)

20. **D. counseling, students.** A comma is needed to set off this phrase from the rest of the sentence. Therefore, Choices (A) and (C) are incorrect. Choice (B) creates a sentence fragment.

21. **A. both challenges and opportunities never.** Choice (A) uses correct parallel structure, and so is correct. Choices (B) and (C) use faulty parallel structure. There is no reason to use *ever* in this sentence, so Choice (D) is incorrect.

22. **C. that.** This item tests your ability to use pronouns correctly. An organization is a thing, so it needs the relative pronoun *that*. Therefore, Choice (C) is correct and Choices (A) and (B) are incorrect. This sentence is not a question, so Choice (D) is incorrect.

23. **B. has been working.** CanLearn Study Tours is a single entity because it's one company. Therefore, it's a singular noun and needs the singular verb *has*. Therefore, Choice (A), which uses the plural verb *have*, is incorrect. There is no reason to use the verb tenses in Choices (C) or (D).

WARNING

People like to refer to companies as *them* when, in fact, a company is always an *it*. Even if a company has a plural noun in its name, such as this one, CanLearn Study Tours, it's still singular.

24. **B. explore.** A punctuation mark is not needed before this list of items in parallel structure, so Choice (B) is the only correct choice.

25. **D. incorporate.** The sentence is about the present and the subject, *tours*, is plural so Choice (D) is correct.

RLA Reading Comprehension Practice

The Reading component of the RLA test consists of excerpts from nonfiction and fiction prose. Multiple-choice and drag-and-drop questions based on the reading material follow each excerpt.

You have two choices of how to approach the items on this part of the test. You can read each excerpt first, read the question to make sure you understand what's being asked, and then answer the questions (referring back to the reading material as often as necessary). Or you can read the questions first and then look for the answers in the passage as you read. If you can remember the questions, reading the text with the questions in mind is much easier and faster. You save time because you know what's being asked of you. Try both ways to see which approach is more effective for you.

For the multiple-choice questions in this section, choose the one best answer to each question. For the drag-and-drop items, write the letters of the answers in the boxes. Work carefully, but don't spend too much time on any one question. Be sure you answer every question. You can find the answers for these questions later in this section.

The questions

Questions 1–8 refer to the following article from the United States Geological Service Newsroom (www. usgs.gov).

(1) USGS scientists and Icelandic partners found avian flu viruses from North America and Europe in migratory birds in Iceland, demonstrating that the North Atlantic is as significant as the North Pacific in being a melting pot for birds and avian flu. A great number of wild birds from Europe and North America congregate and mix in Iceland's wetlands during migration, where infected birds could transmit avian flu viruses to healthy birds from either location.

(2) By crossing the Atlantic Ocean this way, avian flu viruses from Europe could eventually be transported to the United States. This commingling could also lead to the evolution of new influenza viruses. These findings are critical for proper surveillance and monitoring of flu viruses, including the H5N1 avian influenza that can infect humans.

(3) "None of the avian flu viruses found in our study are considered harmful to humans," said Robert Dusek, USGS scientist and lead author of the study. "However, the results suggest that Iceland is an important location for the study of avian flu. . .."

(4) During the spring and autumn of 2010 and autumn of 2011, the USGS researchers and Icelandic partners collected avian influenza viruses from gulls and waterfowl in southwest and west Iceland. . .. By studying the viruses' genomes . . . the researchers found that some viruses came from Eurasia and some originated in North America. They also found viruses with mixed American-Eurasian lineages.

(5) "For the first time, avian influenza viruses from both Eurasia and North America were documented at the same location and time," said Jeffrey Hall, USGS co-author and principal investigator on this study. "Viruses are continually evolving, and this mixing of viral strains sets the stage for new types of avian flu to develop."

1. How dangerous is this new potential source of avian flu to humans?

   (A) very dangerous

   (B) not at all dangerous

   (C) a concern but not particularly dangerous

   (D) serious enough that it requires monitoring

2. Before this discovery, where did scientists believe most birds carrying the avian flu intermingled with North American birds?

   (A) South Pacific

   (B) Central America

   (C) Eurasia

   (D) North Pacific

3. Why was the finding of Eurasian, North American, and mixed virus genomes in the same locale significant?

   (A) It proved avian flu viruses comingle only in the North Pacific.

   (B) It proved that the avian flu is a risk to humans.

   (C) It proved that avian flu viruses had mingled in Iceland.

   (D) It proved that Iceland is the origin of the avian flu.

4. Why is the mixing of avian flu viruses in Iceland an important concern?

   (A) It can lead to a new, dangerous strain of avian flu.

   (B) Cold viruses are constantly evolving.

   (C) It provides lead time to develop new vaccines.

   (D) It suggests tourists avoid that area.

5. Which of these terms best describes the tone of this passage?

   (A) light-hearted

   (B) deeply concerned

   (C) factual and straightforward

   (D) gloomy

6. Which strain of the avian flu virus can infect humans?

   (A) the bird flu

   (B) the H5N1 strain

   (C) the avian H5 flu

   (D) the Eurasian avian flu

7. How does the word *however* in Paragraph 3 function in the passage?

   (A) It indicates that avian flu is not a risk to humans.

   (B) It contrasts the situation in Iceland and the North Pacific.

   (C) It indicates the writer's skepticism about the scientists' claims.

   (D) It shifts the focus from risk to humans to the need for continued monitoring.

8. Which of these statements is essential to a summary of the article? Which are not essential? Write the letters of the statements in the correct boxes.

Essential to a Summary	Not Essential to a Summary

   (A) The scientists studied gulls in southwest Iceland.

   (B) Analysis revealed viruses with mixed Asian and American genomes.

   (C) None of the viruses found to date are harmful to humans.

   (D) The birds congregated in Iceland's wetlands.

Questions 9–16 refer to the following excerpt from Robert Bloch's short story, "This Crowded Earth" (1958).

(1) The telescreen lit up promptly at eight a.m. Smiling Brad came on with his usual greeting. "Good morning — it's a beautiful day in Chicagee!"

(2) Harry Collins rolled over and twitched off the receiver. "This I doubt," he muttered. He sat up and reached into the closet for his clothing. Visitors — particularly feminine ones — were always exclaiming over the advantages of Harry's apartment. "So convenient," they would say. "Everything handy, right within reach. And think of all the extra steps you save!"

(3) Of course most of them were just being polite and trying to cheer Harry up. They knew damned well that he wasn't living in one room through any choice of his own. The Housing Act was something you just couldn't get around; not in Chicagee these days. A bachelor was entitled to one room — no more and no less. And even though Harry was making a speedy buck at the agency, he couldn't hope to beat the regulations.

(4) There was only one way to beat them and that was to get married. Marriage would automatically entitle him to two rooms — *if* he could find them someplace. More than a few of his feminine visitors had hinted at just that, but Harry didn't respond. Marriage was no solution, the way he figured it. He knew that he couldn't hope to locate a two-room apartment any closer than eighty miles away. It was bad enough driving forty miles to and from work every morning and night without doubling the distance. If he did find a bigger place, that would mean a three-hour trip each way on one of the commutrains, and the commutrains were murder. The Black Hole of Calcutta, on wheels. But then, everything was murder, Harry reflected, as he stepped from the toilet to the sink, from the sink to the stove, from the stove to the table.

(5) Powdered eggs for breakfast. That was murder, too. But it was a fast, cheap meal, easy to prepare, and the ingredients didn't waste a lot of storage space. The only trouble was, he hated the way they tasted. Harry wished he had time to eat his breakfasts in a restaurant. He could afford the price, but he couldn't afford to wait in line more than a half-hour or so. His office schedule at the agency started promptly at ten-thirty. And he didn't get out until three-thirty; it was a long, hard five-hour day. Sometimes he wished he worked in the New Philly area, where a four-hour day was the rule. But he supposed that wouldn't mean any real saving in time, because he'd have to live further out. What was the population in New Philly now? Something like 63,000,000, wasn't it? Chicagee was much smaller — only 38,000,000, this year.

(6) *This* year. Harry shook his head and took a gulp of the Instantea. Yes, this year the population was 38,000,000, and the boundaries of the community extended north to what used to be the old Milwaukee and south past Gary. What would it be like *next* year, and the year following?

(7) Lately that question had begun to haunt Harry. He couldn't quite figure out why. After all, it was none of his business, really. He had a good job, security, a nice place just two hours from the Loop. He even drove his own car. What more could he ask?

9. This story is set sometime in the future. Which of the following clues confirms that this story is set in the future?

    (A) the number of rooms in his apartment

    (B) the population of Chicagee

    (C) the affordability of cars

    (D) the affordable price of a restaurant meal

10. This story was published in 1958. What image did Bloch have of the future?

    (A) incredibly crowded

    (B) suffering from food shortages

    (C) well-organized commutes

    (D) long working hours

11. Besides population numbers, how does the author build up the idea of a crowded world?

    (A) descriptions of bad-tasting food

    (B) communication using telescreens

    (C) descriptions of enormous cities

    (D) descriptions of long, hard workdays

12. Why does Harry sometimes wish he worked in the New Philly area?

    (A) shorter commute times

    (B) shorter working hours

    (C) better pay

    (D) better food

13. Why does Harry live in a one-room apartment when he could afford a two-room apartment?

    (A) He likes the efficiency of the small space.

    (B) His lady friends like the convenience of the apartment.

    (C) He is not married.

    (D) He can't afford a larger apartment.

14. What's the population Harry mentions for Chicagee?

    (A) 38 million

    (B) 63 million

    (C) 38 billion

    (D) 63 billion

15. Which of the following statements can be inferred about Harry from Paragraph 7?

    (A) He feels more fortunate than others but still has vague worries.

    (B) He doesn't like Chicagee and feels his life would be better in another city.

    (C) He feels overwhelmed by life's challenges but still feels optimistic.

    (D) He hates his life but feels that marriage will make his life better.

16. Which of the following details support the generalization that Harry believes that life is difficult and unsatisfying? Write the letters in the box.

    [   ]

    (A) travel on commutrains

    (B) the flavor of his breakfast

    (C) the price of meals in restaurants

    (D) the taste of Instantea

Questions 17–22 refer to the following excerpt taken from the Environmental Protection Agency website (www.epa.gov) and the subsequent passage about climate change.

Weather Versus Climate

- Weather is a specific event or condition that happens over a period of hours or days. For example, a thunderstorm, a snowstorm, and today's temperature all describe the weather.

- Climate refers to the average weather conditions in a place over many years (usually at least 30 years). For example, the climate in Minneapolis is cold and snowy in the winter, while Miami's climate is hot and humid in the summer. The average climate around the world is called "global climate."

Weather conditions can change from one year to the next. For example, Minneapolis might have a warm winter one year and a much colder winter the next. This kind of change is normal. But when the average pattern over many years changes, it could be a sign of climate change.

The Greenhouse Effect

The greenhouse effect is the process by which certain gases in the atmosphere trap heat and radiate it back to earth. The greenhouse effect is a natural process that is necessary to life on earth. That's because the greenhouse effect traps heat that otherwise would dissipate into outer space. Heat is trapped by greenhouse gases — mainly carbon dioxide, methane, and water vapor — in the atmosphere, which radiate heat in all directions, including back to earth. Without the greenhouse effect, earth would be a cold, cold place.

So what is the relationship between the greenhouse effect and global warming? When there is a normal amount of greenhouse gases in the atmosphere, earth maintains the warm climate that we know. Studies show that earth's climate has been relatively stable for the last 10,000 years — until about 200 years ago, when technology resulted in more greenhouse gases, especially carbon dioxide, being released into the atmosphere. The amount of methane has increased because of other human activities. For example, large quantities of methane can be released from oil wells and landfills used for trash disposal.

This overabundance of greenhouse gases causes more heat to be trapped than before, which results in rising temperatures. This has led to climate change, which has all sorts of negative consequences, from rising ocean temperatures, to increases in tropical storms and rising sea levels. We are already seeing ways in which climate change is affecting the supply of food and water around the world. Scientists say that climate change is linked to human release of greenhouse gases and not to increased energy from the sun, which has remained constant.

17. When scientists consider climate, what length of time is involved, according to "Weather Versus Climate"?

   (A) 30 years or more.

   (B) a decade

   (C) probably a few months

   (D) whatever is going on today

18. Which of the following is indicative of climate change, according to "Weather Versus Climate"?

   (A) Chicago has two weeks of subzero weather in January.

   (B) A light dusting of snow falls overnight in Tampa, Florida, in December.

   (C) Northern Maine experiences a day or two of 90-degree weather in August every few years.

   (D) The number of Atlantic hurricanes each year has been steadily increasing for decades.

19. According to "The Greenhouse Effect," which of the following is a cause of global warming?

   (A) The amount of heat received from outer space has increased.

   (B) Gases that trap heat in the atmosphere have increased.

   (C) Oceans are releasing more heat into the atmosphere.

   (D) The amount of energy reaching earth from the sun has increased.

20. From "The Greenhouse Effect," which of these actions can we infer would reduce global warming?

   (A) increasing the amount of trash buried in landfills

   (B) reducing the amount of oxygen released into the atmosphere by photosynthesis in plants

   (C) reducing the amount of methane released into the atmosphere by oil pumps

   (D) increasing the amount of water vapor released into the atmosphere by oceans

21. Which of these sentences most accurately describes the relationship between the two passages?

   (A) "Weather Versus Climate" defines weather, climate, and climate change, while "The Greenhouse Effect" explains the cause of climate change.

   (B) "Weather Versus Climate" gives the cause of climate change, while "The Greenhouse Effect" explains its consequences for life on earth.

   (C) "Weather Versus Climate" contrasts weather and climate, while "The Greenhouse Effect" explains that climate change is a natural process we do not need to worry about.

   (D) "Weather Versus Climate" says climate change is not a problem, while "The Greenhouse Effect" asserts that climate change is a crisis situation.

22. Which of these conclusions are supported by both passages?

(A) Global warming is a crisis we must address.

(B) Global warming is the cause of climate change.

(C) We do not need to worry about climate change.

(D) Climate change can be observed in long-term changes in climate we are seeing around the world.

Items 23–25 are based on this passage, which includes an excerpt from the U.S. Constitution.

The Bill of Rights is the first ten amendments to the United States Constitution. These amendments were added to the Constitution because some states were leery of ratifying the Constitution without them. They were afraid that the new government would be too powerful. They felt that the Constitution needed to guarantee fundamental liberties and freedoms that they had fought for and believed in. Some of the most important of these rights are in the First Amendment.

Congress shall make no law respecting an establishment of religion, or prohibiting the free exercise thereof; or abridging the freedom of speech, or of the press; or the right of the people peaceably to assemble, and to petition the government for a redress of grievances.

23. Which of these actions are rights or liberties of all Americans, according to the First Amendment?

(A) complaining to their representative in Congress

(B) owning a firearm

(C) voting in elections

(D) having a trial by jury

24. What does the word *leery* mean in this sentence in Paragraph 1?

These amendments were added to the Constitution because some states were leery of ratifying the Constitution without them.

(A) apprehensive

(B) angry

(C) unwary

(D) confident

25. A television news channel wants to report a story that is critical of the government. The government believes the information in the story is untrue. Which of these sentences describes an action permitted under the First Amendment in this situation?

(A) The government can seize the TV news channel to get it to stop reporting lies.

(B) The news channel must postpone the story until it convinces a court that the story is accurate.

(C) The news channel can show the story whenever it wants to.

(D) The government can force the channel to show another story that presents its point of view.

The answers

1. **D. serious enough that it requires monitoring.** The text states that the comingling of the virus strains is serious enough to require monitoring. Now that a new area of possible comingling has been found, the text implies it, too, should be monitored. Choice (A) isn't supported by the text, and even though Choices (B) and (C) are possible, they're not as clear and important statements as Choice (D).

   Your preparation for the science test can help you with RLA passages and questions like these, and vice versa. That gives you a leg up on both tests!

   TIP

2. **D. North Pacific.** The text states that this finding shows the North Atlantic is as significant a melting pot for birds and avian flu as the North Pacific. Choice (B) isn't mentioned; and although *Eurasia* is mentioned, it isn't mentioned as a place where birds from Europe and North America mingle.

3. **C. It proved that avian flu viruses had mingled in Iceland.** According to the text, only this statement is true. The other statements are contradicted by information in the text.

4. **A. It can lead to a new, dangerous strain of avian flu.** The text states that the virus evolves readily, and that the mingling of North American and Eurasian strains can lead to new varieties that are dangerous to humans. Cold viruses and flu viruses aren't the same, so Choice (B) has nothing to do with the topic of this text. Choices (C) and (D) are not supported by information in the passage.

5. **C. factual and straightforward.** The tone of the passage is very calm, very factual. It isn't *lighthearted, deeply concerned,* or *gloomy*.

6. **B. the H5N1 strain.** The text refers only to the H5N1 strain as a possible human flu. The term *bird flu* refers to the entire category of disease, not just the version dangerous to humans. There's no mention in the text of an *H5 flu*, and *Eurasian avian flu* simply refers to one part of the world where many strains of avian flu originate.

7. **D. It shifts the focus from risk to humans to the need for continued monitoring.** Choice (D) is correct because the paragraph indicates that the situation currently doesn't pose a high risk to humans but should be further monitored. The other choices are not supported by information in the paragraph.

8. **Essential: B, C; Not Essential: A, D.** Choice (B) is one of the key findings of the study, and Choice (C) is relevant for public health around the world, so both statements are essential to the summary. The types of birds, the exact locations in Iceland, and the type of land where the birds gathered are less important, so (A) and (D) are not essential to the summary.

9. **B. the population of Chicagee.** The urban population listed is well beyond anything existing today. The other details are possible today, and so do not indicate that the story is set in the future.

10. **A. incredibly crowded.** The overwhelming view that Bloch sees is a future of incredible overcrowding. There doesn't appear to be a food shortage based on the content of the story, so Choice (B) is wrong. Working hours appear to be shorter, so Choice (D) is also incorrect. And the passage indicates that the commutes are long and hard, so Choice (C) is incorrect.

11. **C. descriptions of enormous cities.** The author says that cities have expanded greatly from their original borders, which is an indication of massive population growth. The other details are mentioned in the passage, but do not indicate that the population has grown so large.

12. **B. shorter working hours.** Harry states that he sometimes wishes he worked there because of the shorter working hours but doesn't say anything about better pay. The text also states that the commuting times would be longer there.

13. **C. He is not married.** The text mentions legal restrictions on accommodations. Harry would have to be married to be entitled to a two-room apartment. Harry states that he makes a good income, so money isn't an issue, which means that Choice (D) is incorrect. His lady friends claim to like the convenience, but Harry knows they're just being polite, which rules out Choice (B). He certainly doesn't like the small space, despite its efficiency, so Choice (A) is incorrect.

14. **A. 38 million.** The text states that the population is 38,000,000 people. The population of New Philly is 63,000,000, which makes Choice (B) incorrect. Choices (C) and (D) are too large.

15. **A. He feels more fortunate than others but still has vague worries.** The third and fourth sentences of the paragraph say that Harry feels fortunate for having a good job, security, and a nice home, yet he can't figure out what is haunting him about the future.

16. **A, B. travel on commutrains** and **the flavor of his breakfast.** The passage says that commutrains and powdered eggs are "murder," so Choices (A) and (B) support the generalization. Choice (C) is not possible because he can afford to eat in restaurants. The passage does not give information on the flavor of Instantea, so this choice does not support the generalization.

17. **A. 30 years or more.** The text states that climate refers to the average weather conditions over many years.

TIP

These two passages are examples of the kinds of textbook materials that may appear on the Reading component of the GED. In these cases, skills you develop for social studies and science tests can help you.

18. **D. The number of Atlantic hurricanes each year has been steadily increasing for decades.** Of the choices, only Choice (D) shows a change over time, so only this choice is possible.

TIP

When you come to readings with two passages, the questions will often tell you which passage(s) they refer to. Use that as a clue to help you look for the answer in the right reading.

19. **B. Gases that trap heat in the atmosphere have increased.** Choice (B) is directly stated in the passage as the cause of global warming. The other choices are not named as causes or are contradicted by the information in the passage.

20. **C. reducing the amount of methane released into the atmosphere by oil pumps.** According to the passage, methane is a greenhouse gas. Reducing emissions of it would reduce global warming. Therefore, Choice (C) is correct. Choice (A) would likely increase the release of methane gas, since the passage says that this gas is released from landfills. Choice (B) is incorrect because oxygen is not a greenhouse gas. In addition, reducing the amount of oxygen released into the air would likely have other negative consequences. Choice (D) is incorrect because water vapor is a greenhouse gas, so releasing increased quantities would increase global warming, not reduce it.

21. **A. "Weather Versus Climate" defines weather, climate, and climate change, while "The Greenhouse Effect" explains the cause of climate change.** Of the choices, only Choice (A) is possible: the first article contains definitions of the terms. The second article explains how the greenhouse effect works. The other options are contradicted by the information in the passages.

22. **D. Climate change can be observed in long-term changes in climate we are seeing around the world.** Of the choices, only Choice (D) is supported by both passages. Choice (A) is not stated in either passage. Choice (B) is supported in only the second passage. Choice (C) is contradicted by the second passage.

23. **A. complaining to their representative in Congress.** Only Choice (A) is mentioned in the First Amendment, so it is correct. The other options are mentioned in other parts of the Constitution.

TIP

This passage is also an example of the kinds of textbook materials that may appear on the Reading component of the GED. In these cases, skills you develop for social studies and science tests can help you on the RLA test, and vice versa. Talk about efficiency!

24. **A. apprehensive.** You can figure out that *leery* means "apprehensive" (Choice A) from the sentences that follow it, which indicate that the states were fearful of losing these rights. Choice (B) does not make sense, and Choices (C) and (D) are the opposite of the states' feelings.

25. **C. The news channel can show the story whenever it wants to.** The First Amendment protects freedom of the press. Choice (C) is the only choice that reflects this fundamental right. The actions in the remaining choices are forbidden by the First Amendment, and so are incorrect.

Chapter **8**

Preparing for the Extended Response Component

The Extended Response item is one of the components of the GED test that test-takers worry about the most. Let's face it, not everyone likes to write, and you may even have bad memories of writing essays in school. I can't make all of that go away, but I can give you some strategies and tips that will help you on test day — and in further education, if you decide to go to college. In this chapter, I give you tips and strategies to help you write a passing GED essay in 45 minutes. And in Chapter 9, I walk you through the entire process, so you will know exactly what to do on test day. You can then use the Extended Response items in the practice tests to develop your skills and get some experience. None of us will ever be William Shakespeare, but by test day, you will at least be ready to pass!

Examining the Extended Response Item

Despite its name, the Extended Response doesn't consist of a long research essay so much as a series of four to five related paragraphs. You aren't expected to produce a book-length opus, complete with documented research. Rather, you're expected to write a coherent series of inter-related paragraphs on a given topic and use the rules of grammar and correct spelling. Part of that essay will be an analysis of two short readings that are presented to you, and part will be preparation of your own logical argument on the topic of the readings. Examiners look for an essay that's well organized, logical, and relevant to the topic given. They also look at how you adhere to standards of English writing, but there is some good news: The focus is largely on complete sentences and overall understandability. You will not be graded down for small errors as long as your overall essay is clear and you use complete sentences.

In the following sections, I will show you what you need to know about the Extended Response and give you some tools for writing a passing essay.

Looking at the skills the Extended Response covers

The evaluation of your essay focuses on three major areas. By having a clear understanding of the main skills covered in this part of the test, you can ensure that you will address all of them when writing your essay; that will translate into success in terms of your essay score. The GED Testing Service defines the three essay criteria you need to address as follows:

>> **Creation of an argument and use of evidence.** This criterion refers to how well you answer the topic, including whether the focus of the response shifts as you write. Stay on topic.

>> **Development and organizational structure.** This criterion refers to whether you show the reader through your essay that you have a clear idea about what you're writing and that you're able to establish a definable plan for writing the essay. The evaluation expects that you'll present your arguments in a logical sequence and back those arguments with specific supporting evidence from the source texts. Remember, you must use specific details from the source texts; you can elaborate, but your answer must be based on the source texts.

>> **Clarity and command of standard English conventions.** This criterion refers to your ability to appropriately use what might be called "on-demand draft writing" — that is, writing an essay in a single draft in 45 minutes on a topic you didn't choose. That includes the application of the basic rules of grammar, such as sentence structure, mechanics, usage, and so forth. It's also looking for stylistic features, such as transitional phrases, varied sentence structure, and appropriate word choices. But as I said before, you will not be graded down for small errors as long as they don't interfere too much with understandability.

The evaluation grades your essay on a three-point scale. You receive 2, 1, or 0 points, depending on your success in each of these three categories. You can check the Educator Handbook and the Assessment Guide for Educators at `https://ged.com/educators_admins/teaching/teaching_resources/` for some valuable learning tools as well as detailed information on how the Extended Response is scored.

WARNING

To pass the entire RLA test, you need to score well on all three parts. If you don't pass the essay, you probably won't accumulate a high enough score on the other sections to pass the RLA test, and that means you'll have to retake the entire test. So use the following information to do your best on the Extended Response.

Understanding the Extended Response format

This 45-minute part of the Reasoning through Language Arts (RLA) test has only one item: a prompt on which you have to write a short essay.

For this part of the test, you're given one topic and a few instructions. Your task is to write an essay of four or more paragraphs on that topic. Remember that you can't write about another topic or a similar topic — if you do, you'll receive zero points for your essay, and you'll have to retake the entire RLA test.

REMEMBER

While you cannot choose the topic of your essay, keep in mind that the test developers look for topics that most adults will know something about and be able to relate to. The topics will avoid areas that are sensitive or controversial. You can be sure that politics, religion, and other areas of personal belief will not come up.

The focus for the evaluation of this part of the GED test is on your reading comprehension, analysis and organization, and writing skills.

The test presents you with two passages of argumentation. That means each of the writers takes a position on an issue. You must examine the positions, determine which is the stronger and best-defended one, and write an essay explaining why you made that choice. You have to do that regardless of how you feel about the issue. The point is to analyze and show that you understand the strategies used to defend these positions.

As part of that process, you must analyze the arguments for logical consistency, illogical conclusions, and false reasoning. This is where your critical thinking skills come into play. Does Point A from the author really make sense? Is it valid and backed by facts?

Finally, you must write your answer in a clear, concise, and well-organized response. The evaluation examines how well you write, including the following aspects:

>> Your style

>> Varied sentence structure and vocabulary

>> Use of transitional sentences

>> Appropriate vocabulary

>> Correct spelling and grammar, including word usage and punctuation

For in-person testing, you will have an erasable tablet for rough notes, points, and organization. On the online-proctored test, you will have an onscreen, erasable whiteboard to do these tasks. Use them to help you prepare your answer. You will write your essay on a computer screen that has a mini–word processor with some basic functions, such as cut, paste, undo, and redo. However, it doesn't offer a spell-checker or grammar-checker.

REMEMBER

For some test takers, having access to an erasable tablet for writing notes and organizing ideas is very handy. Other test takers may prefer the onscreen, erasable whiteboard. Try using the onscreen whiteboard. If you feel you need the erasable tablet to do your best work, you may want to take the RLA test at a testing center.

Preparing to succeed on the Extended Response

The Extended Response essay requires some very specific skills, ranging from grammar and proper language usage to comprehension and analysis skills. If you've ever had an argument about who has the best team or which employer is better, you already know how to assess arguments and respond. Now you need to hone those skills. As you prepare for the RLA Extended Response, do the following:

>> **Read, read, and read some more.** Just as for the other parts of the RLA test (and most other tests on the GED), reading is important. Reading exposes you to well-crafted sentences, which can help you improve your own writing. Reading also expands your horizons and provides you with little bits of information that you can work into your essay.

TIP

As you read, make an outline of the paragraphs or chapters you read to see how the material ties together. Try rewriting some of the paragraphs from your outline, and compare what you write to the original. Your results may not be ready for prime time, but this little exercise gives you practice in writing organized, cohesive sentences and paragraphs, which can go a long way in this part of the test.

>> **Review how to plan an essay.** Few people can sit down, write a final draft of an essay without planning, and receive a satisfactory grade. Instead, you have to plan what you're going to write. The best way to start is to jot down your ideas about the topic without worrying about the order. From there, you can organize your thoughts into groups. Later in this chapter, you will find help on planning your essay.

>> **Practice writing on a topic (and not going off topic!).** Your essay must relate to the given topic as closely as possible. If the test asks you to analyze two positions about daylight savings time and you write about how much you love the summertime, you can kiss your good score on this part of the test goodbye.

TIP

To help you practice staying on topic, read the newspaper and write a letter to the editor or a response to a columnist. Because you're responding to a very narrow topic that appeared in a particular newspaper article, you have to do so clearly and concisely — if you ever want to see it in print. (You can also practice staying on topic by picking a newspaper article's title and writing a short essay about it. Then read the actual story and see how yours compares.)

>> **Think about, and use, appropriate examples.** You're dealing with information presented in the source text. You'll find information in the source text that will support or contradict the position you are to argue. When you take a position, you need to use materials from the source text to support your position. Use that information. Look for flaws in the logic. You can find good examples of such arguments in the editorial section of a newspaper or in blogs. Look at how the writers develop their arguments, use logic to support their positions, and perhaps use false logic or flawed reasoning to persuade the readers.

>> **Practice editing your own work.** After the test starts, the only person able to edit your essay is you. If that thought scares you, practice editing your own work now. Take a writing workshop or get help from someone who knows how to edit. Practice writing a lot of essays, and don't forget to review and edit them as soon as you're done writing.

>> **Practice general writing.** If writing connected paragraphs isn't one of your strengths, practice doing so! Write long e-mails. Write long letters. Write to your member of Congress. Write to your friends. Write articles for community newspapers. Write short stories. Write anything you want — whatever you do, just keep writing.

>> **Write practice essays.** Check out the practice tests in Chapters 19 and 27 for some essay prompts (in actual test format). Write essays based on the topics given, and then ask a knowledgeable friend or former teacher to grade them for you. You can also read a couple of sample essays based on the same topics you're given in Chapters 20 and 28. You may also want to take a preparation class in which you're assigned practice topics to write about. When you think you're finished practicing, practice some more.

>> **Practice keyboarding.** To write an essay in 45 minutes, you need to be ready to type quickly and accurately. So use a computer as much as possible. To simulate real testing conditions, turn off the spell-checker and grammar-checker. When you finish, turn them back on to get some instant feedback about your work. If you don't own a computer, try to find one at your public library or an adult education center. If the center has classes or tutorials on keyboarding, take advantage of them!

Writing the RLA Extended Response

The RLA Extended Response item asks you to write an essay in 45 minutes on an assigned topic. This part of the test assesses your literacy and understanding. Even if you can understand the essay topic, you must now demonstrate that you're thoroughly familiar with the process of writing an essay, that you know how to spell correctly, and that you understand the rules of grammar and language usage. You're asked to read two source texts that present different viewpoints on an issue. You must determine which argument is better supported and write an essay explaining why the position you chose is the better-supported one.

REMEMBER

Keep in mind that writing this essay isn't that different from writing a letter or a blog — except that you must explain and clarify the subject for the reader without rambling on until you run out of space.

WARNING

The way the RLA test is scored, you most likely won't pass if you don't receive a passing mark on the Extended Response. That means if you don't do well on the Extended Response, you'll have to take the entire RLA test over again. That fact alone should be all the incentive you need to practice writing.

In the following sections, I walk you through the four steps to writing an effective Extended Response and provide a few pointers for making sure you ace this part of the RLA test.

Managing your time

You have 45 minutes to finish your essay for the Extended Response on the RLA test, and, in that time, you have four main tasks:

>> Reading the passages

>> Planning your essay

>> Writing your essay

>> Revising and editing your essay

The following sections take a closer look at these tasks and explain how you can successfully complete each one in the time allotted.

TIP

A good plan of action is to spend 5 minutes reading, 10 minutes planning, 20 minutes writing, and 10 minutes editing and revising. This schedule is a tight one, though, so if your keyboarding is slow, consider allowing more time for writing. And remember, no one but you will see anything but the final version, so don't worry if you make mistakes while you type. Keep moving and correct these mistakes when you edit and revise.

Reading and planning (15 minutes total)

Before you begin writing your essay, read the topic carefully several times and ask yourself what the topic means to you. Determine what the two positions presented in the source texts are. Then, gather ideas. There are several ways to gather ideas. On the reading screen, you can highlight key pieces of evidence you want to use in your essay. You can also write notes on the erasable tablet or type them into the on-screen whiteboard. Don't worry about the order in which you write your ideas, You can sort through all the information in the next phase. Don't worry about correct grammar or spelling, either. No one but you will see your notes.

For example, if the essay item presents you with two source texts, one in favor of daylight savings time and the other opposed, and then asks you to evaluate the arguments, you need to begin by considering which text is more convincing, that is, which text presents the better and stronger argument. Then you need to look at and evaluate all the supporting evidence presented by the two sides of the argument. The planning stage of your essay writing begins when you highlight or jot down key pieces of supporting evidence you find about the issue in the source texts. It's important to stick with the points presented in the source texts and not wander off into your own opinions about the topic.

After you write down these points, sit back for a moment to reflect. (Don't reflect too long, though, because you still have an essay to write! Just take a few minutes.) Look over your points and find an introduction, such as, "The argument that daylight savings time has outlived its usefulness makes the stronger case." Write this sentence above your brainstorming notes. Then look at the points you came up with earlier that strongly back up your position. Number them in the most effective order. Add some ideas from the reading that you think are false or flawed, so you can address them in your essay too. All these ideas will be the body of your essay.

Now, write a concluding sentence, such as, "The argument against daylight savings time is stronger. Although once useful, the enormous cost, confusion, and lack of clear benefits show that it's an idea past its time." Glancing at your introduction and the essay topic itself, select points that strengthen your conclusion. Some of these points may be the same ones you used in your introduction.

Your plan will likely look something like this.:

> >> **Introduction.** "The argument that daylight savings time has outlived its usefulness makes the stronger case."
>
> >> **Body.**
>
> - List the appropriate supporting evidence in order of importance.
>
> - List false arguments or flawed arguments made by either side of the discussion.
>
> >> **Conclusion.** "Although daylight savings time was helpful in a bygone day, the changeover twice a year costs Americans billions of dollars in needless expense, lost wages, and inconvenience without any clear benefit to people's lives."

Now reflect again. Can you add any more points to improve the essay? Don't just add points to have more points, though. This isn't a contest for who can come up with the most points. You want to have logically written points that support your argument.

Look over your outline again. Can you combine any parts to make it tighter? Do you want to add an example? Or change the organization? Now's the time!

When you are satisfied with your outline, you're ready to go on to the next step: drafting your essay.

Writing (20 minutes)

During the writing stage, you think in more detail about the points you came up with in the planning stage, and you get your words typed out onscreen. Begin writing, and keep going. Don't get bogged down on spelling or grammar. You can fix those later. Just write organized paragraphs and logical sentences.

Each paragraph starts with an *introductory sentence*, which sets up the paragraph content, and ends with a *transition sentence* that leads from the paragraph you're on to the next one. If you put your sentences in a logical order from introduction to transition, you start to see paragraphs — as well as your essay — emerge.

Editing and revising (10 minutes)

Now comes the hard part. You have to be your own editor. Turn off your ego and remember that every word is written on a computer screen, not carved in stone. Make your work better by editing and revising it. Make this the best piece of writing you've ever done — in a 45-minute time block, of course.

When you're ready to edit and revise, scroll through your essay twice: once for content and again for standards of conventional English. First, read it to make sure that you are satisfied with the content of the essay. Does it make sense? Does it use good examples from the passages? Does it follow a logical order? If it doesn't, you may need to revise. Ask yourself whether each paragraph contributes to your argument. If it doesn't, you may need to do more revising. It could be something as simple as changing the order of the paragraphs, deleting something, or adding transitional phrases.

Then reread your essay for standards of conventional English. Look for errors in spelling, capitalization, subject–verb agreement, and punctuation. If you quote directly from one of the articles, make sure you use quotation marks correctly. Check for these errors last because this area is the least important of the criteria used to score your essay. If your essay has good ideas, is written in sentences and paragraphs, flows logically, and has only a few small errors that do not interfere with understanding, you are 90-percent there!

Putting together a winning essay

Some of the key points in the essay evaluation appear in the following list. If you have all these characteristics in your essay, your chances of receiving a high score are pretty good:

>> You've read and understood the two source texts and selected the position that has the best support.

>> Your essay clearly explains why you made your choice, using proof from the source texts.

>> Your essay is clearly written and well organized.

>> The evidence you present is developed logically and clearly.

>> You use transitions throughout the essay for a smooth flow among ideas.

>> You use appropriate vocabulary, varied sentence structure, and good grammar and spelling.

Here are a few other tips and ground rules to keep in mind as you prepare for the Extended Response:

>> **You have only 45 minutes to write an essay based on a single topic and very specific source text.** An essay usually consists of a number of paragraphs, each of which contains a topic sentence stating a main idea or thought. Be sure each paragraph relates to the overall topic of the essay. And, for the most part, make sure to place a topic sentence at the beginning of each paragraph to help readers focus on the main point you want them to understand.

» **You can prepare your essay by highlighting the source material and using the erasable tablet provided at the test center or the on-screen whiteboard.** As you read the source material, you can highlight ideas you want to include. Use the erasable tablet or on-screen whiteboard to gather and organize ideas, By using these tools, your final essay will be well-supported, logical, and organized. No one will look at the tablet or whiteboard, so what you write there is just for you.

» **You must write about the topic and only about the topic.** You're graded for writing an essay on the topic, so make sure you really do write on the topic you're given. One of the easiest ways to fail this test is to write about something that isn't on topic. The source text presents divergent views. Your job is to analyze, reflect, and respond.

» **The essay tests your ability to write about an issue that has positive and/or negative implications.** Whether you agree or disagree with the issue presented is immaterial. The essay doesn't test how much you know about a given topic or your personal opinions. Rather, it tests your ability to analyze and express yourself in writing.

» **Effective paragraphs use a variety of sentence types: statements, questions, commands, exclamations, and even quotations.** Vary your sentence structure and choice of words to spark the readers' interest. Some sentences may be short, and others may be long to catch the readers' attention. Just make sure that your sentences are complete and well constructed. Avoid fragments and run-ons!

» **Paragraphs create interest in several ways: by developing details, using illustrations and examples, presenting events in a time or space sequence, providing definitions, classifying persons or objects, comparing and contrasting, and demonstrating reasons and proof.** Organize your paragraphs and sentences in a way that both expresses your ideas and creates interest.

» **Don't obsess about spelling, capitalization, and mechanics as you write.** Try to get your ideas on the screen. Later, you can go back and fix those small errors.

» **The evaluation requires you to express your ideas clearly and logically.** Make sure you stick to the topic.

Chapter 9

Writing an Extended Response Item

In this chapter, I provide an example of an Extended Response prompt with two passages that present arguments in favor of and against daylight savings time. Your task is to practice writing an essay, analyzing both positions presented in the passages to determine which one is best supported. Be sure to use relevant and specific evidence from each article to support your response.

Getting Familiar with RLA Extended Response

On test day, the Reasoning Through Language Arts (RLA) Extended Response component is presented to you on a single screen, with the directions at the top. The reading passages are on the left and a word processing box is on the right. You can scroll the passages to read everything, and you can use the highlight feature to mark ideas in the passages that you want to use in your essay.

The word processing box is very similar to a regular word processor, but does not have grammar or spell check, or other advanced features. The only features available are cut, copy, and paste. These features are handy if you decide you want to reorder sentences or paragraphs as you write or revise. On test day, you will also have an online whiteboard you can use to take notes and organize ideas. At test centers only, you will be handed an actual erasable tablet and dry-erase pen for the same purpose. It's big enough for note-taking, but not for writing a whole first draft of your essay in order to keyboard later. For now, have a couple of sheets of paper handy for organizing and writing.

TIP

To become accustomed to the real testing conditions, try to write your essay on a computer, if possible. On many word processing programs, you can simulate test conditions by turning off the spell checker, grammar checker, and auto-correct. (These controls are frequently found under "Preferences.") Then, after you write, you can turn the features back on to get some free, instant feedback on your work. Just remember, mechanics and spelling are not the most important criteria for evaluating your essay!

A Sample Extended Response Prompt

Your task: Analyze the arguments presented in the two passages. Then, develop an argument in which you explain how one position is better supported than the other. In your response, include relevant and specific evidence from both passages to support your argument.

Remember, you don't have to agree with the position you consider the better-argued position.

You have 45 minutes to complete this task.

Passage One

In the Good Old Summer Time!

For most of us, setting our clocks forward one hour in March is a sure sign that spring is coming, followed by summer! After a long, hard winter, particularly in the cold northern states, summer is a welcome time. Kids are out of school, it may be time for a vacation, and we can barbecue, hike, and enjoy the great outdoors. It's time for patios, porches, parks, and back yards!

One of the big advantages of daylight savings time is that it gives us more time to enjoy the great outdoors in summer. Studies show that people are more active on summer evenings if they have an extra hour of daytime to enjoy. And because of the crisis of obesity in America, more exercise is better for everyone, and the country!

Daylight savings time has some other advantages, too. Traffic studies show that accidents go down during daylight savings time because of the longer daylight hours. And daylight savings time helps the economy, too, because longer hours of daylight in the afternoon encourage people to go out and spend. Malls, shopping centers, and downtowns are more likely to be filled when it's light outside.

So daylight savings time is really beneficial! We should definitely keep this longstanding practice so that everyone can reap the benefits.

Passage Two

Spring Forward, Fall Back — Far Back!

Daylight savings time is a relatively new idea that is now past its prime. Daylight savings time was started only during World War I. Its purpose was to reduce the consumption of important supplies, such as fuel and candles, by allowing for an extra hour of daylight each day. Later, it was reimposed to encourage shopping and outdoor activities in summer. However, this practice is now outmoded.

Studies show that the transition to daylight savings time costs our country billions as companies, computer systems, and schedules have to be adjusted twice a year on such a massive scale. Medical studies show that disrupted sleep patterns have all sorts of negative consequences. Heart attacks and strokes go up right after the switchover because of the related stress. And everyone's circadian rhythms are disrupted twice a year, which causes symptoms similar to jet lag. This also causes auto accidents to soar in the days after the transitions as groggy drivers get into needless traffic accidents. Workplace accidents increase too, as sleep-deprived workers make careless mistakes. In addition, studies of workplaces show that productivity goes down in the days after the twice-annual change-overs. Orders are messed up, and work has to be redone as workers recover from disrupted rest patterns.

Daylight savings time has also lost the energy savings that once made it attractive. Because people nowadays run their air conditioners day and night, energy consumption will not be much affected.

Keeping daylight savings time is also bad for international business. Globally, fewer countries than ever before continue to observe daylight savings time. The European Union recently decided to do away with daylight savings time for just the reasons already mentioned. Each year, the U.S. airline industry loses an average of $150 million realigning schedules to those of countries that don't observe daylight savings time. All of the disruption puts the United States at a disadvantage with the rest of the world.

It's time for the United States to align with a growing number of countries around the world and abolish this annual folly. Families, health, and the economy will only benefit.

Evaluating Your Response

After writing your own response to the essay prompt in the previous section (and before you read the sample essay in the next section), evaluate your answer with these key points in mind:

>> Do you clearly state which position was stronger and better argued?

>> Are the arguments presented in the two source texts credible?

>> Do you explain which position you selected as the better-supported position?

>> Do you explain why you came to that conclusion? (You don't have to agree with the position.)

>> Does your introduction clearly state your position?

>> Do you include multiple pieces of evidence from the passages to support your position?

>> Is your evidence presented in a logical order to build your case?

>> Does your conclusion contain an appropriate summary of the evidence and why you took the stand you did?

>> Is your essay written in a clear, concise manner?

>> Does your essay stay on point?

>> Do you use proper linkages between paragraphs?

>> Do you use varied and clear sentences and sentence structure?

>> Is your use of grammar, spelling, and language correct?

Checking Out a Sample Response

Here's an example of a solid RLA Extended Response for the given prompt. Compare it to yours. Then review both against the following criteria the GED Testing Service uses to evaluate your writing. (For more information on the criteria, see Chapter 8.)

>> Creation of argument and use of evidence

>> Development and organizational structure

>> Clarity and command of Standard English conventions

Switching to and from daylight savings time each year has many pros and many cons. While some people may enjoy some benefits from the switchover, the argument that daylight savings time has outlived its usefulness makes the stronger case.

Changing to daylight savings time has a few advantages. People can get outdoors more, and the added daylight is nice for summer fun. But few people really take advantage of this extra time. Most of my friends go to indoor gyms all year, so the extra daylight doesn't make much difference. And to tell the truth, in the southern U.S., where I live, it's too hot to exercise outside anymore, as summer temperatures have increased due to global warming. As the article states, people just stay inside in cool, air-conditioned comfort.

There are many more negatives to daylight savings time. The change-over has all kinds of costs. It has very bad effects on our health, including a big increase in heart attacks, as reported in some medical studies. Other medical studies show that people get into more car accidents. Accidents and errors go up at work, too, which is costly. Daylight savings time also puts us out of kilter with the rest of the world. Fewer countries observe it now than before, so American businesses have to make a lot of effort to stay in sync. My company buys parts from other countries. Each year, we have trouble ordering parts around daylight savings time because we are on different schedules. Daylight savings time gets airline schedules out of whack, too, which costs those companies billions of dollars.

As you can see, although daylight savings time was helpful in a bygone day, the change-over twice a year costs Americans billions of dollars in needless expense, lost wages, poor health, and inconvenience, with few clear benefits to people's lives.

3

Finding Your Way: The Social Studies Test

IN THIS PART . . .

Find out what skills you need to succeed on the test, what subject areas the test covers, and how the test is laid out.

Take advantage of key test-taking strategies so that you're prepared to deal with any question type and evaluate any passage or visual material presented to you.

Chapter 10

A Graph, a Map, and You: Getting Ready for the Social Studies Test

Do you enjoy knowing about how events in the past may help you foretell the future? Do the lives of people in faraway places interest you? Are politics something you care about? If you answered yes to any of these questions, then you're going to like the Social Studies test! After all, social studies helps you discover how humans relate to their environment and to other people.

The GED Social Studies test assesses your skills in understanding and interpreting concepts and principles in civics, history, geography, and economics. Consider this test as a kind of crash course in where you've been, where you are, and how you can continue living there. You can apply the types of skills tested on the Social Studies test to your experience in community, school, and workplace situations as a citizen, a consumer, or an employee.

This test includes questions based on a variety of written passages and visual content taken from academic, community, and workplace materials, including both primary and secondary sources. The materials in this test are like those you see in most online news content. Reading well-written, reliable news sources regularly can help you become familiar with the style and vocabulary of the passages you find on the GED. Pay attention to articles on politics, the government, the Supreme Court, and the economy. For history, any number of websites have articles on U.S. or world history.

The Social Studies test consists of 50 multiple-choice questions on civics and government (about 50 percent of the test), U.S. history (about 20 percent of the test), economics (about 15 percent of the test), and geography and the world (about 15 percent of the test). You have 70 minutes to complete this section. In this chapter, you take a look at the skills required for the Social Studies section of the GED test, the format of the test, and what you can do to prepare.

Looking at the Skills the Social Studies Test Covers

The questions on the Social Studies test evaluate several specific skills, including the ability to read and understand complex text, interpret and relate graphs to text, and relate descriptive text to specific values in graphs. For example, a question could ask about the relationship between a description of unemployment in text and a graph of the unemployment rate over time.

REMEMBER

You don't have to study a lot of new content to pass this test. Everything you need to know is presented to you with the questions. In each case, you see some content, either a passage or a visual, a question or direction to tell you what you're expected to do, and a series of answer options.

The questions do require you to draw on your previous knowledge of events, ideas, terms, and situations that may be related to social studies. From a big-picture perspective, you must demonstrate the ability to

>> Identify information, events, problems, and ideas and interpret their significance or impact.

>> Use the information and ideas in different ways to explore their meanings or solve a problem.

>> Use the information or ideas to do the following:

- Distinguish between facts and opinions

- Summarize major events, problems, solutions, and conflicts

- Arrive at conclusions based on information provided to you

- Influence other people's attitudes

- Find other meanings or mistakes in logic

- Identify causes and their effects

- Recognize how writers may have been influenced by the times in which they lived

- Compare and contrast differing events and people, and their views

- Compare places, opinions, and concepts

- Determine what impact views and opinions may have both at this time and in the future

- Analyze similarities and differences in issues or problems

- Locate examples that illustrate ideas and concepts

- Evaluate solutions

>> Make judgments about the material's appropriateness, accuracy, and differences of opinion. Some questions will ask you to interpret the role information and ideas play in influencing current and future decision making. These questions ask you to think about issues and events that affect you every day. That fact alone is interesting and has the potential to make you a more informed citizen. What a bonus for a test!

Many questions test your ability to read and interpret text in a social studies context. That means you'll be tested on the following:

>> Identifying and interpreting information from sources

>> Isolating central ideas or specific information

>> Determining the meaning of words or phrases used in social studies

>> Identifying points of view, differentiating between fact and opinion, and identifying properly supported ideas

Other questions ask you to interpret graphical information and apply mathematical reasoning to social studies. Much of that relates to your ability to do the following:

>> Interpret graphs

>> Use charts and tables as source data and interpret the content

>> Interpret information presented visually

>> Differentiate between correlation and cause and effect

On the GED Social Studies test, a calculator icon appears on the top right of the computer screen for questions that involve math. When the icon appears, you may click on the calculator icon to use the online calculator or use your own TI-30XS MultiView calculator (at a test center only).

TIP

Since only a few items on the social studies test involve math, you might want to take social studies at home, if that is more convenient. Going to the test center in order to use a real calculator on only a few items may not be worth the extra trouble.

Other questions deal with applying social studies concepts. These concepts include the following:

>> Understanding how specific evidence supports conclusions

>> Comprehending the connections between people, environments, and events

>> Putting historical events into chronological order

>> Analyzing documents to examine how ideas and events develop and interact, especially in a historical context

>> Examining cause-and-effect correlations

>> Identifying bias and evaluating validity of information, in both modern and historical documents

Being aware of what skills the Social Studies test covers can help you get a more accurate picture of the types of questions you'll encounter. The next section focuses more on the specific subject materials you'll face.

Understanding the Social Studies Test Format and Content

You have 70 minutes to complete the Social Studies test. The questions come in various forms and are of varying difficulty. Most are in the standard multiple-choice-question format that you know from your school days. Other formats include fill-in-the-blank, drag-and-drop, and drop-down menu items. For a general overview of the types of questions on the Social Studies test, check out Chapter 2. For a deeper look, see Chapter 11.

In the following sections, you explore the subject areas the Social Studies test covers, and I give you an overview of the types of passages you can expect to see.

Checking out the subject areas on the test

Most of the information you need to answer these questions will be presented in the text or graphics accompanying the questions, so it's important to read and analyze the materials carefully but quickly. The questions focus on the following subject areas.

>> **Civics and government:** About 50 percent of the Social Studies test includes topics such as rights and responsibilities in democratic governance and the forms of governance. Many of these questions are about fundamental documents, such as the U.S. Constitution, the Declaration of Independence, and other writings. But don't worry — you don't need to memorize these documents. You will always be provided with excerpts to read.

>> **American history:** About 20 percent of the test covers a broad outline of the history of the United States from pre-colonial days to the present, including topics such as the War of Independence, the Civil War, the Great Depression, and the challenges of the 20th and 21st centuries.

>> **Economics:** Economics involves about 15 percent of the test and covers two broad areas: economic theory and basic principles. These include topics such as how various economic systems work, as well as topics related to consumer economics, such as inflation, the minimum wage, and other bread-and-butter subjects you can relate to.

>> **Geography and the world:** In broad terms, the remaining 15 percent covers the relationships between the environment and societal development; the concepts of borders, region, place, and diversity; and, finally, human migration and population issues.

The test materials cover these four subject areas through two broad themes.

>> **Development of modern liberties and democracy:** How did the modern ideas of democracy and human and civil rights develop? What major events have shaped democratic values, and what writings and philosophies are the underpinning to American views and expressions of democracy?

>> **Dynamic systems:** How have institutions, people, and systems responded to events, geographic realities, national policies, and economics?

If you're a little worried about all of these subject areas, relax. You're not expected to have detailed knowledge of all the topics listed. Although it helps if you have a general knowledge of these areas, the test is based on your ability to reason, interpret, and work with the information presented in the reading passages and visual material. Knowing basic concepts, such as checks and balances in a representative democracy, will help, but you don't need to know a detailed history of the United States.

Identifying the types of passages

The passages in the Social Studies test are taken from two types of sources.

» **Academic material:** The type of material you find in a school — textbooks, maps, newspapers, magazines, software, and Internet material. This type of passage also includes extracts from speeches or historical documents.

» **Workplace and community material:** The type of material found on the job — manuals, documents, business plans, advertising and marketing materials, company announcements, letters, emails, and so on.

The material may be from primary sources (the original documents, such as the Declaration of Independence) or secondary sources (material written about an event or person, such as someone's opinions or interpretation of original documents, historic events, or historic figures, sometimes long after the event takes place or the person dies).

Examining Preparation Strategies That Work

To improve your skills and get better results, I suggest you try the following strategies when preparing for the Social Studies test:

» **Take as many practice tests as you can get your hands on.** The best way to prepare is to answer all of the sample Social Studies test questions you can find. Work through practice questions (see Chapter 12), the practice tests in this book (see Chapters 21 and 29), and the online test included with this book. You can also find sample items for the Social Studies test at ged.com and at https://ged.com/study/free_online_ged_test/.

Consider taking a preparation class to get your hands on even more sample Social Studies test questions, but remember that your task is to pass the test — not to collect every question ever written.

» **Read a variety of different documents.** The documents you need to focus on include historic passages from original sources (such as the Declaration of Independence and the U.S. Constitution), as well as practical information for citizens and consumers (such as voter guides, atlases, budget graphs, political speeches, almanacs, and tax forms). Read about the evolution of democratic forms of government. Read about climate change and migration, about food and population, and about American politics in the post-9/11 world. Read newspapers and news magazines about current issues, especially those related to civics and government, and social and economic issues.

» **Prepare summaries of the passages you read in your own words.** After you read these passages, summarize what you've read. Doing so can help you identify the main points of the passages, which is an important part of succeeding on the Social Studies test. Ask yourself the following two questions when you read a passage or something more visual like a graph:

- **What's the passage about?** The answer is usually in the first and last paragraphs of the passage. The rest is usually explanation. If you don't see the answer there, you may have to look carefully through the rest of the passage.

- **What's the visual material about?** Look for the answer in the title, labels, captions, and any other information that's included.

After you get an initial grasp of the main idea, determine what to do with it. Some questions ask you to apply information you gain from one situation in another similar situation. If you know the main idea of the passage, you'll have an easier time applying it to another situation.

» **Draft a series of your own test questions that draw on the information contained in the passages you read.** Doing so can help you become familiar with social studies questions. Look in newspapers and magazines for articles that fit into the general passage types that appear on the Social Studies test. Find a good summary paragraph and develop a question that gets to the point of the summary.

» **Compose answers for each of your test questions.** Write down four answers to each of your test questions, only one of which is correct based on the passage. Creating your own questions and answers helps reduce your stress level by showing you how answers are related to questions. It also encourages you to read and think about material that could be on the test. Finally, it gives you some idea of where to look for answers in a passage.

» **Discuss questions and answers with friends and family to make sure you've achieved an understanding and proper use of the material.** If your friends and family understand the question, then you know it's a good one. Discussing your questions and answers with others gives you a chance to explain social studies topics and concepts, which is an important skill to have as you get ready to take this test.

» **Don't assume.** Be critical of visual material and read it carefully. You want to be able to read visual material as accurately as you read text material, and doing so takes practice. Don't assume something is true just because it looks that way in a diagram, chart, or map. Visual materials can be precise drawings, with legends and scales, or they can be drawn in such a way that, at first glance, the information appears to be different than it really is. Manipulating the scale for graphs is one way to skew the information and distort its meaning. At first glance, you never know the purpose for which the visual was created. Even visuals can be biased, so "read" them carefully. Verify what you think you see by making sure the information looks correct and realistic. Finally, before coming to any conclusions, check the scale and legend to make sure the graph is really showing what you think it is showing you.

» **Be familiar with general graphical conventions.** Maps and graphs have conventions. The top of a map is almost always north. The horizontal axis is always the x-axis, and the vertical axis (the y-axis) is dependent on the x-axis. Looking at the horizontal axis first usually makes the information clearer and easier to understand. Practice reading charts and tables in an atlas or check out government websites where information is displayed in tables, charts, and maps.

See Chapter 4 for general test–taking strategies that apply to all the GED test sections.

Chapter **11**

Social Studies Question Types and Solving Strategies

The Social Studies test consists of 50 questions on civics and government (about 50 percent of the test), U.S. history (about 20 percent of the test), economics (about 15 percent of the test), and geography and the world (about 15 percent of the test). You have 70 minutes to complete this section. Having a basic understanding of what's in this section can help you prepare and avoid any surprises when you sit down to the take the test.

The Social Studies test requires you to read a passage or study a visual, analyze the information, evaluate its accuracy, and draw conclusions. It doesn't measure your ability to recall information, such as dates, facts, or events. In most cases, you select an answer from four choices. So although there's not much you can do to study for this test, you can improve your chances of passing by answering practice questions, reading and writing summaries of what you've read — and by checking out my test-taking strategies in this chapter.

In this chapter, we explore the types of materials and questions you encounter on the Social Studies test, and I offer you advice on how to solve them with ease.

Answering Questions about Text and Visual Materials

There are two broad categories of source materials for the questions on the test. These source materials consist of textual materials, something with which you're probably already quite familiar; and visuals, like maps, diagrams, graphs, and tables. Each kind of material requires careful reading, even the visuals, because information can be buried anywhere, and you need to extract it. The materials require you to read thoughtfully, make inferences, come to conclusions, and then determine the answer.

Questions about text passages

About half of the questions on the Social Studies test are based textual passages, followed by a question or a series of questions. Your job is to read the passage and then answer the question or questions about it.

When you're reading these passages on the test (or in any of the practice questions or tests in this book), read between the lines and look at the implications and assumptions in the passages. An *implication* is something you can understand from what's written, even though it isn't directly stated. An *assumption* is something you can accept as the truth, even though proof isn't directly presented in the text.

REMEMBER

Be sure to read each question carefully so you know exactly what it's asking. Read the answer choices and go through the text again, carefully. If the question asks for certain facts, you'll be able to find them right in the passage. If it asks for opinions, you may find those opinions stated directly in the passage or they may simply be implied (and they may not match your own opinions, but you still have to answer with the best choice based on the material presented).

Answer each question using *only* the information given. An answer may be incorrect in your opinion, but according to the passage, it's correct (or vice versa). Go with the information presented and select the best answer choice.

Questions about visual materials

To make sure you don't get bored, many of the questions on the Social Studies test are based on maps, graphs, tables, political cartoons, diagrams, photographs, and artistic works. You need to be prepared to deal with all these types of visual materials. Some questions combine visual material and text.

If you're starting to feel overwhelmed about answering questions based on visual materials, consider the following:

>> **Maps aren't there only to show you the location of places.** They also give you information, and knowing how to decode that information is essential. A map may show you where Charleston is located, but it can also show you how the land around Charleston is used, what the climate in the area is like, or whether the population there is growing or declining. Start by examining the print information with the map, the *legend* (the table explaining the symbols used on the map), title, and key to the colors or symbols on the map. Then look at what the question requires you to find. Now you can find that information quickly by relating the answer choices to what the map shows.

For example, the map in Figure 11-1 shows you the following information:

● The population of the United States for 2020

● The population by state, by size range

Indirectly, the map also shows you much more. It allows you to compare the population of states with a quick glance. For example, you can see that Florida has a larger population than Montana, North Dakota, South Dakota, and Wyoming combined. If you were asked what the relationship is between a state's size and population, you could argue, based on this map, that there isn't much relationship. You could also show that the states in the northeast have a higher population density than the states in the Midwest. This is part of the skill of analyzing maps.

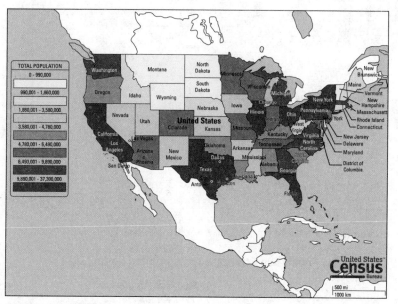

FIGURE 11-1:
Population of U.S. states, District of Columbia, and Puerto Rico, 2020 Census Map.

Source: U.S. Census Bureau

» **Every time you turn around, someone in the media is trying to make a point with a graph.** The types of graphs you see in Figure 11-2 are very typical examples. The real reason people use graphs to explain themselves so often is that a graph can clearly show trends and relationships between different sets of information. The three graphs in Figure 11-2 are best suited for a particular use. For example, bar graphs are great for comparing items over time, line graphs show changes over time, and pie charts show you proportions. The next time you see a graph, such as the ones in Figure 11-2, study it. Be sure to look carefully at the scale of graphs; even visual information can fool you. A bar graph that appears to show a rapid rise of something may in fact show no such thing. It may only look that way because the bottom of the chart doesn't start with values of zero. Check carefully to make sure you understand what the information in the graph is telling you.

» **Tables are everywhere.** If you've ever looked at the nutrition label on a food product, you've read a table. Study any table you can find, whether in a newspaper or on the back of a can of tuna. The population data table in Figure 11-3 is an example of the kinds of data you may see on the test. That table shows you a lot of information, but you can extract quite a bit more information that isn't stated. Some mental math tells you that according to the data in the table, around 236,000 people were serving outside the United States in the armed forces in December, 2020. How do you know that? Just subtract the number in the *Resident Population* column from the *Resident Population Plus Armed Forces Overseas* column. You can also calculate the change in the overall population, the rate of increase of the population, and even the size of the armed forces stationed in the United States compared to serving overseas.

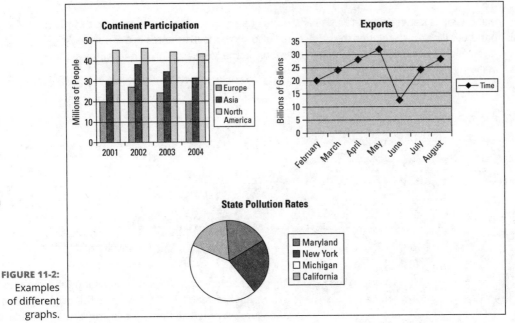

FIGURE 11-2:
Examples
of different
graphs.

© John Wiley & Sons, Inc.

Monthly Population Estimates for the United States, 2020

Month	Resident Population	Resident Population Plus Armed Forces Overseas	Civilian Population
January 1	329,135,084	329,371,559	327,948,163
February 1	329,237,661	329,474,136	328,050,740
March 1	329,342,883	329,579,358	328,155,962
April 1	329,459,499	329,695,974	328,272,578
May 1	329,588,430	329,824,905	328,401,509
June 1	329,726,295	329,962,770	328,539,374
July 1	329,877,505	330,113,980	328,690,584
August 1	330,047,526	330,284,001	328,860,605
September 1	330,215,986	330,452,461	329,029,065
October 1	330,382,026	330,618,501	329,195,105
November 1	330,528,990	330,765,465	329,342,069
December 1	330,656,950	330,893,425	329,470,029

FIGURE 11-3:
Population
data table.

Source: U.S. Census Bureau

REMEMBER

Tables are also sometimes called charts, which can be a little confusing, because graphs can also be called charts. Regardless of what they're called, you need to be prepared to extract information, even if it isn't stated directly. That's what makes maps and tables and graphs such fun.

>> **Political cartoons appear in the newspapers and online every day.** If you don't read political cartoons in the daily newspaper (usually located in the "Editorial," "Op-Ed," or "Opinion" pages in print or online), give them a try. Some days, they're the best entertainment in the paper. Political cartoons are usually based on an event in the last day or week. They can be nasty or funny and are always biased. To get the most out of political cartoons, look for small details, facial expressions, and background clues. The cartoons on the test are obviously older than the ones in daily newspapers, and may include political cartoons from America's past. Then you need to use your knowledge of American history. But don't worry — whether the cartoon is about war, politics, or the economy, the context will be clear. To become more

familiar with past cartoons, search for "political cartoons" online. You can also find websites that build skills for interpreting political cartoons.

» **You've no doubt seen countless photographs in your day.** Photos are all around you. All you need to do to prepare for the photograph-based questions on the test is to begin getting information from the photographs you see. Start with the newspapers or magazines, where photos are chosen to provide information that connects directly to a story. See whether you can determine what message the photograph carries with it and how it relates to the story it supports. Use the caption to help you understand the photo. If you don't understand a word or two in the caption, use information from the photo to help you figure it out.

» **You probably like to look at works of art.** On the Social Studies test, you have a chance to "read" works of art. You look at a work of art and gather information you can use to answer the item. To get yourself ready to gather information from works of art on the test, visit an art museum (in person or online), go on the Internet, or check out some library books. Lucky for you, books and websites even give background and other explanations for these works.

TIP

If you're unsure of how to read a map, go to any search engine and search for "map reading help" or "map reading skills" to find sites that explain how to read a map. If any of the other types of visual materials cause you concern, try similar searches, such as "graph reading skills," "understanding tables," or "interpreting political cartoons." You will get lots of tips and advice, plus plenty of maps, graphs, tables, and political cartoons to look at.

All the visual items you have to review on this test should be familiar to you. Now all you have to do is practice until your skills in reading and understanding them increase. Then you, too, can discuss the latest political cartoon or pontificate about a work of art.

Acing the Social Studies Items

The types of questions you encounter on the Social Studies test include multiple-choice, fill-in-the-blank, drag-and-drop, and drop-down-menu. In the following sections, I provide strategies for examining information, whether a passage or visual, and for answering sample questions in each of these formats.

Choosing an answer from multiple choices

Multiple-choice questions basically ask you to choose a correct answer from four choices. First, read the questions and the answer choices, and then read the passage looking for the answers.

If you can't decide based on that reading, review the answer choices. You can probably eliminate one or two of them because they're obviously wrong. Then skim the text again, looking for information based on the choices that are left. If that doesn't provide you with an answer, then you may have to guess. If you've eliminated the improbable choices, you may have to choose from only two or three options, which improves the odds of picking the correct one.

In the rest of this section, I walk you through answering some multiple-choice questions based on the following passage.

> Bridging both temperate and tropical regions, Mexico's terrain includes mountains, plains, valleys, jungles, rainforest, lakes and rivers, glaciers, and plateaus. Snow-capped volcanoes slope down to pine forests, deserts experience intense heat, and tourists play in the surf on balmy, tropical beaches. This diverse topography supports a variety of industries, including manufacturing, mining,

petroleum, agricultural production, and tourism. A member of the United States-Mexico-Canada Agreement, Mexico has the United States and Canada as its main export partners. In economic terms, Mexico has a GDP (gross domestic product) of $1.269 trillion ($8,421 per person), which ranks it 15th in the world. Beginning in 1985, Mexico began a process of trade liberalization and privatization. From 1982 to 1992, government-controlled enterprises were reduced from 1,155 to 217.

EXAMPLE

Which of the following is a feature of Mexico's terrain?

(A) volcanoes

(B) inland seas

(C) a polar ice cap

(D) earthquakes

The answer to this question is Choice (A), volcanoes, which is stated directly in the passage. Notice that even if you cannot find this answer quickly, you can eliminate Choice (C), since Mexico is not in a polar region. Inland seas (Choice B) are found in Canada and Europe, but not in Mexico. Mexico experiences earthquakes (Choice D), but they are not a topographical feature and are not mentioned in the passage.

EXAMPLE

Which words or phrases demonstrate that Mexico's climate represents extremes in temperature?

(A) sunny and rainy

(B) dark and misty

(C) plains and valleys

(D) snow-capped and intense heat

Here's an example of answer choices that can be misleading unless you read the question carefully. The question asks for the answer choice that represents extremes in *temperature.* So the only choice that works here is Choice (D) because it's the only one that deals with temperatures. *Snow-capped* volcanoes represent an extremely low temperature, while *intense heat* represents the opposite extreme. The other choices don't refer to temperature. *Sunny* and *rainy* and *dark* and *misty* refer to weather. *Plains* and *valleys* refer to terrain.

EXAMPLE

The phrase, *diverse topography*, refers to

(A) differences in terrain

(B) uniqueness in manufacturing

(C) differences in agriculture

(D) diversity of tropical beaches

This question shows why understanding subject-appropriate vocabulary is important. *Topography* is another word for "terrain." *Diverse* means "different," so Choice (A) is correct. *Manufacturing* and *agriculture* are types of industries, and *tropical beaches* are just one type of terrain.

EXAMPLE

Which countries are Mexico's top export partners?

(A) the United States and Britain

(B) France and Germany

(C) the United States and Canada

(D) Canada and Britain

The answer is Choice (C). The passage states this information directly. Britain, France, and Germany aren't mentioned in the passage.

EXAMPLE

What happened in Mexico between 1982 and 1992?

(A) Government control of enterprises increased.

(B) The government controlled fewer enterprises.

(C) Mexico achieved the highest GDP in the world.

(D) Mexico's growth rate was less than 6 percent.

The answer is Choice (B). According to the passage, during the decade from 1982 to 1992, Mexico's government reduced its control of enterprises from 1,155 to 217. Therefore, Choice (A) is incorrect. Notice that when two answer choices are opposites, usually one of them is correct. Mexico's GDP ranking (Choice C) is 15th in the world, and is given for a more recent year than the period between 1982 and 1992. Mexico's growth rate (Choice D) is not stated in the passage.

Coming up with an answer for fill-in-the-blank questions

Fill-in-the-blank questions require you to insert the answer, usually a word, phrase, or number, into a blank. No answer choices are provided, so you have to extract the information carefully from the passage or visual.

For practice, find the information you need in order to answer fill-in-the-blank questions based on the following graph.

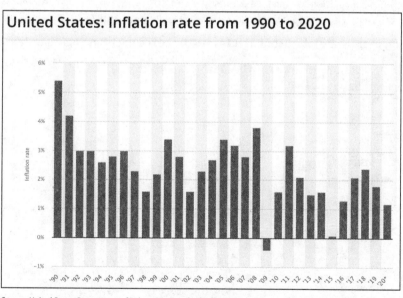

Source: United States Department of Labor, Bureau of Labor Statistics

EXAMPLE

In what year was the inflation rate the lowest? ⬚

The graph shows the annual inflation rate from 1990 to 2020. You need to identify that the vertical scale on the right refers to the inflation data. Every year is listed on the horizontal axis. To answer this question, you need to find the lowest bar on the graph. That bar is −0.4. Because the question asks for the year, write the corresponding year, 2009.

EXAMPLE

What was the difference between the inflation rate in 2015 and 2016? ⬚

To answer this item, you need to find two values on the chart and then subtract. Inflation in 2015 was 0.1%. Inflation in 2016 was 1.3%. Subtract to find the difference: 1.3 − 0.1 = 1.2, so write 1.2% in the box. This calculation was easy and you could do it in your head, but for more complicated calculations, remember to use your calculator or the onscreen calculator.

EXAMPLE

The inflation rate in 1992 was ⬚.

To answer this question, find the bar that corresponds to 1992. Then find the inflation rate for that year. The rate is 3%, so write that value in the box.

Dragging and dropping answers where they belong

Drag-and-drop questions require more understanding than basic multiple-choice questions because, in most instances, you need to prioritize, sequence, or sort answer choices, not just pick the answer.

Here's an example of a drag-and-drop item based on the following excerpt from *U.S. History For Dummies,* by Steve Wiegand (John Wiley & Sons, Inc.).

> As time passed, however, the country began to side more often with Britain, France, and other countries that were fighting Germany. The sinking of the British passenger ship, *Lusitania,* by a German submarine in 1915, which resulted in the deaths of 128 Americans, inflamed U.S. passions against "the Huns." Propagandistic portrayals of German atrocities in the relatively new medium of motion pictures added to the heat. And finally, when it was revealed that German diplomats had approached Mexico about an alliance against the United States, Wilson felt compelled to ask Congress for a resolution of war against Germany. He got it on April 6, 1917.

EXAMPLE

Drag (or write, in this case) the list of events into the boxes in chronological order. Write the letters.

Order of Events

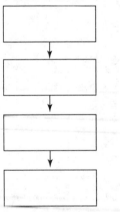

© *John Wiley & Sons, Inc.*

(A) sinking of the *Lusitania*

(B) declaration of war against Germany

(C) anti-German propaganda in the movies

(D) Germany negotiates with Mexico to attack the United States

The correct sequence of events is Choice (A), (C), (D), and then (B): the sinking of the *Lusitania*, anti-German propaganda in the movies, Germany negotiates with Mexico to attack the United States, and then declaration of war against Germany. The only somewhat tricky part of these choices is the timing for the anti-German propaganda, but the key phrase is in the sentence, "Propagandistic portrayals. . .added to the heat." The word *added* implies that it happened after the sinking of the *Lusitania*, which already generated anti-German "heat."

Choosing from a drop-down menu

A drop-down item is similar to a multiple-choice question because you select your answer from several options by clicking on your choice. Unlike multiple-choice questions, drop-down answer choices are not identified by letters. In this book, I use letters for the answer choices, for ease of use.

Drop-down items are frequently used together with graphics. The question usually asks you to complete a caption or a sentence about the graphic.

Try this example about the inflation graph from the previous section.

EXAMPLE

The chart shows the annual _____ of inflation over a 20-year period.

(A) rate

(B) percentage

(C) index

(D) number

The answer is Choice (A). The table is about the rate of inflation. The other choices do not make sense.

Managing Your Time for the Social Studies Test

You have a total of 70 minutes to answer 50 questions. So that means you have 84 seconds for each one. Answering easy questions first should allow you to progress faster, leaving you a little more time per item at the end so that you can come back to work on the harder ones.

To help you keep moving, you can skip questions or flag them for later if you are unsure of your answer. The Flag for Review button, in the upper-left corner of the screen, lets you flag questions that you are not sure about. When you finish the last question, you move to the Review screen, which shows a list of all the questions that are flagged or skipped. You can also go to the Review screen at any time by pressing the Review screen button in the lower-left corner of your screen. This way, you can return to items you flagged or skipped.

The questions on the Social Studies test are based on both regular textual passages and visual materials, so, when you plan your time for answering the questions, you have to consider the amount of time it takes to read both types of materials. (See the earlier section, "Questions about visual materials," for advice on how you can get more comfortable with questions based on graphs, tables, and the like.)

Each time you come to a new passage or visual, read the questions first and then skim the passage to find the answers. If you still can't answer one or more questions, then read the passage carefully, looking for the answers. This way, you take more time only when necessary.

Because you have such little time to gather all the information you can from visual material and answer questions about it, you can't study the map, graph, or cartoon for long. You have to skim it the way you skim a paragraph. Reading the questions that relate to a particular visual first, helps you figure out what you need to look for as you skim the material. The practice tests in Chapters 21 and 29 contain plenty of examples of questions based on visual materials, and so do the sample questions in Chapter 12.

TIP

If you're unsure of how quickly you can answer questions based on visual materials, time yourself on a few and see. If your time comes out to be more than 1.5 minutes, you need more practice.

Realistically, you have about 20 seconds to read the question and the possible answers, 50 seconds to look for the answer, and 10 seconds to select the correct answer. Dividing your time in this way leaves you about 3 minutes for review or for time at the end of the test to spend on difficult items. To finish the Social Studies test completely, you really have to be organized and watch the clock. Check out Chapter 4 for more general time-management tips.

TIP

You don't have to answer all the questions correctly to pass the GED, but you shouldn't leave any answers blank. There is no penalty for guessing on the GED, so even if you guess at random on four items, odds are you will get at least one point. That could be the point that puts you over the top!

Chapter 12

Practicing Social Studies Questions

This chapter provides sample Social Studies test questions to help you prepare for taking that section of the GED test.

Record your answers directly in this book or on a sheet of paper, if you think you'll want to revisit these practice questions at a later date. Mark only one answer for each item, unless otherwise indicated.

At the end of this chapter, I provide detailed answer explanations to help you check your answers. Take your time as you move through the explanations. They can help you understand why you missed the answers you did, and confirm or clarify the thought process for the answers you got right.

Remember, this is just preliminary test practice. I want you to get used to answering different types of Social Studies test questions. Use the complete practice tests in Chapters 21 and 29 to time your work and replicate the real test-taking experience. Then take the online test provided with this book — which closely duplicates the experience of taking the real GED.

Social Studies Practice Questions

The official Social Studies test consists mainly of multiple-choice items but also has some technologically enhanced items of the type I outline in Chapters 3 and 11. They measure general social studies concepts. The items are based on short readings that often include a map, graph, chart, cartoon, or figure. Study the information given and then answer the items following it. Refer to the information as often as necessary in answering. Work carefully, but don't spend too much time on any one question. Be sure you answer every question. Remember, on the real test, you can use the onscreen calculator (or your own calculator if you take the test at a testing center).

Questions 1 and 2 refer to the following excerpt from a U.S. government publication.

Democracies fall into two basic categories, direct and representative. In a direct democracy, citizens, without the intermediary of elected or appointed officials, can participate in making public decisions. Such a system is clearly most practical with relatively small numbers of people — in a community organization, tribal council, or the local unit of a labor union, for example — where members can meet in a single room to discuss issues and arrive at decisions by consensus or majority vote.

Some U.S. states, in addition, place "propositions" and "referendums" — mandated changes of law — or possible recall of elected officials on ballots during state elections. These practices are forms of direct democracy, expressing the will of a large population. Many practices may have elements of direct democracy. In Switzerland, many important political decisions on issues, including public health, energy, and employment, are subject to a vote by the country's citizens. And some might argue that the Internet is creating new forms of direct democracy, as it empowers political groups to raise money for their causes by appealing directly to like-minded citizens.

However, today, as in the past, the most common form of democracy, whether for a town of 50,000 or a nation of 50 million, is representative democracy, in which citizens elect officials to make political decisions, formulate laws, and administer programs for the public good.

1. The federal government of the United States is an example of a ☐☐☐☐ (direct *or* representative) democracy.

2. Which of the following is an example of allowing the population as a whole to vote on an issue?

(A) a vote on issuing library bonds

(B) the election of a local mayor

(C) the election of the president

(D) a school board election

Questions 3 and 4 refer to the following excerpt from a U.S. government publication.

In a democracy, government is only one thread in the social fabric of many and varied public and private institutions, legal forums, political parties, organizations, and associations. This diversity is called pluralism, and it assumes that the many organized groups and institutions in a democratic society do not depend upon government for their existence, legitimacy, or authority. Most democratic societies have thousands of private organizations, some local, some national. Many of them serve a mediating role between individuals and society's complex social and governmental institutions, filling roles not given to the government and offering individuals opportunities to become part of their society without being in government.

In an authoritarian society, virtually all such organizations would be controlled, licensed, watched, or otherwise accountable to the government. In a democracy, the powers of the government are, by law, clearly defined and sharply limited. As a result, private organizations are largely free of government control. In this busy private realm of democratic society, citizens can explore the possibilities of peaceful self-fulfillment and the responsibilities of belonging to a community — free of the potentially heavy hand of the state or the demand that they adhere to views held by those with influence or power, or by the majority.

3. Which of the following is an example of an authoritarian society?

   (A) Canada

   (B) Kingdom of Sweden

   (C) the former USSR

   (D) the Republic of Korea (South Korea)

4. All United States citizens have the right to elect

   (A) their senator.

   (B) Supreme Court justices.

   (C) cabinet secretaries.

   (D) army generals.

Questions 5–9 refer to the following excerpt from U.S. History For Dummies, *by Steve Wiegand (John Wiley & Sons, Inc.).*

Partly because of error and partly because of wishful thinking, Columbus estimated the distance to the Indies at approximately 2,500 miles, which was about 7,500 miles short. But after a voyage of about five weeks, he and his crew, totaling 90 men, did find land at around 2:00 a.m. on October 12, 1492. It was an island in the Bahamas, which he called San Salvador. The timing of the discovery was good; it came even as the crews of the *Nina, Pinta,* and *Santa Maria* were muttering about a mutiny.

Columbus next sailed to Cuba, where he found a few spices and little gold. Sailing on to an island he called Hispaniola (today's Dominican Republic and Haiti), the *Santa Maria* hit a reef on Christmas Eve, 1492. Columbus abandoned the ship, set up a trading outpost he called Navidad, left some men to operate it, and sailed back to Spain in his other two ships.

So enthusiastically did people greet the news of his return that on his second voyage to Hispaniola, Columbus had 17 ships and more than 1,200 men. But this time he ran into more than a little disappointment. Natives had wiped out his trading post after his men became too grabby with the local gold and the local women. Worse, most of the men he brought with him had come only for gold and other riches, and they didn't care about setting up a permanent colony. Because of the lack of treasures, they soon wanted to go home. And the natives lost interest in the newcomers after the novelty of the Spanish trinkets wore off.

5. By how much was Columbus in error in guessing the distance to the Indies? Write the answer in the box. [ ]

6. On what date did Columbus arrive in the Bahamas?

   (A) October 2, 1492

   (B) October 12, 1492

   (C) December 12, 1493

   (D) Christmas Eve, 1492

7. Why did so many people want to sail with Columbus on his second trip?

   (A) They were eager to settle new lands.

   (B) They wanted adventure.

   (C) They had heard stories about amazing cities.

   (D) They had heard stories of the gold Columbus had found.

8. Why did Columbus cut his first voyage short?

   (A) The *Santa Maria* had hit a reef and sank.

   (B) His men were ready to mutiny.

   (C) He had completed his task by setting up a small colony.

   (D) Disease decimated his crew.

9. Columbus's goal was to sail to the continent of [   ].

   Questions 10 and 11 refer to the following excerpt from U.S. History For Dummies, *by Steve Wiegand (John Wiley & Sons, Inc.).*

   On his second trip to the Americas in 1493, Columbus stopped by the Canary Islands and picked up some sugar cane cuttings. He planted them on Hispaniola, and they thrived. In 1516, the first sugar grown in the New World was presented to King Carlos I of Spain. By 1531, it was as commercially important to the Spanish colonial economy as gold.

   Planters soon discovered a by-product as well. The juice left over after the sugar was pressed out of the cane and crystallized was called *melasas* by the Spanish (and *molasses* by the English). Mixing this juice with water and leaving it out in the sun created a potent and tasty fermented drink. They called it *rum* — perhaps after the word for sugar cane, *Saccharum officinarum*. The stuff was great for long sea voyages because it didn't go bad.

   Sugar and rum became so popular that sugar plantations mushroomed all over the Caribbean.

10. What is molasses?

    (A) juice pressed out of sugar cane

    (B) leftover juice after sugar was pressed out of the cane

    (C) sugar cane mixed with water

    (D) *Saccharum officinarum*

11. How many years did it take before the first sugar cane grown in the New World was presented to the king of Spain?

    (A) 33 years

    (B) 23 years

    (C) 13 years

    (D) 1 year

Educational Attainment of the Population 25 Years and Over, by Selected Characteristics: 2019
(Numbers in thousands. Civilian noninstitutionalized population.[1])

Both sexes	Total	None - 8th grade	9th - 11th grade	High school graduate	Some college, no degree	Associate's degree	Bachelor's degree	Master's degree	Professional degree	Doctoral degree
Total	2,21,478	8,603	13,372	62,259	34,690	22,738	49,937	22,214	3,136	4,529
Marital Status										
Married, spouse present	1,26,768	4,476	6,069	32,493	18,378	13,410	31,280	15,096	2,240	3,327
Married, spouse absent, not separated	3,633	294	339	1,063	468	293	692	355	39	89
Separated	4,643	342	585	1,618	759	454	617	206	34	28
Widowed	14,852	1,218	1,414	5,459	2,411	1,284	1,960	872	100	134
Divorced	25,235	697	1,645	7,790	4,815	3,038	4,707	1,983	235	327
Never married	46,348	1,576	3,320	13,836	7,858	4,259	10,681	3,704	488	625
Household Relationship										
Family householder	80,502	2,608	4,497	20,288	13,436	8,923	18,642	9,004	1,232	1,872
Married, spouse present	61,073	1,865	2,683	14,226	9,613	6,630	15,539	7,705	1,097	1,714
Other family householder	19,429	742	1,814	6,062	3,823	2,293	3,103	1,299	136	157
Nonfamily householder	41,973	1,494	2,646	11,553	7,323	4,281	9,321	4,045	513	795
Living alone	34,952	1,333	2,284	9,880	6,149	3,552	7,347	3,306	432	668
Living with nonrelatives	7,020	161	362	1,673	1,174	729	1,974	739	82	127
Relative of householder	86,578	3,972	5,399	26,395	12,019	8,459	19,187	8,181	1,266	1,699
Spouse	61,000	2,029	2,897	16,692	8,220	6,379	14,984	7,117	1,102	1,579
Other	25,577	1,943	2,501	9,703	3,799	2,081	4,203	1,064	163	121
Nonrelative	12,426	529	830	4,022	1,912	1,074	2,786	985	125	162
Citizenship, Nativity, and Year of Entry										
Native born	1,81,283	2,767	9,420	52,024	31,198	19,984	41,686	18,120	2,568	3,515
Native parentage[2]	1,63,644	2,382	8,627	47,620	28,126	18,083	37,290	16,212	2,208	3,096
Foreign or mixed parentage[3]	17,639	385	793	4,404	3,072	1,901	4,396	1,907	361	419
Foreign born	40,195	5,836	3,952	10,235	3,492	2,754	8,250	4,095	568	1,014
Naturalized citizen	20,751	1,856	1,427	5,263	2,246	1,794	5,036	2,102	394	634
Not a citizen	19,444	3,980	2,525	4,972	1,245	960	3,214	1,993	174	380
Year of entry										
2010 or later	7,963	766	560	1,845	568	446	2,145	1,329	96	207
2000-2009	10,252	1,636	1,224	2,732	747	620	1,943	929	162	259
1990-1999	9,796	1,413	1,086	2,578	822	771	1,870	876	138	242
1980-1989	6,414	1,064	692	1,597	684	464	1,208	480	82	142
1970-1979	3,446	653	245	807	356	238	672	311	51	112
Before 1970	2,324	303	146	676	314	216	412	168	38	52
Labor Force Status										
Employed	1,37,478	3,597	5,726	34,453	20,731	15,235	35,820	16,050	2,425	3,440
Unemployed	4,531	169	464	1,403	860	450	809	293	45	37
Not in civilian labor force	79,470	4,837	7,182	26,403	13,099	7,053	13,307	5,871	666	1,052
Occupation (Employed Civilians Only)	**1,37,478**	**3,597**	**5,726**	**34,453**	**20,731**	**15,235**	**35,820**	**16,050**	**2,425**	**3,440**
Management, business, and financial occupations	25,465	170	329	3,412	3,315	2,342	10,185	4,848	323	540
Professional and related occupations	34,622	37	117	2,204	2,575	3,677	12,658	8,720	1,914	2,721
Service occupations	20,981	1,191	1,816	7,926	3,913	2,557	2,940	525	61	52
Sales and related occupations	12,598	148	447	3,450	2,388	1,390	3,908	787	36	44
Office and administrative occupations	15,040	95	331	4,586	3,672	2,122	3,385	768	30	51
Farming, forestry, and fishing occupations	929	256	140	314	88	54	62	15	-	-
Construction and extraction occupations	7,283	741	864	3,238	1,016	691	641	69	18	5
Installation, maintenance, and repair occupations	4,132	119	250	1,751	816	783	370	36	6	2
Production occupations	7,705	490	621	3,496	1,422	850	699	105	13	8
Transportation and material moving occupations	8,723	349	811	4,078	1,526	769	972	178	23	17
Industry (Employed Civilians Only)	**1,37,478**	**3,597**	**5,726**	**34,453**	**20,731**	**15,235**	**35,820**	**16,050**	**2,425**	**3,440**
Agricultural, forestry, fishing, and hunting	2,017	297	194	657	254	193	317	80	6	18
Mining	704	14	33	263	115	60	142	65	-	11
Construction	9,849	775	982	3,948	1,458	956	1,384	289	39	17
Manufacturing	14,450	517	746	4,663	2,203	1,608	3,280	1,212	49	172
Wholesale and retail trade	15,893	307	798	5,240	3,155	1,794	3,601	771	81	146
Transportation and utilities	8,009	175	403	2,972	1,676	959	1,447	327	27	25
Information	2,455	11	31	391	385	218	985	390	12	31
Financial activities	9,847	43	120	1,621	1,495	979	4,036	1,312	120	122
Professional and business services	17,821	448	520	3,009	2,183	1,549	6,119	2,689	724	579
Educational and health services	33,060	222	670	5,019	3,756	4,281	9,078	6,895	1,102	2,037
Leisure and hospitality	9,980	503	755	3,299	1,801	928	2,143	500	34	17
Other services	6,590	255	400	2,223	1,018	862	1,171	515	57	90
Public administration	6,802	29	73	1,147	1,232	847	2,117	1,005	176	175

Source: U.S. Census Bureau

12. How many foreign-born individuals who entered the United States after 2010 were high school graduates? [   ] Write your answer in thousands.

13. Comparing educational attainment of employed and unemployed individuals, the data shows a [   ] (high *or* low) correlation between education and employment.

Question 14 refers to the following graph.

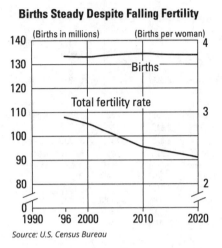

Births Steady Despite Falling Fertility

Source: U.S. Census Bureau

14. The graph shows the total number of births around the entire world in one year as compared to the total fertility rate (TFR). The graph shows a steady decline in the TFR — that is, the number of children born to the average woman — yet the total number of births in the world remains the same. Why is that?

(A) Birth rates have fallen in Europe, the United States, and Japan.

(B) The TFR counts only live births.

(C) The growing world population means that each woman having fewer children is offset by the fact that there are more women to have children.

(D) In China, families are again allowed to have more than one child.

Questions 15–17 refer to the following excerpt from The Declaration of Independence, 1776.

After a long list of grievances, the Declaration of Independence concludes with these words.

In every stage of these Oppressions We have Petitioned for Redress in the most humble terms: Our repeated Petitions have been answered only by repeated injury. A Prince whose character is thus marked by every act which may define a Tyrant, is unfit to be the ruler of a free people.

Nor have We been wanting in attentions to our British brethren. We have warned them from time to time of attempts by their legislature to extend an unwarrantable jurisdiction over us. We have reminded them of the circumstances of our emigration and settlement here. We have appealed to their native justice and magnanimity, and we have conjured them by the ties of our common kindred to disavow these usurpations, which would inevitably interrupt our connections and correspondence. They too have been deaf to the voice of justice and of consanguinity. We must, therefore, acquiesce in the necessity, which denounces our Separation, and hold them, as we hold the rest of mankind, Enemies in War, in Peace Friends.

We, therefore, the Representatives of the united States of America, in General Congress, Assembled, appealing to the Supreme Judge of the world for the rectitude of our intentions, do, in the Name, and by Authority of the good People of these Colonies, solemnly publish and declare, That these United Colonies are, and of Right ought to be Free and Independent States; that they are Absolved from all Allegiance to the British Crown, and that all political connection between them and the State of Great Britain, is and ought to be totally dissolved; and that as Free and Independent States, they have full Power to levy War, conclude Peace, contract Alliances, establish Commerce, and to do all other Acts and Things which Independent States may of right do. And for the support of this Declaration, with a firm reliance on the protection of divine Providence, we mutually pledge to each other our Lives, our Fortunes and our sacred Honor.

15. Why did the authors of the Declaration of Independence believe the king was a tyrant?

(A) The king's only answer to their complaints was more repression.

(B) Appeals to British parliament failed.

(C) The king had taxed them without representation.

(D) They rejected the king's authority.

16. How did the authors feel about British parliament making laws for the Colonies?

(A) The laws were usurpations.

(B) The laws were magnanimous.

(C) The laws are examples of justice and consanguinity.

(D) The parliament heeded the authors' concerns.

17. Why is the word *united* in "united States of America" not also capitalized?

(A) The states viewed themselves as independent entities.

(B) The representatives saw themselves as belonging to one country.

(C) This Congress was a meeting of independent states united for action.

(D) The authors of the Declaration were following old-fashioned rules for writing.

Questions 18 and 19 refer to the following passage from U.S. History For Dummies, *by Steve Wiegand (John Wiley & Sons, Inc.).*

By 1787, it was apparent to many leaders that the Articles of Confederation needed an overhaul, or the union of states would eventually fall apart. So Congress agreed to call a convention of delegates from each state to try to fix things. The first of the delegates (selected by state legislatures) to arrive in Philadelphia in May 1787 was James Madison, a 36-year-old scholar and politician from Virginia who was so frail, he couldn't serve in the army during the Revolution. Madison had so many ideas on how to fix things, he couldn't wait to get started.

Not everyone else was in such a hurry. Although the convention was supposed to begin May 15, it wasn't until May 25 that enough of the delegates chosen by the state legislatures showed up to have a quorum. Rhode Island never did send anyone.

Eventually, 55 delegates took part. Notable by their absence were some of the leading figures of the recent rebellion against England: Thomas Jefferson was in France, Thomas Paine was in England, Sam Adams and John Hancock weren't selected to go, and Patrick Henry refused.

18. What was the name of the original constitution of the United States?

   (A) the Articles of Confederation

   (B) the Constitution of the Confederation

   (C) the Declaration of Independence

   (D) The Declaration of the Rights of Man

19. Why was James Madison especially important to this convention?

   (A) He was eager to get started.

   (B) He represented one of the southern states, which made him very important.

   (C) He had never served in the military.

   (D) He had many ideas on how to fix things.

Questions 20–22 are based on this excerpt from a speech by James Madison on the ratification of the new Constitution of the United States.

What has brought on other nations those immense debts, under the pressure of which many of them labor? Not the expenses of their governments, but war. . .. How is it possible a war could be supported without money or credit? And would it be possible for government to have credit, without having the power of raising money? No, it would be impossible for any government, in such a case, to defend itself. Then, I say, sir, that it is necessary to establish funds for extraordinary exigencies, and give this power to the general government; for the utter inutility of previous requisitions on the States is too well known. Would it be possible for those countries, whose finances and revenues are carried to the highest perfection, to carry on the operations of government on great emergencies, such as the maintenance of a war, without an uncontrolled power of raising money? Has it not been necessary for Great Britain, notwithstanding the facility of the collection of her taxes, to have recourse very often to this and other extraordinary methods of procuring money? Would not her public credit have been ruined, if it was known that her power to raise money was limited?. . . [N]o government can exist unless its powers extend to make provisions for every contingency.

If we were actually attacked by a powerful nation, and our general government had not the power of raising money, but depended solely on requisitions, our condition would be truly deplorable: if the revenues of this commonwealth were to depend on twenty distinct authorities, it would be impossible for it to carry on its operations.

20. According to Madison, what was the major reason for allowing the government to raise revenue?

   (A) to provide a single economic market

   (B) to have the ability to fund extraordinary exigencies

   (C) to limit the power of the states

   (D) to limit the power of the national government

21. What was Madison referring to by "the utter inutility of previous requisitions on the States is too well known"?

   (A) Under the Articles of Confederation, it was easy to convince all the states to contribute money.

   (B) Under the Articles of Confederation, the government had very unlimited powers to tax.

   (C) Under the Articles of Confederation, the states controlled the government.

   (D) Under the Articles of Confederation, the government had only very limited powers to tax.

22. How many states were part of the original Confederation? [   ]

Questions 23–25 refer to the following passage, excerpted from "A Look Back . . . The Black Dispatches: Intelligence During the Civil War," a CIA Feature Story (www.cia.gov).

William A. Jackson

African-Americans who could serve as agents-in-place were a great asset to the Union. They could provide information about the enemy's plans instead of reporting how the plans were carried out. William A. Jackson was one such agent-in-place who provided valuable intelligence straight from Confederate President Jefferson Davis.

Jackson served as a coachman to Davis. As a servant in Davis' home, Jackson overheard discussions the president had with his military leadership. His first report of Confederate plans and intentions was in May 1862 when he crossed into Union lines. While there are no records of the specific intelligence Jackson reported, it is known that it was important enough to be sent straight to the War Department in Washington.

Harriet Tubman

When it comes to the Civil War and the fight to end slavery, Harriet Tubman is an icon. She was not only a conductor of the Underground Railroad, but also a spy for the Union.

In 1860, she took her last trip on the Underground Railroad, bringing friends and family to freedom safely. After the trip, Tubman decided to contribute to the war effort by caring for and feeding the many slaves who had fled the Union-controlled areas.

A year later, the Union Army asked Tubman to gather a network of spies among the black men in the area. Tubman also was tasked with leading expeditions to gather intelligence. She reported her information to a Union officer commanding the Second South Carolina Volunteers, a black unit involved in guerrilla warfare activities.

After learning of Tubman's capability as a spy, Gen. David Hunter, commander of all Union forces in the area, requested that Tubman personally guide a raiding party up the Combahee River in South Carolina. Tubman was well prepared for the raid because she had key information about Confederate positions along the shore and had discovered where they placed torpedoes (barrels filled with gunpowder) in the water. On the morning of June 1, 1863, Tubman led Col. James Montgomery and his men in the attack. The expedition hit hard. They set fires and destroyed buildings so they couldn't be used by the Confederate forces. The raiders freed 750 slaves.

The raid along the Combahee River, in addition to her activities with the Underground Railroad, made a significant contribution to the Union cause. When Tubman died in 1913, she was honored with a full military funeral in recognition for work during the war.

23. What made William Jackson an excellent intelligence source?

(A) He was an African-American.

(B) He had military experience.

(C) He worked in the home of Jefferson Davis.

(D) He was in direct contact with Washington.

24. What is Harriet Tubman best known for?

(A) the Underground Railroad

(B) the drinking gourd song

(C) being a guerilla leader

(D) spying on the president of the Confederacy

25. Harriet Tubman led a raid on ☐ in South Carolina.

(A) the Combahee River

(B) Montgomery

(C) Union-controlled areas

(D) Atlanta

Questions 26 and 27 refer to the following excerpt from U.S. History For Dummies, *by Steve Wiegand (John Wiley & Sons, Inc.).*

Despite conflict in war, civilians and soldiers around the world had at least one thing in common in 1918 — a killer flu. Erroneously dubbed "Spanish Influenza" because it was believed to have started in Spain, it more likely started at U.S. Army camps in Kansas and may not have been a flu virus at all. A 2008 study by the National Institute of Allergy and Infectious Diseases suggested bacteria might have caused the pandemic.

Whatever caused it, it was devastating. Unlike normal influenza outbreaks, whose victims are generally the elderly and the young, the Spanish flu often targeted healthy young adults. By early summer, the disease had spread around the world. In New York City alone, 20,000 people died. Western Samoa lost 20 percent of its population, and entire Inuit villages in Alaska were wiped out. By the time it had run its course in 1921, the flu had killed from 25 million to 50 million people around the world. More than 500,000 Americans died, which was a greater total than all the Americans killed in all the wars of the 20th century.

26. Where did the Spanish flu begin?

(A) Spain

(B) army camps

(C) New York City

(D) Western Samoa

27. How many Americans died of the Spanish flu?

(A) 20% of its population

(B) over 20,000 people

(C) over 500,000 people

(D) 25 to 50 million people

Questions 28–30 are based on the following graphs.

Population by Age and Sex: 2012, 2035 and 2060

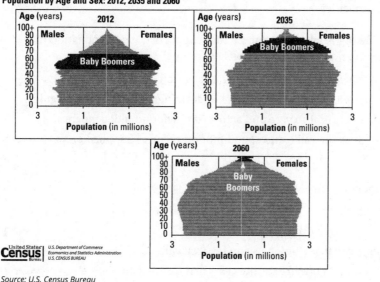

Source: U.S. Census Bureau

28. Look at the population pyramid for the year 2012. Notice that the edges appear ragged. Shorter lines mean fewer people in that age group. There are noticeably fewer people in the 30-to-40 age group. In approximately what time period would these people have been born?

(A) 1960 to 1970

(B) 1970 to 1980

(C) 1980 to 1990

(D) 1990 to 2000

29. Which of the following reasons best explains why there are fewer people in the 30-to-40 age group in the 2012 graph?

(A) Economic troubles and the Vietnam War were going on at the time of their birth.

(B) The Korean War was going on at the time of their birth.

(C) The first Gulf War was going on at the time of their birth.

(D) The invasion of Grenada was going on at the time of their birth.

30. Look at the top of the three pyramids. Are there more men or women in the age group of 80+?

Questions 31 and 32 refer to the following passage about the 1920s, excerpted from U.S. History For Dummies, *by Steve Wiegand (John Wiley & Sons, Inc.).*

Below the veneer of prosperity, there were indications of trouble. More and more wealth was being concentrated in fewer and fewer hands, and government did far more for the rich than the poor. It was estimated, for example, that federal tax cuts saved the hugely wealthy financier Andrew Mellon (who also happened to be Hoover's treasury secretary) almost as much money as was saved by all the taxpayers in the entire state of Nebraska.

Supreme Court decisions struck down minimum wage laws for women and children and made it easier for big business to swallow up smaller ones and become *de facto* monopolies. And union membership declined as organized labor was unable to compete with the aura of good times.

Probably worst off were American farmers. They had expanded production during World War I to feed the troops, and when demand and prices faded after the war, they were hit hard. Farm income dropped by 50 percent during the 1920s, and more than 3 million farmers left their farms for towns and cities.

31. Which of the following is another example that supports the generalization that, "Below the veneer of prosperity, there were indications of trouble"?

   (A) Prohibition outlawed alcohol despite the opposition of many people.

   (B) Stock prices soared many times over the underlying value of the companies.

   (C) Women gained the right to vote and achieved newfound independence.

   (D) Inventions such as the radio and sound motion pictures supplied entertainment to millions.

32. Why did union membership decline in the 1920s?

   (A) Unions were illegal.

   (B) Unions were no longer necessary.

   (C) Growing prosperity made unions seem less relevant.

   (D) The government did far more for the rich than for the poor.

Questions 33–35 are based on the following excerpt from The Wealth of Nations, *by Adam Smith (Thrifty Books).*

The increase of revenue and stock is the increase of national wealth. . . . Is this improvement in the circumstances of the lower ranks of the people to be regarded as an advantage or as an inconvenience to the society? The answer seems at first sight abundantly plain. Servants, laborers, and workmen of different kinds, make up the far greater part of every great political society. But what improves the circumstances of the greater part can never be regarded as an inconvenience to the whole. No society can surely be flourishing and happy, of which the far greater part of the members are poor and miserable. It is but equity, besides, that they who feed, clothe, and lodge the whole body of the people, should have such a share of the produce of their own labor as to be themselves tolerably well fed, clothed, and lodged. The liberal reward of labor, as it encourages the propagation, so it increases the industry of the common people. The wages of labor are the encouragement of industry, which, like every other human quality, improves in proportion to the encouragement it receives. A plentiful subsistence increases the bodily strength of the laborer, and the comfortable hope of bettering his condition, and of ending his days perhaps in ease and plenty, animates him to exert that strength to the utmost. Where wages are high, accordingly, we shall always find the workmen more active, diligent, and expeditious than where they are low.

33. What does Smith mean by "what improves the circumstances of the greater part can never be regarded as an inconvenience to the whole"?

   (A) Paying the working class more is an inconvenience to everyone.

   (B) Whatever improves conditions for most people cannot be regarded as bad for society as a whole.

   (C) Only circumstance that helps some improves life for all.

   (D) Company owners don't need to share profits with their employees.

34. According to Adam Smith, how should employers treat the financial well-being of their employees?

   (A) Keep wages as low as possible.

   (B) Reward a laborer liberally.

   (C) Under no circumstances consider changes.

   (D) Avoid the issue.

35. When Henry Ford's Model T car proved to be a success, he doubled his workers' wages, even when all other car manufacturers at the time would not raise wages. Would he and Adam Smith have agreed on this issue?

   (A) Yes. Well-paid workers are more active and diligent.

   (B) No. Paying workers more only encourages sloth.

   (C) Yes. It is only fair.

   (D) No. A business must remain competitive.

Questions 36 and 37 refer to the following passage about the Cuban Missile Crisis, excerpted from U.S. History For Dummies, *by Steve Wiegand (John Wiley & Sons, Inc.).*

During the summer of 1962, the Soviets began developing nuclear missile sites in Cuba. That meant they could easily strike targets over much of North and South America. When air reconnaissance photos confirmed the sites' presence on October 14, President John F. Kennedy had to make a tough choice: Destroy the sites and quite possibly trigger World War III, or do nothing, and not only expose the country to nuclear destruction but, in effect, concede first place in the world domination race to the USSR.

Kennedy decided to get tough. On October 22, 1963, he went on national television and announced the U.S. Navy would throw a blockade around Cuba and turn away any ships carrying materials that could be used at the missile sites. He also demanded the sites be dismantled. Then the world waited for the Russian reaction.

On October 26, Soviet leader Nikita Khrushchev send a message suggesting the missiles would be removed if the United States promised not to invade Cuba and eventually removed some U.S. missiles from Turkey. The crisis — perhaps the closest the world came to nuclear conflict during the Cold War — was over, and the payoffs were ample.

36. Why was the placement of Soviet missiles in Cuba so important to both the Soviet Union and the United States?

   (A) This was the only way missiles of that time could reach into North and South America.

   (B) The Soviets wanted to show their support for Fidel Castro.

   (C) It provided an important trade opportunity.

   (D) The Soviet Union wanted to start a nuclear war.

37. What triggered the Soviet move to put missiles capable of attacking the United States into bases in Cuba?

   (A) The Soviet Union was preparing to attack the United States.

   (B) Fidel Castro demanded them as protection against an American invasion of Cuba.

   (C) The United States had placed its own missiles in Turkey on the border of the Soviet Union.

   (D) The Soviets wanted to divert attention from Vietnam.

Source: Library of Congress (Photograph of David Woodbury traveling photo studio wagon and tent)

The American Civil War is the first major conflict documented in photos. American photographer Matthew Brady, noted for his photographs of Abraham Lincoln, is often credited with the large number of photos taken during and after key battles of the Civil War. However, while the idea was his, nearly all of the photos were taken by a team of photographers Brady assembled and embedded with the Union army. He sent them with special darkroom wagons and tents, such as the one in the photo, which they used to develop compelling photos of battles and their aftermath. After the photographer developed the photo, the glass plate negative could be easily and swiftly transported to Brady's studio in Washington without risk of being exposed and ruined. The photo shows one of the photographers, David Woodbury, camping with Grant's army, taken after the Battle of Cold Harbor. He's holding a developed glass photographic plate. Exhibitions of the photos became hugely popular, and Brady's studios sold many copies of the images. The photos were later donated to the U.S. government, where they became an invaluable historic record.

38. What does the word "embedded" mean as used in this passage?

(A) Kept in a safe location far from the action.

(B) Assigned to fight as a front-line soldier.

(C) Attached to a military unit involved in the action.

(D) Assigned to a desk job that supported the troops in the field.

39. How did the wagons help the photographers document the war?

    (A) They had all the tools and equipment needed to take and develop photos.

    (B) They could transmit the photos to Brady by telegraph.

    (C) They had a comfortable place to sleep.

    (D) They could store their undeveloped photos until they got back to Washington.

40. Why is the wagon covered with a dark cloth?

    (A) to camouflage the wagon from the enemy

    (B) to keep the wagon warm

    (C) to match the soldier's tents

    (D) to block sunlight from entering the darkroom

Questions 41–44 are based on the following tables.

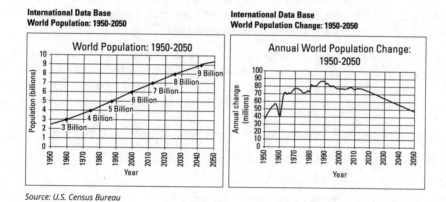

Source: U.S. Census Bureau

41. The total population of the world continues to ⬚.

42. The number of children born each year has ⬚ since 1990.

43. What does the graph entitled "Annual World Population Change" actually show?

    (A) the change in the world total population over time

    (B) the actual net change in world population by year

    (C) the actual number of children born each year

    (D) the rate of change in births each year

44. Considering the chart shows that the annual world population change is declining, why is the world population continuing to climb?

    (A) Chart B ignores children who die in the first year of life.

    (B) More people means more children, even if individual women have fewer children.

    (C) The rate of growth is still climbing.

    (D) Families in China are now allowed to have more than one child again.

Question 45 and 46 are based on the following excerpt from U.S. History For Dummies, *by Steve Wiegand (John Wiley & Sons, Inc.).*

While the war on terrorism dominated Bush's presidency, he did attempt to make changes on domestic issues as well. Within a few days of taking office, Bush proposed an ambitious education reform program, called the No Child Left Behind Act. Approved by Congress, the plan posted federal education funding; increased standards expected of schools, including annual reading and math skills testing; and gave parents more flexibility in choosing schools. The program was variously praised for making schools more accountable and criticized for forcing educators to take cookie-cutter approaches to teaching.

In late 2003, Bush pushed a plan through Congress to reform Medicare, the federal health insurance program for the elderly. The plan gave senior citizens more choice when picking a private insurance plan through which they received medical services, as well as in obtaining prescription drugs.

Bush had far less success in trying to reform Social Security and the U.S. immigration policies. Bush proposed to replace the government-run pension program with a system of private savings accounts. But the plan died in the face of criticism that it would put too much of a burden on individuals and be too expensive in the transition.

Bush also supported a bipartisan plan that would allow an estimated 12 million illegal immigrants to remain in the country on a temporary basis and to apply for citizenship after returning to their own countries and paying a fine. The plan was crushed by the weight of opposition from those who thought it was too draconian and those who thought it was too soft.

45. Why were some people opposed to the No Child Left Behind Act?

(A) Some objected to standardized reading and math tests.

(B) Some felt it would reduce education choices.

(C) It was considered too expensive by some in Congress.

(D) Congress would not approve the plan.

46. Which of Bush's proposals were passed by Congress? Not passed? Write the letter in the correct place. Passed: [   ]   Not Passed: [   ]

(A) education reform

(B) Medicare reform

(C) immigration reform

(D) Social Security reform

Questions 47 and 48 refer to the following excerpt, taken from the CIA's World Factbook *(www.cia.gov).*

Canada resembles the U.S. in its market-oriented economic system, pattern of production, and high living standards. Since World War II, the impressive growth of the manufacturing, mining, and service sectors has transformed the nation from a largely rural economy into one primarily industrial and urban. Canada has a large oil and natural gas sector with the majority of crude oil production derived from oil sands in the western provinces, especially Alberta. Canada now ranks third in the world in proved oil reserves behind Venezuela and Saudi Arabia and is the world's seventh-largest oil producer.

The 1989 Canada-U.S. Free Trade Agreement and the 1994 North American Free Trade Agreement (which includes Mexico) dramatically increased trade and economic integration between the U.S. and Canada. Canada and the U.S. enjoy the world's most comprehensive bilateral trade and investment relationship, with goods and services trade totaling more than $680 billion in 2017, and two-way investment stocks of more than $800 billion. Over three-fourths of Canada's merchandise exports are destined for the U.S. each year. Canada is the largest foreign supplier of energy to the U.S., including oil, natural gas, and electric power, and a top source of U.S. uranium imports.

Given its abundant natural resources, highly skilled labor force, and modern capital stock, Canada enjoyed solid economic growth from 1993 through 2007. The global economic crisis of 2007-08 moved the Canadian economy into sharp recession by late 2008, and Ottawa posted its first fiscal deficit in 2009 after 12 years of surplus. Canada's major banks emerged from the financial crisis of 2008-09 among the strongest in the world, owing to the financial sector's tradition of conservative lending practices and strong capitalization. Canada's economy posted strong growth in 2017 at 3%.

47. How does the CIA's World Factbook describe Canada's economy before World War II?

(A) primarily industrial and urban

(B) a modern capitalist society

(C) largely rural

(D) a major petroleum power

48. According to the passage, how is Canada's economy linked with that of the United States?

(A) Canada is a large importer of American products.

(B) Canada is the largest supplier of energy to America.

(C) Canada's economic growth rate was 3% in a recent year.

(D) Canada's banks are among the strongest in the world.

Questions 49 and 50 refer to the following excerpt from the Australian War Memorial website on the topic of the Australian contribution to the Vietnam War, 1962–1975 (www.awm.gov.au).

[A]lmost 60,000 Australians, including ground troops and air force and navy personnel, served in Vietnam; 521 died as a result of the war and over 3,000 were wounded. . ..

Australian support for South Vietnam in the early 1960s was in keeping with the policies of other nations, particularly the United States, to stem the spread of communism in Europe and Asia. . ..

By early 1965,. . .the U.S. commenced a major escalation of the war. By the end of the year, it had committed 200,000 troops to the conflict. As part of the build-up, the U.S. government requested further support from friendly countries in the region, including Australia. The Australian government dispatched the 1st Battalion, Royal Australian Regiment (1RAR), in June 1965, to serve alongside the U.S. 173rd Airborne Brigade in Bien Hoa province. . ..

By 1969, anti-war protests were gathering momentum in Australia. Opposition to conscription mounted, as more people came to believe the war could not be won. . .. The U.S. government began to implement a policy of "Vietnamisation," the term coined for a gradual withdrawal of U.S. forces that would leave the war in the hands of the South Vietnamese. With the start of the phased withdrawals, the emphasis of the activities of the Australians in Phuoc Tuy province shifted to the provision of training to the South Vietnamese Regional and Popular Forces.

In early 1975, the communists launched a major offensive in the north of South Vietnam, resulting in the fall of Saigon on 30 April. During April, a RAAF detachment of 7–8 Hercules transports flew humanitarian missions to aid civilian refugees displaced by the fighting and carried out the evacuation of Vietnamese orphans (Operation Babylift), before finally taking out embassy staff on 25 April.

49. In what way was the Australian experience in their participation in the Vietnam War similar to that of America?

   (A) They were reluctant to become involved.

   (B) They contributed only humanitarian aid.

   (C) There was strong popular opposition on the home front to participation in this war.

   (D) They supported the spread of Communism.

50. Which of the following is an example of humanitarian assistance to the people of Vietnam?

   (A) Australia sent a battalion to Vietnam.

   (B) Australia turned from military engagement to training.

   (C) The Australian government evacuated its embassy.

   (D) Australian forces evacuated orphans.

Answers and Explanations

1. **representative.** In America, citizens elect officials, from state representatives to federal senators, who represent the interests of individual citizens in the administration of the country.

2. **A. a vote on issuing library bonds.** Choices (B), (C), and (D) are all examples of indirect or representative democracy, where someone is elected to *represent* the voter. For example, mayors, who citizens elect directly, are in office to represent them. The voters don't make political decisions; the mayor does. Only in a referendum is the voters' voice directly applied to a decision.

3. **C. the former USSR.** The former USSR, also known as the Soviet Union, was run by a government that allowed elections but with only one political party. The party, not the people, decided who would run for office. Although the form resembled democracy, it didn't allow for pluralism or political choice. The other countries are all pluralist. Canada is a parliamentary democracy with five major political parties. Sweden is also a parliamentary democracy, and like Canada, has a Monarch as head of state. It, too, has several political parties contending for office in free elections. South Korea is a republic, run by a legislative assembly and a president elected by popular vote.

4. **A. their senator.** Of the offices in the list, only senators are elected. The others are appointed by the president.

5. **7,500 miles.** Columbus miscalculated by 7,500 miles. He thought the world was considerably smaller than it actually is.

6. **B. October 12, 1492.** The Christmas Eve date refers to his subsequent arrival at the island he called Hispaniola. The other two dates are not mentioned in the text.

7. **D. They had heard stories of the gold Columbus had found.** According to the text, they were all focused on gold. Choice (B) may be partially correct, that they were looking for adventure, but Choices (A) and (C) are not supported by the text.

8. **A. The *Santa Maria* had hit a reef and sank.** Choice (B) is incorrect at this stage of his trip, and although Choices (C) and (D) may be partially correct, they're not the best answers.

9. **Asia.** Columbus wanted to find a shorter route to Asia. He never dreamed that other continents existed.

10. **B. leftover juice after sugar was pressed out of the cane.** The text states that molasses is "the juice left over after the sugar was pressed out of the cane and crystalized." The juice pressed out of the cane still contains sugar to be extracted. The cane isn't mixed with water, but rather the extracted juices are. And the name *Saccharum officinarum* is simply the Latin name for the sugar cane plant.

11. **B. 23 years.** This problem requires some simple arithmetic. The first crop, assuming Columbus' workers planted the cane as soon as they landed, was planted in 1493. The first sugar cane was presented to the King in 1516. Subtract 1493 from 1516, and you get 23. The correct answer is 23 years.

12. **1,845.** To find this number in the table, first find the row on the left that shows foreign-born individuals who entered the U.S. after 2010. Then find the column at the top that shows high school graduates. The cell in the table where they come together shows that 1,845 thousand is the answer.

13. **high.** The data in the table consistently shows higher educational attainment in every category for employed individuals. This data shows that your decision to get your GED is the right one. *Keep going!*

14. **C. The growing world population means that each woman having fewer children is offset by the fact that there are more women to have children.** Even though the number of children women are having has declined, far more women exist and are available to have children. That balances out the individual birth rate decline and results in a steady number of births.

15. **A. The king's only answer to their complaints was more repression.** The first line of the text states the answer. Choice (B) has nothing to do with the belief that the king was a tyrant. Choice (C) may be correct but also has nothing to do with the reasons the king was considered a tyrant. Choice (D) does not make sense.

16. **A. The laws were usurpations.** The colonial states felt that the king and British parliament were taking upon themselves powers to which they had no right. They certainly didn't feel that the laws were magnanimous (Choice B) or examples of justice and consanguinity (Choice C), or that the parliament was paying attention to their concerns (Choice D).

17. **A. The states viewed themselves as independent entities.** At this time, the various states considered themselves as having the same rights as independent countries loosely joined in the Confederation.

18. **A. the Articles of Confederation.** The original constitution of the United States was called the *Articles of Confederation,* not *the Constitution of the Confederation* or *the Declaration of Independence.*

19. **D. He had many ideas on how to fix things.** The text describes Madison as a man of many ideas about how to fix the Articles of Confederation. Choice (A) is a minor consideration, and Choices (B) and (C) are irrelevant.

20. **B. to have the ability to fund extraordinary exigencies.** Madison had seen that one of the major shortcomings of the Articles of Confederation was that the federal government depended on the states to raise money. It was the need to raise money in the face of extraordinary dangers that was a key element.

21. **D. Under the Articles of Confederation, the government had only very limited powers to tax.** This information is stated directly in the passage.

22. **13.** The Confederation of 1776 consisted of the original 13 colonies — Connecticut, Delaware, Georgia, Maryland, Massachusetts, New Hampshire, New Jersey, New York, North Carolina, South Carolina, Pennsylvania, Rhode Island, and Virginia. These were the first states in the union. Other states were added at later dates.

23. **C. He worked in the home of Jefferson Davis.** The most important element of the choices offered is the fact that William Jackson worked in the home of Jefferson Davis, where he had direct access to all the discussions that took place. There's no suggestion that Jackson had any military experience, and his direct contact with Washington grew out of his service in

Davis's home. The fact that he was African-American is relevant only to the extent that he was a servant in that home.

24. **A. the Underground Railroad.** Harriet Tubman is best known for her key work in the Underground Railroad. Choice (B) is a song associated with the Underground Railroad but is not mentioned in the passage. Choice is (C) is a less well-known accomplishment. Though Harriet Tubman acted as a spy, Choice (D) is an accomplishment of William A. Jackson.

25. **A. the Combahee River.** *Montgomery* was the name of a military officer working with Tubman, and she was attacking Confederate-controlled areas, not Union areas.

26. **B. army camps.** This information is stated directly in the passage. Spain (Choice A) was erroneously named as the origin of the epidemic. The places in the other choices are mentioned in the passage as having notably high death counts, not as the disease's place of origin.

27. **C. over 500,000 people.** This information is stated directly in the passage. The other numbers are for other parts of the world or the entire world.

28. **B. 1970 to 1980.** Subtract 30 and 40 from 2012 to get the high and low end of the range, 1970 to 1980.

29. **A. economic troubles and the Vietnam War were going on at the time of their birth.** The period of 1970 to 1980 was a time of economic difficulty and the winding down of the Vietnam War. With a controversial war, rising inflation, and worries about money, people were less likely to have children at that time. The Korean War (Choice B) had ended many years earlier, and the Gulf War (Choice C) and invasion of Grenada (Choice D) were still to come.

30. **women.** If you look at the top of the three pyramids, you can see that the right side is wider than the left. The right side reflects the number of females in the population.

31. **B. Stock prices soared many times over the underlying value of the companies.** The high value of stocks covered up the fact that the stocks were trading at many times the true value of the companies. This is an example of a veneer of prosperity covering up an underlying problem.

32. **C. Growing prosperity made unions seem less relevant.** For most people, times appeared to be good. As long as that was the feeling, there seemed to be no real need for labor to organize. Unions were no longer illegal, so Choice (A) is incorrect. Choice (B) is contradicted by the information in the passage; the defeat of minimum wage laws showed that unions still had a role to play. Choice (D) is a reason that made unions relevant, despite people's perception of them at the time, and so is incorrect.

33. **B. Whatever improves conditions for most people cannot be regarded as bad for society as a whole.** Adam Smith proposes that anything that helps those less well-off can only improve society as a whole.

34. **B. Reward a laborer liberally.** According to Smith, employers should reward their laborers generously. The other options are contradicted by the text, when Smith states, "no society can surely be flourishing and happy, of which the far greater part of the members are poor and miserable."

35. **A. Yes. Well-paid workers are more active and diligent.** Smith and Ford would have been of one mind on this issue. Ford came under attack by other wealthy industrialists for granting his workers this pay increase, but he argued that paying his workers well allowed them to buy his cars, thereby improving his own business while making the workers happy.

36. **A. This was the only way missiles of that time could reach into North and South America.** At that time, missiles couldn't cross intercontinental distances. As a result, locations close to your intended target were important. That's why the United States placed missiles in Turkey that could attack the Soviet Union. The USSR was simply responding in kind when it decided to build missile bases in Cuba. There was no trade benefit to the Soviet Union, and although the Soviet Union may have wanted to show support for Fidel Castro, that wasn't the main reason for deploying the missiles. The Soviet Union didn't want to start a nuclear war; they wanted to be able to counter the United States' missiles in Turkey.

37. **C. The United States had placed its own missiles in Turkey on the border of the Soviet Union.** The United States had placed missiles in Turkey that directly threatened the Soviet Union. Soviet actions in Cuba were a direct response. There is no evidence in the passage that the Soviet Union wanted to distract attention from Vietnam. Although Castro may have demanded the missiles as protection, that wasn't the key element in the Soviets' decision, nor is that argument supported by the text.

38. **C. Attached to a military unit involved in the action.** From the context, you can figure out that this option is correct. The photographers were sent to take photos of the war and its aftermath, so they needed to be close to the action, but not directly participating in the fighting. In fact, the photo shows the photographer camping with the rest of the army. The other options do not make sense.

39. **A. They had all the tools and equipment needed to take and develop photos.** The passage makes it clear that they used the "darkroom wagons" to develop photos on the spot, so that the developed plates could be returned quickly and safely to Brady's studio in Washington. The other choices do not make sense. Telegraphic transmission of photos was not developed until several years later (Choice B), though many of the photos were converted into wood engravings that appeared in newspapers of the day. The wagon does not look comfortable, so Choice (C) is incorrect. Choice (D) is contradicted by information in the passage and the photo: the photographer is seen holding a developed photographic plate.

40. **D. to block sunlight from entering the darkroom.** This answer can be inferred from the photo and the purpose of the wagon. Black absorbs sunlight, whereas light-colored canvas tends to allow light to enter. Therefore, a black covering would block sunlight from entering the darkroom and spoiling the photographs. None of the tents seem to be camouflaged, so Choice (A) does not make sense. Choice (B) is not supported by information in the passage or photo. In addition, the Civil War was fought mostly in the summer in very hot weather, so staying warm would not be a consideration. Choice (C) is contradicted by the color of the other tents in the photograph.

41. **increase.** The line for *World Population* continues to climb upward to the right. Using the scale, that shows an increasing population. The number values on the line confirm that.

42. **declined.** The chart shows the change in the net world population. Because all the numbers on the scale are in the positive domain, the world population is growing. However, the growth peaks around 1990, and declines — unevenly — after that. People are living longer in some parts of the world, and life expectancy in most other parts of the world hasn't changed. So the decline in the growth of the world population must mean that there are fewer children being born.

43. **B. the actual net change in world population by year.** That is, it shows the number of births minus the number of deaths. Choice (A) is partially correct, but Choice (B) is the best option. Choices (C) and (D) are wrong because they don't take into account both birth and death rates.

44. **B. More people means more children, even if individual women have fewer children.** Although the actual number of children by individual women is declining, the population as a whole is growing. That means there are more women available to have children. So even with fewer children for women, the population continues to grow.

45. **A. Some objected to standardized reading and math tests.** The only option mentioned in the text is Choice (A). According to the text, the act increased parental choice, and the plan was passed by Congress. Although some people in Congress may have considered it too expensive, there's nothing in the text to support that point.

46. **Passed: A, B. Not Passed: C, D.** The success of each policy initiative is stated directly in the passage. While No Child Left Behind and Medicare reform (Choices A and B) were passed, immigration reform and Social Security reform (Choices C and D) were not successful in Congress.

47. **C. largely rural.** You have to read carefully to find this answer. The text states that since World War II, Canada became an industrial society. Then it states that this transformed it from a largely rural economy. Choices (A), (B), and (D) are all true, but only after World War II.

48. **B. Canada is the largest supplier of energy to America.** This information is stated directly in the passage. The passage does not give information on exports from the U.S. to Canada, so Choice (A) is incorrect. Choices (C) and (D) are not related to the U.S.-Canada economic relationship.

49. **C. There was strong popular opposition on the home front to participation in this war.** According to the text, some people in Australia strongly objected to participation in Vietnam, very much like what happened in the United States. The reluctance to become involved isn't the best choice, there's no evidence that there was a demand to contribute only humanitarian aid, and both countries were trying to stop the spread of Communism.

50. **D. Australian forces evacuated orphans.** Evacuating orphans (Choice D) is an example of humanitarian aid, which helps people. Choices (A) and (B) are examples of military assistance. Choice (C) safeguarded the lives of Australian diplomats assigned to Vietnam. This item is a good example of why it's important to read each answer choice carefully. If you just scan for the word "evacuated," you could select Choice (C) by mistake.

4

Peering at Your Specimen: The Science Test

Chapter **13**

From Aardvarks to Atoms: Confronting the Science Test

D id you know that the passing rate for the GED Science test is 90 percent? That's because the GED Science test doesn't test you on the depth of your knowledge of science. You're not expected to memorize any scientific information to do well on this test. Instead, this test assesses your ability to ferret out information presented in passages or visual materials. However, you should have at least a passing background knowledge of science and scientific vocabulary.

One of the best ways to improve your understanding of science material and scientific vocabulary is to read scientific material, science magazines, websites, and even old textbooks. Look up any words you don't know. Rest easy that you aren't expected to know the scientific difference between terms like *fission* and *fusion* — but just being familiar with them can help you on the test.

And there's more good news! Since the science test is based on your ability to read and interpret textual material, your preparation for the Reading Comprehension section of the Reading and Language Arts test will help you on the Science test — and vice versa!

The Science test covers material from life science, physical science (chemistry and physics), and earth and space science. Don't panic — you don't need to memorize material from those subjects. You just need to be able to read and understand the material and answer questions correctly. In this chapter, I help you get a feel for the Science test, the skills it requires, and some techniques you can use to prepare.

Looking at the Skills the Science Test Covers

If you're totally unfamiliar with science and its vocabulary, you'll likely have trouble with the questions on the Science test. You're expected to have some basic knowledge about how the physical world works, how plants and animals live, and how the universe operates. This material tests you on ideas that you observe and develop throughout your life, both in and out of school. You probably know a little about traction, for example, from driving and walking in slippery weather. On the other hand, you may not know a lot about equilibrium aside from what you read in school.

As you prepare to take the Science test, you're expected to understand that science is all about inquiry. In fact, inquiry forms the basis of the *scientific method* — the process every good scientist follows when faced with an unknown. The steps of the scientific method are as follows:

1. **Ask questions.**
2. **Gather information.**
3. **Do experiments.**
4. **Think objectively about what you find.**
5. **Look at other possible explanations.**
6. **Draw one or more possible conclusions.**
7. **Test the conclusion(s).**
8. **Tell others what you found.**

TIP

Look at your studying for the Science test as a scientific problem. The question you're trying to answer is, "How can I increase my scientific knowledge?" Follow the scientific method to come up with a procedure to fix the problem. Your solution should include reading, reading, and more reading! In addition to this book, one or more high-school science books can be a great tool to use, or even a course that teaches the basics of high-school science. (Go to your local library to get your hands on a copy of one of these books, and check with your local adult education program or community college to find basic science courses that are available in your area.) If several people are preparing for the GED tests at the same time as you are, forming a study group may also be helpful.

Understanding the Test Format and What Topics Are Covered

The Science test contains about 50 questions of different formats, which you have 90 minutes to answer. As with the other test sections, the information and questions on the Science test are straightforward — no one is trying to trick you. To answer the questions, you have to read and interpret the passages or other visual materials provided with the questions (and you need a basic understanding of science and the words scientists use when they communicate).

In terms of organization, some of the items are grouped in sets. Some items are stand-alone questions based on one issue or topic. Some questions follow a given passage, chart, diagram, graph, map, or table. Your job is to read or review the material and decide on the best answer for each question based on the given material.

In terms of subject matter, the questions on the Science test check your knowledge in the following areas.

>> **Physical science:** About 40 percent of the test is about *physical science,* which is the study of atoms, chemical reactions, forces, and what happens when energy and matter get together. As a basic review, keep the following in mind:

- Everything is composed of atoms even the paper or computer screen you're reading right now!

- When chemicals get together, they have a reaction — unless they're *inert* (which means they don't react with other chemicals; inert chemicals are sort of like antisocial chemicals).

- You're surrounded by forces and their effects. (If the floor didn't exert a force up on you when you stepped down, you would go through the floor.)

For more information about physical science (which includes basic chemistry and basic physics), read and review a basic science textbook. You can borrow one from your local library. You can also find one on the Internet. When reading this material, you may need definitions for some of the words or terms to make understanding the concepts easier. Use a good dictionary, a dictionary phone app, or the Internet to find these definitions. (If you use the Internet, type any of the topics into a search engine and add "definition" after it. Become amazed at the number of hits produced, but don't spend time reading them all!)

>> **Life science:** Another 40 percent of the test covers *life science* — the study of cells, heredity, and other processes that occur in living systems. All life is composed of *cells,* which you can see under a microscope. Don't worry — you aren't expected to have access to a microscope and a set of slides with cells on them. Most life science–related books and websites have photographs of cells that you can study. When someone tells you that you look like your parents or that you remind them of another relative, they're talking about *heredity.* Reading a bit about heredity in biology-related books can help you practice answering some of the questions on the Science test.

Use a biology textbook to help you prepare for this portion of the test. (Get your hands on a copy of one at your local library, a nearby adult education center, or online.)

>> **Earth and space science:** The remaining 20 percent of the test covers earth and space science. This area of science looks at the earth and the universe, specifically weather, astronomy, geology, rocks, erosion, and water.

When you look down at the ground as you walk, you're interacting with earth science. When you look up at the stars on a clear night and wonder what's really up there, you're thinking about space science. When you complain about the weather, you're complaining about earth science. In a nutshell, you're surrounded by earth and space sciences, so you shouldn't have a problem finding materials to read on this subject.

The topics on the Science test are focused on two main themes, both of which you probably deal with on some level every day.

>> **Human health and living systems:** Who isn't concerned with being safe and healthy? After all, it's your body and you need it. Most people try to eat nutritious meals, get some exercise, and avoid getting sick. Understanding the human body and other living organisms is an important part of science knowledge.

>> **Energy and related systems:** Energy powers your cars, cooks your food, heats your home, turns on your lights, and keeps the planet going. Understanding how energy flows through organisms and ecosystems can help you navigate your daily life and succeed on the Science test.

REMEMBER

You don't have to memorize everything you read about science before you take the test. All the answers to the test questions are based on information provided in the passages, or on the basic knowledge about science that you've acquired over the years. However, any science reading you do prior to the test not only helps you increase your basic knowledge but also improves your vocabulary. An improved science vocabulary increases your chances of being able to read the passages and answer the related questions on the test quickly.

Examining Preparation Strategies That Work

To get better results from the time and effort you put into preparing for the Science test, I suggest you try the following strategies:

>> **Take practice tests.** Take as many practice tests as you can. You can find two full length practice tests in this book (in Chapters 23 and 31), as well as a full-length online test. Follow the time limits, and check the answers and explanations when you're finished. If you still don't understand why some answers are correct, ask a tutor, take a preparation class, or look up the information in a book or on the Internet. Be sure you know why every one of your answers is right or wrong.

>> **Create your own dictionary.** Get a small notebook and keep track of all the new words (and their definitions) that you discover as you prepare for the Science test. Make sure you understand all the science terminology you see or hear. Of course, this goal isn't one you can reach in one night. Take some time to build your vocabulary. You don't need to start talking like a scientist, but you should be able to recognize and understand science-related words when you read them.

>> **Read as many passages as you can.** I may sound like a broken record, but reading is the most important way to prepare for the Science test. After you read a paragraph from any source (textbook, newspaper article, website, and so on), ask yourself some questions about what you read. You can also ask friends and family to ask you questions about what you read.

Check out Chapter 3 for some general test-taking strategies to help you prepare for all the sections of the GED test.

FINDING SCIENCE ON THE INTERNET

The Internet can increase your scientific knowledge or simply introduce you to a new area of interest. If you don't have an Internet connection at home, try your local library or community center.

To save yourself time as you begin your online search for additional practice in reading science material, I suggest you check out the following sites.

- `www.els.net`: Contains tons of information about life sciences.

- `www.earth.nasa.gov`: Contains lots of intriguing earth- and space-related information.

- `www.chemistry.about.com`: Contains interesting information related to chemistry. (Note that this is a commercial site, which means you'll see pesky banners and commercial links amidst the interesting and helpful information.)

- `www.thoughtco.com/physics-4133571`: Contains some interesting physics lessons that are presented in an entertaining and informative manner.

- `ged.com`: The GED Testing Service's site, which contains a great deal of information, both general and specific, regarding the Science test.

To explore on your own, go to your favorite search engine and type the science keywords you're most interested in (*biology, earth science,* and *chemistry,* just to name a few examples). You can also use the same keywords for a YouTube search and find many excellent videos explaining these topics.

Chapter 14

Science Question Types and Solving Strategies

The Science test is one long 90-minute test. It shares most of the same features and question formats as the other GED test sections. Although the items are mostly in the traditional multiple-choice format, you'll also find fill-in-the-blank, drop-down, and drag-and-drop question formats. The questions are based on scientific text passages or visual images, including diagrams, graphs, maps, and tables. In this chapter, I explore the different question types and strategies for solving them.

Tackling the Science Test Questions

The Science test questions are based on two types of information: textual passages and visual materials. A few questions may be based on both. Having a basic understanding of these two types of information can help you avoid any surprises when you sit down to take the test.

You want to make sure that you read and understand every chart, diagram, graph, map, table, passage, and question that appears on the GED Science test. Information — both relevant and irrelevant — is everywhere, and you never know where you'll find what you need to answer the questions quickly and correctly, especially when dealing with visuals, graphs, tables, and diagrams. Don't skip something because it doesn't immediately look important. And make sure you use the tabs and scroll bars to view all the information. For a review of these important features, see Chapter 2. In this section, I'll show you how to answer questions about textual passages and visual materials.

Questions about text passages

The text passages on this test — and the questions that accompany them — are very similar to a reading-comprehension test: You're given textual material, and you have to answer questions about it. The passages present everything you need to answer the questions, but you usually have to understand all the words used in those passages to figure out what they're telling you (which is why I recommend that you read as much science information as you can prior to the test).

The difference between the text passages on the Science test and other reading-comprehension tests is that the terminology and examples are all about science. Thus, the more you read about science, the more science words you'll know, understand, and be comfortable seeing on the test — which, as you may imagine, can greatly improve your chances of success.

TIP

Keep the following tips and tricks in mind when answering questions about text passages:

>> **Read each passage and question carefully.** Some of the questions on the Science test assume that you know a little bit from past experience. For example, you may be expected to know that a rocket is propelled forward by an engine firing backward. (On the other hand, you won't have to know the definition of *nuclear fission* — thank goodness!)

Regardless of whether an item assumes some basic science knowledge or asks for an answer that appears directly in the passage, you need to read each passage and corresponding question carefully. As you read, do the following:

- Try to understand the passage and think about what you already know about the subject.

- If a passage has only one question, read that question extra carefully.

- If the passage or question contains words you don't understand, try to figure out what those words mean from the rest of the sentence, the entire passage, or any graphic or illustration. However, if you still understand the overall main idea without knowing that word, you can skip the word and go on.

>> **Read each answer choice carefully.** Doing so helps you get a clearer picture of your options. If you select an answer without reading all the choices, you may end up picking the wrong one because, although that answer choice may seem right at first, it may be only partially correct. Another answer choice may be more complete or accurate. As you read the answer choices, do the following:

- If one answer choice is right from your reading and experience, select it and go on to the next item.

- If you aren't sure which answer choice is right, exclude the choices you know are wrong, and then exclude choices that may be wrong.

- If you can exclude all but one answer choice, it's probably correct, so choose it.

- If you can only exclude one or two answer choices, guess and go on to the next item. Use the flag feature in the online interface to mark any items you cannot answer or want to return to if you have more time.

Try out these tips on the sample passages and questions in the later section, "Practicing with Sample Items."

Questions about visual materials

Visual materials are images that contain information you use to answer the corresponding questions. Visual materials can include tables, graphs, diagrams, photos, and maps. A graphic image can contain as much information as — or more information than — a passage. As the saying goes, "A picture is worth a thousand words." This section (and the practice tests) can help you get the practice you need to get the most out of visual materials.

REMEMBER

Any visual object is like a short paragraph. It has a topic and makes comments or states facts about that topic. When you come across a question based on visual material, the first thing to do is to figure out the content or topic of the material. Usually, visual objects have titles or captions that help you understand their meanings, so read those first. If you don't understand any of the words, use the image to help you figure out the words. After you understand the main idea behind the visual object, ask yourself what information you're being given and what information you need to find out; reading the question can be helpful. After you know these two pieces of information, you're well on your way to answering the question.

The following sections take a more detailed look at the different visual materials that you may find on the Science test. As a bonus, this advice also applies to the Social Studies test. (Check out Chapter 11 for examples of all the visual materials mentioned below.)

Tables

A *table* is a graphical way of organizing information. This type of visual material allows for easy comparison between two or more sets of data. Some tables use numbers and symbols to represent information; others use words.

TIP

Most tables have titles that tell you what they're about. Always read the titles first so you know right away what information the tables include. If a table gives you an explanation (or *key*) of the symbols, read the explanation carefully, too; doing so helps you understand how to read the table.

Graphs

A *graph* is a picture that shows how different sets of numbers are related. On the Science test, you can find the following three main types of graphs.

>> **Bar or column graphs:** Bar (horizontal) or column (vertical) graphs present and often compare numbers or quantities.

>> **Line graphs:** On line graphs, one or more lines connect points drawn on a grid to show the relationships between data, including changes in data over time.

>> **Pie graphs (also called pie charts or circle graphs):** Arcs of circles (pieces of a pie) show how data relates to a whole. Often, data in pie charts is expressed as a percent of a whole.

All three types of graphs usually share the following common characteristics.

>> **Title:** The title tells you what the graph is about, so always read the title before reviewing the graph.

>> **Horizontal axis and vertical axis:** Bar, column, and line graphs have a horizontal axis and a vertical axis. (Pie graphs don't.) Each axis is a vertical or horizontal reference line that's labeled to give you additional information.

>> **Label:** The labels on the axes of a graph usually contain units, such as feet or dollars. Read all axis labels carefully; they can either help you with the answer or lead you astray (depending on whether you read them correctly). The labels in a pie chart will indicate the unit of measurement and the quantities (often percent).

>> **Legend:** Graphs usually have a *legend,* or printed material that tells you what each section of the graph is about. They may also contain labels on the individual parts of the graph and explanatory notes about the data used to create the graph, so read carefully.

Graphs and tables are both often called *charts*, which can be rather confusing. To help you prepare for problems with graphs, make sure you look at and understand plenty of graphs before the test. Remember that graphs show relationships. If the numbers represented on the horizontal axis are in millions of dollars and you think they're in dollars, your interpretation of the graph will be more than a little incorrect.

Diagrams

A *diagram* is a drawing that helps you understand how something works. Diagrams on the Science test often have the following two components.

>> **Title:** Tells you what the diagram is trying to show you.

>> **Labels:** Indicate the names of the parts of the diagram.

When you come to a question based on a diagram, read the title of the diagram first to get an idea of what the diagram is about. Then carefully read all the labels to find out the main components of the diagram. These two pieces of information can help you understand the diagram well enough to answer questions about it.

Photos

A *photo* may sometimes appear on the GED. You can use these features of photos to help you understand them.

>> **Caption:** The caption tells you the subject of the photo. For example, a photo of the planet Mars may identify the planet and say how the photo was taken: "A space probe took this close-up photo of the planet Mars."

>> **Labels:** Labels may mark or identify people or objects in the photo. For example, a photo of Mars may have its ice cap labeled.

When you come to a question based on a photo, read the caption first. Then carefully read any labels. Then look at the photo. If you don't understand any words in the label, use the photo to figure them out.

Maps

A *map* is a drawing of some section — large or small — of the earth or another planet. People even call images of the solar system or of the stars in the night sky a map. Because the entire world is too large to depict on one piece of paper, maps are drawn to scale.

Most maps give you the following information.

>> **Title:** Tells you what area of the world the map focuses on and what it shows.

>> **Legend:** Gives you general information about the meaning, colors, symbols, or other graphics used on the map.

>> **Compass:** Indicates the map's orientation. In general, north is at the top of a map, but for certain maps, this may not be the case. On many maps, a small compass will show which way is north. (Sometimes this compass may be omitted if the map is very familiar. A map of the United States likely would not have a compass, as most people know the north is at the top.)

>> **Labels:** Indicate what the various points on the map represent.

>> **Scale:** Tells you what the distance on the map represents in real life. (For example, a map with a scale of 1 inch = 100 miles shows a distance of 500 miles on the real earth as a distance of 5 inches on the map.)

Although maps are seldom used in science passages, they are used occasionally, so you want to be familiar with them. And you will certainly encounter them on the Social Studies test. The best way to get familiar with maps is to spend some time looking at road maps and world atlases, which you can find in your local library or online.

REMEMBER

The exact meaning of any visual materials may not be obvious or may even be misleading if not examined carefully. You must understand what the legends, scale, labels, and color-coding are telling you. Numbers on a table also may be misleading or even meaningless unless you read the legend and labels carefully. Colors on a map aren't just for decoration; each color has a meaning. Each piece of a visual represents meaning from which you can put together the information you need to determine the answers to test questions.

Practicing with Sample Items

To help increase your odds of doing well on the Science test, you want to be as familiar as you can be with the kinds of questions you'll encounter on the real GED test. The following sections show the different kinds of questions that may appear on the Science test. Not all of the item types here will appear on the test, but you can be sure that there will be plenty of multiple-choice questions and a few fill-in-the-blank questions. Get familiar with each question type. I'll give you some tips and tricks to help you answer each kind.

Multiple-choice questions

Most of the questions on the Science test are in the traditional multiple-choice format, where you get four answer choices. Your job is to pick the best answer that's supported by the passage or visual material. If the material is in the form of a text passage, read the passage quickly to answer the question. If the material is in the form of a visual, read the title and the verbal information so you understand what the visual is all about.

REMEMBER

If one answer must be correct, then three answers must be wrong. If you can exclude the wrong answers, you'll be left with the right one. Read the passage carefully to figure out the right or wrong choices.

The example questions in this section refer to the following passage.

> One of the great discoveries in earth science is rocks. Rocks have many useful purposes in science. They can be used as paperweights to keep academic papers from flying away in the wind. Rocks can be used to prop laboratory doors open when the experiments go wrong and horrible smells are produced. Smooth rocks can be rubbed when pressure builds and you just need a mindless activity to get through the day.

EXAMPLE

According to the passage, one of the great discoveries in science is

(A) atomic energy.

(B) static electricity.

(C) rocks.

(D) DNA.

The correct answer is Choice (C). The important words in the question are *According to the passage*. When you see this phrase, you know to look in the passage for the answer. Because none of the answers except rocks is even remotely mentioned, rocks must be the best answer.

EXAMPLE

How do rocks help scientists when experiments go horribly wrong and produce terrible odors?

(A) They can be used to smash the windows.

(B) They can prop open the doors.

(C) They can be thrown in anger.

(D) They can be rubbed.

The correct answer is Choice (B). According to the passage, the rocks can be used to hold open the door of the lab. Rocks can also be used to smash windows and can be thrown in anger, but the passage doesn't specifically mention these uses. The passage mentions rubbing rocks as one of their uses, but it does so in another context.

Fill-in-the-blank questions

For science fill-in-the-blank questions, you have to provide your own answer(s) — a specific calculation, a word, or words — to show that you understand a concept, to complete a definition, or to describe a trend on a graph. This is another example of why you should read as much scientific material as possible. A misspelled word is scored as incorrect. Keeping that vocabulary list I suggest as a review method before the test will really help.

The following fill-in-the-blank question is based on this excerpt from a job posting on the Federal Government Jobs website (www.federalgovernmentjobs.us).

> A career with the Forest Service will challenge you to manage and care for more than 193 million acres of our nation's most magnificent lands, conduct research through a network of forest and range experiment stations and the Forest Products Laboratory, and provide assistance to State and private forestry agencies.
>
> It's an awesome responsibility — but the rewards are as limitless as the views.

EXAMPLE

Based on the information in the passage, what would the person hired for this job do in conjunction with range experiment stations? ⬚

The correct answer is *conduct research*. The successful applicant would conduct research with the range experiment stations as part of their duties. This is stated explicitly in the passage.

Try another fill-in-the-blank question on for size, based on the following excerpt from the USDA Animal and Plant Health Inspection Service website (www.aphis.usda.gov).

> The Lacey Act combats trafficking in "illegal" wildlife, fish, and plants. The 2008 Farm Bill (the Food, Conservation, and Energy Act of 2008), effective May 22, 2008, amended the Lacey Act by expanding its protection to a broader range of plants and plant products. The Lacey Act now, among other things, makes it unlawful to import certain plants and plant products without an import declaration.

EXAMPLE

The Lacey Act is a piece of government legislation to control the transportation and selling of ⬚ plants.

The passage states that this act was passed to combat the trafficking of illegal wildlife, fish and plants. So the correct answer is *illegal.*

Because math is used in science, some items may test math skills. These items are frequently fill-in-the-blank items or multiple-choice items. Here is an example:

> To calculate density, you divide mass by volume. A sample of ice at 0°C has a volume of 64 cm³ and a mass of 58.7 g.

EXAMPLE

What is the density of the sample, rounded to three decimal points? [_____] g/cm³ You may use numbers, a decimal point (.), and/or a negative sign in your answer.

The information says that to calculate density, you divide mass by volume: 58.7/64 = 0.9171875. Rounded to three decimal places, the answer is 0.917 g/cm³. Because *g/cm³* is already provided, you just need to type 0.917.

TIP

A calculator icon appears on the top right of the computer screen for some questions on the Mathematical Reasoning, Science, and Social Studies tests. You may click on the calculator link to help you compute your answers. If you have a handheld Texas Instruments TI-30XS calculator, you may use it when testing at a test center.

TIP

Pay careful attention to the instructions when answering a fill-in-the-blank question with a number. Even small errors, such as not rounding to the number of places specified, can cost you the answer. On the previous item, the test software will also accept .917, but not 0.9172, which has too many decimal places. With math questions, always read and follow the directions!

Drag-and-drop questions

For this question format, you have to drag answer choices from a list to a designated position — whether that's placing labels on a graph or diagram or dropping words or images on a specific location on a chart or other type of visual. This question format requires a bit more than just picking the correct answer. In drag-and-drop questions, you may have to sort and prioritize your selections. Although you're given a list of possible answers, more than one may be correct. Read the passage carefully to either eliminate wrong answers or choose correct ones.

Here's an example of a question in the drag-and-drop format.

EXAMPLE

In Ms. Fleming's graduating class, three of her students want to specialize in science:

>> Gilda wants to study physics.

>> Domenic wants to study biology.

>> Freida wants to learn everything she can about NASA's missions.

Drag (or write, in this case) the appropriate name into the column labeled with the general area each student wants to study.

(A) Gilda

(B) Domenic

(C) Freida

Earth and Space Science	Life Science	Physical Science

The correct response here is that Gilda wants to study physical science, Domenic wants to study life science, and Freida wants to study earth and space science. General knowledge from your experience and reading would enable you to fit the specific interests into the general areas.

Drop-down menu questions

The drop-down menu is a type of multiple-choice question, in that you're given a number of answer choices to choose from to complete a sentence so it reads correctly and accurately. Usually, drop-down menu questions involve more science vocabulary, so your reading in science will help you choose the correct answer. As with most multiple-choice items, the drop-down menu includes correct and incorrect answers.

The following drop-down menu question refers to this excerpt from the Missions page on NASA's website (www.nasa.gov).

> The Post-landing Orion Recovery Tests (PORT) began in late March at the Naval Surface Warfare Center, Carderock Division in Bethesda, Md. This first round took place in a controlled water environment. Testing near Kennedy Space Center in April will be done in the rougher, uncontrolled waters of the Atlantic Ocean. Crews will head out over several days and at varying distances from land to assess the vehicle's performance in open water landing conditions. Recovery teams will gain experience dealing with Orion in water. The tests will also help NASA understand the motions astronauts will experience within the craft. The same boats that have been used to recover the space shuttle's solid rocket boosters will tow the capsule for these tests.

EXAMPLE

The Orion will be tested in open waters in the Atlantic to

(A) ensure that the astronauts can swim.

(B) ensure the safety and security of the astronauts.

(C) assess the Orion's ability to travel far in space.

(D) allow the astronauts to fish to provide them with provisions.

The answer is Choice (B), *ensure the safety and security of the astronauts.* Dropping a sealed capsule into the ocean wouldn't test swimming ability (Choice A), assess the ship's ability to travel far in space (Choice C), or offer fishing possibilities (Choice D).

Drop-down questions are frequently used with visual materials. In these questions, you have to complete a caption for the visual material. For example, the test might present you with a graph of the average global temperature for each year from 1900 to the present, with the graph showing a steadily rising temperature.

EXAMPLE

This graph of average global temperatures since 1900 shows a generally [＿＿＿＿＿] pattern year over year. (*Note:* Since this is an example of a question type, the graph is not shown).

(A) rising

(B) falling

(C) stable

(D) unpredictable

Choice (A) is correct. According to the description, the graph shows a generally increasing global temperature, so only this choice is possible.

Managing Your Time for the Science Test

The Science test has about 50 questions (the exact number varies from test to test) that you must answer in 90 minutes, which means you have about 100 seconds (or about a minute and three quarters) to read each textual or visual passage and its corresponding question(s) and determine the correct answer. If a passage has more than one question, you have slightly more time to answer those questions because you should read the passage only once.

To help you manage your time, check out Chapters 2 and 3 for some general time-management strategies that you can use on all the test sections. For the Science test, specifically, I suggest you focus on these two time-saving strategies:

>> **For questions about passages, read the question first and then scan the material for the answer.** The passage always contains the answer, but your background knowledge in science and your familiarity with scientific terms can help you understand the material more easily and quickly. Reading the question first provides you with a guide to what's being asked and what the passage is about so you know what to look for as you read it.

>> **For questions about a visual material, such as a graph or table, read the question first and then scan the visual material.** Look at the visual material to see the big picture; questions usually don't ask about minute details.

As a general tip, answer the easiest questions first. Use the Flag button (in the upper-right corner of your screen) to mark questions you want to return to. Remember, when you finish all the items, you will be offered the opportunity to see a list of all the questions you answered, skipped, and flagged in the Review screen. You can use that list to return to items you had questions about or skipped earlier. If you run out of time or want to see the list of skipped and flagged items at any time, press Review in the lower-right corner of your screen.

And don't panic! Your worst enemy on this or any other test is panic. Panicking takes time and energy, and you don't have a surplus of either one. Use a calming technique (such as inhaling deeply) and then keep moving forward. If you find yourself spending too much time on one question, flag it and keep moving. Return to the question at the end of the test when you know exactly how much time is left.

Chapter **15**

Sampling Some Science Practice Questions

This chapter provides sample Science test questions to help you prepare for taking this section of the GED test.

Record your answers directly in this book or on a sheet of paper, if you think you'll want to revisit these practice questions at a later date. Mark only one answer for each item. At the end of the chapter, I provide detailed answer explanations for you to check against your answers.

Remember, this is just preliminary practice. I want you to get used to answering different types of Science test questions. Use the complete practice tests in Chapters 23 and 31 to time your work and replicate the real test-taking experience.

Science Practice Questions

The Science test consists of a series of items intended to measure general concepts in science. The items are based on short readings that may include a graph, chart, or figure. Study the information given and then answer the question(s) following it. Refer to the information as often as necessary in answering the questions. Work carefully, but don't spend too much time on any one question. Be sure you answer every question.

Questions 1 and 2 refer to the following diagram and excerpt adapted from NASA's Glenn Research Center website for Space Flight Systems.

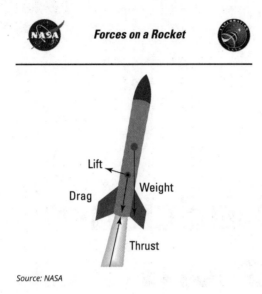

Source: NASA

Many differences exist between the forces acting on a rocket and those acting on an airplane.

- On an airplane, the **lift force** (the aerodynamic force perpendicular to the flight direction) is used to overcome the **weight**. On a rocket, **thrust** is used in opposition to weight. On many rockets, **lift** is used to stabilize and control the direction of flight.

- On an airplane, most of the aerodynamic forces are generated by the wings and the tail surfaces. For a rocket, the aerodynamic forces are generated by the fins, nose cone, and body tube. For both airplane and rocket, the aerodynamic forces act through the center of pressure (the dot with the black center on the figure), while the weight acts through the center of gravity (the solid dot on the figure).

- While most airplanes have a high lift-to-drag ratio, the drag of a rocket is usually much greater than the lift.

- While the magnitude and direction of the forces remain fairly constant for an airplane, the magnitude and direction of the forces acting on a rocket change dramatically during a typical flight.

1. In the diagram, which force must be the greatest for the rocket to leave the earth?

(A) drag

(B) lift

(C) thrust

(D) weight

2. Which statement most accurately describes lift on airplanes and rockets?

(A) On airplanes, lift holds the airplane in the air; on some rockets, lift helps steer the rocket.

(B) On airplanes, lift helps steer the plane; on rockets, lift holds the rocket in the air.

(C) Rockets and planes both use lift to leave the earth.

(D) Rockets use lift; planes use thrust.

Questions 3 and 4 refer to the following excerpt adapted from the U.S. Environmental Protection Agency's website on climate change (www.epa.gov/climatechange).

As temperatures increase, the habitat ranges of many North American species are moving northward in latitude and upward in elevation. While this means a range expansion for some species, for others it means a range reduction or a movement into less hospitable habitat or increased competition. Some species have nowhere to go because they are already at the northern or upper limit of their habitat.

For example, boreal forests are invading tundra, reducing habitat for the many unique species that depend on the tundra ecosystem, such as caribou, arctic fox, and snowy owl. Other observed changes in the United States include expanding oak-hickory forests, contracting maple-beech forests, and disappearing spruce-fir forests. As rivers and streams warm, warmwater fish are expanding into areas previously inhabited by coldwater species. Coldwater fish, including several trout species valued by many people for their high protein content, are losing their habitats. As waters warm, the area of feasible, cooler habitats to which species can migrate is reduced. Range shifts disturb the current state of the ecosystem and can limit opportunities for fishing and hunting.

3. As temperatures become warmer and ranges move, the new territory may prove to be less ☐ for specific species.

4. Which of the following is a consequence of the warming of the habitats of coldwater fish?

(A) coldwater fish migrate to new habitats

(B) warmwater fish move into the habitats of coldwater fish

(C) coldwater fish adjust to warmer water

(D) opportunities for fishing increase

Question 5 refers the following excerpt from Womenshealth.gov.

"Mirror, Mirror on the wall. . .who's the thinnest one of all?" According to the National Eating Disorders Association, the average American woman is 5 feet 4 inches tall and weighs 140 pounds. The average American model is 5 feet 11 inches tall and weighs 117 pounds. All too often, society associates being "thin" with "hard-working, beautiful, strong and self-disciplined." On the other hand, being "fat" is associated with being "lazy, ugly, weak and lacking will-power." Because of these harsh critiques, rarely are women completely satisfied with their image. As a result, they often feel great anxiety and pressure to achieve and/or maintain an imaginary appearance.

Eating disorders are serious medical problems. Anorexia nervosa, bulimia nervosa, and binge-eating disorder are all types of eating disorders. Eating disorders frequently develop during adolescence or early adulthood but can occur during childhood or later in adulthood. Females are more likely than males to develop an eating disorder.

5. Which of the following would add further support to the passage?

(A) Images of unusually thin women are pervasive in media.

(B) Women have trouble losing weight.

(C) Males are generally taller and weigh more.

(D) Males are not subject to the same pressure about weight as women.

Question 6 refers to the following statement by the U.S. Surgeon General (www.surgeongeneral.gov).

We must increase our efforts to educate and encourage Americans to take responsibility for their own health. Over the past 20 years, the rates of overweight doubled in children and tripled in adolescents. Today nearly two out of every three American adults and 15 percent of American kids are overweight or obese. That's more than 9 million children — one in every seven kids — who are at increased risk of weight-related chronic diseases. These facts are astounding, but they are just the beginning of a chain reaction of dangerous health problems — many of which were once associated only with adults.

6. The percentage of children who are overweight or obese is estimated at

   (A) 9 percent

   (B) 15 percent

   (C) 20 percent

   (D) 30 percent

Question 7 refers to the following definition from the U.S. Environmental Protection Agency's climate change glossary (www.epa.gov/climatechange).

Black carbon (BC) is the most strongly light-absorbing component of particulate matter (PM), and is formed by the incomplete combustion of fossil fuels, biofuels, and biomass. It is emitted directly into the atmosphere in the form of fine particles.

7. Based on this information, why would reducing automobile use result in a cleaner environment?

   (A) Traffic would be lighter.

   (B) Most automobiles run on fossil fuel.

   (C) Subways are a more efficient form of moving people.

   (D) Electricity is less expensive than fossil fuels.

Question 8 refers to the following definition from the U.S. Environmental Protection Agency's climate change glossary (www.epa.gov/climatechange).

The greenhouse effect is the trapping and build-up of heat in the atmosphere (troposphere) near the Earth's surface. Some of the heat flowing back toward space from the Earth's surface is absorbed by water vapor, carbon dioxide, ozone, and several other gases in the atmosphere and then reradiated back toward the Earth's surface. If the atmospheric concentrations of these greenhouse gases rise, the average temperature of the lower atmosphere will gradually increase.

8. Heat reradiated from the Earth's surface is absorbed by several _____ in the Earth's atmosphere.

Question 9 refers to the following excerpt from NASA's Science website (science.nasa.gov).

Examples of the types of forecasts that may be possible are: the outbreak and spread of harmful algal blooms, occurrence and spread of invasive exotic species, and productivity of forest and agricultural systems. This Focus Area also will contribute to the improvement of climate projections for 50–100 years into the future by providing key inputs for climate models. This includes projections of future atmospheric CO_2 and CH_4 concentrations and understanding of key ecosystem and carbon cycle process controls on the climate system.

9. Long-term forecasts of this type are important to people because

   (A) they will help hunters know when their favorite sport will become impossible
   (B) they will allow scientists to develop research projects that will address the consequences of dramatic climate change
   (C) people will know what type of winter clothing to buy for their children
   (D) it will spur research into more efficient subway systems

Question 10 refers to the following excerpt from NASA's Science website (science.nasa.gov).

Throughout the next decade, research will be needed to advance our understanding of and ability to model human-ecosystems-climate interactions so that an integrated understanding of Earth System function can be applied to our goals. These research activities will yield knowledge of the Earth's ecosystems and carbon cycle, as well as projections of carbon cycle and ecosystem responses to global environmental change.

10. This type of research should lead to advances in our understanding of how the carbon cycle and our ecosystem respond to [   ].

Questions 11 and 12 refer to the following excerpt from NASA's Jet Propulsion Laboratory website (www.jp.nasa.gov).

We live on a restless planet. Earth is continually influenced by the Sun, gravitational forces, processes emanating from deep within the core, and by complex interactions with oceans and atmospheres. At very short time scales we seem to be standing on terra firma, yet many processes sculpt the surface with changes that can be quite dramatic (earthquakes, volcanic eruptions, landslides), sometimes slow (subsidence due to aquifer depletion), seemingly unpredictable, and often leading to loss of life and property damage.

Accurate diagnosis of our restless planet requires an observational capability for precise measurement of surface change, or deformation. Measurement of both the slow and fast deformations of Earth are essential for improving the scientific understanding of the physical processes, and for optimizing responses to natural hazards, and for identifying potential risk areas.

11. Although people often talk about standing on solid ground, the truth is that

   (A) the Earth is capable of supporting huge buildings anywhere on its surface
   (B) the ground is solid and stable
   (C) the ground is capable of sudden, dramatic movement
   (D) people should not live near an active volcano

12. Accurate scientific research into surface change is essential to

   (A) offset the physical processes
   (B) warn people about volcanoes
   (C) ensure better responses to natural hazards
   (D) make more accurate weather forecasts

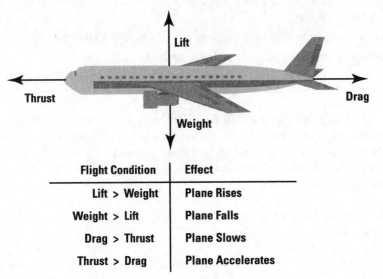

Flight Condition	Effect
Lift > Weight	Plane Rises
Weight > Lift	Plane Falls
Drag > Thrust	Plane Slows
Thrust > Drag	Plane Accelerates

Source: NASA

13. For the plane to take off, ☐ and ☐. Write the appropriate answers in the boxes.

(A) lift > weight

(B) weight > lift

(C) drag > thrust

(D) thrust > drag

Question 14 refers to the following excerpt from NASA's website (www.nasa.gov).

It would be impractical, in terms of volume and cost, to completely stock the International Space Station (ISS) with oxygen or water for long periods of time. Without a grocery store in space, NASA scientists and engineers have developed innovative solutions to meet astronauts' basic requirements for life. The human body is two-thirds water. It has been estimated that nearly an octillion (1,000,000,000,000,000,000,000,000,000) water molecules flow through our bodies daily. It is therefore necessary for humans to consume a sufficient amount of water, as well as oxygen and food, on a daily basis in order to sustain life. Without water, the average person lives approximately three days. Without air, permanent brain damage can occur within three minutes. Scientists have determined how much water, air, and food a person needs per day per person for life on Earth. Similarly, space scientists know what is needed to sustain life in space.

14. Why is it necessary to recycle air and water on a space ship?

(A) to keep the interior smelling clean

(B) to keep the ISS moving

(C) to keep the astronauts alive

(D) so that they don't get thirsty between meals

Question 15 refers to the following diagram from NASA's Glenn Research Center website (www.grc.nasa.gov).

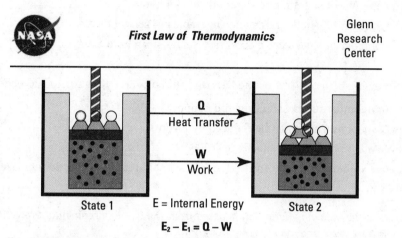

Any thermodynamic system in an equilibrium state possesses a state variable called the internal energy (E). Between any two equilibrium states, the change in internal energy is equal to the difference of the heat transfer <u>into</u> the system and work done <u>by</u> the system.

Source: NASA

15. Circle the vessel on the diagram with the higher temperature.

Questions 16 and 17 refer to the following excerpt from the Department of Agriculture website (www.usda.gov).

As the centerpiece of First Lady Michelle Obama's Let's Move! initiative to raise a healthier generation of kids, USDA led the effort to pass the Healthy, Hunger-Free Kids Act, historic legislation to allow us, for the first time in 30 years, the chance to make real reforms to the school lunch and breakfast programs by improving the critical nutrition and hunger safety net for nearly 32 million children who eat school lunch each day and the 12 million who eat breakfast at school.

The USDA's efforts to improve and enhance the school food environment include the following:

- Updated science-based school meal standards for the National School Lunch Program to increase fruits, vegetables, whole grains, and low-fat dairy while reducing fats, sodium, and sugars;

- Performance-based funding increases of 6 cents per lunch for schools meeting the new meal standards; this is the first real increase in 30 years;

- Implemented new snack-food standards in schools that preserve flexibility for time-honored traditions like fundraisers and bake sales, and provide ample transition time for schools;

- Provision of training and technical assistance to help schools meet improved standards. USDA is working closely with schools to move swiftly to make these reforms a reality in every school.

16. The Healthy, Hunger-Free Kids Act includes efforts to

(A) increase free breakfasts

(B) increase the amount of sodium and sugars in school meals

(C) increase the amount of whole grains and vegetables in school meals

(D) increase the number of bake sales elementary schools can hold

17. Which of the following is necessary for the Healthy, Hunger-Free Kids Act to succeed?

(A) School personnel must receive training and support.

(B) The price of school lunches must be reduced by 6 cents.

(C) More schools must provide free snacks to students.

(D) The number of students who are entitled to free school breakfasts should increase to 32 million.

Question 18 refers to the following definition adapted from the U.S. Environmental Protection Agency's climate change glossary (www.epa.gov/climatechange).

Weather is an atmospheric condition at any given time or place. It is measured in terms of such things as wind, temperature, humidity, atmospheric pressure, cloudiness, and precipitation. In most places, weather can change from hour-to-hour, day-to-day, and season-to-season. Climate is usually defined as the "average weather," or more rigorously, as the statistical description in terms of the mean and variability of relevant quantities over a period of time ranging from months to thousands or millions of years. The classical period is 30 years, as defined by the World Meteorological Organization (WMO). These quantities are most often surface variables such as temperature, precipitation, and wind. Climate in a wider sense is the state, including a statistical description, of the climate system. A simple way of remembering the difference is that climate is what you expect (e.g., cold winters) and weather is what you get (e.g., a blizzard).

18. If you were sitting around with a group of friends complaining about how the rain forecast for tomorrow was going to ruin your baseball game, you would be complaining about the ⬚.

Question 19 refers to the following definition from the U.S. Environmental Protection Agency's climate change glossary (www.epa.gov/climatechange).

Atmospheric lifetime is the average time that a molecule resides in the atmosphere before it is removed by chemical reaction or deposition. This can also be thought of as the time that it takes after the human-caused emission of a gas for the concentrations of that gas in the atmosphere to return to natural levels. Greenhouse gas lifetimes can range from a few years to a few thousand years.

19. Why is it important for humans to become more aware of the pollution they are causing by overuse of fossil fuels?

(A) Gasoline is becoming expensive.

(B) The greenhouse gases can remain in the atmosphere for many years.

(C) Traffic congestion is causing health problems.

(D) Humans are turning the blue sky gray.

Question 20 refers to the following excerpt from the U.S. Department of Energy's website (www.energy.gov).

In 2009, President Barack Obama signed an Executive Order creating the White House Council on Women and Girls. In his remarks at the signing, the President underscored that the purpose of the Council is "to ensure that each of the agencies in which they're charged takes into account the needs of women and girls in the policies they draft." The Energy Department's chapter of the Council continues to pull program offices and National Laboratories together to work on confronting the challenges faced by women and girls.

At the Clean Energy Ministerial held in London in April 2012, the Department launched the U.S. Clean Energy, Education, and Empowerment (C3E) program to advance the careers and leadership of women in clean energy fields. The program, led by the Department in partnership with the MIT Energy Initiative, includes an ambassador network, annual symposium and the C3E Awards program.

A year later, inspired by the success of C3E, Energy Secretary Ernest Moniz launched the Minorities in Energy (MIE) Initiative. The initiative includes a network of more than 30 senior-level Ambassadors across the public and private sector working alongside the Department to increase the participation of minorities in energy careers as well as support their advancement to leadership positions.

20. The effect of President Obama's initiative was to ⬚ the participation of women and minorities in careers in energy-related fields.

Question 21 refers to the following excerpt from NASA's Earth Observatory website (www.earthobservatory.nasa.gov).

If Kepler's laws define the motion of the planets, Newton's laws define motion. Thinking on Kepler's laws, Newton realized that all motion, whether it was the orbit of the Moon around the Earth or an apple falling from a tree, followed the same basic principles. "To the same natural effects," he wrote, "we must, as far as possible, assign the same causes." Previous Aristotelian thinking, physicist Stephen Hawking has written, assigned different causes to different types of motion. By unifying all motion, Newton shifted the scientific perspective to a search for large, unifying patterns in nature. Newton outlined his laws in *Philosophiae Naturalis Principia Mathematica* ("Mathematical Principles of Natural Philosophy"), published in 1687.

21. Newton was inspired by

(A) Hawking

(B) Aristotle

(C) Kepler

(D) Einstein

Question 22 refers to the following information, taken from the U.S. Department of Labor's Occupational Safety & Health Administration website (www.osha.gov).

Unexpected releases of toxic, reactive, or flammable liquids and gases in processes involving highly hazardous chemicals have been reported for many years. Incidents continue to occur in various industries that use highly hazardous chemicals which may be toxic, reactive, flammable, or explosive, or may exhibit a combination of these properties. Regardless of the industry that uses these highly hazardous chemicals, there is a potential for an accidental release any time they are not properly controlled. This, in turn, creates the possibility of disaster.

Recent major disasters include the 1984 Bhopal, India, incident resulting in more than 2,000 deaths; the October 1989 Phillips Petroleum Company, Pasadena, TX, incident resulting in 23 deaths and 132 injuries; the July 1990 BASF, Cincinnati, OH, incident resulting in 2 deaths, and the May 1991 IMC, Sterlington, LA, incident resulting in 8 deaths and 128 injuries.

22. Of the incidents reported in the passage, which one caused the most fatalities?

   (A) Bhopal, India
   (B) Pasadena, Texas
   (C) Cincinnati, Ohio
   (D) Sterlington, Louisiana

Question 23 is based on the following excerpt from the National Oceanic and Atmospheric Administration's Office of Response and Restoration website (`response.restoration.noaa.gov`*).*

Reactivity is the tendency of substances to undergo chemical change, which can result in hazards — such as heat generation or toxic gas by-products. The CRW (Chemical Reactivity Worksheet) predicts possible hazards from mixing chemicals and is designed to be used by emergency responders and planners, as well as the chemical industry, to help prevent dangerous chemical incidents.

The chemical datasheets in the CRW database contain information about the intrinsic hazards of each chemical and about whether a chemical reacts with air, water, or other materials. It also includes case histories on specific chemical incidents, with references.

23. What is the most important contribution of the CRW to the prevention of hazardous accidents?

   (A) provides information
   (B) enforces the regulations
   (C) creates laws
   (D) closes companies for infractions

Question 24 refers to the following excerpt from the U.S. Environmental Protection Agency's website on climate change (`www.epa.gov/climatechange`*).*

Climate change, along with habitat destruction and pollution, is one of the important stressors that can contribute to species extinction. The IPCC estimates that 20–30% of the plant and animal species evaluated so far in climate change studies are at risk of extinction if temperatures reach levels projected to occur by the end of this century. Projected rates of species extinctions are 10 times greater than recently observed global average rates and 10,000 times greater than rates observed in the distant past (as recorded in fossils).

24. One of the great dangers to the earth as a result of climate change is the ⬚ of species.

Question 25 refers to the following excerpt from the U.S. Environmental Protection Agency's website on climate change (`www.epa.gov/climatechange`*).*

When coral reefs become stressed, they expel microorganisms that live within their tissues and are essential to their health. This is known as coral bleaching. As ocean temperatures warm and the acidity of the ocean increases, bleaching and coral die-offs are likely to become more frequent. Chronically stressed coral reefs are less likely to recover.

25. Coral bleaching refers to

(A) a chemical reaction between the ocean waters and microorganisms in the coral

(B) expulsion of microorganisms from within coral reefs

(C) the effect of extremely strong sunlight on coral reefs

(D) coral die-offs

Question 26 refers to the following excerpt from the U.S. Environmental Protection Agency's website on climate change (`www.epa.gov/climatechange`).

For many species, the climate where they live or spend part of the year influences key stages of their annual life cycle, such as migration, blooming, and mating. As the climate has warmed in recent decades, the timing of these events has changed in some parts of the country. Some examples are:

- Warmer springs have led to earlier nesting for 28 migratory bird species on the East Coast of the United States.

- Northeastern birds that winter in the southern United States are returning north in the spring 13 days earlier than they did in the early 20th century.

- In a California study, 16 out of 23 butterfly species shifted their migration timing and arrived earlier.

Changes like these can lead to mismatches in the timing of migration, breeding, and food availability. Growth and survival are reduced when migrants arrive at a location before or after food sources are present.

26. Severe climate changes can lead to extinction of a species through ⬚⬚⬚⬚⬚ in aspects of their lives upon which their survival depends.

Question 27 refers to the following excerpt from NASA's Science website (`science.nasa.gov`).

New remote sensing technologies are empowering scientists to measure and understand subtle changes in the Earth's surface and interior that reflect the response of the Earth to both the internal forces that lead to volcanic eruptions, earthquakes, landslides and sea-level change and the climatic forces that sculpt the Earth's surface. For instance, InSAR [interferometric synthetic aperture radar] and LiDAR [light detection and ranging] measurements from satellite and airborne sensors are used to provide images of millimeter scale surface changes that indicate an awakening of volcanic activity long before seismic tremors are felt. Ground based geodetic GPS instruments provide time continuous measurements of this activity though they are often lost during intense volcanic activity. Thermal infrared remote sensing data from NASA satellites signal impending activity by measuring ground temperatures and variations in the composition of lava flows as well as the sulfur dioxide in volcanic plumes. The combination of instruments provides accurate information that can be used for both long term and short hazard assessment. These same LiDAR, InSAR and thermal instruments also provide accurate information on the velocity of ice steams, sub glacial lake activity, glacial rebound of the Earth's crust, and the retreat and advance of mountain glaciers that are related to climatic changes.

27. New remote sensing technologies provide ⬚⬚⬚⬚⬚ that may lead to long- and short-term hazard assessment.

Question 28 refers to the following excerpt from the National Science Foundation website (`www.nsf.gov`).

By observing galaxies formed billions of years ago, astronomers have been able to paint an increasingly detailed picture of how the universe evolved. According to the widely accepted Big Bang theory, our universe was born in an explosive moment approximately fifteen billion years ago. All of the universe's matter and energy — even the fabric of space itself — was compressed into an infinitesimally small volume and then began expanding at an incredible rate. Within minutes, the universe had grown to the size of the solar system and cooled enough so that equal numbers of protons, neutrons, and the simplest atomic nuclei had formed.

28. Astronomers believe that the universe evolved about [   ] billion years ago.

Question 29 refers to the following excerpt from NASA's Earth Observatory website (www.earth observatory.nasa.gov).

Within a single frame of reference, the laws of classical physics, including Newton's laws, hold true. But Newton's laws can't explain the differences in motion, mass, distance, and time that result when objects are observed from two very different frames of reference. To describe motion in these situations, scientists must rely on Einstein's theory of relativity.

At slow speeds and at large scales, however, the differences in time, length, and mass predicted by relativity are small enough that they appear to be constant, and Newton's laws still work. In general, few things are moving at speeds fast enough for us to notice relativity. For large, slow-moving satellites, Newton's laws still define orbits. We can still use them to launch Earth-observing satellites and predict their motion. We can use them to reach the Moon, Mars, and other places beyond Earth. For this reason, many scientists see Einstein's laws of general and special relativity not as a replacement of Newton's laws of motion and universal gravitation, but as the full culmination of his idea.

29. Einstein's theory provides a frame of reference for explanations of differences in time, length, and mass from

  (A) two very different speeds

  (B) two very different scales

  (C) observations from two very different frames of reference

  (D) two very different perspectives

Question 30 refers to the following excerpt from NASA's Science website (science.nasa.gov).

As basic research leads to prediction of solid Earth processes, so does the need to adapt this research to real societal problem-solving. Knowledge that improves human abilities to prepare and respond to disasters involving the dynamism of the Earth's interior offers the immediate benefit of saving lives and property. The Earth Surface and Interior focus area (ESI) seeks to coordinate the efforts of NASA's Research and Analysis Program in Solid Earth with the Applied Sciences Disaster Management Program to provide a continuum of development from re-search to applications that will enable first responders, planners, and policy makers to improve decision-making tools through NASA science and technology.

30. ESI provides first responders with [   ] to improve their decision-making in the event of a disaster.

Question 31 refers to the following excerpt from the U.S. Environmental Protection Agency's website on climate change (www.epa.gov/climatechange).

A food web is made up of predators and prey that interact in a habitat or ecosystem. The impact of climate change on a particular species can ripple through a food web and affect a wide range of other organisms. . . .. Declines in the duration and extent of sea ice in the Arctic leads to declines in the abundance of ice algae, which thrive in nutrient-rich pockets in the ice. These algae are eaten by zooplankton, which are in turn eaten by Arctic cod, an important food source for many marine mammals, including seals. Seals are eaten by polar bears.

31. The information in the passage implies that a rise in Arctic temperature may result in

(A) an increase in the nutrient-rich pockets in the ice

(B) a decline in the number of polar bears

(C) an extension of the sea ice

(D) an increase in the species of zooplankton

Question 32 refers to the following excerpt from the U.S. Environmental Protection Agency's stratospheric ozone glossary (www.epa.gov/ozone).

Consumer aerosol products in the United States have not used ozone-depleting substances (ODS) since the late 1970s because of voluntary switching followed by federal regulation. The Clean Air Act and EPA regulations further restricted the use of ODS for non-consumer products. All consumer products, and most other aerosol products, now use propellants that do not deplete the ozone layer, such as hydrocarbons and compressed gases.

32. The propellants that are currently used in aerosol products are [   ] and [   ].

Question 33 refers to the following definition from the U.S. Environmental Protection Agency's climate change glossary (www.epa.gov/climatechange).

Biofuels are gas or liquid fuels made from plant material (biomass). They include wood, wood waste, wood liquors, peat, railroad ties, wood sludge, spent sulfite liquors, agricultural waste, straw, tires, fish oils, tall oil, sludge waste, waste alcohol, municipal solid waste, landfill gases, other waste, and ethanol blended into motor gasoline.

33. Biofuels are ecologically sound because

(A) they are inexpensive

(B) they do not pollute the Earth

(C) they are made from indestructible materials

(D) they can be used as fuels

Question 34 refers to the following definition from the U.S. Environmental Protection Agency's climate change glossary (www.epa.gov/climatechange).

The carbon cycle is all parts (reservoirs) and fluxes of carbon. The cycle is usually thought of as four main reservoirs of carbon interconnected by pathways of exchange. The reservoirs are the atmosphere, terrestrial biosphere (usually includes freshwater systems), oceans, and sediments (includes fossil fuels). The annual movements of carbon, the carbon exchanges between reservoirs, occur because of various chemical, physical, geological, and biological processes. The ocean contains the largest pool of carbon near the surface of the Earth, but most of that pool is not involved with rapid exchange with the atmosphere.

34. The largest pool of carbon on Earth is the [   ].

Questions 35 and 36 refer to the following definition from the U.S. Environmental Protection Agency's climate change glossary (www.epa.gov/climatechange).

Carbon footprint is the total amount of greenhouse gases that are emitted into the atmosphere each year by a person, family, building, organization, or company. A person's carbon footprint includes greenhouse gas emissions from fuel that an individual burns directly, such as by heating a home or riding in a car. It also includes greenhouse gases that come from producing the goods or services that the individual uses, including emissions from power plants that make electricity, factories that make products, and landfills where trash gets sent.

35. Which of the following would increase people's individual carbon footprint?

   (A) walking more and driving less

   (B) lowering their thermostats during the cold weather

   (C) not barbequing

   (D) taking airplanes more frequently

36. People's personal carbon footprints are also affected by processes out of their control, such as

   (A) grocery shopping

   (B) recycling depots

   (C) power plants

   (D) driving less

Question 37 refers to the following image of a human nerve cell.

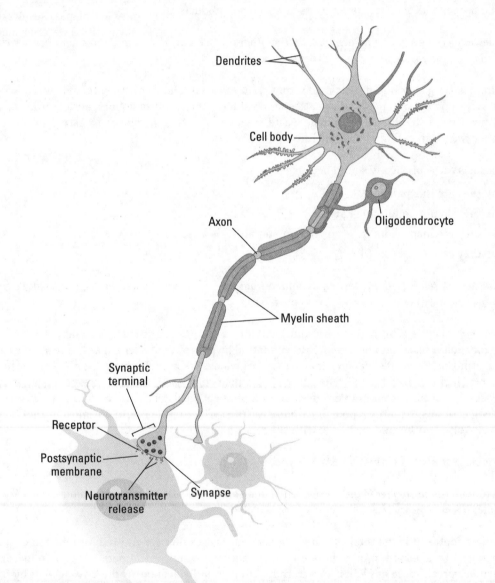

Source: U.S. Department of Health and Human Services

37. The nerve cells in your body carry messages in the form of electrical signals. The signals travel from the cell body along the axon, which is protected by the ⬚.

Question 38 refers to the following excerpt from NASA's website (www.nasa.gov).

Saving lives does not have to be as complex as robotic surgery but can be as simple as providing the life-giving source of clean water. This specifically is of utmost importance to a community in rural Mexico, showing the far-reaching benefits of the water purification component of NASA's Environmental and Life Control Support System (ECLSS). ECLSS provides clean water for drinking, cooking and hygiene aboard the space station. This technology has been adapted on Earth to aid remote locations or places devastated by natural disaster that do not have access to clean drinking water.

In Chiapas, Mexico, many people are at risk of illness from drinking contaminated water from wells, rivers or springs not treated by municipal water systems. Children in Chiapas, previously sickened by parasites and stomach bugs, now have access during school to clean, safe drinking water. This is due to the installation of the ECLSS-derived water purification plant. Renewable solar energy powers the water treatment technology for the community in Chiapas. Results include improved overall health and cost-savings from not having to buy purified water or medication to treat water-borne illnesses.

38. How do innovations by NASA help a little town in Mexico?

(A) by setting up space industries

(B) by providing for clean water

(C) by supplying food

(D) by ridding the area of parasites

Question 39 refers to the following excerpt from the U.S. Department of Labor's Occupational Safety & Health Administration website (www.osha.gov).

Chemicals have the ability to react when exposed to other chemicals or certain physical conditions. The reactive properties of chemicals vary widely, and they play a vital role in the production of many chemical, material, pharmaceutical, and food products we use daily. When chemical reactions are not properly managed, they can have harmful, or even catastrophic consequences, such as toxic fumes, fires, and explosions. These reactions may result in death and injury to people, damage to physical property, and severe effects on the environment.

39. What is the main idea of this passage?

(A) Chemicals can poison the food supply.

(B) Chemicals can have dire consequences if not handled properly.

(C) Chemicals play a vital role in our lives.

(D) Chemicals have many advantages, but also pose serious risks.

Question 40 refers to the following chart.

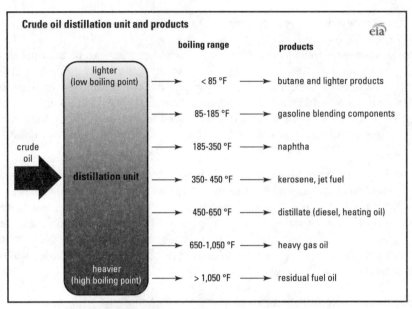

Crude oil distillation unit and products

	boiling range	products
lighter (low boiling point)	< 85 °F	butane and lighter products
	85-185 °F	gasoline blending components
crude oil → distillation unit	185-350 °F	naphtha
	350- 450 °F	kerosene, jet fuel
	450-650 °F	distillate (diesel, heating oil)
	650-1,050 °F	heavy gas oil
heavier (high boiling point)	> 1,050 °F	residual fuel oil

Source: U.S. Energy Information Administration

40. Why is it easier to obtain naphtha from crude oil in a distillation unit than diesel oil?

(A) It naturally floats to the surface where it can be skimmed off.

(B) It has a lower boiling point, so it evaporates sooner than diesel oil.

(C) It has a higher boiling point, so it remains behind as diesel is evaporated.

(D) Naphtha can be filtered out.

Questions 41 and 42 refer to the following chart.

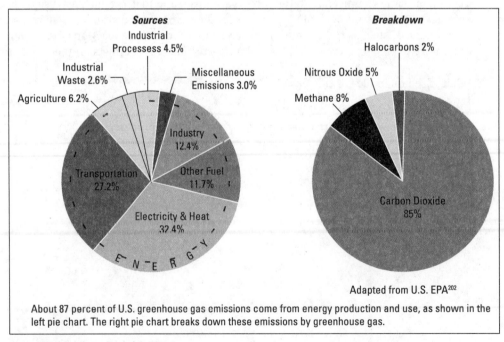

Sources

Industrial Processsess 4.5%
Industrial Waste 2.6%
Agriculture 6.2%
Miscellaneous Emissions 3.0%
Industry 12.4%
Transportation 27.2%
Other Fuel 11.7%
Electricity & Heat 32.4%
ENERGY

Breakdown

Halocarbons 2%
Nitrous Oxide 5%
Methane 8%
Carbon Dioxide 85%

Adapted from U.S. EPA[202]

About 87 percent of U.S. greenhouse gas emissions come from energy production and use, as shown in the left pie chart. The right pie chart breaks down these emissions by greenhouse gas.

Source: U.S. Global Change Research Program

41. What is the largest single source of greenhouse gas emissions in the United States?

(A) electricity and heat

(B) transportation

(C) industry

(D) agriculture

42. According to the Intergovernmental Panel of Climate Change, methane gas has 34 times the effect of carbon dioxide, pound for pound, over a 100-year period. Based on the chart, how does methane compare to carbon dioxide as an issue in climate change?

(A) It is a bigger problem than carbon dioxide.

(B) It is approximately equal to carbon dioxide as a problem.

(C) It is less of a problem than carbon dioxide.

(D) Cannot be determined from the table.

Questions 43 to 45 refer to the following diagram.

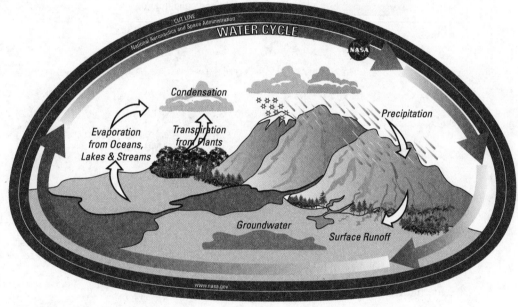

Source: NASA

43. What is the energy source that powers the water cycle?

(A) wind

(B) solar energy

(C) geothermal energy

(D) hydroelectric power

44. How does surface runoff of water eventually return to the atmosphere?

    (A) It collects in lakes and streams and evaporates.

    (B) It is absorbed into the ground.

    (C) It is used by plants to make food.

    (D) It falls as precipitation.

45. Based on the diagram of the water cycle, the purest water would be found in which of the following?

    (A) the rivers

    (B) the groundwater

    (C) the ocean

    (D) the mountain ice caps

Question 46 refers to the following diagram.

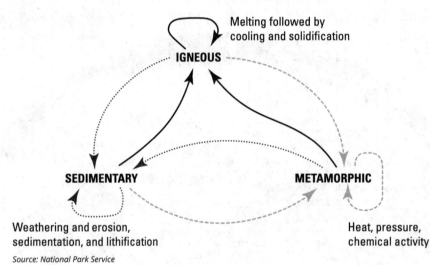

Source: National Park Service

46. According to the diagram, how is igneous rock created?

    (A) weathering and erosion

    (B) chemical activity

    (C) lithification

    (D) melting, cooling, and solidification

Questions 47 and 48 refer to the following diagram.

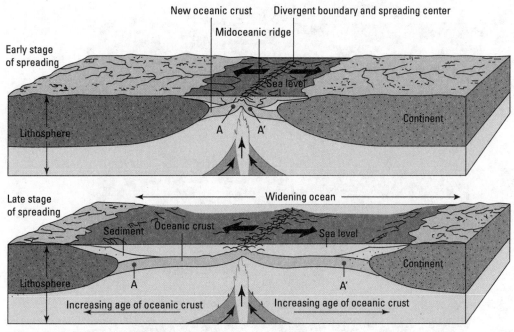

New oceanic crust   Divergent boundary and spreading center
Midoceanic ridge

Early stage
of spreading

Sea level

Lithosphere

Continent

A   A'

Late stage
of spreading

Widening ocean

Sediment   Oceanic crust   Sea level

Continent

Lithosphere

A   A'

Increasing age of oceanic crust   Increasing age of oceanic crust

Source: U.S. Geological Survey and National Park Service

47. The diagram shows an area where a "hot spot" in the lithosphere allows magma to work its way through the Earth's crust to the surface. Because this is taking place under the ocean, it has resulted in a ridge that runs most of the way from Antarctica to the arctic down the middle of the North and South Atlantic. Write the letters of the steps in order to describe the process.

(A) Repeated intrusions of magma widen the gaps, fill them in, and then create new gaps.

(B) The magma creates gaps in the sea floor, which are filled by fresh magma.

(C) The magma cools, forming ridges, which break open as new magma pushes its way up.

48. How have scientists been able to confirm that this spreading of the sea floor is actually happening and has gone on for millions of years?

(A) Core samples of the ocean sediments show evidence of increasing age the farther away the samples were taken from the mid–ocean ridge.

(B) Scientists have been able to use lasers to measure the distance between continental coasts.

(C) Satellite observation has shown continuing movement of the Earth's crust.

(D) Seismic monitors detect movement in the sea floor.

Questions 49 and 50 refer to the following diagram and excerpt from the U.S. Environmental Protection Agency website (www.epa.gov).

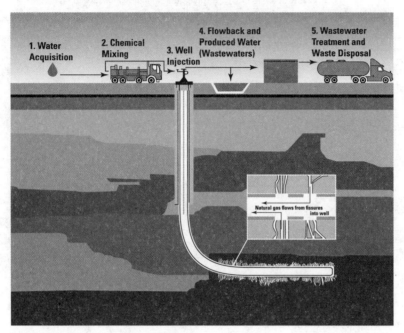

Source: U.S. Environmental Protection Agency

This diagram shows a process for obtaining a natural gas by a method called "fracking" or hydraulic fracturing. In the process, water mixed with chemicals is injected into a well under high pressure. The pressure fractures the earth around the well and allows natural gas to seep into the well. The natural gas, along with waste water, comes to the surface where it is separated, treated, and processed.

49. Which of the following is a way that fracking can contaminate groundwater?

(A) The process uses a large quantity of both surface and groundwater.

(B) The natural gas released in the process can accidentally enter aquifers.

(C) Methane can be released into the atmosphere.

(D) Fracking can trigger a seismic event.

50. What effect has the hydraulic fracturing process had on the availability of crude oil and natural gas in the United States?

(A) Fracking has resulted in a large increase in crude oil and natural gas production.

(B) Fracking has had very little effect to date.

(C) Fracking has had no effect to date.

(D) The effect cannot be determined from the information given.

Answers and Explanations

1. **C. thrust.** The thrust of the rocket engines must provide more energy than the weight of the rocket for it to leave the earth. The other forces have an effect, but the thrust lifts it off the ground.

2. **A. On airplanes, lift holds the airplane in the air; on some rockets, lift helps steer the rocket.** This information is stated directly in the passage. Therefore, the other choices are incorrect.

3. **hospitable.** As the passage states, the new territory may be less *hospitable* because of the natural conditions of the territory.

4. **B. warmwater fish move into the habitats of coldwater fish.** Only Choice (B) is supported by information in the passage. The other choices are either contradicted by the passage or cannot be concluded from it.

5. **A. Images of unusually thin women are pervasive in media.** Choice (A) provides another reason that would make women dissatisfied with their images, and so is correct.

6. **B. 15 percent.** The passage clearly states, "15 percent of American kids are overweight or obese."

7. **B. Most automobiles run on fossil fuel.** Most automobiles run on gasoline, which is a fossil fuel, the incomplete combustion of which forms black carbon. The other choices may be important from a traffic congestion or economic point of view but aren't mentioned in the passage.

8. **gases.** The passage states that water vapor, carbon dioxide, ozone, and several other gases are responsible for the reradiation of heat from the Earth's surface.

9. **B. they will allow scientists to develop research projects that will address the consequences of dramatic climate change.** More accurate forecasts will allow scientists to work on experiments to address the changes that may be coming. Choices (A) and (C) may be possibilities but aren't mentioned in the passage. Choice (D) is probably a good general idea but has nothing to do with the passage.

10. **global environmental change.** The passage states this as one of the results of this research.

11. **C. the ground is capable of sudden, dramatic movement.** Some of the examples given to support this choice are volcanic eruptions, earthquakes, and landslides. The other choices aren't supported by any content in the passage, although Choice (D) is probably a good idea.

12. **C. ensure better responses to natural hazards.** The other choices aren't mentioned in the passage.

13. **A. lift > weight; D. thrust > drag.** For a plane to take off, it must accelerate and rise. In order to do that, lift must be greater than weight and thrust must be greater than drag.

14. **C. to keep the astronauts alive.** Without a constant supply of air and water, the astronauts couldn't survive in space, and because carrying a sufficient supply of air and water would be impossible given weight restrictions, they must be recycled.

15. **State 1.** State 1 should be circled because it has the higher temperature. According to the diagram, the heat transfer, Q, would be from State 1 to State 2, indicated by the arrow labeled Q.

16. **C. increase the amount of whole grains and vegetables in school meals.** The passage states that new school meal standards for the National School Lunch Program aim to increase fruits, vegetables, whole grains, and low-fat dairy while reducing fats, sodium, and sugars.

17. **A. School personnel must receive training and support.** One of the provisions of the Act is training and technical assistance to help schools meet improved standards.

18. **weather.** *Weather* is current and is a short-term condition. *Climate* is the average weather over a period of time. So *weather* refers to the condition on any given day.

19. **B. The greenhouse gases can remain in the atmosphere for many years.** The passage states that the lifetime of greenhouse gases ranges from a few years to a few thousand years, and these gases are a danger to people's health. Choice (A) is a *truism* (a commonly heard true statement) and Choice (C) may be true but not in the context of the passage. Choice (D) may be a symptom of the increase in pollution but isn't the best choice.

20. **increase.** President Obama's initiative was aimed at increasing the participation of the two groups in science-related careers.

21. **C. Kepler.** The passage is very clear about Kepler's influence on Newton. Hawking and Einstein both lived after Newton's publication, and Aristotle differed from Newton's conclusion.

22. **A. Bhopal, India.** According to the passage, this incident resulted in over 2,000 fatalities, which is larger than the number of fatalities at the other locations. Note that this question is a good illustration of how reading the question first can help you save time. To answer this question, you do not need to read the entire passage. You only have to find the largest number.

23. **A. provides information.** The CRW provides information about hazardous materials so companies can use them safely. The other choices are incorrect according to the passage.

24. **extinction.** The passage states that climate change will cause species to become extinct at an accelerated rate.

25. **B. expulsion of microorganisms from within coral reefs.** Stressed coral reefs expel micro-organisms essential to their health. Choice (A) sounds correct if you skim the passage, but it's incorrect. Choice (C) is also wrong because there's no mention of the effect of sunlight on the reefs, and Choice (D) does not make sense.

26. **mismatches.** These mismatches can lead to dramatic changes in the lives of a species, which could lead to eventual extinction.

27. **information.** According to the passage, all the technologies mentioned provide information that may help scientists in assessing the potential for impending hazards.

28. **15.** The Big Bang theory says that this series of occurrences took place about 15 billion years ago.

29. **C. observations from two very different frames of reference.** As the passage states, Einstein's theory is relevant under these circumstances. The other choices are either incomplete or incorrect.

30. **information** (or **knowledge**). ESI provides information to the people and departments in charge of making decisions in the case of a disaster.

31. **B. a decline in the number of polar bears.** The passage explains the ripple effect of a food web: It can be reasonably inferred that a rise in Arctic temperature will cause a decline in the extent of sea ice, which will lead to fewer ice algae. Fewer ice algae will lead to fewer zooplankton, which will lead to fewer cod, which will lead to fewer seals. Without a sufficient diet of seals, polar bear populations will decline.

32. **hydrocarbons; compressed gases.** These two propellants are used because they don't deplete the ozone.

33. **B. they do not pollute the Earth.** Materials made from biomass tend to be made from recycled materials, making them less polluting.

34. **ocean.** Although you may not usually think of water as containing carbon, the ocean is the largest pool of carbon on Earth because the ocean isn't pure water.

35. **D. taking airplanes more frequently.** Only this action would increase people's carbon footprint. Walking more and driving your car less, lowering your thermostat during the cold weather, and not barbequing all would reduce people's carbon footprint.

36. **C. power plants.** Power plants may increase or decrease pollution depending on the process used, which tends to affect your carbon footprint positively or negatively.

37. **myelin sheath.** You can see in the diagram that the axon is surrounded by the myelin sheath, a protective coating.

38. **B. by providing for clean water.** NASA used a form of its water purification process to provide the village with clean water.

39. **D. Chemicals have many advantages, but also pose serious risks.** The passage gives the advantages and dangers of chemicals, so this choice sums up the passage best. The other choices are either advantages or disadvantages.

40. **B. It has a lower boiling point, so it evaporates sooner than diesel oil.** Naphtha is a component of crude oil. It has a lower boiling point than diesel fuel and thus evaporates at a lower temperature than diesel fuel. This allows it to be separated from the crude oil before diesel fuel.

41. **A. electricity and heat.** The production of energy and heating in the United States produces more greenhouse gases than any other single activity.

42. **D. Cannot be determined from the table.** The key term here is *by weight.* The pie chart doesn't indicate whether the emissions are by weight or by volume. Therefore, it's impossible to calculate a comparative value.

43. **B. solar energy.** The basic source that drives the water cycle on Earth is solar energy. Heat from the Sun causes water to evaporate. Heat from the Sun causes movement of air mass on Earth, thus creating winds and evaporation. Winds carry the evaporated moisture from place to place on Earth. Eventually, the evaporated moisture condenses, forming rain or other forms of precipitation.

44. **A. It collects in lakes and streams and evaporates.** Of the choices, only this one results in water returning to the atmosphere.

45. **D. the mountain ice caps.** The purest water would be found in the ice caps of the mountains because it would be the least contaminated. Water in surface runoff picks up minerals from the soil as it runs down the mountains and flows into groundwater, rivers, and oceans.

46. **D. melting, cooling, and solidification.** The diagram states right beside the word *igneous* that the process consists of melting, cooling, and solidification. The other choices refer to processes involved in creating or changing sedimentary or metamorphic rocks.

TIP

Don't be distracted by Choice (C). You don't need to know the word *lithification* to answer the question but might be attracted to this answer choice and choose it anyway kbecause it's a fancy, "five dollar" word. You can exclude this option because according to the diagram, lithification goes with sedimentary rock, and the question is about igneous rock.

47. **B, C, A.** Sea floor spreading is caused when magma forces its way into faults or thinner or softer areas of the Earth's crust. The thinnest areas are typically located under an ocean. As the magma forces its way to the sea floor, filling cracks in the crust, it forces the crust apart slightly and creates ridges. It cools, solidifies, and then is subjected to pressure from underneath yet again. More cracks are filled with magma, and in the process, ridges are created, the sea floor is forced further and further apart, and the gap is filled with magna. This question is a good example of a drag-and-drop item. On the actual test, you would drag the statements into boxes in the correct order.

48. **A. Core samples of the ocean sediments show evidence of increasing age the farther away the samples were taken from the mid-ocean ridge.** The question asks for evidence that this process has been going on for millions of years. The only choice that has any evidence over such a time period is Choice (A). The remaining choices offer evidence that the continents are continuing to move in the present time, and you can extrapolate from that information that this process has been going on for a long time. However, there's no proof, because you can't measure historical data in the present. Therefore, core samples of sediments on the ocean floor are the only useful evidence among the choices presented.

49. **B. The natural gas released in the process can accidentally enter aquifers.** According to the EPA, Choices (A), (C), and (D) are all concerns about fracking, but only Choice (B) is related to groundwater contamination.

50. **D. The effect cannot be determined from the information given.** The diagram shows how the process works but offers no information on the volume of natural gas or oil products produced by this process.

5

Counting All the Possible Solutions: The Mathematical Reasoning Test

Chapter **16**

Safety in Numbers: Facing the Mathematical Reasoning Test

Welcome to the dreaded Mathematical Reasoning test (or Math test for short). Although you may have done everything to avoid math in high school, you can't escape this test if you want to pass the GED. To tell you the truth, test takers really do have nightmares about this test, but don't worry! This chapter helps you prepare, not for having nightmares, but for taking the test successfully!

Most of the questions on the other GED test sections are about reading comprehension: You're given a passage and are expected to understand it well enough to answer the questions that follow. Although you can prepare for the other tests by doing a lot of reading and taking sample tests, you don't have to come in with a lot of knowledge or great skills in the test areas themselves.

The Mathematical Reasoning test is different. It tests your understanding of mathematical concepts and your ability to apply them to situations you may find in the real world. That means you have to spend time solving as many problems as you can and improving your math skills as much as possible before you take this test. This chapter gets you started by introducing the test format and the skills it covers and then providing some tips and tricks for tackling the test.

Looking at the Skills the Math Test Covers

To do well on the Math test, you need to have a general understanding of numbers, their relationships to one another, measurements, geometry, data analysis and statistics, probability, patterns, functions, and algebra. (If you don't know what I mean by these terms, check out the next section, "Understanding the Test Format.") In essence, to be successful on this test, you need to have the mathematical knowledge base that most high-school graduates have, and you need to know how to apply it to solve real-life problems.

REMEMBER

The GED Math test provides a formula sheet for you to use during the test. Keep in mind that you may not need all the formulas provided, and you will not need a formula for every question. Part of the fun of math is knowing which formula to use for which problems and figuring out when you don't need one at all. You may want to memorize some of the more common formulas to save time. But when you need a formula, you can look it up. You don't have to memorize them all! That makes preparing easier.

The Math test assesses the following four areas.

» **Basic math:** This area of math covers, you guessed it, the basics! Here's a breakdown of the two topics in this category:

- *Number operations* are the familiar actions you take in math problems and equations, such as addition, subtraction, multiplication, and division. You probably mastered these operations in grade school; now all you have to do is practice them.

- *Number sense* is the ability to understand numbers. You're expected to be able to recognize different kinds of numbers (such as fractions, decimals, percentages, and square roots), know their relative values, and know how to use them (which takes us back to number operations).

» **Geometry:** Here, you get a chance to play with mathematical shapes and manipulate them in your head — and on the GED's new onscreen whiteboard. You get to use the Pythagorean Theorem to do all sorts of interesting calculations, and you get to use measurements to do things like find the volume of ice cream in a cone or the amount of wall you need to cover with paint. If you relax, you can have fun with these questions and then maybe even use a lot of the knowledge in real life. This category breaks down into two topics:

- *Measurement* involves area, volume, time, and the distance from here to there. Measurement of time is a good thing to know when taking any test because you want to make sure you run out of questions before you run out of time!

- *Geometry* deals with relationships and properties of points, lines, angles, and shapes (such as squares, circles, and triangles). This branch of math requires you to draw, use, and understand diagrams.

» **Basic algebra:** Algebra is used to solve problems by using letters to represent unknown numbers, creating equations from the information given, and solving for the unknown numbers — thus, turning them into known numbers. If you ever said something like, "How much more does the $10 scarf cost than the $7.50 one?" you were really solving this equation: $\$7.50 + x = \$10.00$.

» **Graphs and functions:** Graphs and functions allow you to analyze data. You can learn how to analyze data in graphs, tables, and the coordinate plane.

- *Data analysis* is when you see a graph of the stock market's performance (or lack of performance), calculate or read about baseball statistics, or figure out how many miles per gallon your car gets.

- *Functions* are part of mathematics. They involve the concept that one number can be determined by its relationship with another. A dozen always consists of 12 units, for example. If you were buying two dozen eggs, you'd be buying $12 \times 2 = 24$ eggs.

- *The coordinate plane* graphically shows the location of points on the plane or a line and helps you to determine such things as the slope, or steepness, of a line.

Make sure you understand how to solve problems involving these four math concepts. (Check out Chapter 17 for practice problems, where I walk you through strategies on solving each type of math question you'll see on the GED test.)

If you already have a firm grasp on these topics, go ahead and take the practice tests in Chapters 25 and 33 and the included online-only practice test. However, if you need more preparation, read the following section and Chapter 17, and then take the mini–practice test in Chapter 18. You can check your answers and read the explanations when you're done. If you need to review certain concepts even more, be sure to do so. Then you can take the full practice tests in Chapters 25 and 33 and the included online full practice test.

Understanding the Test Format

Math isn't scary, and it has yet to appear as the villain in any major Hollywood horror films (at least that I know about). In fact, math can even be fun when you put your mind to it. In any case, the Mathematical Reasoning test assesses your abilities in math, so you have to be ready for it. This is the one GED test subject that requires a special way of thinking and understanding — improving your ability to think mathematically will make passing this test easier.

The Mathematical Reasoning test is 115 minutes long and consists of multiple-choice, drop-down, drag-and-drop, and fill-in-the-blank questions, but it doesn't have any type of essay question. You really have to be thankful for small mercies!

REMEMBER

To get ready for the Math test, you first have to relax and realize that math is your friend — perhaps not a lifetime friend, but a friend at least until you finish the test. You also need to consider that you've been using math all your life (and probably didn't even know it). When you tell a friend that you'll be over in 20 minutes, for example, you use math. When you see a sale sign in the store and mentally figure out whether you can afford the sale-priced item, you use math. When you complain about the poor mileage your car gets (and can prove it), you use math. You already know more math than you thought, and I show you the rest in this chapter.

Revealing Some Helpful Prep Pointers

As you prepare for the Mathematical Reasoning test, do the following:

>> **Master arithmetic fundamentals.** About half of the Math test depends on basic arithmetic (addition, subtraction, multiplication, division, decimals, and fractions). The better you know the fundamentals, the better you can do on the test.

>> **Understand how to solve problems.** To get a handle on how to solve basic mathematical problems, do a lot of practice problems before the test. The more problems you solve, the more natural solving problems will become. Borrow or buy as many math books as you can, or find some online, and use the questions in them to develop your problem-solving skills. (Be sure to get books that also provide the answers so you can check your work.) Check every answer immediately after you work the question. If you answered it incorrectly, figure out why.

If you still have trouble with that problem, ask someone to explain the solution to you. You can also look online for short instructional videos on solving various math problems. YouTube is a particularly good source.

>> **Understand the rules and formulas of math.** Textbooks are full of rules, theorems, formulas, and so on. Read over as many of these rules as you can, focusing on the formulas in the formula sheet. Try to explain the main ones to a friend. If you can explain a particular rule (the Pythagorean Theorem, for example) to a friend and they understand it, you've mastered the rule. If you can't explain it, ask someone to help you better understand the rule. If you're not sure where to start, begin by looking at the formula sheet provided on the GED test (check out an example in Chapter 25 or 33). Try to explain what each formula does and how it works.

>> **Sign up for a math prep class or a math study group.** The loneliest experience is sitting in a room staring at a wrong answer without anyone to ask why it's wrong. If you're having trouble with math, swallow your pride and enroll in a math class or study group where you can get some help and have access to someone who can answer your questions.

>> **Take practice tests and check your answers.** See Chapters 25 and 33 in this book for two full-length practice tests, as well as the included online full practice test. As you take the practice tests, answer every question and adhere to the time limits. If you run out of time, mark where you stopped, and then continue answering the remaining items. Be sure to check your answers. Going through the answer explanations can help you figure out which areas you need more work on. Even if you get an answer correct, reading the explanation can be helpful.

The only part of the test you can't duplicate is the feeling of sitting in the examination room just before you start the test. But the more practice tests you take, the more comfortable you'll be when the test day finally arrives.

>> **Get familiar with the onscreen calculator ahead of time.** You're probably familiar with calculators that add, subtract, multiply, and divide. The calculator used on the GED test is a scientific calculator, the TI-30XS MultiView calculator, which means it does all those operations and a whole lot more, such as calculating fractions, percentages, exponents, and problems involving parentheses. In the test, you access the on-screen calculator by clicking the calculator icon at the top of the screen. Usually, you will see a short film on how to use the calculator before taking the Math test. But for the best results, watch the film online as you prepare, at www.youtube.com/watch?v=VoLZLsRXuKE. It's well worth the time. You can also get hands-on practice with the onscreen calculator using the tutorial on the GED website at https://ged.com/practice-test/en/calculator/. Note that you won't be able to use the calculator on the first five questions of the test, and you won't necessarily use all the keys on the calculator to take the test.

TIP

If you take the GED in person at a testing center, you can use the onscreen calculator or buy and bring your own TI-30XS MultiView calculator with you. If using your own calculator is faster or easier for you, you might consider taking the Math test at a testing center.

>> **Learn to use the GED test's onscreen whiteboard.** Sometimes, when solving a math problem, it helps to write down the numbers or draw a diagram. You can use the onscreen whiteboard or the erasable tablet (at a test center only). Get familiar with the whiteboard on the GED Testing Service's website, ged.com. As with the calculator, if the online whiteboard is difficult for you to use, you might consider taking the test in person at a testing center so you can use the erasable tablet.

>> **Learn to use the GED test's Æ Symbol tool.** You use this tool to insert special symbols such as > (greater than) into answers to short-answer questions or the online whiteboard. You can see an explanation of the tool on the Mathematics Formula Sheet at the beginning of Chapter 25. You can access the Symbol tool by clicking the Æ icon on the test screen.

>> **Make sure you understand what you read.** What all the GED test sections have in common is that they all assess, in one way or another, reading comprehension; if you can't read and understand the items, you can't answer them. As I mention time and time again in this book, just reading isn't always enough — you have to stop and ask yourself questions about what you read. A good way to practice this skill is to find an old math textbook. Read through each problem and ask yourself these questions: What does this problem want me to find? How can I calculate it? What is the answer in general terms?

TIP

If you need more practice reading and understanding math problems, check out one of the following books (all published by Wiley):

>> *Basic Math and Pre-Algebra For Dummies* by Mark Zegarelli

>> *Basic Math and Pre-Algebra Workbook For Dummies* by Mark Zegarelli

>> *Math Word Problems For Dummies* by Mary Jane Sterling

IN THIS CHAPTER

» Checking out the different Math
  test question types and strategies

» Getting familiar with the
  calculator and formula sheet

» Doing a little math to help manage
  your time on the test

Chapter **17**

Mathematical Reasoning Question Types and Solving Strategies

The Mathematical Reasoning (Math) test is 115 minutes long. The first five questions are designed to be done without a calculator and must be attempted before you can continue. For the rest of the items, you may or may not need a calculator to complete them. If you see the calculator icon on the screen, you can use the onscreen calculator (or your own if you've brought one to the test center) to solve the problem. You will use a special calculator — more on that later! Getting a basic understanding of the question formats helps you avoid any surprises when you sit down to the take the test. The Math test presents you with questions from every area of math. It ranges from arithmetic calculations, which you have to do without a calculator, to basic algebra, and more. In this chapter, I explain the question formats you encounter on this test and offer advice on how to solve them with ease.

Perfecting Your Approach with Sample Questions

This may be your first experience taking a math test on a computer, but don't worry! The test is still about math — the same old math that has been around for several thousand years. Be careful of the format and pay particular attention to the math. The basic operations are still addition, subtraction, multiplication, and division, but you have to know how to use them to solve problems. Practice doesn't make perfect but will increase your chances of getting the correct answer to the question.

TIP

Because you're not penalized for guessing, if you don't know the answer to a question, go ahead and guess. Although you can't get a point for a blank answer, you can get a point for eliminating all but the most possible answer and marking it (if you get it right, of course).

Making the most of multiple-choice questions

Most of the questions on the Math test are a form of multiple-choice. You're given four possible answers, and all you have to do is choose the one best answer.

Answering basic multiple-choice questions

The multiple-choice questions on the Math test are pretty straightforward. You're given some information or a figure and asked to solve the problem based on that information. Here are a couple of examples.

EXAMPLE

Milton wanted to be taller than his father, who was 2 yards tall. Milton was 5 feet 10 inches tall even when he stretched. How much taller would Milton have to grow to be taller than his father by at least an inch?

(A) 1 inch

(B) 2 inches

(C) 3 inches

(D) 4 inches

The first thing you have to do with questions like this one is make sure all measurements are in the same format. Two yards equals 6 feet (1 yard = 3 feet). So Milton is 2 inches shorter than his father. The question asks how much he would have to grow to be at least 1 inch taller than his father. If he were to grow 3 inches, he would have reached that goal. Choice (C) is correct.

EXAMPLE

Samantha was a super salesperson and by far the best salesperson at Industrial Chemicals Inc. She was so good that she knew that she had to work for only three months not only to beat the sales records of her fellow salespeople but also to boost the total sales for the company substantially. The following chart appeared in the company's annual report. In which quarter do you think Samantha made all her sales?

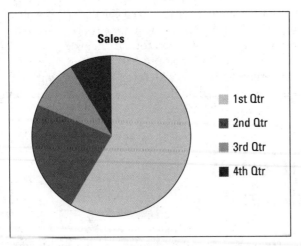

© John Wiley & Sons, Inc.

(A) 1st

(B) 2nd

(C) 3rd

(D) 4th

The graph shows that the majority of sales were made in the first quarter, and if Samantha's boasts were correct, she would have made the majority of those sales. In the other nine months of the year, without her sales, overall sales slipped considerably. In a graph such as this one, the area of the segment of the circle represents the data. Thus, the answer is Choice (A).

Extracting the information you need

Some of the questions on the Math test may have extra information that you don't need; in those cases, just ignore it. Of course, you have to make sure that the information you think is extra really is. For example, if the last question in the previous section said that Irving was the poorest salesperson the company had ever employed, that information really would be extra and would make no difference to the rest of the question.

The people who write the test questions include extra information for a reason: extra information can make guessing more difficult and separate the test-takers who are paying attention from those who aren't. Sometimes, extra information is put in to make the question a bit more realistic: in real life, you figure out the relevant information to solve problems all the time. You don't want to disregard anything essential to solving the problem.

While reading the following question, try to visualize the situation and consider where the plot takes an extreme turn. This is usually the place where the information turns from important to irrelevant or vice versa.

EXAMPLE

Kenny, Dharma, and Sophie went out for an early lunch. The wall of their favorite burger place had the following menu:

Item	Calories (kcal)	Fat (g)	Cost ($)
Hamburger	780	44	4.09
Cheeseburger	793	56	4.09
Vegetable Wrap	450	25	3.69
French Fries	360	17	1.59
Blueberry Muffin	450	15	2.10
Chocolate Chip Cookies	160	7	1.00
Soda	220	0	1.49

Their total bill came to $24.31, and after a long discussion, they decided to tip the server 15%. What was the server's tip?

(A) $2.92

(B) $3.00

(C) $3.65

(D) $4.86

The menu may be interesting, but it's irrelevant for answering this question. The relevant information is the part about the server's tip. The only important information is the amount of the bill and the percentage of the tip. So you multiply the total bill by 15% to get a tip of $24.31 \times 0.15 = \$3.65$, rounded to the nearest penny. Thus, Choice (C) is the answer.

In other items, you may have to find and extract the details you need from the information and the item and combine them. Take a look at this example.

EXAMPLE

A hamburger meal combo at the restaurant includes French fries and a soda for $6.49. If you order before 12 p.m. noon, you get a free cookie. How much can Dharma save from the menu prices by ordering the special, not counting tax or tip, at 11:45 a.m.?

(A) $0.68

(B) $1.00

(C) $1.68

(D) $2.68

In this item, you have to use information from the item to figure out what's included in the combo when ordered before noon (hamburger, French fries, soda, and a free cookie). Next, you use the menu to determine the total cost of items and then subtract the cost of the special: $4.09 + 1.59 + 1.49 + 1.00 - 6.49 = \$1.68$. Thus, Choice (C) is the answer.

Providing the answer in fill-in-the-blank items

Fill-in-the-blank items require that you fill in the answer without the benefit of four answer choices to choose from. On the Math test, these questions will always involve some calculation, and the answer is always a number. I walk you through answering two fill-in-the-blank questions in this section.

EXAMPLE

Demitri wanted to buy a new LCD television. His old one had a diagonal measurement of 32 inches, but he wanted to buy a 50-inch diagonal television. The new one would be [   ] inches larger, measured diagonally. You may use numbers, a decimal point (.), and/or a negative sign (−) in your answer.

To answer this question, you have to find the difference between the two televisions. The new one would be $50 - 32 = 18$ inches larger, measured diagonally.

EXAMPLE

Carol found a part-time job to augment her scholarship. She was paid $13.45 an hour and was promised a 15% raise after three months. Business had been very poor during that period, and the owner of the business called Carol in to explain that he could afford only an 11% raise but would reassess the raise in the next quarter, depending on how business was. With this raise, Carol's new hourly rate would be [   ]. You may use numbers, a decimal point (.), and/or a negative sign (−) in your answer.

To calculate the amount of an 11% raise, multiply by 111% ($100\% + 11\% = 111\%$, or 1.11 expressed as a decimal). Carol's new salary would be calculated at the rate of $13.45 times 111%, or $13.45 \times 1.11 = \$14.93$ (rounded to the nearest penny).

Answering other special item types

Some special items will ask you to select an answer from a drop-down menu or drag numbers or words into the correct position using your cursor and mouse. You can see how these questions on the GED test in Chapter 2. You can try your hand on these items in the practice questions in Chapter 18, the two full length practice tests in Chapters 25 and 33, and the included full-length online practice test.

Occasionally, items on the GED will ask you to use the cursor to indicate a point on a table or graph. This item format, called hot-spot, is seldom tested, and happens mostly with items that use the coordinate plane. We mention it here "just in case." Look at the sample item:

EXAMPLE

Mark the point (1,1) on the coordinate plane.

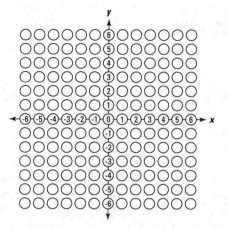

© John Wiley & Sons, Inc.

In this case, use the mouse to place the cursor over the correct point, and click.

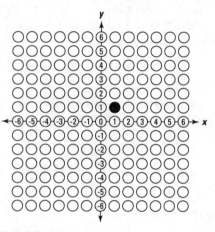

© John Wiley & Sons, Inc.

Using the Mathematical Reasoning Test's Special Features

During the Mathematical Reasoning test, you can use the on-screen (or your own) TI-30XS MultiView calculator for all but the first five questions. Before you start celebrating, remember that the calculator is an instrument that makes calculations easier. It doesn't solve problems or perform other miracles. You still have to solve the problems, using the computer between your ears.

The test also has a formula sheet. This feature also isn't a miracle that can work out problems for you. It's just a memory aid if you don't remember the formulas. And as a special treat, the Math test also provides symbols for you to use in the fill-in-the-blank items as needed. I explore all these features in the following sections. You can find a tutorial on these special features on the GED website, at `https://app.ged.com/portal/tips`.

REMEMBER

One of the most valuable tools for preparing for the GED is an account at ged.com. Besides being the place where you sign up to take the test, this website offers tools and study aids. You have to be logged into your account to access many of the special features I reference in this chapter.

Solving questions with and without a calculator

For all but the first five items in the Math test, you can use a calculator. You have to finish the first five items before you go on to questions that use the calculator. To pull up the calculator on the computerized GED Math test, click the calculator icon. A calculator — a Texas Instruments TI-30XS MultiView calculator to be exact — appears onscreen.

It's a good idea to get familiar with the calculator before taking the GED test. You can either use the one on the GED Testing Service website for practice or find an identical hand-held one. (The computer version of the calculator operates just like the hand-held device.) Then make sure you know how to solve the various types of mathematical problems, and only depend on the calculator to do mechanical operations more quickly and easily.

TIP

Keep the calculator in mind when you decide where to take the Math test. If you test at home, you can only use the on-screen calculator. At a testing center, you can bring your own TI-30XS MultiView calculator. If using a handheld calculator is easier for you, consider taking the Math test at a testing center, even if it is less convenient for you in other ways. A few points on the Math test can make a big difference! And don't worry about the other tests — you can take any of the tests online or at a test center — it's your choice!

Often, solving a problem without a calculator is faster than using a calculator, especially with multiple-choice questions where you have four answer choices to choose from. And the more questions you practice in your head, the easier it will be. Here are some ways to practice solving problems in your head (without a calculator):

>> When you go shopping, add up the prices as you put items in your cart. Check your total at the cash register.

>> Calculate discounts off items you see or buy when you shop.

>> Be the first at your table in a restaurant to figure out the tip. And for bonus practice, figure out different tip percentages on your bill, such as 15, 18, and 20 percent tips.

TIP

For multiple-choice questions, sometimes estimating the answer to a question is easier and faster. For example, 4.2×8.9 is almost 4×9, which equals 36. If only one answer choice is close to 36, that choice is probably correct. If you see that two or more answer choices are close to 36, however, you need to spend time calculating the exact answer.

Refreshing your memory with the formula sheet

The GED Math test includes a formula sheet with a list of formulas you may need for the test. You simply click on the formula icon to make the page of formulas appear. Unfortunately, no genie will appear to tell you which formula to use. Figuring out which formula you need is your job.

To get familiar with the formulas you may need on the GED test, study the formulas in this book (you can find a list of formulas in the practice tests in Chapters 25 and 33), and make sure you know their purpose. Then make sure you understand what kind of problem you can use each formula for. For example, if you have a formula for the volume of a rectangular cube and the question asks you how many cubic feet of water a swimming pool contains, you know this formula will enable you to work out the answer. If the question asks you how many tiles it'd take to go around the rim of the pool, you need another formula.

Inserting special symbols

When answering fill-in-the-blank items, you sometimes need to insert special symbols. These formulas are mainly math symbols, such as add or subtract, greater than or less than, equals, pi (π), and so on. You can see all the symbols at the beginning of Practice Test 1. To make a symbol appear in the fill-in-the-blank box on the test, click the symbols icon at the top of the screen (Æ), and then click the symbol you want to include in the box. You can also use the symbols in the online whiteboard. You can find a tutorial on these special features on the GED website, at https://app.ged.com/portal/tips.

Managing Your Time for the Math Test

Try not to be intimidated by the word *math* or the subject as a whole. A math teacher once said that mathematicians are lazy people — they always use the easiest way to find the right answer. I don't want to insult or irritate any mathematicians by calling them lazy, but finding the easiest way to solve a problem is usually the right way. If your way is too long and complicated, it's probably not right.

The Mathematical Reasoning test allows you 115 minutes to complete 50 questions. That's less than 1 and ½ minutes per question, so you have to keep moving. You must answer the first five items without using the calculator, and then the rest follow after you have answered these five questions.

To help you manage your time for the Math test, check out the following suggestions (refer to Chapters 3 for some general time-management tips):

REMEMBER

>> **Stay on schedule.** Being able to manage your time is the most important indicator of success on the Math test. If you can keep to your schedule of less than 1-1/2 minutes per question, you'll have enough time to go over your answers and make any changes necessary after you finish solving all the questions. If a question is hard for you or involves a lot of time-consuming calculations, click the flag feature in the test. That will mark the item for you to return to later, if you have time. Spending all your time trying to solve one problem at the expense of the others isn't a good idea.

With such a tight schedule for taking the Math test, you have no time to panic. Aside from the fact that panicking distracts you from your overall goal, it also takes time — and you have very little time to spare. So relax and just do your best — save the panicking for another day.

>> **Know when to move ahead.** If you don't see what's being asked by a question within a few seconds, reread the question and try again. If it still isn't clear, skip the question or use the Flag feature and go on to the next question. Later you can use the Review screen to return to these questions — even only to guess!

>> **Keep an eye on the time.** The timer on the computer screen is your only time-management tool. You're not allowed to bring any electronics into the testing area except your calculator, and then only if you test at a testing center.

Chapter **18**

Practicing Sample Mathematical Reasoning Problems

The best way to get ready for the Mathematical Reasoning (Math) test is to practice. The questions on this test evaluate your skills in a wide variety of areas, so check out the sample questions in this chapter to help you prepare for all of them. At the end of this chapter, you find detailed answer explanations where you can check your answers.

Record your answers either directly in this book or on a sheet of paper, if you think you might want to try these practice questions again at a later date. The Mathematical Reasoning test doesn't include an Extended Response item, so there's no need for extra sheets of lined paper. (Writing an essay about quadratic equations or the beauty of exponents — now *that* would be painful!) Get out a couple pieces of scratch paper, though, to calculate, write down formulas, or draw simple sketches to help you visualize a question. And remember to use your calculator when you think it can help you work more quickly and accurately. For these questions, you can use any calculator, including the one on your phone, though using a real TI-30XS MultiView calculator is the best preparation for the real test.

Remember, this is just preliminary practice. I want you to get used to answering different types of Mathematical Reasoning questions. Use the complete practice tests in Chapters 25 and 33 and online to time your work and replicate the real test-taking experience.

Mathematical Reasoning Practice Questions

The following math practice questions test your knowledge of mathematical operations and reading skills in math. Read the questions carefully, making sure you understand what's being asked. You may have to convert some units of measurement to another, but in all cases, they'll make sense. For example, if you see the measurement for a wall is 120-something high, read the problem carefully because the wall was probably measured in inches and not feet.

1. Vlad is shopping for new shirts because all the stores are having end-of-season sales. Sam's Shirts offers Vlad 20% off all his purchases, while Harry's Haberdashery has a special sale offering five shirts for the price of four. Tim & Tim's Clothes' offers buy four, get one free. The regular price for shirts is the same at all three stores. Vlad decides to get 5 shirts. Which is the better deal?

   (A) Tim & Tim's Clothes

   (B) Sam's Shirts

   (C) Harry's Haberdashery

   (D) The are all the same.

2. Olga designed a company logo, consisting of an equilateral triangle in a circle. She designed the logo with one vertex of the triangle pointing northeast. The client said she liked the design but preferred that the vertex of the triangle point due south. What rotation would Olga have to perform to satisfy her client?

   (A) 90 degrees to the right

   (B) 110 degrees to the right

   (C) 135 degrees to the left

   (D) 135 degrees to the right

3. Solve the following equation for x:

   $x = 2y + 6z - y^2$, if $y = 6$ and $z = 2$

   (A) 12

   (B) 11

   (C) −11

   (D) −12

Question 4 refers to the following table of prices for new vacuum cleaners.

Make and Model	Price
Hopper Model A1	$249.99
Vacuous Vacuum Company Model ZZ3	$679.99
Clean-R-Up Special Series	$179.00
Electrified Home Upright	$749.99
Super Suction 101	$568.99

4. Nate is looking for a new vacuum cleaner for his apartment. He has been told by his best friend that spending around the average price will get him an adequate unit. Which vacuum cleaner is closest to the average price for vacuum cleaners? ☐

5. Evaluate the following formula:

$N = a + c - 2ac$, if $a = 5$ and $c = 3$

(A) -22

(B) 22

(C) 28

(D) 38

6. Solve the following equation for x.

$3x + 12 = 24$

(A) 3

(B) 4

(C) 5

(D) 12

7. Rachel and Ronda were planning for their first apartment, and they decided to split the required shopping tasks. Rachel was responsible for finding out how much it would cost to carpet their living room, and Ronda was responsible for finding out how much it would cost to paint the bedroom walls. What formula would each of them need to use to get an answer that would let them figure out the price for each job?

(A) $P = 2(l + w)$

(B) $A = l \times w$

(C) $V = l \times w \times d$

(D) $A = \pi r^2$

8. Lillian is drawing a scale diagram of her apartment to take with her while shopping for rugs. If she has taken all the measurements in the apartment, what mathematical relationship would she use to draw the scale drawing?

(A) decimals

(B) exponents

(C) ratios

(D) addition

9. Sylvia couldn't fall asleep one night and got to wondering how much water her bedroom would hold if she filled it to the ceiling. She had previously measured all the walls and knew all the measurements, including length, width, and height. She should use _____ to calculate how many cubic feet of water would be needed to fill the room.

(A) addition

(B) subtraction

(C) multiplication

(D) division

10. Alvin is drawing a diagram of his room. He has drawn the line representing the floor and is ready to draw the line representing the wall. This line would be _____ to the line representing the floor.

(A) congruent

(B) parallel

(C) similar

(D) perpendicular

11. Aaron wants to paint the floor of his apartment. His living room/dining room is 19 feet by 16 feet, his bedroom is 12 feet by 14 feet, and his hallways are 6 feet by 8 feet. Bowing to pressure from his friends, he has decided not to paint the floor of the kitchen or the bathroom. How many square feet of floor must he paint?

(A) 520

(B) 304

(C) 250

(D) 216

Question 12 refers to the following table.

Week	Calories Consumed Per Week	Weight (Pounds)	Height (Feet/Inches)
1	12,250	125	5 ft. 1.5 in.
2	15,375	128	5 ft. 1.5 in.
3	13,485	128	5 ft. 1.5 in.
4	16,580	130	5 ft. 1.5 in.
5	15,285	129	5 ft. 1.5 in.

12. Alan kept track of his caloric intake, his weight, and his height for a period of five weeks. What conclusion can you draw from his observations?

(A) Eating a lot makes you taller.

(B) Eating more calories will make you gain weight.

(C) Gaining weight will make you taller.

(D) There's no correlation between the data presented.

13. On Monday, Mary walked 12 blocks. On Tuesday, she walked 10 blocks, and on Wednesday, she walked 14 blocks. If she wants to walk more than her average trip for those three days on Thursday, at least how many blocks must she walk?

(A) 9

(B) 10

(C) 11

(D) 13

14. Hassan has developed a new trick to play on his classmates. He asks them to write down their ages and multiply by 4, divide by 2, then subtract 6, and, finally, add 8. When they tell him the resulting number, Hassan can always tell them their age. If one of his friends tells Hassan the resultant number is 52, how old is he?

(A) 24

(B) 25

(C) 33

(D) 52

Question 15 refers to the following table.

a	b	F
1	2	–16
2	1	–3
3	2	–18
2	3	–35
3	4	x

15. Herman developed the following function to amuse himself: $F = 2a + 3b^2 - 2ab$. He kept track of his results in this table.

Using Herman's function, what is the value of x?

(A) –82

(B) 30

(C) 53

(D) 88

16. Calvin and Kelvin, carpenters extraordinaire, are building an attic staircase for their client, Ms. Coleman. The stairway is to bridge a space 10 feet high, and the distance from the front of the bottom step to the back of the top step is 14 feet. What is the slope of the attic staircase to 2 decimal places?

(A) 0.69

(B) 0.70

(C) 0.71

(D) 0.72

Questions 17 and 18 refer to the following information.

April is considering two apartments. They are of equal size except for the bedrooms. Bedroom A is 19 feet by 14 feet, and bedroom B is 17 feet by 16 feet.

17. How many square feet larger is the larger bedroom?

(A) 8

(B) 7

(C) 6

(D) 5

18. April wants an area rug for the larger bedroom that would cover the floor, leaving a space 1 foot from each wall. If the rug had a 1-inch fringe all the way around it, how many feet long would the fringe be?

(A) 85

(B) 58

(C) 55

(D) 29

19. The school nurse made this table, which shows the results he got from asking several students about their heights and birth months.

Month of Birth	Height
March	5 ft. 4 in.
June	5 ft. 6 in.
March	5 ft. 1 in.
January	5 ft. 8 in.
August	5 ft. 5 in.
January	5 ft. 6 in.

In which month was the shortest person born?

(A) January

(B) March

(C) June

(D) August

20. Order these numbers from smallest (1) to largest (4).

$\sqrt{4}$ 0.75   1/3 1^3

21. Susie is shopping for a few groceries. She buys a loaf of bread for $1.29 and a half gallon of milk on sale for $1.47. She sees her favorite cheese on sale for $2.07. If she has $5.00 in her purse, she **can / cannot** (circle one) buy the cheese if there is no tax on food.

Question 22 refers to the following table.

Annual Sales of the Wonderful World of Widgets

Year	Annual Sales (In Million Units)
2021	43
2020	29
2019	72
2018	70
2017	71

22. The general manager of the Wonderful World of Widgets wants to present these figures in a visual, easily understood way to the board of directors to help them understand the effect that the downturn in the economy in 2020 had on the sales of widgets. What would be the best way to present the figures?

(A) a graph

(B) a series of tables

(C) verbal descriptions

(D) a movie of how widgets are used in America

23. Mark the points $(3,1)$, $(-4,-3)$, and $(-5,5)$ on the graph to draw a geometric figure and identify the figure _____.

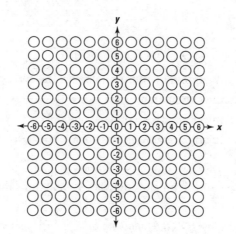

24. Georgio leaned a 25-foot ladder on the side of his house. The bottom of the ladder is 7 feet from the wall. Therefore, the top of the ladder is touching a point _____ feet above the ground. You may use numbers, a decimal point (.), and/or a negative sign (−) in your answer.

25. Where are all the points with an x-coordinate of -4 located on a graph?

(A) 4 units above the x-axis

(B) 4 units below the x-axis

(C) 4 units to the right of the y-axis

(D) 4 units to the left of the y-axis

26. In a recent 10-year period, the average age of Americans claiming Social Security went up from 63.6 to 64.7 for men, and from 63.6 to 64.6 for women. How much was the age increase for women claiming Social Security over that period?

(A) 0 years

(B) 0.1 year

(C) 1 year

(D) 1.1 years

27. The students in a math class are looking at the equation $A = l \times w$. The teacher asks what result doubling the length (l) would have on the area (A). What answer is correct?

   (A) makes it two times larger

   (B) makes it three times larger

   (C) makes it four times larger

   (D) makes it five times larger

28. Herman is going to paint a wall that is 20 feet long and 8 feet high. If all of it is to be covered with one coat of primer, how many square feet of wall have to be covered with primer?

   (A) 28

   (B) 56

   (C) 160

   (D) 610

29. Where on a graph would the point $(-4, -4)$ be?

   (A) four units to the right and four units below the corresponding axis

   (B) four units to the left and four units below the corresponding axis

   (C) four units to the left and four units above the corresponding axis

   (D) four units to the right and four units above the corresponding axis

30. Roger and Ekua went shopping together. Ekua spent twice as much for clothing as Roger did. If their total expenditure for clothing was $90.00, how much did Roger spend for clothing? $

   [   ]

   Questions 31 and 32 refer to the following table, which shows the median age of marriage for men and women in the United States over several years.

Year	Men	Women
2018	29.8	27.8
2017	29.5	27.4
2016	29.5	27.4
2015	29.2	27.1
2014	29.3	27.0

31. Althea saw this table in her social studies book. According to the table, which of these statements is a logical conclusion?

   (A) Women tend to get married later in life than men.

   (B) Men tend to get married earlier in life than women.

   (C) Men and women are getting married later in life as time goes by.

   (D) Fewer people are getting married now than in the past.

32. In which year did the median age of marriage for men go down over the previous year?

(A) 2014

(B) 2015

(C) 2016

(D) 2018

33. The reading on the illustrated meter is [   ] .

© John Wiley & Sons, Inc.

Question 34 refers to the following table, which shows Sheila's marks in her final year of high school.

Subject	Grade (%)
Literature	94
Mathematics	88
Physical Education	86
Science	92
Spanish	90

34. The result on Sheila's average grade after a 6-point drop in her Spanish grade would be [   ] .

35. Barry earns $1,730 per month after taxes. Each month, he spends $900 for rent and $600 for living expenses like food and utilities. After all his expenses are paid, he has $[____] left over to buy luxuries and spend on entertainment.

Questions 36 and 37 refer to the following table.

Car Manufacturer	Sales — July 2021 (In Thousands)	Sales — July 2020 (In Thousands)	% Change
Commonwealth	90	105	–14
Frisky	175	147	+19
Goodenough	236	304	–22
Horsesgalore	99	64	+55
Silkyride	24	16	+50

36. From the table, which car manufacturer showed the greatest percentage increase in sales?

(A) Commonwealth

(B) Frisky

(C) Goodenough

(D) Horsesgalore

37. Which car manufacturer had the largest increase in the number of cars sold?

(A) Frisky

(B) Goodenough

(C) Horsesgalore

(D) Silkyride

Question 38 refers to the following table.

Person	Flavor Preference			
	Chocolate	Vanilla	Strawberry	Rocky Road
Donalda's mother	Yes	Yes	Yes	No
Donalda's father	No	No	Yes	No
Donalda's brother	No	No	No	Yes
Donalda's sister	Yes	Yes	Yes	No

38. Donalda loves all flavors of ice cream, but her other family members are fussier than she is. She wants to buy some ice cream for a family barbecue. She wrote down every family member's preferences in this table. She wants to buy only two flavors. Which two flavors will satisfy everyone in her family?

(A) Chocolate and vanilla

(B) Chocolate and strawberry

(C) Vanilla and rocky road

(D) Strawberry and rocky road

Answers and Explanations

1. **D. The are all the same.** In this case, all the offers are for 20% off. They are just expressed differently. "Five shirts for the price of four" and "buy four and get one free" are the same deal expressed differently. Consider buying four shirts for $10 each and getting one more free. Five shirts would cost $40, or an average price of $8 each, which is 20% off the regular price ($10). Keep in mind that the same prices are often stated in different ways.

2. **D. 135 degrees to the right.** If you visualize the equilateral triangle drawn within the circle with one vertex pointing northeast, you can see that the vertex is 45 degrees above the horizontal, which is due east. Due south would be at the halfway point of the circle or at 180 degrees. Simply subtract 45 degrees (the initial position) from 180 degrees (the final position) to discover that the vertex has traveled 135 degrees to the right. Another way to answer this question is with addition. To go from due east to due south requires a rotation of 90 degrees to the right. The entire rotation would consist of 45 degrees + 90 degrees = 135 degrees to the right. If reading about this problem is confusing, draw it. Diagrams often make problems easier to visualize.

3. **D. –12.** You can solve this equation by substituting 6 for y and 2 for z, which produces this equation: $2(6) + 6(2) - 6^2 = -12$.

4. **Super Suction 101.** You can calculate the average price by adding all the prices and dividing the sum by the number of prices. To simplify the calculations, you can round to the nearest dollar. $($250 + $680 + $179 + $750 + 569)/5 = 485.60. The machine that comes closest is the Super Suction 101 because the difference between the price of the Super Suction 101 and the average price is $569 - $486 = 83. The difference between the price of the Hopper Model A1 and the average price is $486 - $250 = 236, leaving the Super Suction 101 the clear selection, using the friend's criteria.

   TIP

   Note that this question is a clear example of the advantage of using rounding to make a question fast and easy to solve. That can help you keep moving from item to item on test day!

5. **A. –22.** Only this result follows the correct order of operations.

   TIP

   Always remember to follow the correct order of operations, which is Parentheses, Exponents, Multiplication and Division, and Addition and Subtraction. You always work from left to right, and always work multiplication and division together and addition and subtraction together. A good way to remember is with the letters PEMDAS.

6. **B. 4.** If $3x + 12 = 24$, you can subtract 12 from both sides so that $3x = 24 - 12$, or $3x = 12$; then divide both sides by 3 to find x, or $x = 4$. Again, remember the cardinal rule of equations: Whatever you do to one side, you must do to the other.

   REMEMBER

   As you prepare for the Mathematical Reasoning section of the GED test, you definitely want to remember this rule about equations: Whatever you do to one side of the equation, you must do to the other side.

7. **B. $A = l \times w$.** In each case, Rachel and Ronda have to calculate the area of the space they're dealing with to get a price for the carpet and the paint. The formula for area is $A = l \times w$.

8. **C. ratios.** A scale drawing involves representing one dimension with a smaller one, while keeping the shape of the room the same. Lillian may have decided to represent 1 foot in real life by 1 inch on her drawing (a ratio of 1 foot to 1 inch), resulting in a 12-foot wall being represented by a 12-inch line. None of the other three choices are mathematical relationships, and would therefore have to be excluded immediately.

9. **C. multiplication.** The formula to calculate the volume of a room is to multiply the length by the width by the height. (On the GED test, the formula for calculating volume is listed on the formula sheet.)

10. **D. perpendicular.** The line is perpendicular because walls are perpendicular to floors (if they weren't perpendicular, the room would probably collapse).

11. **A. 520.** To find the total area, you must multiply the length by the width for each area. The area of the living room/dining room is $19 \times 16 = 304$ square feet, the area of the bedroom is $12 \times 14 = 168$ square feet, and the area of the hallway is $6 \times 8 = 48$ square feet. The total area is the sum of the room areas or $304 + 168 + 48 = 520$ square feet.

12. **B. Eating more calories will make you gain weight.** The more Alan ate, the heavier he became (which represents a possible causal relationship). The table provides no basis for the other answers.

    If two values change in tune with each other, they have a *correlating* relationship. For example, there's a positive correlation between height and age during the teenage years. In other words, you get taller as you get older. If one event leads to another or causes another, the events form a *causal* relationship. For example, eating all the red jellybeans alters the percentage of orange jellybeans in a mixture of equal numbers of different colors because eating a red jellybean removes it from the pool of jellybeans. As a result, the percentage of orange jellybeans (and of every other remaining color) increases.

13. **D. 13.** Mary's average trip for those three days was $(12 + 10 + 14) / 3 = 36 / 3 = 12$ blocks. To beat her average, she has to walk 13 blocks on Thursday. If she walks 12 blocks, she will equal (not beat) her average trip. All the other answers are less than her average.

14. **B. 25.** Hassan knows that multiplication and division are opposite operations, which means that multiplying by 4 and dividing by 2 produces a number twice the original. Addition and subtraction are opposites, too, so subtracting 6 and adding 8 results in a number 2 larger than the original. If the number Hassan's friend tells him is 52, Hassan simply has to subtract 2 from the resultant number (52) and divide by 2, giving him an answer of 25. Or Hassan could start with 52 and then work backward (first subtracting 8, then adding 6, and so on) through the directions to arrive at the correct answer.

15. **B. 30.** Using Herman's function, $x = 2(3) + 3(4)(4) - 2(3)(4) = 6 + 48 - 24 = 30$.

16. **C. 0.71.** To calculate the slope, you have to divide the rise by the run. That is $\frac{10}{14} = 0.7142857$, or 0.71 to 2 decimal places.

TIP

The *slope* of a line is rise over run. Thus, the slope of a stairway is equal to the distance above the floor of the last step over the distance from the front of the first step to the back of the top step.

17. **C. 6.** The area of bedroom A is $19 \times 14 = 266$ square feet. The area of bedroom B is $17 \times 16 = 272$ square feet. Bedroom B is larger by $272 - 266 = 6$ square feet.

18. **B. 58.** The measure of the fringe is the perimeter of the rug. Because the rug would cover the floor 1 foot in from each wall, the length of the rug would be $17 - 2 = 15$ feet, and the width would be $16 - 2 = 14$ feet. The reason you have to subtract 2 from each measurement is that the rug would be 1 foot from each wall, resulting in a rug that was 2 feet shorter than the room in each dimension. Perimeter $= 2(l + w)$, where l is the length and w is the width, so the perimeter of the rug is $2(15 + 14) = 2(29) = 58$ feet.

19. **B. March.** The shortest person in the survey is 5 ft. 1 in. tall. That person was born in March.

20. **The** correct order is (1) 1/3, (2) 0.75, (3) 1³, and (4) $\sqrt{4}$. The largest number is $\sqrt{4}$, which is equal to 2. The exponent 1³ is equal to 1 ($1 \times 1 \times 1 = 1$). And the fraction 1/3 (0.33) is smaller than 0.75.

21. **can.** The simplest way to solve this problem is to add the cost of the bread and milk to get $2.76, and then add the price of the cheese ($2.07) to get a total of $4.83, which is less than $5.00. You can also estimate the result by rounding and adding $1.30 and $1.50 to get $2.80, and then adding $2.10 for the cheese for a total of $4.90, which is less than $5.00. Using rounding can help you answer some questions quickly and move on to the next ones.

22. **A. a graph.** A graph is a visual representation of data; it's easily understood and can be used to compare data visually. You could use some of the other choices to represent the data, but they would all be more complex than a graph.

23. **Because** there are only three points on the graph, the figure is a triangle.

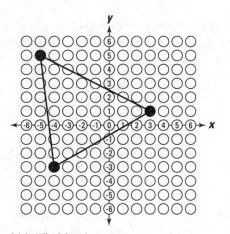

© John Wiley & Sons, Inc.

TIP

Questions where you mark your answer on the quadrant plane come up from time to time on the GED. Good mousing skills are essential to answering these questions correctly.

24. **24.** You can represent the ladder leaning against a house as a right triangle with an hypotenuse of 25 feet and a base of 7 feet. You can use the Pythagorean Theorem to solve this problem. The Pythagorean Theorem states that $a^2 + b^2 = c^2$, where c is the measure of the hyoptenuse. You can set up the problem as $25^2 = 7^2 + \text{height}^2$, and solve for the height. You can simplify to $625 - 49 = \text{height}^2$. The answer is 24 = height. (The square root of 576 is 24.)

REMEMBER

Pythagoras, a Greek mathematician, is credited with the discovery that the square of the hypotenuse of a right-angled triangle is equal to the sum of the squares of the other two sides. The *hypotenuse* is the side opposite the right angle. You'll find the Pythagorean Theorem on the formula sheet you get with your test.

25. **D. 4 units to the left of the** *y*-axis. All points with *x*-coordinates that are negative are located to the left of the *y*-axis (the vertical axis). Therefore, if a point has an *x*-coordinate of −4, it's located on a line 4 units to the left of the *y*-axis.

26. **C. 1 year.** The average age for women claiming Social Security increased from 63.6 to 64.6 during that period. That's an increase of exactly 1 year, which makes Choice (C) the correct answer. This item shows that it pays to read the information and the question carefully, and focus only on the information needed to answer the question. In this case, you only need to pay attention to the information about women. That's why Choice (D) is incorrect. Choice (D) shows the increase for men.

27. **A. makes it two times larger.** In this linear equation, any multiple of one term results in the same multiple of the answer. Multiplying l by 2 results in increasing A by 2.

28. **C. 160.** You can use the formula for area to calculate the number of square feet Herman has to cover in primer. The dimensions of the wall are 20 feet by 8 feet, which is 160 square feet. If your first choice for the answer was Choice (A), you added the length and height instead of multiplying. If you picked Choice (B), you confused perimeter with area. Remember that *perimeter* is the distance all the way around an object — in this case, $2(20+8) = 56$. Choice (D) is the answer with the first two digits reversed. This item is a good illustration of making sure that you use the correct formula (in this case, area of a rectangle, not perimeter) and then apply it correctly. It's also a good reminder to select your answer carefully. Reversing digits under the stress of time limits isn't impossible or unusual.

29. **B. four units to the left and four units below the corresponding axis.** Because both coordinates are negative, the point would have to be the corresponding distance to the left and below the corresponding axis.

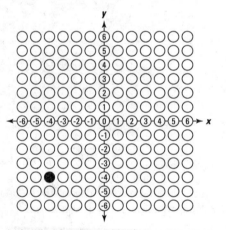

30. **30.00.** If you use x to represent the amount of money Roger spent, the amount of money that Ekua spent is $2x$. You can represent their total spending by the equation $90 = x + 2x$ or $3x = 90$, in which case $x = 30$. So Roger spent $30.00 for clothing.

31. **C. Men and women are getting married later in life as time goes by.** The data in the table shows that in most years, the average age for marriage increased. Therefore, this option is the only one that is correct.

32. **B. 2015.** Of the four years, in the table, this was the only year in which the average age declined. Therefore, it is correct.

33. **1,483.** Read the gauge carefully to find the answer.

34. **88.8.** The average grade, with Sheila's grade in Spanish falling 6 points, would be $(94 + 88 + 86 + 92 + 90 - 6)/5 = 88.8$.

35. **230.** Barry spends $\$900 + \$600 = \$1,500$ for rent and living expenses. He has $\$1,730 - \$1,500 = \$230$ left over.

36. **D. Horsesgalore.** The greatest percentage increase was experienced by Horsesgalore, with a 55% increase in sales.

37. **C. Horsesgalore.** To find the increase in cars sold in July over those two years, subtract the number sold in 2020 from the number sold in 2021. The biggest increase was for Horsesgalore, with an increase of 35 thousand cars ($99 - 64 = 35$). Note that you don't have to calculate for Goodenough, which had a decline in sales.

38. **D. Strawberry and rocky road.** This combination of flavors is the only one with at least one flavor that everyone in the family likes. For all the other combinations, at least one person in the family doesn't like either flavor.

6

Putting Your Skills to the Test: GED Practice Test 1

Chapter 19

Practice Test 1: Reasoning through Language Arts

You're ready to take a crack at a full-blown practice GED Reasoning through Language Arts test. You're feeling good and ready to go! (Well, maybe not, but you're at least smart enough to know that this practice is good for you!)

You have 95 minutes to complete the question-and-answer section and then another 45 minutes to write the Extended Response (a separate item). You get a ten-minute break before starting the Extended Response. Remember, you can't save time from one section to use in the other, Use the timer on your mobile phone to keep track of time. If you run out of time, mark the last item you completed. Then finish the remaining items. This will give you an idea of how faster you must work to complete all the items on the real test.

The answers and explanations to this test's questions are in Chapter 20. Go through the explanations to all the questions, even for the ones you answered correctly. The explanations are a good review of the techniques I discuss throughout the book.

REMEMBER

Whether you take the online-proctored GED at home or take the test at a testing center, you'll be taking the test on a computer. Instead of marking your answers on an answer sheet, like you do for the practice tests in this book, you'll see clickable ovals, and you'll be able to click with your mouse to answer drop-down and drag-and-drop items where indicated. I formatted these special items in this book to make them appear as similar as possible to the real GED test, but I had to retain A, B, C, and D choices for marking your answers on the answer sheet. Also, to make it simpler for you to time yourself, I present the questions for the Reading Comprehension and Grammar and Language components together in one section rather than separately (as on the real GED), with the Extended Response at the end of the test. If possible, write the essay on a computer to simulate conditions on test day. Have one or two sheets of paper to use to jot down notes and organize your ideas. Otherwise, use the lined paper I provide for you.

Answer Sheet for Practice Test 1, Reasoning through Language Arts

1. _____

2. _____

3. _____

4. _____

5. _____

6. _____

7. _____

8. _____

9. _____

10. _____

11. _____

12. _____

13. _____

14. _____

15. _____

16. _____

17. _____

18. _____

19. _____

20. _____

21. _____

22. _____

23. _____

24. _____

25. _____

26. _____

27. _____

28. _____

29. _____

30. _____

31. _____

32. _____

33. _____

34. _____

35. _____

36. _____

37. _____

38. _____

39. _____

40. _____

41. _____

42. _____

43. _____

44. _____

45. _____

46. _____

47. _____

48. _____

49. _____

50. _____

51. _____

52. _____

53. _____

54. _____

55. _____

56. _____

57. _____

58. _____

59. _____

60. _____

TIME: 95 minutes

ITEMS: 60

DIRECTIONS: You may answer the questions in this section in any order. Mark your answers on the answer sheet provided.

Questions 1–7 refer to the following excerpt, written by Dale Shuttleworth (originally printed in the Toronto Star).

(1) The Centre for Social Innovation, a renovated warehouse in the Spadina Ave. area of Toronto, houses 85 "social enterprises," including organizations concerned with the environment, the arts, social justice, education, health, technology, and design. Tribute has been paid to the "social enterprise movement" in Quebec and Vancouver for providing the impetus for this very successful venture.

(2) Toronto, Ontario, also has provided leadership in the areas of community education and community economic development — essential components in the creation of social enterprises. In 1974, the Toronto Board of Education assisted in the establishment of the Learnxs Foundation as part of its Learning Exchange System.

(3) The foundation represented an additional source of support for the burgeoning "alternatives in education" movement. In 1973, the Ontario government had imposed ceilings on educational spending and, together with reduced revenue due to declining enrollment, the Toronto board had limited means to fund innovative and experimental programs. The Learnxs Foundation was an independent, "arms-length" nonprofit charitable enterprise, which could solicit funds from public and private sources and generate revenue through the sale of goods and services to support innovative programs within the Toronto system.

(4) What followed during the 1970s was a series of Learnxs-sponsored demonstration projects as a source of research and development in such areas as: school and community programs to improve inner-city education; a series of small enterprises to employ 14- to 15-year-old school leavers; Youth Ventures — a paper recycling enterprise employing at-risk youth; Artsjunction — discarded material from business and industry were recycled for use as craft materials for visual arts classes; Toronto Urban Studies Centre — a facility to encourage the use of the city as a learning environment; and Learnxs Press — a publishing house for the production and sale of innovative learning materials.

(5) The York Board of Education and its school and community organizations jointly incorporated the Learning Enrichment Foundation (LEF), modeled on Learnxs. Originally devoted to multicultural arts enrichment, LEF during the 1980s joined with parental groups and the school board to establish 13 school-based childcare centers for infants, pre-school and school-age children.

(6) In 1984, LEF was asked by Employment and Immigrant Canada to convene a local committee of adjustment in response to York's high rate of unemployment and plant closures. Outcomes of the work of the Committee included:

(7) York Business Opportunities Centre: In 1985, with support from the Ontario Ministry of Industry, Trade and Technology, LEF opened the first small business incubator operated by a nonprofit charitable organization.

(8) Microtron Centre: This training facility was devoted to micro-computer skills, word and numerical processing, computer-assisted design, graphics and styling, and electronic assembly and repair.

(9) Microtron Bus: This refurbished school bus incorporated eight workstations from the Microtron Centre. It visited small business, industry and service organizations on a scheduled basis to provide training in word and numerical processing for their employees and clients.

(10) In 1996, the Training Renewal Foundation was incorporated as a nonprofit charity to serve disadvantaged youth and other displaced workers seeking skills, qualifications, and employment opportunities. Over the years, TRF has partnered with governments, employers, and community organizations to provide a variety of services including job-creation programs for: immigrants and refugees, GED high school equivalency, café equipment technicians, coffee and vending service workers, industrial warehousing and lift truck operators, fully expelled students, youth parenting, construction craft workers and garment manufacturing.

1. The Center for Social Innovation is

   (A) a new restaurant.
   (B) a center housing social enterprises.
   (C) the head office of a charity.
   (D) a small enterprise to employ high school dropouts.

2. The Learnxs Foundation supported

   (A) homeless people.
   (B) scholarships for computer studies students.
   (C) innovative programs.
   (D) art programming.

3. Artsjunction specialized in

   (A) providing opportunities for local at-risk youth.
   (B) recycling discarded materials for use in crafts.
   (C) encouraging environmental learning in the city.
   (D) publishing progressive educational materials.

4. The Microtron bus helped

   (A) provide transportation for computer science students to their labs.
   (B) provide training in word and numerical processing to employees and clients.
   (C) train auto mechanics in the digital controls of new cars.
   (D) the center establish social enterprises.

5. The Training Renewal Foundation serves

   (A) as a social innovator for youth disadvantaged youth and displaced workers.
   (B) as a patron of the center.
   (C) dinner to the homeless.
   (D) as a business incubator.

6. What does *arm's-length* mean in this sentence from Paragraph 3?

   The Learnxs Foundation was an independent, "arms length" nonprofit charitable enterprise, which could solicit funds from public and private sources and generate revenue through the sale of goods and services to support innovative programs within the Toronto system.

   (A) The foundation actively opposes the school board.
   (B) The foundation promotes alternative education strategies the school board opposes.
   (C) The foundation is opposed to public education.
   (D) The foundation can act free from influence from the school board.

7. Based on the details in the passage, which of these conclusions is supported?

(A) The school board doesn't believe in alternative education strategies.

(B) The school board didn't want to address the needs of school-leavers.

(C) The school board started the foundation to expand offerings it couldn't otherwise afford.

(D) The school board started the foundation because its traditional programs were not working.

Questions 8–14 refer to the following excerpt from an employee handbook.

It is expected that employees behave in a respectful, responsible, professional manner. Therefore, each employee must do the following:

- Wear appropriate clothing and use company-supplied safety equipment where required.
- Behave appropriately and professionally in the workplace and refrain from unauthorized use of telephones, computers, and copiers.
- Address all other employees and supervisors with courtesy and respect, using non-offensive language.
- Accept the authority of supervisors without argument. If you consider an action unfair, inform the Human Resources department.
- Respect the work environment of the company and conduct oneself in a manner conducive to the growth and the enhancement of our business.
- Refrain from inviting visitors to our place of work to keep the premises secure.
- Promote the dignity of all persons, regardless of gender, race or ethnicity, sexual orientation/gender identity, ability, creed, or culture.

    If the employee chooses *not* to comply:

- On the first offense, the employee meets with their supervisor. A representative from Human Resources may choose to attend.
- On the second offense, the employee meets with the Vice President of Human Resources before returning to work.
- On the third offense, the employee is automatically dismissed. Depending on the severity of the infraction, an employee can be dismissed on a first or second offense.

8. Which requirement relates to employee appearance?

(A) The employee must refrain from making personal phone calls.

(B) The employee must keep the premises secure.

(C) The employee must wear appropriate clothing.

(D) The employee must use courtesy and respect.

9. Which requirement addresses relations with supervisors?

(A) Accept authority.

(B) Contribute to business growth and enhancement.

(C) Refrain from inviting guests to visit the facility.

(D) Refrain from unauthorized use of telephones and computers.

10. Which requirement is concerned with the growth and enhancement of the business?

   (A) computer and phone usage

   (B) promoting the dignity of all persons

   (C) dress code

   (D) personal conduct and respect of the work environment

11. How are safety and security protected?

   (A) by promoting dignity

   (B) by not inviting others in

   (C) by the types of interaction

   (D) through meetings with supervisors

12. What is the penalty for continued noncompliance?

   (A) You meet with the president of the company.

   (B) You must avoid your supervisor.

   (C) You have to take behavior management classes.

   (D) You are fired.

13. Which of the following is Marge allowed to do?

   (A) Make a copy of a form from her son's school.

   (B) Call her husband from her office phone.

   (C) Not wear a company-supplied hair net because it messes up her hair.

   (D) Make copy of a form she completed for human resources.

14. Which of these phrases best describe the tone of the passage?

   (A) clear and legalistic

   (B) friendly and easy-going

   (C) unclear and confusing

   (D) harsh and unfair

Questions 15–24 refer to the following business letter.

Mr. Speedy Home Appliances
11 Peach Lane
Atlanta, GA 30303

Ms. Jessica North
733 Brower Ave.
Atlanta, GA 30303

Dear Mr. Speedy Home Appliances,

I [Select... ▾] draw your attention to an issue that I am having with your company. Last month on July 1st, I purchased a washing [Select... ▾] a dryer from Mr. Speedy Home Appliances. Your salesman assured me that the appliances and all the parts necessary for [Select... ▾] installation would arrive by the next Wednesday, July 6th. The appliances did arrive on July 6th, and the washing machine was successfully installed. [Select... ▼] the dryer did not come with the proper vent for installation. Your installer immediately called the store and [Select... ▼] the necessary vent was out of stock and wouldn't be available for ten days.

[Select... ▼] waited ten days for your installer to call me with a new date for installation. When no one called by the tenth day, I called your store. I was told that a manager wasn't [Select... ▼] but would call me back before the end of the day. I never received that phone call.

I originally patronized your store because of [Select... ▼] reputation for speedy and reliable service. I don't think that I should continue to be [Select... ▼] have three small children and, needless to say, a lot of laundry. I have been taking the laundry to a local laundromat [Select... ▼] an unnecessary expense because of your poor service.

Please call me as soon as possible with a solution to this problem.

Very truly yours,

Jessica North

15. I [Select... ▼] draw your attention to an issue that I am having with your company.

(A) would of liked to

(B) would have liked to

(C) would like to

(D) would like

16. Last month on July 1st, I purchased a washing [Select... ▼] a dryer from Mr. Speedy Home Appliances.

(A) machine, and

(B) washing machine, dryer

(C) washing machine and

(D) washing machine dryer

17. Your salesman assured me that the appliances and all the parts necessary for [Select... ▼] installation would arrive by the next Wednesday, July 6th.

(A) your

(B) their

(C) my

(D) its

18. [Select... ▼] the dryer did not come with the proper vent for installation.

(A) Indeed,

(B) However,

(C) For example,

(D) In addition,

19. Your installer immediately called the store and [Select... ▼] the necessary vent was out of stock and wouldn't be available for ten days.

(A) told

(B) were told

(C) had been told

(D) was told

20. [Select... ▼] waited ten days for your installer to call me with a new date for installation.

(A) I

(B) While I

(C) When I

(D) After I

21. I was told that a manager wasn't [Select... ▼] but would call me back before the end of the day.

(A) theirs

(B) there

(C) they're

(D) their

22. I originally patronized your store because of [Select... ▼] reputation for speedy and reliable service.

(A) it's

(B) its'

(C) its

(D) their

23. I don't think that I should continue to be [Select... ▼] have three small children and, needless to say, a lot of laundry.

(A) inconvenienced,

(B) inconvenienced. I

(C) inconvenienced I

(D) inconvenienced, I

24. I have been taking the laundry to a local laundromat [Select... ▼] an unnecessary expense because of your poor service.

(A) and incurring

(B) and had been incurring

(C) and I will incur

(D) incurred

Questions 25–30 refer to the following excerpt from Washington Irving's "Rip Van Winkle" (1819).

(1) Whoever has made a voyage up the Hudson must remember the Kaatskill Mountains. They are a dismembered branch of the great Appalachian family, and are seen away to the west of the river, swelling up to a noble height, and lording it over the surrounding country. Every change

of season, every change of weather, indeed, every hour of the day, produces some change in the magical hues and shapes of these mountains, and they are regarded by all the good wives, far and near, as perfect barometers. When the weather is fair and settled, they are clothed in blue and purple, and print their bold outlines on the clear evening sky; but, sometimes, when the rest of the landscape is cloudless, they will gather a hood of gray vapors about their summits, which, in the last rays of the setting sun, will glow and light up like a crown of glory.

(2) At the foot of these fairy mountains, the voyager may have descried the light smoke curling up from a village, whose shingle-roofs gleam among the trees, just where the blue tints of the upland melt away into the fresh green of the nearer landscape. It is a little village of great antiquity, having been founded by some of the Dutch colonists, in the early times of the province, just about the beginning of the government of the good Peter Stuyvesant, (may he rest in peace!) and there were some of the houses of the original settlers standing within a few years, built of small yellow bricks brought from Holland, having latticed windows and gablefronts, surmounted with weather-cocks.

25. How would you set out to find the Kaatskill Mountains?

(A) Turn left at the Mississippi River.

(B) Journey up the Hudson.

(C) Look for a dismembered branch.

(D) Notice fresh green.

26. According to the narrator, wives tell the weather

(A) with perfect barometers.

(B) by the clear evening sky.

(C) by checking with each other.

(D) with colors and shapes of the mountains.

27. What is the first sign that you are close to the village?

(A) fairy mountains

(B) shingle-roofs

(C) light smoke curling

(D) blue tints

28. Who originally founded the village?

(A) Peter Stuyvesant

(B) a group of married women

(C) Dutch colonists

(D) the great Appalachian family

29. Why is the phrase, "May he rest in peace!" used after Peter Stuyvesant in Paragraph 2?

(A) He has since died.

(B) He was a settler.

(C) He was a soldier.

(D) He was the governor.

30. According to the passage, which of these materials came from Holland?

   (A) small yellow bricks

   (B) window glass

   (C) weather-cocks

   (D) river boats

Questions 31–36 refer to the following excerpt from Seventeen, written by Booth Tarkington (1916). At the time the novel takes place, many drugstores had counters that served soft drinks and ice cream.

William Sylvanus Baxter paused for a moment of thought in front of the drugstore at the corner of Washington Street and Central Avenue. He had an internal question to settle before he entered the store: he wished to allow the young man at the soda-fountain no excuse for saying, "Well, make up your mind what it's goin' to be, can't you?" Rudeness of this kind, especially in the presence of girls and women, was hard to bear, and though William Sylvanus Baxter had borne it upon occasion, he had reached an age when he found it intolerable. Therefore, to avoid offering opportunity for anything of the kind, he decided upon chocolate and strawberry, mixed, before approaching the fountain. Once there, however, and a large glass of these flavors and diluted ice-cream proving merely provocative, he said, languidly — an affectation, for he could have disposed of half a dozen with gusto: "Well, now I'm here, I might as well go one more. Fill 'er up again. Same."

Emerging to the street, penniless, he bent a fascinated and dramatic gaze upon his reflection in the drug-store window, and then, as he turned his back upon the alluring image, his expression altered to one of lofty and uncondescending amusement. That was his glance at the passing public. From the heights, he seemed to bestow upon the world a mysterious derision — for William Sylvanus Baxter was seventeen long years of age, and had learned to present the appearance of one who possesses inside information about life and knows all strangers and most acquaintances to be of inferior caste, costume, and intelligence.

He lingered upon the corner awhile, not pressed for time. Indeed, he found many hours of these summer months heavy upon his hands, for he had no important occupation, unless some intermittent dalliance with a work on geometry (anticipatory of the distant autumn) might be thought important, which is doubtful, since he usually went to sleep on the shady side porch at his home, with the book in his hand. So, having nothing to call him elsewhere, he lounged before the drugstore in the early afternoon sunshine, watching the passing to and fro of the lower orders and bourgeoisie of the middle-sized midland city which claimed him (so to speak) for a native son.

31. According to the story, the internal question William has to settle is

   (A) whether or not to enter the drugstore.

   (B) whether to be rude or polite to the young women inside.

   (C) what flavor ice cream soda to order.

   (D) how he should address the young man working at the soda fountain.

32. The clerk dislikes

   (A) rudeness.

   (B) indecision.

   (C) pride.

   (D) laziness.

33. Which of the following statements can be supported by the evidence in the story?

(A) William's favorite flavor of ice cream is chocolate.

(B) William is considering taking a job at the drugstore.

(C) William is a good friend of the young man who works at the soda fountain.

(D) William spent all the money he had with him on ice cream sodas.

34. The *alluring image* refers to

(A) a young woman in the drugstore.

(B) William's reflection in the glass window of the drugstore.

(C) the ice cream flavors lined up in the display case.

(D) the glittering glasses for ice cream and sodas arranged on the shelves.

35. Which of the following best describe William?

(A) quiet and shy

(B) self-impressed and smug

(C) polite and energetic

(D) hard-working and ambitious

36. Choose the answer that arranges the events in the order in which they occur in the story.

1. William lingers outside the drugstore, watching the people pass by.
2. William says, "Fill 'er up again."
3. William decides on a chocolate and strawberry ice cream soda.
4. William ponders an internal question.
5. William approaches the soda-fountain.

    (A) 1, 3, 2, 5, 4

    (B) 4, 3, 5, 2, 1

    (C) 3, 5, 1, 2, 4

    (D) 5, 4, 3, 2, 1,

Questions 37–46 refer to the following excerpt, which is adapted from Customer Service For Dummies, by Karen Leland and Keith Bailey (John Wiley & Sons, Inc.).

This step requires you to listen to each [Select... ▼] assessment of the problem. When she explains the situation from her [Select... ▼] job is to fully absorb what she is saying about her unique set of circumstances. After you identify the customer's problem, the next step, obviously, is to fix it. Sometimes, you can easily remedy the situation by changing an invoice, redoing an order, [Select... ▼] refunding charges, or replacing a defective product. [Select... ▼] the problem is more complex because the damage or mistake cannot be repaired simply. In these instances, [Select... ▼] compromises need to be reached.

[Select... ▼] this step begins to remedy the situation and gives the customer what she needs to resolve the source of the conflict. Don't waste time and effort by putting the cart before the horse and [Select... ▼] to fix the wrong problem. It's easy to jump the gun and think that you know what the customer is about to say [Select... ▼] you've heard it all a hundred times before. Doing so [Select... ▼] you ground on the recovery front and further annoys the customer. [Select... ▼] what you think the problem is at first glance, is different from what it becomes upon closer examination.

37. This step requires you to listen to each [Select... ▼] assessment of the problem.

    (A) customers

    (B) customers'

    (C) customers's

    (D) customer's

38. When she explains the situation from her [Select... ▼] job is to fully absorb what she is saying about her unique set of circumstances.

    (A) perspective, your

    (B) perspective your

    (C) perspective. Your

    (D) perspective; you

39. Sometimes, you can easily remedy the situation by changing an invoice, redoing an order, [Select... ▼] refunding charges, or replacing a defective product.

    (A) waiving, or

    (B) waving, or

    (C) waiving or

    (D) waving or

40. [Select... ▼] the problem is more complex because the damage or mistake cannot be repaired simply.

    (A) At other times, fixing

    (B) At other times. Fixing

    (C) At other times fixing

    (D) At other times: fixing

41. In these instances, [Select... ▼] compromises need to be reached.

    (A) mutually acceptable

    (B) mutual acceptable

    (C) mutual exceptable

    (D) mutually exceptable

42. [Select... ▼] this step begins to remedy the situation and gives the customer what she needs to resolve the source of the conflict.

    (A) Whatever the problem,

    (B) Be it as it may,

    (C) Nevertheless,

    (D) While

43. Don't waste time and effort by putting the cart before the horse and [Select... ▼] to fix the wrong problem.

    (A) try

    (B) trying

    (C) tried

    (D) have tried

44. It's easy to jump the gun and think that you know what the customer is about to say [Select... ▼] you've heard it all a hundred times before.

    (A) because

    (B) while

    (C) although

    (D) until

45. Doing so [Select... ▼] you ground on the recovery front and further annoys the customer.

    (A) lose

    (B) loses

    (C) loose

    (D) looses

46. [Select... ▼] what you think the problem is, at first glance, is different from what it becomes, upon closer examination.

    (A) Very infrequently,

    (B) Instead,

    (C) Moreover,

    (D) More often than not,

Questions 47–53 refer to the following business letter.

Caffeinated Enterprises LLC 1 Caffeinated Way, Kansas City, MO 64105

To Whom It May Concern:

We are delighted [Select... ▼] a reference for Gregory Jackson. He was employed by the training division of our company for six [Select... ▼] recruiting and training clients to participate in our coffee vending machine repair division for the period of June 2017 to October 2021.

As part of that program, he prepared PowerPoint presentations for new recruits, revised and upgraded training [Select... ▼] communications with other companies in the industry.

Mr. Jackson [Select... ▼] an excellent representative for our company, which has trained some 45 new repair personnel in the past year. His concerted efforts to network with others in the coffee industry contributed greatly to his success. He [Select... ▼] a high level of commitment to his job here. I am confident that he [Select... ▼] to do his work with both competence and efficiency at your organization.

I have developed a great respect for Mr. [Select... ▼] personal communication skills and dedication to his work. I recommend him enthusiastically and with no reservations whatsoever.

Sincerely,

Jules Klaus,
Director, Training

47. We are delighted [Select... ▼] a reference for Gregory Jackson.

    (A) provide

    (B) provided

    (C) providing

    (D) to provide

48. He was employed by the training division of our company for six [Select... ▼] recruiting and training clients to participate in our coffee vending machine repair division for the period of June 2017 to October 2021.

(A) years, he provided excellent services. Both

(B) years, he provided excellent services, both

(C) years. He provided excellent services, both

(D) years he provided excellent services, both

49. As part of that program, he prepared PowerPoint presentations for new recruits, revised and upgraded training [Select... ▼] communications with other companies in the industry.

(A) procedures and organizes

(B) procedures, and organized

(C) procedures, organizes

(D) procedures, and had organized

50. Mr. Jackson [Select... ▼] an excellent representative for our company, which has trained some 45 new repair personnel in the past year.

(A) had always been

(B) always had been

(C) always was

(D) has always been

51. He [Select... ▼] a high level of commitment to his job here.

(A) has shown

(B) has been shown

(C) have shown

(D) has showed

52. I am confident that he [Select... ▼] to do his work with both competence and efficiency at your organization.

(A) would continue

(B) continued

(C) will continue

(D) continues

53. I have developed a great respect for Mr. [Select... ▼] personal communication skills and dedication to his work.

(A) Jackson's

(B) Jacksons'

(C) Jacksons

(D) Jacksons's

(1) If you've ever had to figure out where to stick batteries in your child's latest electronic acquisition, then loading batteries in your point-and-shoot shouldn't be a challenge. Turn off your camera when you install them; the camera may go crazy opening and closing its lens. (Some cameras turn themselves off after you install new batteries, so you have to turn them back on to shoot.)

(2) With big point-and-shoot models, you typically open a latched cover on the bottom to install batteries. More compact models have a battery compartment under a door or flap that is incorporated into the side or grip of the camera. You may have to pry open such doors with a coin.

(3) More annoying are covers on the bottom that you open by loosening a screw. (You need a coin for this type, too.) And most annoying are battery covers that aren't hinged and come off completely when you unscrew them. If you have one of these, don't change batteries while standing over a sewer grate, in a field of tall grass, or on a pier.

(4) Whether loading four AAs or a single lithium, make sure that the batteries are correctly oriented as you insert them. You'll find a diagram and/or plus and minus markings, usually within the compartment or on the inside of the door.

(5) If your camera doesn't turn on and the batteries are correctly installed, the batteries may have lost their punch from sitting on a shelf too long. Which is where the battery icon comes in.

(6) If your camera has an LCD panel, an icon tells you when battery power is low.

54. In what will you be installing the batteries?

(A) an electronic acquisition

(B) a children's toy

(C) a big point-and-shoot

(D) a camera

55. What is the easiest model in which to replace the batteries?

(A) compact models

(B) big point-and-shoots

(C) screw bottoms

(D) covers not hinged

56. Why should locations such as sewer grates and tall grass be avoided when changing batteries?

(A) Water can get in the camera.

(B) Your lens may get dirty.

(C) Your card might be ruined.

(D) The battery cover may be lost.

57. How do you ensure that the batteries are correctly oriented?

(A) Use four AAs.

(B) Use a single lithium.

(C) Empty the compartment.

(D) Find a diagram.

58. What tells you whether the batteries are low?

    (A) the diagram

    (B) the battery icon

    (C) the battery compartment

    (D) a single lithium battery

59. How does the author most likely feel about changing batteries?

    (A) It makes him go crazy.

    (B) He hates it because batteries are too expensive.

    (C) He feels it's necessary but mildly annoying.

    (D) He thinks it's so easy it's child's play.

60. What does the phrase "lost their punch" mean in this sentence from Paragraph 5?

If your camera doesn't turn on and the batteries are correctly installed, the batteries may have lost their punch from sitting on a shelf too long.

    (A) become damaged

    (B) been misplaced

    (C) already been used

    (D) become run down

At this point, you may take a 10-minute break before beginning the Extended Response.

Extended Response

TIME: 45 minutes

YOUR ASSIGNMENT: The following articles present arguments both for and against banning cars from city centers. In your response, analyze the positions presented in each article and explain which you think is best supported. Use specific and appropriate evidence to support your arguments. If possible, write your essay on a computer with spell-check, grammar-check and autocorrect turned off. Otherwise, use the following sheets of lined paper to prepare your response. Spend up to 45 minutes in reading the passages and planning, writing, revising, and editing your response.

Article 1 **Let's Ban Cars**

The proliferation of cars in every major city is an inevitable product of modern society. Increased salaries, more disposable income, and lower vehicle prices mean that almost everyone can own a car. This translates into more cars, more traffic, more pollution, and more space taken up for parking lots. There are some very pressing reasons to ban cars from metropolitan areas.

The number of cars in the world today exceeds 1 billion and is estimated to exceed 2 billion by the year 2035. Considering how congested cities are now, this paints a staggering picture of clogged streets and gridlocked intersections. In addition, automobile congestion creates a health hazard to city dwellers. The constant stop and go of city driving burns more gas and spews more dangerous pollutants into the air. While the Environmental Protection Agency has set limits on exhaust emissions, these limit only a small percentage of chemicals that are emitted. Unregulated particulates in the air cause widespread harm. High levels of nitrogen oxide are toxic to humans; carbon dioxide contributes to global warming; and ozone can exacerbate asthma. It is little wonder that the number of asthma sufferers in cities is steadily increasing.

Furthermore, cars use up valuable resources, both economic and natural. Cars are expensive to run because the price of gas is so high. Cars also burn precious fossil fuels, and the processes required to extract the raw petroleum necessary are costly and dangerous. Think of the explosions of oil rigs in the Gulf of Mexico and the catastrophic oil spills that have destroyed sea plants and wildlife. Maybe it's time to admit that the impact of too many cars goes beyond the city and affects us globally.

Along with the environmental and health dangers caused by traffic comes the quality-of-city-life issues. So much space is required to provide parking spaces and lots to house the thousands of cars, limousines, and taxis. Think of how much better it would be to use that space to benefit human beings rather than machines. Pedestrian walks, small parks, and gardens could be enjoyed by so many people. And, how much more attractive is a garden than a four-story concrete parking garage!

It is true that everybody needs to get to work, and that city centers are the hubs of commercial activity. But, there are so many better options than driving a car into the city. Public transportation is widely available and is often far more economical than owning a gas-guzzling vehicle. With a ban on private cars, more people will ride buses and trains, freeing up traffic congestion and decreasing health hazards. Some may even find that they can accomplish some work on the bus and train, thus using their time more efficiently. Pedestrians will also be able to navigate the city streets without fear of being run over by a car trying to beat a red light. And perhaps, some people will sit in a garden on the site of a former parking lot and enjoy some fresh air and sunshine.

Article 2 **Cars are Necessary**

Banishing the private automobile from urban areas may seem like an easy solution to traffic jams and air pollution, but the actual dynamics are far more complex. The simple fact is that people need to get to work, and city centers are often epicenters of finance, shopping, and banking. Without cars, how will people get to work every day? The economy will suffer as workers and consumers struggle to find their way to business and retail centers.

Those who support a ban on private cars in city centers point to public transportation as the solution to all the problems associated with urban traffic. What they fail to consider is that most public transportation systems rely on buses and trains that aren't used efficiently. During peak hours, they become so crowded that they create uncomfortable and even unsafe conditions for users as the system copes with the temporary surge in demand. Moreover, because people are reluctant to travel on unsanitary, overcrowded, and seedy public transport, low ridership makes many services financially unsustainable, particularly in suburban areas. In spite of significant subsidies and cross-financing, very few public transit systems can generate sufficient income to cover the costs of operating. While in the past, deficits were considered acceptable because of the essential service public transit was providing for urban mobility, its financial burden is increasingly controversial. Moreover, as people struggling to find affordable housing move farther and farther out into suburbs, access to public transportation dwindles, and driving to work is the only option.

Proponents of banning automobiles also cite statistics on the dangerous emissions of car exhausts, but this is becoming less of a valid argument every day. Increased technology has reduced emissions significantly — the goal is to build cars that emit no pollution — and alternative fuel, hybrid development, and electrical technology have reduced reliance on fossil fuels. And, self-driving cars, which add a measure of safety, are on the horizon. The addition of high-occupancy vehicle lanes (HOVs) has encouraged car-pooling to further reduce traffic. In addition, urban planners are designing new roadways and reworking existing ones to decrease inner-city traffic congestion, which will result in lower exhaust emissions.

It is also important to note that owing a car is a cultural symbol of status and personal freedom. In the U.S., where only eight percent of the population does not own a car, most people see car ownership as a necessity rather than a convenience. Indeed, 88 percent of all commuting in this country is done by car. Most people reject the need to rely on schedules and inconvenient transport systems that may not be suitable for their lifestyles. With your own car, you can come and go when and where you please. This privilege is one that most people value highly.

Chapter **20**

Answers for Practice Test 1, Reasoning through Language Arts

In this chapter, I provide the answers and explanations to every question in the Reasoning through Language Arts practice test in Chapter 19. If you just want a quick look at the answers, check out the abbreviated answer key at the end of this chapter. However, if you have the time, be sure to read the answer explanations. Doing so will help you understand why some answers were correct and others not, especially when the choices were really close. You can discover just as much from your errors as from the correct answers.

Answers and Explanations

1. **B. a center housing social enterprises.** The first paragraph of the passage specifically states that the center houses 85 social enterprises. Choice (A) is totally wrong and can be instantly eliminated on the first reading. The other answers have a ring of correctness because the passage is about social enterprises, charities, and school leavers, but they have nothing to do with the center and, thus, are wrong.

2. **C. innovative programs.** The passage states that the Learnxs Foundation supports innovative programs. All the other answers except for Choice (A) are mentioned or implied in the passage; however, they aren't correct answers to the question. You have to read carefully and double-check the facts. Just because something is mentioned or is familiar doesn't mean it's the right answer to the question.

3. **B. recycling discarded materials for use in crafts.** The passage clearly spells out that Artsjunction's function is to distribute discarded materials to visual arts classes.

4. **B. provide training in word and numerical processing to employees and clients.** The column is very specific about the purpose of the Microtron bus. It provided services to employees and clients of small businesses in word and numerical processing. The other answers sound like they could be right, but after rereading the passage, you can see that they aren't.

TIP

When you're trying to answer these questions under time constraints, try to remember exactly what the passage said. If you only think you remember, go back and look for key words as quickly as you can. In this case, the key word is *Microtron.* This item is a good example of why it can help to read the question first, before reading the passage.

5. **A. disadvantaged youth and displaced workers.** The passage very precisely spells out the mandate of the Training Renewal Foundation: to serve disadvantaged youth and displaced workers. Choices B and D may be worthy activities for any charity, but they aren't stated as part of the mandate and, thus, are wrong as answers. Choice (C) is just wrong and is a play on another meaning of *serves.* You can immediately exclude this answer and have only three others to consider.

6. **D. The foundation can act free from influence from the school board.** The sentence says that the foundation is independent from the school board. That means it can act free from influence.

7. **C. The school board started the foundation to expand offerings it couldn't otherwise afford.** The information is in the third paragraph. The school board had funding and other limitations for a variety of reasons and used the foundation as a way to offer needed innovations it could not otherwise afford.

8. **C. The employee must wear appropriate clothing.** Employees must wear appropriate clothing to project a professional appearance and maintain safety standards. The other requirements — such as refraining from making phone calls, keeping the premises secure, and being respectful — don't relate to appearance.

9. **A. Accept authority.** Employees must accept the authority of supervisors, as is stated clearly in the passage. The other choices may be partially correct, but they are not the best answers.

10. **D. personal conduct and respect of the work environment.** Employees must conduct themselves professionally so that the business grows and improves.

11. **B. by not inviting others in.** To ensure safety and security, employees shouldn't invite other people in. The promotion of dignity, interaction, and supervisors' meetings don't relate to ensuring safety and security.

12. **D. You are fired.** Repeated instances of noncompliance lead to dismissal. The other options aren't backed up by the passage.

13. **D. Make a copy of a form she completed for human resources.** Employees can use copiers only for business purposes. Therefore, she is allowed take this action. The other actions are not permitted under the rules.

14. **A. clear and legalistic.** The information in the passage contains direct, uncomplicated rules. Therefore, Choice (A) is correct.

15. **C. would like to.** This choice is correct because *would like* + infinitive is used to express a desire politely. Therefore, Choices (B) and (D) are incorrect. The phrase *would of* (Choice A) is a misspelling of the contraction *would've (would have)*, and so is also incorrect.

16. **C. washing machine and.** Choice (C) is correct because two nouns are joined with a conjunction such as *and*. No comma is needed. Therefore, the remaining options, which include unnecessary commas (Choices A and B) or omit *and* (Choices (B) and (D) are incorrect.

17. **B. their.** *Their* is the correct pronoun because it refers to *appliances*, which is plural. The other choices do not make sense.

18. **B. However,** The logical transitional word to begin the sentence is *however*. You need to indicate contrast between the successful installation of the washing machine and the unsuccessful installation of the dryer.

19. **D. was told.** Choice (D) is correct because this sentence is in the passive voice, which uses a form of the verb *be* plus a past participle. *Was* is the correct choice because the subject of the sentence is singular. Therefore, Choice (A), which is active voice, is incorrect. Choice (B) is incorrect because it has a plural verb. There is no reason to make the change in Choice (C), so it is incorrect.

20. **A. I.** Choice (A) creates an independent clause so is correct. Beginning the sentence with *while, when,* or *after,* all subordinating conjunctions (as in the remaining choices), creates a *dependent clause* — a clause that cannot stand on its own. You can fix this kind of error by deleting the subordinating conjunction (which creates an independent clause) or joining the clause to another sentence with the correct conjunction and punctuation.

21. **B. there.** These homonyms are confusing: Remember to use *their* when a possessive pronoun is needed, *there* when you refer to a place, *they're* as a contraction of *they are,* and *theirs* as a possessive pronoun.

22. **C. its.** The correct choice is the possessive pronoun *its* (Choice C). Remember, *it's* (Choice A) is the contraction of *it is,* and *its'* (Choice B) is never correct. *Their* (Choice D) is incorrect because the pronoun refers to the store, which is singular, and *their* is plural.

23. **B. inconvenienced. I.** Choice (B) creates two concise sentences. Choice (A) creates a comma splice and a sentence fragment. Choice (C) creates a run-on sentence, and Choice (D) creates another comma splice.

24. **A. and incurring.** Choice (A) creates correct parallel structure. Choices (B) and (C) use faulty parallel structure with verb tenses that do not make sense. Choice (D) creates a run-on sentence and a sentence fragment.

25. **B. Journey up the Hudson.** To get to the Kaatskill Mountains, you need to journey up the Hudson (Choice B). The Mississippi River has nothing to do with the Hudson River, so Choice (A) is incorrect. *A dismembered branch* (Choice C) and *fresh green* (Choice D) aren't locations that can better help you locate the mountains.

26. **D. with colors and shapes of the mountains.** The passage says that wives use "the magical hues and shapes of these mountains" (Choice D) to forecast the weather. A barometer (Choice A), an instrument that measures air pressure to predict the weather, is employed as a metaphor for the mountain view being used as a predictor of the weather. The evening sky (Choice B) isn't mentioned as an indicator. The passage says nothing about the wives talking to one another to determine the weather (Choice C).

27. **C. light smoke curling.** To help you locate the village, you first need to look for light smoke curling from chimneys. You can't see the other sign, shingle-roofs (Choice B), until after you can see the smoke. Blue tints (Choice D) aren't signs for locating villages, and neither are fairy mountains (Choice A).

28. **C. Dutch colonists.** The Dutch colonists were the newcomers who founded the village. Although others are mentioned, they're not the founders of the village. Peter Stuyvesant (Choice A) was a leader of the colonial government. The women in the area (Choice B) are mentioned only in relation to the weather. The great Appalachian family (Choice D) refers to the mountains.

29. **A. He has since died.** Peter Stuyvesant, who had headed the government, is now deceased. The other answer choices describe Stuyvesant as a settler (Choice B), a soldier (Choice C), and a governor (Choice D), but they don't refer to his death.

30. **A. small yellow bricks.** The passage states that the yellow bricks were brought from Holland. The sources of the other materials are not mentioned, and are therefore unknown.

31. **C. what flavor ice cream soda to order.** William wants to make the decision before he enters the drugstore, so the young man serving him won't have the opportunity to say, "Well, make up your mind what it's goin' to be, can't you?" William clearly has been through this experience before and doesn't want to repeat it.

32. **B. indecision.** The clerk becomes frustrated with William when he cannot make up his mind about the flavor of soda he wants.

33. **D. William spent all the money he had with him on ice cream sodas.** Because William is *penni-less* when he leaves the store, you can assume he spent all his money to pay for his order. Although he orders two chocolate and strawberry ice cream sodas, you can't assume that chocolate is his favorite flavor, so Choice (A) isn't the best answer. There is no evidence in the story that William is a friend of the server or that he plans to get a job there.

34. **B. William's reflection in the glass window of the drugstore.** William, self-impressed young man that he is, finds his own reflection alluring. The evidence in the story supports none of the other choices.

35. **B. self-impressed and smug.** There are clues in the story that give you a clear picture of William's character. After staring admiringly at his reflection in the store window, he looks at passers-by with "lofty and uncondescending amusement." You learn that "from the heights, he seemed to bestow upon the world a mysterious derision."

36. **B. 4, 3, 5, 2, 1.** The correct order of events is as follows: 4. William ponders an internal question. 3. William decides on a chocolate and strawberry ice cream soda. 5. William approaches the soda-fountain. 2. William says, "Fill 'er up again." 1. William lingers outside the drugstore, watching the people pass by.

37. **D. customer's.** The *assessment* belongs to each customer and requires a possessive form of customer: *customer's.* Because *customer* is singular, you must insert the apostrophe before the *s*.

38. **A. perspective, your.** In this sentence, a dependent clause is followed by an independent clause, so a comma is needed to separate them. Therefore, Choices (B) and (D) are incorrect. Choice (C) is incorrect because a dependent clause cannot stand alone as a sentence.

39. **C. waiving or.** *Waving* means "motioning with the hand," while the homonym *waiving* means "dismissing." It may be interesting to wave at a charge, but the proper meaning of the sentence is "to dismiss (or not collect) the charge." Therefore, Choices (B) and (D) are incorrect. Choice (A) is incorrect because there is no reason to add a comma. Therefore, Choice (C) is correct.

40. **A. At other times, fixing.** The introductory phrase *At other times* should be set off by a comma. Therefore, Choices (C) and (D) are incorrect. Choice (B) creates a sentence fragment.

41. **A. mutually acceptable.** Choice (A) is correct because *mutually acceptable* means "agreeable to both." *Exceptable* is a close homonym that means "fit for excepting." Therefore, Choices (C) and (D) are incorrect. An adverb, *mutually,* is needed to modify an adjective, so Choices (B) and (C) are incorrect. The more reading you do as you prepare for the test, the better your chances are for recognizing homonyms.

42. **A. Whatever the problem,** Only this option makes sense in the sentence. In questions such as this one, it's helpful to say the sentence silently to yourself, substituting each answer choice to find out which one sounds better. Sometimes, you just need to do it by ear!

43. **B. trying.** This choice results in correct parallel structure (*putting* and *trying* are parallel). The other options result in faulty parallel structure.

44. **A. because.** Only this subordinating conjunction indicates the correct relationship between the two clauses in the sentence — the second clause of the sentence is the reason for the first clause of the sentence.

45. **B. loses.** Choice (B) is correct because the subject of the sentence, the phrase *doing so*, is singular so needs a singular verb. Therefore, Choice (A) is incorrect. Choices (C) and (D) don't make sense in the context of the sentence. *Loose* is usually an adjective that means "not tight" or "not fixed in place, or a verb that means "set free."

46. **D. More often than not,** Only this choice indicates the correct relationship among the ideas in the paragraph. The other choices do not make sense.

47. **D. to provide.** An infinitive is required after *be delighted.* Therefore, Choice (D) is correct.

48. **C. years. He provided excellent services, both.** Choice (C) creates two complete sentences. Choice (A) creates a sentence fragment. Choice (B) creates a comma splice. Choice (D) creates a run-on sentence.

49. **B. procedures, and organized.** This is a case of faulty parallelism. Every verb in the series should be in the past tense. The other choices do not correct this error and/or add additional ones.

50. **D. has always been.** Choice (D) uses the correct verb tense. Choices (A) and (B) introduce the wrong tense into the sentence, and Choice (C) is no improvement.

51. **A. has shown.** Choice (A) uses the correct form of *show* in the present perfect tense. Therefore, Choices (B) and (D) are incorrect. Choice (C) introduces a subject-verb agreement error.

52. **C. will continue.** Choice (C) is correct because the sentence is about actions in the future, so the future tense is required.

53. **A. Jackson's.** *Jackson* is singular, so the possessive case is formed by adding an apostrophe and an *s*, as in Choice (A).

54. **D. a camera.** The batteries are installed in a camera. Other answer choices, such as electronics or a children's toy, have no meaning in this excerpt. Point-and-shoot, while another term for a camera, isn't the best answer, because the passage talks about point-and-shoot cameras of all sizes.

55. **B. big point-and-shoots.** The easiest model in which to replace batteries is a big point-and-shoot camera. The other answer choices — compact models, screw bottoms, and different types of covers — aren't the best answers to the question.

56. **D. The battery cover may be lost.** Avoid all the locations mentioned so you don't lose your battery cover if you drop it. Sewer grates and tall grass are places where the cover could easily be lost. The rest of the answer choices refer to issues other than losing battery covers.

57. **D. Find a diagram.** To ensure that the batteries are correctly oriented, you must find the diagram and use it. Other choices, such as using four AAs or a single lithium or emptying the compartment, don't answer the question.

58. **B. the battery icon.** You must check the battery icon to see whether the batteries are low. According to the passage, the *diagram*, *battery compartment*, and *lithium battery* aren't correct answers.

59. **C. He feels it's necessary but mildly annoying.** Choice (C) is correct because he indicates that changing batteries is necessary for cameras and other electronic devices and can pose some minor challenges. Choice (A) is too strong. Choices (B) and (D) are not supported by information in the passage.

60. **D. become run down.** Only Choice (D) is a consequence of batteries sitting on a shelf too long. The other options do not make sense.

Sample Extended Response

The following sample essay would receive solid marks. It isn't perfect, but as the GED Testing Service tells you, you're not expected to write the perfect essay. You're expected to write a good, first-draft-quality response. When you prepare your essay, consider using a schedule similar to this: 5 minutes to read and analyze the source passages; 10 minutes to prepare, 20 minutes to write, and the remaining 10 minutes to revise and edit.

Compare the following sample to the response you wrote, and then compare it to the criteria the GED Testing Service uses to evaluate your writing (review Chapter 8 for more details on the scoring criteria):

» Creation of an argument and use of evidence

» Development and organizational structure

» Clarity and command of standard English conventions

Both articles admit that traffic in the city is terrible, but one article argues that cars should be banned while the other says that cars are necessary. Both sides raise valid points, but the article in favor of banning cars presents a stronger argument because it has more specific examples and more convincing evidence.

The pro automobile banning article is very well organized, and it analyzes the issue very clearly point by point. It begins by addressing health issues, which are very important to every American. Who isn't concerned about the pollutants in the air that we breathe? The main point about traffic congestion causing unhealthy exhaust emissions is backed up by concrete evidence. The specific toxins (nitrogen oxide, carbon dioxide, and ozone) are listed, and these details strengthen the argument. The writer also uses statistics, such as the increasing number of cars on the roads (more than 2 billion by 2035!) and the increase in asthma victims, to add persuasive scientific evidence to the article. On the other hand, the writer of the article against the banning of cars brushes off the health hazards of increased automobiles on the city roads. This article says that emissions are already down due to advancements in technology, and the goal for the future is to reduce emissions completely. Right now, everyone in the city center is breathing in toxic fumes. I am far more convinced by the first article that cars cause unhealthy conditions.

Both articles also address the alternative to cars — public transportation. While Article 2 does offer the opinion that buses and trains can be uncomfortable and crowded, this seems like a very broad, general statement rather than a fact. Many cities have new or refurbished trains and buses, and all cities have clean-up crews at the end of the day. Article 2 also mentions "very few public transit systems can generate sufficient income to cover the costs of operating." While that is most likely true, if fewer people drove their cars into the city and took public transport, the increased ridership would boost profits. Article 1 makes an important point about public transit that Article 2 never addresses: the efficient use of travel time. Public transit riders can use their commuting time to work, to read, to socialize, or just to rest. This can make them more productive in their jobs, which will boost the economy.

Finally, Article 1 discusses a very important issue that Article 2 never even considers: the space used for parking and storing vehicles in the city. Most urban centers have parking space problems. One solution is to construct multi-level parking garages. Not only are these usually very unattractive, but they also use space that could be put to better use for gardens or parks. Article 1 points out that quality of life is so important in modern times. As Article 1 recognizes, everyone needs to spend some down time, smelling the flowers and getting energized by beauty. A park is a far more desirable place to relax than a concrete bunker.

It is easy to fall into the trap of thinking that everyone needs a car to get around. Article 2 points out that "owning a car is a cultural symbol of status and personal freedom." While this may be true, it is a weak argument. How can having a status symbol be reason enough to jeopardize the health and quality of life of so many city dwellers? The truth is that most people who live in cities rely on public transit. It is the people who drive into the city centers from the suburbs who create the dangerous emissions, noise, and traffic jams. One solution might be for cities to set up parking lots outside the city and then provide public transit into the center. A ban on cars from the city centers, as Article 1 convincingly argues, will be beneficial to all by reducing reliance on fossil fuels, cleaning up the air, and improving the quality of life in the city centers.

Answer Key

1.	B	21.	B	41.	A
2.	C	22.	C	42.	A
3.	B	23.	B	43.	B
4.	B	24.	A	44.	A
5.	A	25.	B	45.	B
6.	D	26.	D	46.	D
7.	C	27.	C	47.	D
8.	C	28.	C	48.	C
9.	A	29.	A	49.	B
10.	D	30.	A	50.	D
11.	B	31.	C	51.	A
12.	D	32.	B	52.	C
13.	D	33.	D	53.	A
14.	A	34.	B	54.	D
15.	C	35.	B	55.	B
16.	C	36.	B	56.	D
17.	B	37.	D	57.	D
18.	B	38.	A	58.	B
19.	D	39.	C	59.	C
20.	A	40.	A	60.	D

Chapter **21**

Practice Test 1: Social Studies

The Social Studies test consists of questions that measure general social studies concepts. The questions are based on short readings that often include a map, graph, chart, cartoon, or figure. Study the information given and then answer the question(s) following it. Refer to the information as often as necessary in answering the questions.

The Social Studies test of the GED consists of one section. You have 70 minutes to complete the test. Remember, on the real test you can use the onscreen calculator (or your own TI-30XS MultiView calculator if you take the test at a testing center).

The answers and explanations to this test's questions are in Chapter 22. Go through the explanations to all the questions, even for the ones you answered correctly. The explanations are a good review of the techniques I discuss throughout the book.

REMEMBER

Unless you require accommodations, you'll be taking the GED test on a computer. Instead of marking your answers on an answer sheet, as you do for the practice tests in this book, you'll see clickable ovals and fill-in-the-blank text boxes, and you'll be able to click with your mouse and drag and drop items where indicated. I formatted the questions and answer choices in this book to make them appear as similar as possible to the real GED test, but I had to retain some A, B, C, D choices for marking your answers, and I provide an answer sheet for you to do so.

Answer Sheet for Practice Test 1, Social Studies

1. _____

2. _____

3. _____

4. _____

5. _____

6. _____

7. _____

8. _____

9. _____

10. _____

11. _____

12. _____

13. _____

14. _____

15. _____

16. _____

17. _____

18. _____

19. _____

20. _____

21. _____

22. _____

23. _____

24. _____

25. _____

26. _____

27. _____

28. _____

29. _____

30. _____

31. _____

32. _____

33. _____

34. _____

35. _____

36. _____

37. _____

38. _____

39. _____

40. _____

41. _____

42. _____

43. _____

44. _____

45. _____

46. _____

47. _____

48. _____

49. _____

50. _____

Questions 1–5 refer to the following passage, which is excerpted from Cliffs Quick Review U.S. History I, by P. Soifer and A. Hoffman (John Wiley & Sons, Inc.).

Industry and Trade in the Thirteen Colonies

The colonies were part of an Atlantic trading network that linked them with England, Africa, and the West Indies. The pattern of commerce, not too accurately called the Triangular Trade, involved the exchange of products from colonial farms, plantations, fisheries, and forests with England for manufactured goods and the West Indies for slaves, molasses, and sugar. In New England, molasses and sugar were distilled into rum, which was used to buy African slaves. Southern Europe was also a valuable market for colonial foodstuffs.

Colonial industry was closely associated with trade. A significant percentage of Atlantic shipping was on vessels built in the colonies, and shipbuilding stimulated other crafts, such as the sewing of sails, milling of lumber, and manufacturing of naval stores. Mercantile theory encouraged the colonies to provide raw materials for England's industrializing economy; pig iron and coal became important exports. Concurrently, restrictions were placed on finished goods. For example, Parliament, concerned about possible competition from colonial hatters, prohibited the export of hats from one colony to another and limited the number of apprentices in each hat maker's shop.

1. What did England, Africa, and the West Indies have in common?
   (A) They all had fisheries.
   (B) They all bought slaves.
   (C) They all distilled rum.
   (D) They all exchanged products.

2. What was rum used for?
   (A) colonial farms
   (B) milling of lumber
   (C) purchase of slaves
   (D) molasses and sugar

3. Why were the colonies important to Atlantic trade?
   (A) They built the ships.
   (B) They sewed sails.
   (C) They had naval stores.
   (D) They milled lumber.

4. How did the colonies support British industry?
   (A) They took part in sewing.
   (B) They produced finished goods.
   (C) They developed mercantile theory.
   (D) They provided raw materials.

5. What British product was threatened by colonial competition?

   (A) coal

   (B) pig iron

   (C) hats

   (D) lumber

Questions 6–11 refer to the following passage, which is excerpted from The Declaration of Independence, 1776.

Charges Against the King

He has forbidden his governors to pass laws of immediate and pressing importance, unless suspended in their operation till his assent should be obtained; and when so suspended, he has utterly neglected to attend to them.

He has refused to pass other laws for the accommodation of large districts of people, unless those people would relinquish the right of representation in the legislature — a right inestimable to them, and formidable to tyrants only.

He has called together legislative bodies at places unusual, uncomfortable, and distant from the depository of their public records, for the sole purpose of fatiguing them into compliance with his measures.

He has dissolved representative houses repeatedly, for opposing, with manly firmness, his invasions on the rights of the people.

He has refused, for a long time after such dissolutions, to cause others to be elected; whereby the legislative powers, incapable of annihilation, have returned to the people at large, for their exercise, the state remaining in the meantime exposed to all the dangers of invasion from without, and convulsions within.

He has endeavored to prevent the population of these states; for that purpose obstructing the laws for naturalization of foreigners; refusing to pass others to encourage their migration hither, and raising the conditions of new appropriations of lands.

He has obstructed the administration of justice, by refusing his assent to laws for establishing judiciary powers.

He has made judges dependent on his will alone, for the tenure of their offices, and the amount and payment of their salaries.

He has erected a multitude of new offices, and sent hither swarms of officers, to harass our people, and eat out their substance.

He has kept among us, in times of peace, standing armies, without the consent of our legislature.

He has affected to render the military independent of, and superior to, the civil power.

6. The king neglected the colonies in many ways, especially by

   (A) failing to provide money.

   (B) failing to pass laws.

   (C) removing their right of condemnation.

   (D) giving power to his governors.

7. Which of the following methods did the king use to force legislative bodies to follow his wishes?

   (A) He never called them together.

   (B) He made them comfortable.

   (C) He made sure they were well rested.

   (D) He made meeting places unusual, distant, and uncomfortable.

8. Which of the following actions was seen as a threat to the colonists' rights?

   (A) The king dissolved representative houses.

   (B) The king refused to approve laws to encourage immigration.

   (C) The king sent many new officeholders, who consumed valuable resources.

   (D) The king maintained a large army in the colonies.

9. The king was very concerned about the growth of the colonies, so he

   (A) gave away free land to people willing to settle.

   (B) encouraged people to settle.

   (C) settled there himself.

   (D) discouraged people from settling.

10. How did the king obstruct the judicial system?

    (A) He made it independent of his authority.

    (B) He erected new offices.

    (C) He refused to enact certain laws.

    (D) He harassed the people.

11. According to the colonists, which of the following endangered them?

    (A) Too many immigrants were entering the colonies.

    (B) Armies were available to defend the colonies from attack.

    (C) The king imposed new taxes.

    (D) Representative bodies were closed, so threats couldn't be addressed.

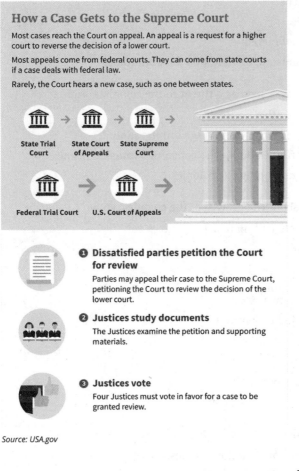

How a Case Gets to the Supreme Court

Most cases reach the Court on appeal. An appeal is a request for a higher court to reverse the decision of a lower court.

Most appeals come from federal courts. They can come from state courts if a case deals with federal law.

Rarely, the Court hears a new case, such as one between states.

State Trial Court → State Court of Appeals → State Supreme Court →

Federal Trial Court → U.S. Court of Appeals →

❶ Dissatisfied parties petition the Court for review

Parties may appeal their case to the Supreme Court, petitioning the Court to review the decision of the lower court.

❷ Justices study documents

The Justices examine the petition and supporting materials.

❸ Justices vote

Four Justices must vote in favor for a case to be granted review.

Source: USA.gov

12. Which branch of government is this illustration about?

(A) executive

(B) legislative

(C) judicial

(D) environmental

13. The most usual way for a case to reach the Supreme Court is through a/an ☐ .

14. The states of Michigan, Minnesota, and Wisconsin sued Illinois over the level of water in the Great Lakes. They believed that actions Illinois was taking were harming their residents. Which court would first hear this case?

(A) State Trial Court

(B) State Supreme Court

(C) Federal Trial Court

(D) U.S. Supreme Court

15. How many of the Supreme Court's nine justices have to vote in favor for a case to be granted review?

(A) 3

(B) 4

(C) 5

(D) 6

16. A company is convicted of a crime in state court. The company wants to appeal the conviction. Which court should the company appeal to first?

(A) State Appeals Court

(B) State Supreme Court

(C) Federal Appeals Court

(D) U.S. Supreme Court

Questions 17–22 refer to the following passage, which is excerpted from President Lincoln's Gettysburg Address, November 19, 1863.

Gettysburg Address

Four score and seven years ago, our fathers brought forth upon this continent a new nation, conceived in liberty and dedicated to the proposition that all men are created equal. Now we are engaged in a great civil war, testing whether that nation or any nation so conceived and so dedicated can long endure. We are met on a great battlefield of that war. We have come to dedicate a portion of that field as a final resting place for those who here gave their lives that that nation might live. It is altogether fitting and proper that we should do this. But, in a larger sense, we cannot dedicate, we cannot consecrate, we cannot hallow this ground. The brave men, living and dead, who struggled here have consecrated it far above our poor power to add or detract. The world will little note nor long remember what we say here, but it can never forget what they did here. . . .

17. Which of the following is of primary importance in the Civil War, according to Lincoln's speech?

(A) happiness and friendship

(B) safety and security

(C) liberty and equality

(D) peace and prosperity

18. Where did President Lincoln deliver this speech?

(A) on a train

(B) at the White House

(C) on a battlefield

(D) in Congress

19. What does "little note nor long remember" mean?

(A) The audience is not taking notes.

(B) Lincoln has a bad memory.

(C) The soldiers are not there to hear the speech.

(D) People around the world will not remember the speech.

20. According to the address, a portion of the battlefield is used for a/an [   ].

21. Who has "hallow[ed] this ground"?

(A) President Lincoln

(B) those who fought there

(C) the Confederate government

(D) the Union government

22. What does the phrase, "four score and seven," refer to?

(A) soldiers

(B) consecration

(C) time

(D) the war

Questions 23–28 refer to the following passage, which is excerpted from Cliffs Quick Review U.S. History II, by P. Soifer and A. Hoffman (John Wiley & Sons, Inc.).

Causes of World War I

On June 28, 1914, a Serbian nationalist assassinated the Archduke Franz Ferdinand, the heir to the throne of Austria-Hungary. Austria demanded indemnities from Serbia for the assassination. The Serbian government denied any involvement with the murder and, when Austria issued an ultimatum, turned to its ally, Russia, for help. When Russia began to mobilize its army, Europe's alliance system, ironically intended to maintain the balance of power on the continent, drew one country after another into war. Austria's ally, Germany, declared war on Russia on August 1 and on France (which was allied with Russia) two days later. Great Britain entered the war on August 4, following Germany's invasion of neutral Belgium. By the end of August 1914, most of Europe had chosen sides: the Central Powers — Germany, Austria-Hungary, Bulgaria, and the Ottoman Empire (Turkey) — were up against the Allied Powers — principally Great Britain, France, Russia, and Serbia. Japan joined the Allied cause in August 1914, in hopes of seizing German possessions in the Pacific and expanding Japanese influence in China. This action threatened the Open Door Policy and led to increased tensions with the United States. Originally an ally of Germany and Austria-Hungary, Italy entered the war in 1915 on the side of Britain and France because they had agreed to Italian territorial demands in a secret treaty (the Treaty of London).

23. The assassin of Archduke Ferdinand came from the country of [   ].

24. Austria initially reacted to the assassination by

(A) denying any involvement.

(B) demanding indemnities.

(C) asking for Russian help.

(D) declaring war.

25. Which country entered the war last?

(A) Italy

(B) France

(C) Germany

(D) Japan

26. What caused Great Britain to enter the war?

   (A) Germany invaded Belgium.

   (B) Russia attacked Serbia.

   (C) Germany declared war on France.

   (D) Austria invaded Hungary.

27. Which country was a member of the Central Powers?

   (A) Great Britain

   (B) France

   (C) Germany

   (D) Serbia

28. Place the events in the proper sequence. Write the letters on the line: [＿＿＿＿].

   (A) France declares war on Germany.

   (B) Austria issues an ultimatum to Serbia.

   (C) Germany invades Belgium.

   (D) Germany declares war on Russia.

   (E) Serbia asks Russia for help, and Russia mobilizes its army.

Questions 29–32 refer to the following political cartoon.

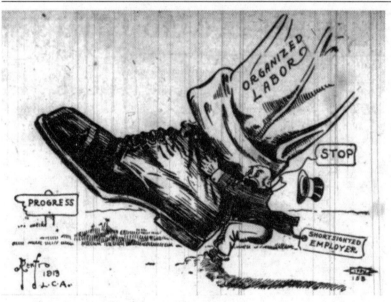

Cartoon by Alfred T. Renfro, Seattle Union Record, November 1, 1913.

29. How is organized labor portrayed in the cartoon?

   (A) an irrelevant idea that's past its time

   (B) an impediment to improving society

   (C) an ineffective voice for reform

   (D) a powerful force for positive change

30. How are employers portrayed in the cartoon?

    (A) supporters of workers

    (B) ineffective opponents of change

    (C) patriotic citizens

    (D) dynamic leaders of a strong economy

31. What is the main idea of the cartoon?

    (A) Labor unions must be stopped from causing more harm to the economy.

    (B) Labor unions are corrupt and ineffective representatives of workers.

    (C) Labor unions are an unstoppable positive force in America.

    (D) Labor unions do not do much positive good for the country.

32. Which of the following actions by a labor union would be most consistent with the way labor is portrayed in the cartoon?

    (A) Obtaining free dental insurance for all employees at a large company.

    (B) Providing legal help when an employee is fired unfairly.

    (C) Encouraging the government to raise the minimum wage.

    (D) All of the above.

Questions 33–36 refer to this pie chart.

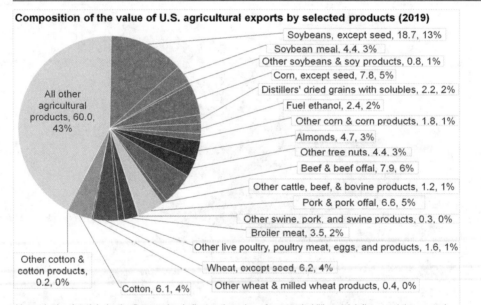

Composition of the value of U.S. agricultural exports by selected products (2019)

- Soybeans, except seed, 18.7, 13%
- Soybean meal, 4.4, 3%
- Other soybeans & soy products, 0.8, 1%
- Corn, except seed, 7.8, 5%
- Distillers' dried grains with solubles, 2.2, 2%
- Fuel ethanol, 2.4, 2%
- Other corn & corn products, 1.8, 1%
- Almonds, 4.7, 3%
- Other tree nuts, 4.4, 3%
- Beef & beef offal, 7.9, 6%
- Other cattle, beef, & bovine products, 1.2, 1%
- Pork & pork offal, 6.6, 5%
- Other swine, pork, and swine products, 0.3, 0%
- Broiler meat, 3.5, 2%
- Other live poultry, poultry meat, eggs, and products, 1.6, 1%
- Wheat, except seed, 6.2, 4%
- Other wheat & milled wheat products, 0.4, 0%
- Cotton, 6.1, 4%
- Other cotton & cotton products, 0.2, 0%
- All other agricultural products, 60.0, 43%

Notes: In the data labels, the first number indicates the value of exports in billions of dollars, and the second number indicates the category's share of total U.S. agricultural exports. The category "All Other Agricultural Products" includes all agricultural products not specified in the other product categories.

Source: Prepared by authors using data from U.S. Department of Commerce, Bureau of the Census data as compiled by USDA, Foreign Agricultural Service, Global Agricultural Trade System.

Source: The U.S. Department of Agriculture

33. Which plant crop provides the largest share of agricultural exports? ⬚

34. What is the total value of exports of "wheat, except seed"?

    (A) $4 million

    (B) $6.2 million

    (C) $4 billion

    (D) $6.2 billion

35. Over 43 percent of all exports are "other agricultural products." Which of these generalizations about American agricultural exports is supported by this statistic?

    (A) The United States does not export a wide number of different agricultural products.

    (B) American agricultural exports are incredibly varied.

    (C) Agricultural products are a significant part of the United States' exports.

    (D) A strong agriculture sector is responsible for the prosperity of the United States.

36. What is the most widely exported tree nut, according to the pie chart? [   ]

Questions 37–41 refer to the following timeline.

Timeline of Major Events in U.S. History

1900: Gold standard for currency adopted by the United States.

1914: World War I begins.

1918: World War I ends.

1929: Stock market crashes; Great Depression begins.

1933: Gold exports banned; daily price established; U.S. citizens ordered to turn in all gold.

1934: Price of gold fixed at $35 per troy ounce.

1939: World War II begins.

1945: World War II ends.

1950: Korean Conflict begins.

1953: Korean Conflict ends.

1965: Vietnam War begins.

1973: Vietnam War ends; gold prices allowed to float; U.S. currency removed from gold standard.

1974: U.S. citizens allowed to own gold again.

1979: Soviet Union invades Afghanistan; U.S. hostages seized in Iran.

1980: Historic high prices for gold.

1987: Stock market crashes.

1989: Berlin Wall falls.

1990: Gulf War begins.

1991: Gulf War ends.

2001: Terrorist attacks on the United States.

2002: Invasion of Afghanistan and Iraq.

2008: United States elects first black president.

2009: United States slips into a recession.

37. Which of the following was the value of the United States' dollar based on in 1900?

   (A) stocks and bonds

   (B) gold

   (C) silver

   (D) trade surpluses

38. What is the connection between the stock market crash and the Great Depression in 1929?

   (A) The crash triggered the Great Depression.

   (B) Very little; economic problems had been building for some time before the crash.

   (C) Pure coincidence.

   (D) The stock market crash delayed the Great Depression.

39. What does "U.S. citizens ordered to turn in all gold" mean?

   (A) Citizens got to keep their gold.

   (B) Citizens had to tell the government about their gold.

   (C) Citizens could buy gold from each other, for profit.

   (D) Citizens had to take all their gold to government offices.

40. When was U.S. currency removed from the gold standard? [_____]

41. Based on what you see in the timeline, what probably caused the price of gold to reach an historic high in 1980?

   (A) Citizens were allowed to buy and sell bullion again.

   (B) The U.S. dollar was removed from the gold standard.

   (C) The Soviet Union invaded Afghanistan.

   (D) The Gulf War began.

Questions 42–44 refer to the following newscast.

Unusual and unseasonable conditions continue to plague cities and countries around the world.

Extreme temperatures, drought, and wildfires are plaguing the western United States. Drought and extreme temperatures are continuing to wreak havoc with farmers and to cause wildfires. Record wildfires are burning in California and Oregon. In addition, the drought is so severe that water supplies are being rationed in several locations. Fires in California have affected wine-producing areas. Several vineyards are reported to be completely ruined. The economic impact of the wildfires and drought shows no sign of abating, as weather conditions are predicted to remain hot and dry.

Floods are affecting Europe and China. While parts of the United States have too little water, parts of Europe and China have too much. Torrential downpours caused major flooding recently in England, Germany, and Belgium. The Netherlands also experienced record storms, but that country's flood control system managed to contain the excess water. Other countries were not so lucky. Flooding also affected major cities in China, and subway systems in both China and England were flooded.

Ash and smoke from a volcanic eruption in Iceland affected air traffic in the country's capital. The volcano, near the capital and its main airport, disrupted flights for several days. Prior to the eruption, weeks of violent tremors terrorized residents in the capital area.

42. In which continents did major flooding take place?

   (A) Europe and North America

   (B) Asia and South America

   (C) Europe and Africa

   (D) Europe and Asia

43. How does extreme drought cause financial problems for farmers?

   (A) Farmers lose their entire year's crop and income.

   (B) Farm equipment is destroyed.

   (C) Floods destroy crops.

   (D) Water is rationed in cities.

44. Which of the following is an example of extreme weather?

   (A) a volcanic eruption

   (B) an earthquake

   (C) a tremor

   (D) a torrential downpour

Question 45 refers to the following passage, which is excerpted from the Central Intelligence Agency website (www.cia.gov).

By the time World War I started in 1914, the United States' ability to collect foreign intelligence had shrunk drastically because of budget cuts and bureaucratic reorganizations in the government. The State Department began small-scale collections against the Central Powers in 1916, but it wasn't until the United States declared war on Germany in 1917 that Army and Navy intelligence finally received more money and personnel. By that time, it was too late to increase their intelligence output to aid the cause very much.

The most significant advance for U.S. intelligence during the war was the establishment of a permanent communications intelligence agency in the Army, what would become the forerunner of the National Security Agency. Meanwhile, the Secret Service, the New York Police Department, and military counterintelligence aggressively thwarted numerous German covert actions inside the United States, including psychological warfare, political and economic operations, and dozens of sabotage attempts against British-owned firms and factories supplying munitions to Britain and Russia.

45. How effective was U.S. foreign intelligence-gathering during World War I?

   (A) Very effective; it stopped much domestic sabotage.

   (B) Not very effective; it depended on the New York Police Department.

   (C) It was limited because of pre-war budget cuts.

   (D) It was excellent at psychological warfare.

Questions 46 and 47 refer to the following excerpt from a speech given by Frederick Douglass (an African-American reformer, statesman, and former enslaved person) on July 5, 1852.

What, to the American slave, is your 4th of July? I answer: a day that reveals to him, more than all other days in the year, the gross injustice and cruelty to which he is the constant victim. To him, your celebration is a sham; your boasted liberty, an unholy license; your national greatness, swelling vanity; your sounds of rejoicing are empty and heartless; your denunciations of tyrants, brass fronted impudence; your shouts of liberty and equality, hollow mockery; your prayers and hymns, your sermons and thanksgivings, with all your religious parade, and solemnity, are, to him, mere bombast, fraud, deception, impiety, and hypocrisy — a thin veil to cover up crimes which would disgrace a nation of savages.

46. Which of the following statements best summarizes the main idea of this excerpt?

(A) Even tyrants should give enslaved people the day off from work to celebrate the Fourth of July.

(B) It is hypocritical to celebrate the Fourth of July when people remain enslaved.

(C) The United States should cancel all patriotic celebrations because the whole idea of independence is fraudulent.

(D) Those who are listening to this speech must give sermons, sing hymns, and persuade their fellow Americans to abolish slavery.

47. Frederick Douglass most likely asks the question in the first line of the excerpt to

(A) make his listeners question their patriotism.

(B) suggest that more celebrations incorporate African-American heritage.

(C) enlist support for his alternative celebration.

(D) point out disparities between ideals and realities.

Questions 48 and 49 are general questions about the United States government.

48. The first ten amendments to the Constitution are called

(A) The Parts of Ten

(B) The Bill of Rights

(C) The Articles of Confederation

(D) We the People of the United States

49. Which of the following individuals is the head of the judicial branch of government?

(A) President

(B) Speaker of the House of Representatives

(C) Senate Majority Leader

(D) Chief Justice of the United States

Question 50 refers to the following excerpt from the Declaration of Sentiments written in 1848 at the Seneca Falls Convention.

We hold these truths to be self-evident: that all men and women are created equal; that they are endowed by their Creator with certain inalienable rights; that among these are life, liberty, and the pursuit of happiness; that to secure these rights governments are instituted, deriving their just powers from the consent of the governed. Whenever any form of government becomes destructive of these ends, it is the right of those who suffer from it to refuse allegiance to it, and to insist upon the institution of a new government, laying its foundation on such principles, and organizing its powers in such form, as to them shall seem most likely to effect their safety and happiness.

50. The authors of the Declaration of Sentiments used which of the following documents to support their claims?

(A) The Declaration of Independence

(B) The Federalist Papers

(C) The Emancipation Proclamation

(D) The Magna Carta

Chapter 22

Answers for Practice Test 1, Social Studies

In this chapter, I provide the answers and explanations to every question in the Social Studies practice test in Chapter 21. If you just want a quick look at the answers, check out the abbreviated answer key at the end of this chapter. However, if you have the time, it's more useful for study purposes to read all the answer explanations carefully. Doing so will help you understand why some answers were correct and others not, especially when the choices were really close. It will also point you to areas where you may need to do more review. Remember, you learn as much from your errors as from the correct answers.

Answers and Explanations

1. **D. They all exchanged products.** England, Africa, and the West Indies all traded products: The West Indies traded molasses, sugar, and slaves with England for food and wood; England (via the New England colonies) then made the molasses and sugar into rum and traded it with Africa for more slaves. But these areas did not all have the same commodities to trade; each had its own strengths.

2. **C. purchase of slaves.** Rum was used to purchase slaves for the colonies. The other answer choices — colonial farms, milling of lumber, and molasses and sugar — were all patterns of commerce but weren't uses of rum.

3. **A. They built the ships.** Ships were built in the colonies to increase Atlantic trade. Sewing sails, naval stores, milled lumber, and other crafts were colonial products that shipbuilding stimulated. However, shipbuilding itself was the primary reason the colonies were important to the Atlantic trade; the other choices were secondary.

4. **D. They provided raw materials.** The colonies provided raw materials for British manufacturing industries. According to the passage, "Mercantile theory encouraged the colonies to provide raw materials for England's industrializing economy. . . ." The British government blocked exports of finished goods from the colonies.

5. **C. hats.** The export of hats — a finished good — from the colonies was prohibited because it threatened British manufacturing. Coal and lumber were raw materials, which didn't threaten English manufacturing. Even pig iron needed further manufacturing to sell, so it was allowed.

6. **B. failing to pass laws.** According to the first paragraph of the passage, the king neglected the colonies in a number of ways. Of the ways listed here, only failing to pass laws (ones that would alleviate grievances) is correct. Although the other choices are grievances, they can't be alleviated until the appropriate laws are passed.

7. **D. He made meeting places unusual, distant, and uncomfortable.** According to the third paragraph of the passage, the charge against the king clearly states that he tries to force compliance by forcing his legislative bodies to meet in uncomfortable and far-off places in an effort to wear them down and make them more agreeable to his wishes.

8. **A. The king dissolved representative houses.** According to the fourth paragraph of the passage, the king dissolved the representative houses because they opposed his attacks on the rights of the people. The remaining choices were problems caused by the king's actions, but they did not affect the colonists' rights.

9. **D. discouraged people from settling.** The sixth paragraph of the passage says, "He has endeavored to prevent the population of these states." In other words, he has discouraged newcomers from settling.

10. **C. He refused to enact certain laws.** The seventh paragraph of the passage states that the king didn't give his approval to laws that would have created a local judicial system.

11. **D. Representative bodies were closed, so threats couldn't be addressed.** According to the document, because the king had closed the representative bodies and refused to reopen them, the colonies were, "exposed to all the dangers of invasion from without, and convulsions within." Choices (A) and (B) are contradicted by the passage. Choice (C) is not supported by the passage, because taxes are not mentioned in the excerpt.

12. **C. judicial.** The judicial branch of government consists of the court system. There is no such branch of government as environmental (Choice D).

13. **appeal.** The information says that most cases reach the Supreme Court through appeal. Only a few cases reach the court directly, and many of those involve states suing other states.

14. **D. U.S. Supreme Court.** According to the information, when states sue one another, the case is heard in the U.S. Supreme Court.

15. **B. 4.** According to the information, four justices are required to vote in favor of reviewing an appeal. Choice (C), 5, is the number of judges required to decide a case. The remaining choices are incorrect.

16. **A. State Appeals Court.** The next court the company could appeal to is the State Court of Appeals.

17. **C. liberty and equality.** As stated in the first two sentences of the passage, the issues of prime importance in the Civil War were liberty and equality. Happiness and friendship (Choice A), safety and security (Choice B), and peace and prosperity (Choice D) aren't the best answers.

18. **C. on a battlefield.** You know from the passage that President Lincoln was delivering his speech on a battlefield at Gettysburg. This fact rules out every answer choice except this one.

19. **D. People around the world will not remember the speech.** Lincoln was saying that the world would remember the soldiers who died but wouldn't remember his speech. (He was wrong about his speech, because the Gettysburg Address is one of the most famous speeches in American history.)

20. **burial ground, cemetery,** or **graveyard.** Some of the battlefield was to become a burial ground for the fallen. Much of the rest has been preserved as a memorial and is one of the most commonly visited of all Civil War battlefields today.

21. **B. those who fought there.** The ground was hallowed by those who fought there. Lincoln doesn't believe the people involved in the dedication of the battlefield can make the place holy or important; the sacrifice of the people who fought on the battlefield makes it so.

22. **C. time.** The word *years* follows *four score and seven*, so you can assume that phrase relates to time. (By the way, a *score* is 20 years, so *four score and seven* is 87 years.)

23. **Serbia.** Archduke Ferdinand was assassinated by a Serbian nationalist, so the correct answer is Serbia.

24. **B. demanding indemnities.** Austria demanded indemnities in response to the assassination. This answer comes directly from the passage.

25. **A. Italy.** According to the passage, Italy joined the war in 1915. The other countries went to war in 1914.

26. **A. Germany invaded Belgium.** You know that Great Britain entered the war when Germany invaded Belgium from the sentence that states, "Great Britain entered the war on August 4, following Germany's invasion of neutral Belgium."

27. **C. Germany.** Germany was a member of the Central Powers. About halfway through the passage is a list of the Central Powers (on one side of the war) and the Allied Powers (on the other side).

28. **B, E, D, A, C (Austria issues an ultimatum to Serbia; Serbia asks Russia for help, and Russia mobilizes its army; Germany declares war on Russia; France declares war on Germany; Germany invades Belgium).** This is the order of events as stated in the passage. Note that this question, which is designed to mimic a drag-and-drop question, can have more than four answer choices.

29. **D. a powerful force for positive change.** The movement toward "progress" shows that the cartoonist views unions as a positive force.

30. **B. ineffective opponents of change.** The overweight, overdressed employer who is unable to stop the unions shows that Choice (B) is correct.

31. **C. Labor unions are an unstoppable positive force in America.** The strength of the leg and foot, the powerful motion toward "progress," and the inability of the businessperson to stop unions show that the cartoonist believes labor unions are a strong, positive force.

32. **D. All of the above.** *All of the above* is the only correct choice because all the actions in Choices (A), (B), and (C) are positive changes. Items with "all of the above" as an answer choice are rare on the GED but sometimes appear. On items like this, the process of elimination works in reverse. If two of the answer choices are correct but you cannot decide about the third, then the most likely answer is "all of the above." Items with "all of the above" can be tricky. If you do not read all of the answer choices, you can easily select the first choice as correct, not realizing that all of them are correct. This is another good reason to always read all the answer choices!

33. **soybeans.** The single largest shaded area after "all other agricultural products" is for soybeans and related products.

34. **D. $6.2 billion.** According to the pie chart, these exports totaled $6.2 billion. Choice (B) is incorrect because the information below the chart makes it clear that the first number is units in billions of dollars and the second number is the percentage of total exports. Choice (A) is the value for the percentage of exports incorrectly written in millions of dollars, and Choice (C) is the same value incorrectly written in billions of dollars.

35. **B. American agricultural exports are incredibly varied.** The fact that 43 percent of American agricultural products are in the "other" category shows that the United States produces a huge variety of agricultural products. Therefore, Choice (A) is incorrect. Choice (C) is true but is not supported by this detail, and so is not the answer to this question. Choice (D) is likely true but is not supported by this pie chart or other information.

36. **almonds.** The only categories for tree nuts in the chart are almonds and other tree nuts. Therefore, almonds are the most widely exported tree nut.

37. **B. gold.** The first item on the list states, "gold standard for currency adopted." That means that the value of the American dollar was directly linked to gold.

38. **A. The crash triggered the Great Depression.** The Great Depression was caused by a variety of issues, but the immediate cause, the trigger, was the crash of the stock market. The other answers are wrong. Although Choice (B) says that problems had been building, the crash started the panic that resulted in the Great Depression. It wasn't coincidence, nor did the crash delay the Great Depression.

39. **D. Citizens had to take all their gold to government offices.** U.S. citizens had to take all their gold to U.S. offices and not keep any in their banks or homes. The timeline and graph don't tell you why they had to do so, just that they did. *Turn in* is the key phrase here.

40. **1973.** The U.S. currency was removed from the gold standard in 1973.

41. **C. The Soviet Union invaded Afghanistan.** The best answer is that gold reached a historic high when the Soviets invaded Afghanistan. Of all the prior events in the timeline, this event is the one closest to the record high. Financial worries caused by the invasion prompted investors to buy gold, raising its price. Choices (A) and (B) are too far in the past to be causes of the increase in gold prices. Choice (D) took place after the price record was set, and so cannot be the cause.

42. **D. Europe and Asia.** According to the passage, the floods occurred in Asia (China) and Europe (England, Germany, and Belgium). The United States (Choice A), a country in North America, is mentioned in the passage, but not in relation to flooding, and so is incorrect. South America (Choice B) and Africa (Choice C) are not mentioned in the passage at all.

43. **A. Farmers lose their entire year's crop and income.** Extreme drought conditions lead to crop failures and financial losses. Therefore, Choice (A) is correct. Droughts don't destroy farm equipment (Choice B) or cause floods (Choice C). Water rationing in cities (Choice D) doesn't affect farmers.

44. **D. a torrential downpour.** Of the four choices, only Choice (D) is related to weather. The remaining choices are related to geography.

45. **C. It was limited because of pre-war budget cuts.** The efforts against sabotage, Choice (A), and psychological warfare, Choice (D), weren't part of foreign intelligence-gathering and are thus wrong. Choice (B) is also related to domestic intelligence. The foreign intelligence work was limited because of budget issues. The text states at the end of the first paragraph that foreign intelligence did not "aid the cause very much."

46. **B. It is hypocritical to celebrate the Fourth of July when people remain enslaved.** Frederick Douglass' main point is that celebrating the Fourth of July, a day honoring independence, freedom from tyranny, and liberty, is cruel and hypocritical while slavery continues to exist.

47. **D. point out disparities between ideals and realities.** Douglass asks the question, "What, to the American slave, is your 4th of July?" to point out that the ideal of "liberty and freedom for all" isn't the reality of life for slaves.

48. **B. The Bill of Rights.** The first ten amendments to the Constitution comprise the Bill of Rights.

49. **D. Chief Justice of the United States.** This is the formal title of the head of the judicial branch, though many people call this person "Chief Justice of the Supreme Court." Choice (A) is the head of the executive branch. Choices (B) and (C) are leaders of the legislative branch.

50. **A. The Declaration of Independence.** The excerpt from the Declaration of Sentiments, written during the Seneca Falls Convention in 1848, makes a direct reference to the words of the Declaration of Independence. It's a direct quote from the second paragraph of the Declaration of Independence.

Answer Key

1.	D	18.	C	34.	D
2.	C	19.	D	35.	B
3.	A	20.	burial ground, cemetery, or graveyard	36.	almonds
4.	D			37.	B
5.	C			38.	A
6.	B	21.	B	39.	D
7.	D	22.	C	40.	1973
8.	A	23.	Serbia	41.	C
9.	D	24.	B	42.	D
10.	C	25.	A	43.	A
11.	D	26.	A	44.	D
12.	C	27.	C	45.	C
13.	appeal	28.	B, E, D, A, C	46.	B
14.	D	29.	D	47.	D
15.	B	30.	B	48.	B
16.	A	31.	C	49.	D
17.	C	32.	D	50.	A
		33.	soybeans		

Chapter 23

Practice Test 1: Science

The Science test consists of multiple-choice, fill-in-the-blank, drop-down, and drag-and-drop questions intended to measure your understanding of general concepts in science. The questions are based on short passages that may include a graph, chart, or figure. Study the information given and then answer the question(s). Refer to the passage as often as necessary when answering the questions, but remember that you have a time limit, and you should try to spend as little time on any item as you can and still get the correct answer.

You have 90 minutes to complete this section of the GED test. The answers and explanations to this test's questions are in Chapter 24. Go through the explanations to all the questions, even for the ones you answered correctly. The explanations are a good review of the techniques I discuss throughout the book.

Remember, you are allowed to use a calculator on the GED Science test. For this test it's OK to use the calculator on your phone, but at some point, you'll want to get used to the TI-30XS MultiView calculator that is used on the test.

REMEMBER

On the real GED, you'll take the test on a computer. Instead of marking your answers on an answer sheet, like you do for the practice tests in this book, you'll use the keyboard and the mouse to indicate your answers. I formatted the questions and answer choices in this book to make them appear as similar as possible to what you'll see on the computer screen, but I had to retain some A, B, C, and D choices and provide an answer sheet for marking your answers. When you're ready for the included online practice test, you'll be able to see and try the actual question types as they appear on the test.

Use the timer on your phone to keep track of time. If you run out of time, mark the last question you answered. Then answer the rest of the questions. This will help you figure out how much more quickly you will have to work to complete the entire test in the time allowed.

Answer Sheet for Practice Test 1, Science

1. _____

2. _____

3. _____

4. _____

5. _____

6. _____

7. _____

8. _____

9. _____

10. _____

11. _____

12. _____

13. _____

14. _____

15. _____

16. _____

17. _____

18. _____

19. _____

20. _____

21. _____

22. _____

23. _____

24. _____

25. _____

26. _____

27. _____

28. _____

29. _____

30. _____

31. _____

32. _____

33. _____

34. _____

35. _____

36. _____

37. _____

38. _____

39. _____

40. _____

41. _____

42. _____

43. _____

44. _____

45. _____

46. _____

47. _____

48. _____

49. _____

50. _____

Science Test

TIME: 90 minutes

ITEMS: 50

DIRECTIONS: Read each question carefully and mark your answer on the answer sheet provided.

Questions 1 and 2 refer to the following passage.

Insulation

During the winter, you need something to keep warmth in the house and cold air out. In the summer, you need something to keep heat outside and cooler air inside. What you need is insulation.

Insulation reduces or prevents the transfer of heat (called *thermal transfer*) from the inside out or the outside in. Fiberglass and plastic foam provide such insulation because they contain trapped air. Normally, air is not a good insulator because the currents in air transfer the heat from one place to another. Trapping the air in small places, however, slows or prevents the transfer of heat. Think about these little packets of air the next time you sit in a warm house, safe from the frigid air of winter.

Joe "JJ" Johnson, the world-famous architect and building supervisor, has developed a standard vacation home that he builds for his clients. This house has one floor-to-ceiling glass wall that overlooks the best feature of the client's lot. The other walls are cinder block covered with a cosmetic coat of concrete. These walls have normal-sized windows in each room.

Mr. Johnson has been hired to build one of his famous designs for a client in Juno, Alaska, on a huge lot with a spectacular view of the Gastineau Channel. The client has requested a variation on the standard design to reduce their carbon footprint.

1. What variation would make the most sense to reduce the carbon footprint and preserve the home's beautiful design?

    (A) Have a floor-to-ceiling window facing away from the channel toward the front of the property.

    (B) Replace the floor-to-ceiling window with a cinder block wall.

    (C) Order curtains to cover the floor-to-ceiling window.

    (D) Use new high-tech insulated glass in all the windows in the house.

2. What other ways could the homeowner consider to reduce the cost of energy to heat the house?

    (A) Add as much additional insulation as possible.

    (B) Use the house only during the winter months.

    (C) Switch to an electric car.

    (D) Have fewer houseguests in winter.

Questions 3–5 refer to the following passage from The Surgeon General's Vision for a Healthy and Fit Nation *(www.surgeongeneral.gov).*

As a society, we have to begin to change our habits one healthy choice at a time. Change starts with the individual choices we as Americans make each day for ourselves and those around us. Balancing good nutrition and physical activity while managing daily stressors is always a challenge, but one that can be achieved. Finding time to shop for and prepare healthful meals after work and between family activities requires planning. Stress and a lack of healthful and available foods are some of the reasons why many people turn to fast food as a regular source for meals. Eating excess calories contributes to obesity, but so does watching too much television and sitting for hours in front of a computer.

This fact is especially true for children and teenagers. Technological advancements have made our lives more convenient — but also more sedentary. Research shows that leading an inactive life not only increases the risk of becoming overweight or obese, but also contributes to an increased risk for disease and disability.

The good news is that we can overcome these challenges — and the reward is the creation of a healthy and fit nation. Healthy choices include the following:

Reducing consumption of sodas and juices with added sugars

Reducing consumption of energy-dense foods that primarily contain added sugars or solid fats

Eating more fruits, vegetables, whole grains, and lean proteins

Controlling your portions

Drinking more water

Choosing low-fat or non-fat dairy products

Limiting television viewing time and considering keeping televisions out of children's rooms

Becoming more physically active throughout the day

3. According to the passage, people turn to fast food because
   (A) they prefer the taste of fast food to home-cooked food.
   (B) eating at fast food restaurants is cheaper than eating at home.
   (C) fast food is just as healthful as home-cooked food.
   (D) they don't have access to healthful and affordable foods.

4. Which of the following will result in children losing weight?
   (A) children eating more calories than they burn
   (B) children spending a lot of time watching TV
   (C) children's lives being sedentary because of technology
   (D) children eating portion-controlled meals

5. According to the passage, a significant psychological contributor to obesity is [_____].

Questions 6 and 7 refer to the following passage.

Velocity and Speed

There is a difference between speed and velocity, though sometimes you see these words used interchangeably. The *velocity* of a body is its rate of motion in a specific direction, such as a bicycle traveling 14 miles per hour due east. Because velocity has both magnitude (14 miles per hour) and direction (due east), it can be represented by a vector.

Speed has magnitude only. If a bicycle travels at a speed of 14 miles per hour, you know its magnitude (14 miles per hour) but not its direction. Because speed has a magnitude but not a direction, it can be represented as a scalar.

6. A force is defined as that which is required to change the state or motion of an object in magnitude and direction. A force has both magnitude and direction. Which of the following is the best way to represent a force?

(A) wavy lines

(B) a straight line

(C) a scalar

(D) a vector

7. If you were involved in a bicycle race over a predetermined route, what would be of greatest interest to you if you wanted to win: your speed, your distance traveled, your direction, or your route? [   ].

Questions 8 and 9 refer to the following diagram, which is excerpted from Physical Science: What the Technology Professional Needs to Know, *by C. Lon Enloe, Elizabeth Garnett, Jonathan Miles, and Stephen Swanson (John Wiley & Sons, Inc.).*

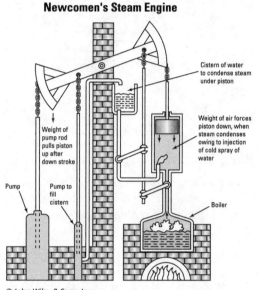

Newcomen's Steam Engine

Cistern of water to condense steam under piston

Weight of air forces piston down, when steam condenses owing to injection of cold spray of water

Weight of pump rod pulls piston up after down stroke

Pump

Pump to fill cistern

Boiler

© *John Wiley & Sons, Inc.*

8. What properties of water and steam allow Newcomen's steam engine to operate?

(A) Water is heavier than steam.

(B) Steam condenses when cooled, occupying less space.

(C) The boiler provides the energy to move the pump.

(D) The pump rod is heavy enough to pull the arm down.

9. What effect does the condensation of steam in the cylinder with the piston have on the pump that fills the cistern?

(A) It controls the fire in the boiler.

(B) It pumps water from the cistern to the boiler.

(C) It causes the pump to fill the cistern with water.

(D) It forces the piston down.

Question 10 refers to the following figure.

The Food Chain

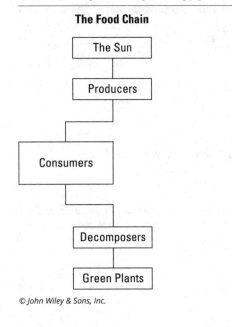

© *John Wiley & Sons, Inc.*

10. In the food chain, producers are ☐ .

Questions 11–14 refer to the following passage.

The Big Bang Theory

It is hard enough to imagine the universe as it is now and even harder to create a theory about how it all began. In the 1940s, George Gamow began to develop such a theory. Georges Lemaitre, another scientist, had also been working on the problem, and Gamow used some of the ideas of Lemaitre to develop his theory.

Gamow proposed the following theory: Somewhere between 10 and 21 billion years ago, there was a giant explosion in space. Before the explosion, the universe was the size of an atomic nucleus, with a temperature of about 10 billion degrees. The explosion started the expansion of the universe. Quarks, or elemental particles, existed in huge numbers.

Within a millisecond, the universe had expanded to the size of a grapefruit. The temperature cooled to 1 billion degrees. The quarks began to clump into protons and neutrons. Minutes later, the universe was still too hot for electrons and protons to form into atoms: a super-hot, fog-like environment.

With passing time and cooling temperatures, nuclear reactions took place, and within 300,000 years, atoms of hydrogen and helium began to emerge. As the atoms formed, light began to shine. The universe was taking shape.

Gravity began to act on the atoms and transform them into galaxies. Within 1 billion years of that first great explosion, galaxies and stars began to form. Within 15 billion years, planets began to emerge from the heavy elements thrown off by the dying of stars. The universe started with a big bang and continues to grow and change according to this theory.

11. The temperature of the first tiny particles was thought to be [   ] billion degrees.

12. For galaxies to have been transformed from atoms, what was necessary?

    (A) heat

    (B) pressure

    (C) centrifugal force

    (D) gravity

13. This theory is called the "Big Bang" because

    (A) an interplanetary war created a void, which the planets were formed to fill.

    (B) an immense explosion created the universe.

    (C) hydrogen causes immense explosions when ignited.

    (D) the explosion was very loud.

14. Which of the following formed planets?

    (A) nuclear reactions

    (B) matter from dying stars

    (C) an explosion

    (D) light

Questions 15–17 refer to the following passage.

The Jellyfish

One of the creatures living in all the world's oceans is the jellyfish. Although it lives in the ocean, it is not a fish. The jellyfish is an invertebrate — that is, an animal lacking a backbone. Not only does it lack a backbone, but the jellyfish also has no heart, blood, brain, or gills and is more than 95 percent water.

Around the bell-like structure of the body, the jellyfish has *tentacles* — long tendrils that contain stinging cells — which are used to capture prey. The movement of the prey triggers the sensory hair in the stinging cell, and the prey is then in trouble.

Unfortunately, people are also in trouble if they get too close to the tentacles of a jellyfish. The stings are not fatal to humans but can cause a great deal of discomfort.

15. Why is a jellyfish classified as an invertebrate?

    (A) It has tentacles.

    (B) It has a small brain.

    (C) It has a primitive circulatory system.

    (D) It has no backbone.

16. What are the possible consequences for a swimmer swimming in the vicinity of a school of jellyfish?

    (A) The jellyfish look weird.

    (B) Swimmers can get caught in the tentacles.

    (C) Swimmers may accidentally swallow a jellyfish.

    (D) The jellyfish may sting the swimmer, and the stings are painful.

17. Why do most small ocean creatures try to avoid jellyfish?

  (A) Jellyfish get in the way of the fish when they are feeding.

  (B) Jellyfish sting and eat small ocean creatures.

  (C) Fish are afraid of the strange-looking creatures.

  (D) Jellyfish and ocean creatures compete for the same food sources.

Questions 18–25 refer to the following passage.

Laws of Conservation

You are faced with laws every day. You cannot speed on the roads, and you cannot park wherever you choose.

Science has its laws as well. One such law states that energy cannot be created or destroyed. This law, called the law of conservation of energy, makes sense because you cannot create something from nothing. If you have an electrical charge, you cannot simply make it disappear.

A further law of conservation is the law of conservation of matter, which says that matter cannot be created or destroyed. This means that when a physical or chemical change occurs, the total mass remains constant. When you melt an ice cube, the water that results is neither heavier nor lighter than the original ice cube.

18. Trees are damaged when struck by lightning, but the lightning is nowhere apparent afterward. Because lightning is a form of energy, what would explain the apparent disappearance of the energy in the lightning?

  (A) The energy in the lightning disappears.

  (B) The energy in the lightning is transformed into another form of energy.

  (C) The tree absorbs the lightning and stores the energy for future use.

  (D) Lightning striking the tree remains in the form of lightning.

19. Which of these statements can be inferred from the passage?

  (A) The scientific method is a law of science.

  (B) Scientific laws prevent scientists from doing dangerous actions.

  (C) Scientific laws encourage scientists to make new discoveries.

  (D) Scientific laws describe phenomena that always happen.

20. When a magician makes a rabbit appear in a hat, it is an example of which of the following?

  (A) conservation of energy

  (B) conservation of matter

  (C) creation of illusion

  (D) conservation of resources

21. When an iceberg melts as a result of temperature changes, the law of science that is being best illustrated is ☐ .

22. When the batteries in a frequently used flashlight run down, what has happened to their original charge?

  (A) It has been converted into light.

  (B) It has disappeared.

  (C) The battery charge has changed from positive to negative.

  (D) The energy has been destroyed.

23. How would a scientist categorize the result of adding 100 grams of water and 20 grams of salt?

   (A) An example of the law of conservation of energy in that the amount of energy would be the same afterward as before.

   (B) You will end up with 100 grams of salty water.

   (C) The salt will disappear, and all that will remain is water.

   (D) An example of the law of conservation of mass in that the total mass will remain the same.

24. A ball rolling down a hill cannot stop by itself. What law of science explains this?

   (A) There is a bump on the road.

   (B) The ball has no brakes.

   (C) The energy from rolling down the hill can't disappear.

   (D) Friction keeps the ball from stopping.

25. A scientist burns a sample of coal in their lab. As the coal burns, carbon atoms in the coal combine with oxygen to form a gas, carbon dioxide. In addition, ash is produced. This is an example of conservation of _____.

Questions 26–28 refer to the following passage.

Why Do Birds Fly South for the Winter?

Every fall, the sky is full of birds flying south for the winter. However, you can still see a few birds in the northern part of the country during the winter. Scientists have advanced theories about this phenomenon.

Some birds eat insects for food. In winter, many species of birds fly south, because that's where the food exists. In southern states, insects are available all year long, providing a banquet for the birds, whereas in the northern parts of the country, insects (as well as other food sources, such as seeds and berries) are scarce or even nonexistent during the winter. The birds fly south for winter to follow the food. In the spring, as insects once again become plentiful in the northern states, the birds still follow the food, this time to the north.

Migration is stressful for birds. It is physically taxing, and migratory flocks are vulnerable to predators. Because birds migrate in large groups, their crowded "rest stops" make them prone to parasitic infections.

26. Why do migratory birds return to the northern states in the spring?

   (A) They miss their summer homes.

   (B) It gets too hot in the southern states.

   (C) They are able to find food again.

   (D) They fly north out of habit.

27. How is the population of insects in a geographical area related to the regular migratory pattern of birds?

   (A) Insects bite the birds.

   (B) The insects migrate in a pattern similar to that of the birds.

   (C) Some birds eat insects.

   (D) Birds have a habit of always eating the same insects.

28. According to the passage, which of the following statements is true?

(A) Migration is haphazard; birds don't follow a specific route.

(B) Parasites follow the same migratory pattern as birds.

(C) Migrating can be dangerous for birds.

(D) Scientists have no explanation for migration patterns.

Questions 29 and 30 refer to the following passage.

The Law of Unintended Consequences

Lake Victoria is the largest freshwater lake in Africa. It once had abundant fish, which provided protein for the local people who ate the fish. Unfortunately, a new species — the Nile Perch — was introduced into the lake by fishermen looking for a challenging fishing experience to attract their share of tourists interested in exploring the area.

The Nile Perch is an aggressive predator and had no natural enemies in Lake Victoria. It quickly ate up large numbers of the smaller fish, which affected the diets of the local population. These smaller fish ate algae and parasite-bearing snails. Without the smaller fish eating them, the live algae spread over the surface of the lake. Dead algae sank to the bottom of the lake and decayed, a process that consumed oxygen necessary for the fish living deep in the lake.

The snails, without natural predators, and the parasites they carried, multiplied, creating a serious health hazard to the population. The introduction of a fish to encourage tourism had a detrimental effect on the lake and the population that depended on it.

29. What human intervention caused the destruction of the ecological balance in Lake Victoria?

(A) growing populations of snails

(B) increasing algae levels

(C) declining populations of smaller fish

(D) introduction of the Nile Perch

30. Why can it be problematic to introduce a new species into a stable environment?

(A) The new species has plenty of predators.

(B) The other species in the environment would not have to compete for food.

(C) The new species is bad for sport fishermen.

(D) The new species can upset the ecological balance.

Questions 31–34 refer to the following table, which is adapted from Hands-On General Science Activities with Real-Life Applications, *by Pam Walker and Elaine Wood (John Wiley & Sons, Inc.).*

Space Travel

Characteristic	Moon	Mars
Distance from Earth	239,000 miles	48,600,000 miles
Gravity	1/6 Earth's gravity	1/3 Earth's gravity
Atmosphere	None	Thin carbon dioxide, 1% air pressure of Earth
Trip time	3 days	1.88 Earth years
Communication time	2.6 seconds, round trip	10 to 41 minutes, round trip

31. If you were an aeronautical engineer planning a journey to Mars, why would you prefer to go to a space station on the Moon and then launch the rocket to Mars instead of going directly from Earth to Mars?

(A) Lower gravity on the Moon means you need less fuel for the launch.

(B) You have more space to take off and land on the Moon.

(C) No atmosphere means an easier takeoff.

(D) The Moon is closer to Earth than Mars.

32. On earth, a certain piece of equipment used in space weighs 120 pounds. How much does it weigh (in pounds) on the moon? [ ] How much does it weigh (in pounds) on Mars? [ ]

33. Why would a trip to the Moon be less challenging than a trip to Mars for space travelers?

(A) You can see the Moon from Earth without a telescope.

(B) The time of the trip is much shorter.

(C) The Moon has a better atmosphere.

(D) There are already space vehicles on the Moon.

34. If you held a pole-vaulting contest on the Moon and Mars, the same contestant would vault higher with the same expenditure of energy on [ ].

Questions 35–37 refer to the following passage.

Heredity, Then and Now

How often have you seen a young child and said, "They take after their parents"? Many traits in a child do come from their parents. Physical characteristics, such as hair color and nose shape, are transmitted from one generation to the next. These transmitted characteristics exist because of genetic code.

The first scientist to experiment with heredity was Gregor Mendel during the 19th century. Mendel experimented with pea plants and noted that characteristics appearing in "child" plants were similar to those of the "parent" plants. Mendel hypothesized that these characteristics were carried from generation to generation by "factors." It took many years of research to understand why children often look like their parents, but genetic code is now the basis of the study of heredity.

35. According to the passage, [ ] is a primary determinant for characteristics of the next generation.

36. The factor that Mendel hypothesized carried traits from one generation to the next is

(A) traits.

(B) protons.

(C) genetic code.

(D) mutation.

37. If you want to grow monster-sized pumpkins, from what kind of pumpkins do you want to get seeds to increase the probability of growing larger-than-average pumpkins?

(A) orange pumpkins

(B) monster-sized pumpkins

(C) average-sized pumpkins

(D) healthy pumpkins

Questions 38 and 39 refer to the following passage.

The Space Shuttle

NASA has designed and built six space shuttles: *Atlantis, Challenger, Columbia, Discovery, Endeavor,* and *Enterprise.* The space shuttles are made up of two distinct parts: the orbiter and the booster rocket. The booster rocket provides the thrust to get the space shuttle away from the gravitational pull of the Earth. The orbiter carries the people and payload as well as the workings of the shuttle. In a space flight, the booster is jettisoned after clearing the Earth's gravitational pull, and the orbiter continues on its way.

38. Why would the booster be jettisoned during flight?

(A) because the shuttle needs to add weight

(B) to increase the size of the shuttle

(C) to make the shuttle less maneuverable for landing

(D) because it is no longer needed

39. Which part of a shuttle carries the payload?

(A) booster

(B) cockpit

(C) orbiter

(D) rocket

Questions 40 and 41 refer to the following figure, which is excerpted from Physical Science: What the Technology Professional Needs to Know, *by C. Lon Enloe, Elizabeth Garnett, Jonathan Miles, and Stephen Swanson (John Wiley & Sons, Inc.).*

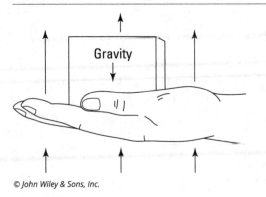

© John Wiley & Sons, Inc.

40. Work is defined as the product of force times displacement. Consider the diagram. If the force of gravity was greater than the forces being exerted by the muscles controlling the hand, what would happen?

(A) Nothing would happen.

(B) The hand would move downward.

(C) The hand would move to the right.

(D) The hand would move upward.

41. If an athlete knows that building muscles requires doing work against a weight, what would the athlete want to change in this diagram?

(A) Move the hand upward faster.

(B) Add weight to the hand.

(C) Close the fist as the arm is raised.

(D) Exhale as the arm is raised.

Questions 42 and 43 refer to the following passage, which is adapted from The Sciences: An Integrated Approach, *3rd Edition, by James Trefil and Robert M. Hazen (John Wiley & Sons, Inc.).*

Copying a DNA Sequence

The polymerase chain reaction (PCR) copies a sequence of DNA. To do this, a strand of DNA is mixed with nucleotides (DNA precursors). Nucleotides target a specific piece of DNA, as well as polymerase, an enzyme that helps to assemble DNA. Heat is applied until the temperature reaches 200°F. The energy from the heating separates the DNA strands. The mixture is then cooled to 140°F. At this temperature, the primers attach themselves to the DNA strands. Raising the temperature to 160°F causes the nucleotides to begin to attach to the DNA strands. After all this, two copies of the DNA are created.

42. To separate the DNA strands during the polymerase chain reaction, nucleotides and polymerase are mixed with a strand of [   ].

43. At what temperature (in Farenheit) does the DNA separate? [   ]

Questions 44 and 45 refer to the following passage.

Dogs and Wolves — Relatives?

Current scientific theory is that the familiar family pet, the dog, descended from the wolf, but the dog has taken a very different path. The dog was the first animal to be domesticated, right around the end of the Ice Age.

Dogs are part of an extended family called *Canidae,* which contains 38 different species. Jackals, foxes, wolves, and dogs are all part of this family. Although they are related, wolves and dogs are different. Wolves have smaller heads for the same body weight. Dogs have smaller teeth, a more curved lower jaw, and eyes that are more rounded and forward looking. At a distance, however, many of these differences are difficult to spot.

44. What feature makes the wolf better adapted to hunting in the wild?

   (A) heavier coat

   (B) larger body

   (C) larger teeth

   (D) larger paws

45. What attribute of dogs makes them a better household pet than other members of the Canidae family?

   (A) Dogs have a curved jaw.

   (B) Dogs were domesticated.

   (C) Dogs have smaller heads.

   (D) Dogs can help the visually impaired.

Questions 46–48 refer to the following passage.

Isotopes

Isotopes are chemical cousins. They are related to each other, but each isotope has slightly different — but related — atoms. Each of the related atoms has the same number of protons but a different number of neutrons. Every element has a different atomic number, which is the number of protons (or electrons) normally found in an atom of the given chemical element. The higher the atomic number, the heavier the atom is. In neutral atoms, the number of protons and electrons is the same, while in "charged atoms," the number is different. Because the number of protons determines the atomic number, isotopes have the same atomic number.

The number of neutrons determines the mass number. Because the number of neutrons in each isotope is different, the mass number is also different. These cousins all have different mass numbers but the same atomic number. Their chemical properties are similar but not the same. Like most cousins, they have family resemblances, but each has a unique personality.

46. Different elements would have different numbers of [　　　　　].

47. Isotopes of a chemical have the same

   (A) number of neutrons.

   (B) mass number.

   (C) atomic number.

   (D) chemical properties.

48. A scientist has found related atoms in two different substances. If both atoms have the same atomic number but different mass numbers, what preliminary conclusion can be reached about the atoms?

   (A) They are the same substance.

   (B) They are isotopes.

   (C) They are different substances.

   (D) One is a compound of the other.

How to Survive the Winter

When the temperature drops and the wind blows cold, you may worry about the survival of animals that don't have homes to protect them from the cold. Not much food is available, temperatures in northern states go into the sub-zero range, and shelter is limited. How do they survive the winter?

Many animals, like skunks, groundhogs, and bears, can find shelter and hibernate for the winter. Hibernation is a sleeplike condition in which the animal's heartbeat, temperature, and metabolism slow down to conserve energy during periods of time when an adequate food supply is unavailable. This dormant condition allows the hibernating animal to live off stored fat to prevent starvation or freezing during the harsh winters.

49. To survive the winter, what do bears do?

    (A) Migrate south to live in warm caves.

    (B) Store food in their caves.

    (C) Absorb the sun's rays to keep warm.

    (D) Find a safe shelter and hibernate.

50. What does the passage indicate about animals that hibernate?

    (A) Animals hibernate to compensate for periods of hyperactivity during warmer months.

    (B) Hibernating animals gain weight because they are so inactive.

    (C) Larger mammals hibernate because they need so much food to survive.

    (D) Before hibernating, animals need to store enough fat to last the winter.

Chapter 24

Answers for Practice Test 1, Science

In this chapter, I provide the answers and explanations to every question in the Science practice test in Chapter 23. If you just want a quick look at the answers, check out the abbreviated answer key at the end of this chapter. However, if you have the time, it's more useful for study purposes to read all the answer explanations carefully. Doing so will help you understand why some answers were correct and others not, especially when the choices were really close. It will also point you to areas where you may need to do more review. Remember, you learn as much from your errors as from the correct answers.

Go through the explanations to all the questions, even for the ones you answered correctly. The explanations offer a good review of the techniques I discuss throughout the book.

Answers and Explanations

1. **D. Use new high-tech insulated glass in all the windows in the house.** A sheet of regular window glass contains no encapsulated air and, thus, does not provide insulation, but a high-tech insulated window provides effective insulation. Therefore, Choice (D) is correct. Replacing the floor-to-ceiling glass walls with a cinder block wall (Choice B) would increase the insulating properties of that wall and reduce the heating costs for the house, but then people would not be able to enjoy the spectacular view. Choices (A) and (C) would not reduce the carbon footprint from heating.

2. **A. Add as much additional insulation as possible.** This choice would result in less energy used to heat the house. The other choices would not decrease energy used to heat the house.

3. **D. they don't have access to healthful and affordable foods.** The passage states that many Americans turn to fast food because of the "lack of healthful and available foods." Choices (A) and (B) are not mentioned in the passage. Choice (C) is contradicted by the passage.

4. **D. children eating portion-controlled meals.** The passage lists Choices (A), (B), and (C) as contributors to childhood obesity. Controlling portion size is helpful to anyone who is concerned about weight gain.

5. **stress.** The passage twice mentions stress as a contributing factor to unhealthy eating habits (*managing daily stressors is always a challenge* and *Stress and a lack of healthful and available foods are some of the reasons why many people turn to fast food*).

6. **D. a vector.** The question states that a force has magnitude and direction. Therefore, it can be represented by a vector (Choice D). The last line of the first paragraph gives you the information you need. Choice (C) is used to represent speed, which has magnitude only, so is incorrect. Choices (A) and (B) are not mentioned in the passage.

7. **your speed.** In most bicycle races, the direction, route, and distance are predetermined. The most important variable for the individual rider is their speed.

8. **B. Steam condenses when cooled, occupying less space.** In the steam engine, water cools the steam, which then condenses, occupying less space. This action starts the entire cycle over again. You can eliminate the other answer choices when guessing is necessary. Choice (A) is incorrect because water and steam are both water, in different states. Their densities may be different, but their weights are the same. Only the volume differs when water turns to steam. Choice (C) is incorrect because the boiler doesn't provide the energy to move the pump, which you can see by looking at the diagram. Choice (D) isn't based on information given in the diagram and is not a property of steam and water, which is what the question is about.

9. **C. It causes the pump to fill the cistern with water.** The pump pushes water into the cistern. The other choices don't answer the question based on the information provided in the diagram. Knowing how to answer questions based on diagrams is a useful skill to have for the GED Science test.

10. **plants.** Plants are the only organisms that can produce food.

11. **10.** The passage states that the temperature of the first tiny particles was 10 billion degrees.

12. **D. gravity.** The last paragraph states that gravity transformed the atoms into galaxies. This question is an example of when a basic knowledge of science-related words can be helpful.

13. **B. an immense explosion created the universe.** The passage states that a "giant explosion in space . . . started the expansion of the universe."

14. **B. matter from dying stars.** This information is stated directly in the passage.

15. **D. It has no backbone.** According to the passage (third sentence in the first paragraph), invertebrates have no backbones. The other choices may be correct, but they don't answer the question. Here, and in all questions on this test, you're looking for the best choice that answers the question posed. Don't get sidetracked by other choices that are correct based on your knowledge or even based on the passage. The answer to the question posed is always the best response on a multiple-choice test.

16. **D. The jellyfish may sting the swimmer, and the stings are painful.** You find this information in the last sentence of the third paragraph. The other choices don't answer the question based on the passage. For example, Choice (C) may be the stuff nightmares are based on, but this information or misinformation isn't in the passage, so you can't consider it.

17. **B. Jellyfish sting and eat small ocean creatures.** Small ocean creatures are always on the menu for jellyfish. Creatures, in general, avoid predators — a fact that's general science knowledge.

18. **B. The energy in the lightning is transformed into another form of energy.** The passage states that energy can't be created or destroyed, so the energy from the lightning must be transformed into another type of energy. The other answer choices imply that the energy has somehow disappeared or isn't transformed, which the passage says can't happen.

19. **D. Scientific laws describe phenomena that always happen.** The two examples are phenomena that always happen naturally, so Choice (D) is correct. The other choices do not make sense.

20. **C. creation of illusion.** Matter can't be created or destroyed. Thus, a rabbit can't appear except by creation of an illusion. The other answer choices seem scientific but have nothing to do with the question. Always read the question carefully to make sure you're answering it with the best selection of the choices provided.

21. **conservation of matter.** When ice melts, it turns into water. This is an example of the law of conservation of matter.

22. **A. It has been converted into light.** Flashlights provide light by using the energy in the battery. The passage says that energy can't be created or destroyed, so the energy in the battery must have been converted or transformed into something else. In fact, chemical energy in the battery is converted to electrical energy and then into light. In reality, even if you don't use a battery for an extended time, the battery grows weaker because of other reactions inside the cell. This tidbit isn't mentioned in the passage and is just a reminder not to leave batteries in your flashlight forever.

23. **D. An example of the law of conservation of mass in that the total mass will remain the same.** If you add 100 grams of water and 20 grams of salt, you have 120 grams of combined ingredients. The combined mass is the same as the sum of the individual masses. Therefore, Choice (B) is incorrect. Choices (A) and (C) are just incorrect.

24. **C. The energy from rolling down the hill can't disappear.** The law of conservation of energy states that energy can't be created or destroyed. Thus, the energy developed by the ball rolling down the hill can't disappear. Choice (C) is more a statement of the meaning of the law of conservation of energy than naming it, but it is still the best answer. In reality, there's friction between the ball and the ground that slows it down, and the hills don't go on forever — so the ball will eventually come to rest. You may have learned this information elsewhere, but it doesn't answer the question based on the passage.

25. **matter.** This example is consistent with how substances behave during a chemical change.

26. **C. They are able to find food again.** The passage states that the lack of food in the winter months makes most birds fly south to find sources of food. When the food returns to the northern states, so do the birds. The other choices don't answer the question based on the information in the passage.

27. **C. Some birds eat insects.** Some birds eat insects for their food supply. If an area has no insects, the birds move to find a new source of food. Choice (A) does not make sense. Choice (B) is not stated in in the passage. And although some birds always eat the same insect (Choice D), that's not the best answer.

28. **C. Migrating can be dangerous for birds.** The last paragraph of the passage lists some of the dangers of migration: physical exhaustion, parasites, and increased vulnerability to predators. The other answers aren't supported by the information in the passage.

29. **D. introduction of the Nile Perch.** Of the potential answers given Choice D, Nile Perch, is correct because it's the only change that is a human intervention. The remaining responses are all results of this human intervention.

30. **D. The new species can upset the ecological balance.** This question asks you to make a general statement about introducing a new species into a stable environment. Although this question doesn't ask you to consider the Lake Victoria example specifically, you're supposed to think about that example as you answer the question. Using the Lake Victoria example, you can safely say that a new species can upset the local ecological balance. You also know from the example that the other three choices are incorrect.

31. **A. Lower gravity on the Moon means you need less fuel for the launch.** The less fuel you need to launch, the less you have to carry. The gravity on the Moon is less than that on Earth, so you need less force and less fuel to break free of gravity.

32. **Moon: 20, Mars, 40.** You can easily answer the question using mental math. Divide the weight on earth by 6 to determine the weight on the moon (120 ÷ 6 = 20). Divide the weight on earth by 3 to determine the weight on Mars (120 ÷ 3 = 40).

33. **B. The time of the trip is much shorter.** According to the table, it takes just 3 days to get to the Moon, which is a much better first choice than the 1.88 years needed to get to Mars. The other choices are irrelevant to the question and the given table.

34. **the Moon.** Gravity on the Moon is less than that on Mars. Because gravity is the force that attracts you to the Moon (or to Earth or to Mars), the less the gravity, the less the attraction between you and the surface on which you stand, and, thus, the higher and farther you can jump — which, as you may know, is the goal of a pole-vaulting contest.

35. **heredity.** The passage states that heredity determines the characteristics of the next generation.

36. **C. genetic code.** The passage states, "These characteristics, passed from one generation to the next, exist because of genetic code." Thus, the best answer Choice (C).

37. **B. monster-sized pumpkins.** If offspring inherit the traits of their parents, you want the desired traits of your pumpkin offspring to be a part of the traits of the parent pumpkins. Monster-sized pumpkin seeds have a better chance of producing extra-large pumpkins than do the seeds from an average-sized pumpkin.

38. **D. because it is no longer needed.** All the choices except Choice (D) — that the booster is no longer needed — are incorrect because they're in direct opposition to the passage. If you can quickly eliminate some or most of the answer choices, you can save time answering the question. In this case, you can eliminate three answers, making the final choice easy and quick.

39. **C. orbiter.** Because the booster is jettisoned after takeoff, the orbiter has to carry everything that continues on the trip. Choices (A), (B), and (D) are wrong and can be quickly eliminated.

40. **B. The hand would move downward.** If the force pushing down was greater than the force pushing up, the hand would move down. Although this question is based on the given diagram, which gives a general idea of what happens when a hand holds weight, the answer to the question is in the first part of the question itself. If the force of gravity (the downward force) was greater than the force of the muscles moving upward, the resultant force would be downward.

41. **B. Add weight to the hand.** A larger weight in the hand would produce a greater force downward. Thus, the athlete would have to work harder against this extra weight (and, as a result, would build more muscle).

42. **DNA.** This information is stated directly in the passage.

43. **200.** This answer is stated directly in the passage.

44. **C. larger teeth.** The larger teeth of the wolf are better for hunting. The fifth sentence of the second paragraph of the passage states that dogs have smaller teeth, which means wolves must have bigger teeth. Although this information isn't stated directly in the passage, it's implied. You're expected to be able to draw conclusions from the information given, so read carefully. The other answer choices are incorrect. True, some dogs have heavier coats, larger bodies, and so on, but this information isn't in the passage. You can answer the question using only information given or implied in the passage — not information from your general knowledge or prior reading.

45. **B. Dogs were domesticated.** The passage states that the dog was domesticated very long ago. A domesticated animal is preferable to a wild one for a household pet. The other answers may be factually correct, but they aren't part of the information included in the passage.

46. **protons.** According to the passage, the atomic number is determined by the number of protons. This question is an example of when skimming the paragraph after reading the question makes finding the correct answer fast and easy.

47. **C. atomic number.** The last sentence of the first paragraph of the passage states that isotopes have the same atomic number.

48. **B. They are isotopes.** The last sentence of the first paragraph of the passage states that isotopes have the same atomic number. The second sentence of the second paragraph tells you that isotopes have different mass numbers. This question requires using two bits of information from two different locations in the passage to decide on the right answer.

49. **D. Find a safe shelter and hibernate.** According to the first sentence of the second paragraph of the passage, animals, including bears, survive the winter by finding a safe shelter and hibernating.

50. D. Before hibernating, animals need to store enough fat to last the winter. Animals hibernate in the winter when food is scarce (a fact implied from the last sentence in the second paragraph). But, to survive a long period of time without food, the animals feed heavily when food is plentiful, and during hibernation, live off their stored fat. Because this is an inference question, you must read between the lines and use "science logic" to figure out the answer.

Answer Key

1. D
2. A
3. D
4. D
5. stress
6. D
7. your speed
8. B
9. C
10. plants
11. 10
12. D
13. B
14. B
15. D
16. D
17. B

18. B
19. D
20. C
21. conservation of matter
22. A
23. D
24. C
25. matter
26. C
27. C
28. C
29. D
30. D
31. A
32. Moon: 20, Mars: 40
33. B

34. the Moon
35. heredity
36. C
37. B
38. D
39. C
40. B
41. B
42. DNA
43. 200
44. C
45. B
46. protons
47. C
48. B
49. D
50. D

Chapter 25

Practice Test 1: Mathematical Reasoning

The Mathematical Reasoning test consists of a series of questions intended to measure general mathematics skills and problem-solving ability. The questions are based on short readings that may include a graph, chart, or figure.

You have 115 minutes to complete this section. The answers and explanations to this section's questions are in Chapter 26. Go through the explanations to all the questions, even for the ones you answered correctly. The explanations are a good review of the mathematical techniques I discuss throughout the book.

The GED formula sheet is on the page before the first test question. Only some of the questions require you to use a formula, and you may not need all the formulas given. *Note:* If you are familiar with the formulas and understand how to use them, you'll save some time on the test; you can then use that time for review or for harder items that give you trouble.

TIP

If you have time before the test, memorize the most commonly tested formulas: area of a square or rectangle, area of a circle, circumference, and the Pythagorean Theorem. Items using these formulas usually appear on the GED test.

On the real test, you will be able to use the online whiteboard (or an erasable tablet, if you test at a test center). For now, have a few pieces of scratch paper ready to calculate, write down formulas, or draw simple sketches to help you visualize a question. And remember to use your calculator when you think it can help you work more quickly and accurately. For these questions, you can use any calculator, including the one on your phone, though using a real TI-30XS MultiView calculator is the best preparation for the real test. You can use the timer on your phone to keep track of time. If you run out of time, mark the last question you answered. Then answer the remaining questions. This will give you an idea of how much faster you should work to answer all the questions on the real test.

REMEMBER

On the real GED, you'll be answering on a computer. Instead of marking your answers on a separate answer sheet, like you do for the practice test sections in this book, you'll see clickable ovals and fill-in-the-blank text boxes. You'll be able to click with your mouse and drag and drop items where indicated. The questions and answer choices in this book are formatted to appear as similar as possible to what you'll see on the actual test, but I had to retain some A, B, C, and D choices for marking your answers, and I provide an answer sheet for you to do so. When you're ready for the included online practice test, you will be able to see and try the actual question types as they appear on the test.

Answer Sheet for Practice Test 1, Mathematical Reasoning

1. _____

2. _____

3. _____

4. _____

5. _____

6. _____

7. _____

8. _____

9. _____

10. _____

11. _____

12. _____

13. _____

14. _____

15. _____

16. _____

17. _____

18. _____

19. _____

20. _____

21. _____

22. _____

23. _____

24. _____

25. _____

26. _____

27. _____

28. _____

29. _____

30. _____

31. _____

32. _____

33. _____

34. _____

35. _____

36. _____

37. _____

38. _____

39. _____

40. _____

41. _____

42. _____

43. _____

44. _____

45. _____

46. _____

47. _____

48. _____

49. _____

50. _____

Mathematics Formula Explanations

This displays formulas relating to geometric measurement and certain algebra concepts and is available on the GED® test — Mathematical Reasoning.

Area of a:

square	$A = s^2$
rectangle	$A = lw$
parallelogram	$A = bh$
triangle	$A = \frac{1}{2}bh$
trapezoid	$A = \frac{1}{2}h(b_1 + b_2)$
circle	$A = \pi r^2$

Perimeter of a:

square	$P = 4s$
rectangle	$P = 2l + 2w$
triangle	$P = s_1 + s_2 + s_3$
Circumference of a circle	$C = 2\pi r$ OR $C = \pi d$; $\pi \approx 3.14$

Surface area and volume of a:

rectangular prism	$SA = 2lw + 2lh + 2wh$	$V = lwh$
right prism	$SA = ph + 2B$	$V = Bh$
cylinder	$SA = 2\pi rh + 2\pi r^2$	$V = \pi r^2 h$
pyramid	$SA = \frac{1}{2}ps + B$	$V = \frac{1}{3}Bh$
cone	$SA = \pi rs + \pi r^2$	$V = \frac{1}{3}\pi r^2 h$
sphere	$SA = 4\pi r^2$	$V = \frac{4}{3}\pi r^3$

(p = perimeter of base with area B; $\pi \approx 3.14$)

Data

mean	mean is equal to the total of the values of a data set, divided by the number of elements in the data set
median	median is the middle value in an odd number of ordered values of a data set, or the mean of the two middle values in an even number of ordered values in a data set

Algebra

slope of a line	$m = \dfrac{y_2 - y_1}{x_2 - x_1}$
slope-intercept form of the equation of a line	$y = mx + b$
point-slope form of the equation of a line	$y - y_1 = m(x - x_1)$
standard form of a quadratic equation	$y = ax^2 + bx + c$
quadratic formula	$x = \dfrac{-b \pm \sqrt{b^2 - 4ac}}{2a}$
Pythagorean theorem	$a^2 + b^2 = c^2$
simple interest	$I = Prt$
	(I = interest, P = principal, r = rate, t = time)
distance formula	$d = rt$
total cost	total cost = (number of units) x (price per unit)

Æ Symbol Tool Explanation

The GED® test on computer contains a tool known as the "Æ Symbol Tool." Use this guide to learn about entering special mathematical symbols into fill-in-the-blank item types.

Symbol	Explanation	Symbol	Explanation	Symbol	Explanation
π	pi	|	absolute value	—	minus or negative
f	function	×	multiplication	(	open or left parenthesis
≥	greater than or equal to	÷	division	)	close or right parenthesis
≤	less than or equal to	±	positive or negative	>	greater than
≠	not equal to	∞	infinity	<	less than
2	2 exponent ("squared")	√	square root	=	equals
3	3 exponent ("cubed")	+	plus or positive		

TIME: 115 minutes

ITEMS: 50

DIRECTIONS: Find the answer to each question. Mark your answers on the answer sheet provided.

1. Madan is making sale signs for the Super Summer Sale at the Super Saver Swim Shop. Sales tax in Madan's town is 5%. He makes a series of signs.
   - Sign A: $\frac{1}{2}$ off all merchandise
   - Sign B: Buy one item, get the second item of equal value free
   - Sign C: 50% off all merchandise
   - Sign D: Nine times your sales tax back

   What would a shrewd consumer notice about the signs?

   (A) Sign A offers the best buy.

   (B) Sign B offers the best deal.

   (C) Sign C offers the worst deal.

   (D) Sign D offers the worst deal.

2. Daryl is framing a picture in a rectangular frame. He draws the following diagram to help him make the frame:

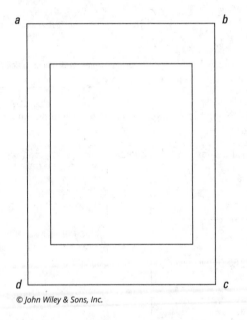

© John Wiley & Sons, Inc.

   Which of the following is true about the diagram?

   (A) *ab* must be perpendicular to *ad*.

   (B) *ab* must be parallel to *bc*.

   (C) *ad* must be parallel to *ab*.

   (D) *ab* and *dc* must be perpendicular.

3. The Hammerhill family is building a deck behind their house. The deck is to be 18 feet long and 24 feet wide, and the decking material was priced at $45.00 a square yard. The cost, in dollars, of the decking material would be [＿＿＿＿＿]. You may use numbers, a decimal point (.), and/or a negative sign (−) in your answer.

4. Margaret Millsford, the Chief Financial Officer of Aggravated Manufacturing Corporation, has to report to the Board of Directors. She has been instructed to analyze the sales of each of the company's product lines and to recommend dropping the least profitable line. She found that although the per-unit profits of grommets and gadgets were the same, moving production of widgets to Texas doubled the profits. She prepared the following graph to demonstrate the relative volumes and made an oral presentation to illustrate the differing profitability of production in Texas to back up her recommendation:

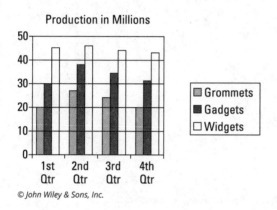

© John Wiley & Sons, Inc.

Based on the graph and Margaret's oral presentation, her recommendation would be to drop

(A) widgets.

(B) grommets.

(C) gadgets.

(D) grommets and widgets.

5. Quan is obsessive about how his grades compare to those of the other students in his class. On Quan's final report, his results were as follows:

- **Computer Studies: 97**
- **English: 98**
- **Mathematics: 99**
- **Physical Education: 87**
- **Science: 97**
- **Social Studies: 94**
- **Spanish: 86**
- **The average for Quan's entire class was 94.27.**

What's the difference between the class average and Quan's average? You may use numbers, a decimal point (.), and/or a negative sign (−) in your answer. [＿＿＿＿＿].

6. Alice was trying to explain how the length of time she could run each morning had improved each month since she started running, except for the month she twisted her ankle. She drew the following graph to show her friends Mary and Kevin the average length of time (in minutes) she ran each day in each month:

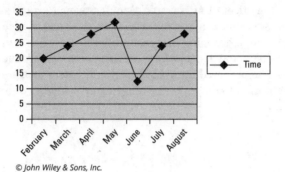

© John Wiley & Sons, Inc.

In which month did Alice likely twist her ankle?

(A) February

(B) June

(C) July

(D) August

7. Dominic and Paula were comparing their report cards, as follows:

Dominic's Report Card

Subject	Grade (%)
Mathematics	63
Social Studies	76
Science	65
Language Arts	84
Physical Education	72

Paula's Report Card

Subject	Grade (%)
Mathematics	80
Social Studies	64
Science	76
Language Arts	72
Physical Education	88

The teacher told them that the ratio of their total marks was very close. What is the ratio of Paula's marks to Dominic's marks on these report cards?

(A) 9:10

(B) 18:19

(C) 10:9

(D) 19:18

8. In the series, 4, 6, 10, 18, . . ., the first term that is a multiple of 11 is [_____]. You may use numbers, a decimal point (.), and/or a negative sign (−) in your answer.

9. Marta follows the stock market very carefully. She has been following Cowardly Corporation the last few weeks, keeping track of her research in the following table:

Date	Closing Price (In U.S. Dollars)
August 7	15.03
August 17	16.12
September 1	14.83
September 9	15.01
September 16	14.94
September 20	15.06
September 23	15.17
September 24	15.19

Marta bought shares of the stock on September 24 and wants to make money before selling it. She paid 3% commission to her broker for buying and will pay the same again for selling. What is the lowest price for which Marta can sell each of her shares to break even?

(A) $15.66

(B) $16.13

(C) $16.48

(D) $20.00

10. If $22.4 = \dfrac{56a}{5a + 10}$, what is the value of a?

(A) 4

(B) 0

(C) −4

(D) −56

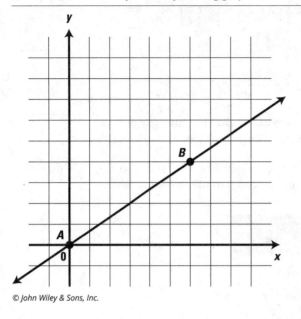

© *John Wiley & Sons, Inc.*

11. Calculate the slope of the line *AB*. The slope of *AB* is [＿＿＿＿＿]. You may use numbers, a decimal point (.), and/or a negative sign (−) in your answer.

12. If the slope of *AB* remains the same, but it intercepts the *y*-axis at $C(0,4)$, where does it intersect the *x*-axis? [＿＿＿＿＿]

13. Janet is ordering pizza for a lunch with friends. One extra-large or two medium pizzas is always enough for them. An extra-large garden pizza at their favorite pizza shop measures 18 inches in diameter and costs $20. Today, two medium garden pizzas are on special for $21. Medium pizzas measure 12 inches in diameter and normally cost $12 each. Which pizza order is a better deal, one extra-large or two mediums? [＿＿＿＿＿]

14. Lydia and Wayne are shopping for carpets for their home and are looking for the best carpet at the best price. Carnie's Carpets offers them a wool carpet for $21.50 per square yard. Flora's Flooring says they will match that same carpet for only $2.45 per square foot, while Dora's Deep Discount offers them an 8×12-foot rug of the same carpet material for $210.24. What is the lowest price per square foot offered to Lydia and Wayne?

(A) $2.19

(B) $2.39

(C) $2.45

(D) $19.71

15. Miscellaneous Appliances Company is concerned about its output at Plant A. Company officials prepared the following graphs to show the output for each quarter of the last two years:

Output at Plant A – 2020

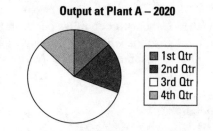

Output at Plant A – 2021

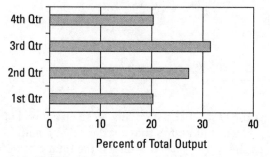

Percent of Total Output

© John Wiley & Sons, Inc.

Which quarter had the highest output during both years?

(A) 1st quarter

(B) 2nd quarter

(C) 3rd quarter

(D) 4th quarter

16. Mr. and Mrs. Nash are looking to expand their house and have calculated that they need at least another 630 square feet to live comfortably. A contractor quotes them $15.80 per square foot for the addition. A real estate agent tells them that they can increase the value of their home by about $18,000 by building the addition. If they want to add as much space as possible for the $18,000 they will recover, the new addition would measure [   ] square feet. (Round your answer to the nearest 10 square feet.) You may use numbers, a decimal point (.), and/or a negative sign (–) in your answer.

17. Graph the point (6,6) on the coordinate plane.

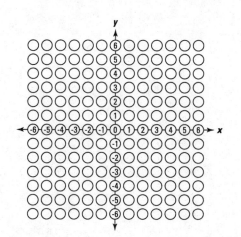

© John Wiley & Sons, Inc.

18. LeeAnne is shopping for a new vehicle. She drives about 18,000 miles per year. She is most concerned about the cost of gasoline. She estimates gasoline will average $3.50 a gallon during the five years she will own the car and is basing her decision on that price. As she shops, she creates a chart:

Type of Vehicle	Miles per Gallon
SUV	12.8
2-door	19.6
Sedan	19.5
SUV	15.2
Sports car	17.2

She notes that a sedan and a 2-door get the best miles per gallon, so she narrows her decision to those two. She wants to save money on gas, but knows that a sedan will be more comfortable for her growing family. She decides she will buy a sedan only if the total cost of fuel over five years is no more than $500 more for the sedan than the 2-door. Which car should she buy?

☐

19. Tom is worried about getting to the GED testing center on time for his test. He knows that he averages 40 miles per hour on the route to the test. If the test site is 50 miles from Tom's house and he wants to arrive 30 minutes early, how much time should he allow for the trip plus waiting time at the center?

(A) 1 hour and 15 minutes

(B) 1 hour and 25 minutes

(C) 1 hour and 45 minutes

(D) 1 hour and 55 minutes

20. Leonora has just received her mid-term report card. Her grades are as follows:

Leonora's Report Card

Subject	Grade (%)
English	84
Geography	78
Mathematics	68
Physical Education	77
Physics	82

Leonora's average grade is 77.8%. To get into the college of her choice, she needs an average of 80%. English is her best subject. By how many percentage points will her English score have to go up, assuming all her other subjects stay the same, in order for her to get into her preferred college?

(A) 8

(B) 9

(C) 10

(D) 11

21. Sonia has an amazing recipe for rice. For each 1 cup of rice, she adds 2 cups of vegetable soup and a quarter cup of lentils. This weekend, Sonia is having a some guests for dinner and figures that she needs to cook 3½ cups of rice for her guests. How much of the other two ingredients should she use?

(A) 7 cups of soup and 7/8 cup of lentils

(B) 3½ cups of soup and ½ cup of lentils

(C) 7 cups of soup and 1 cup of lentils

(D) 1 cup of soup and 7 cups of lentils

22. In drawing cards from a 52-card deck, any single card has an equal chance of being drawn. After six cards have been drawn and removed, what is the probability of drawing an ace of hearts if it has not yet been drawn?

(A) 1:50

(B) 1:48

(C) 1:46

(D) 1:44

23. The Symons are redecorating a room in their house. They have some interesting ideas. They want to put a rug on the floor surrounded by a border of tiles. They are considering teak paneling halfway up each wall. In addition, they may cut away part of the ceiling to put in a skylight. This is a diagram of their room:

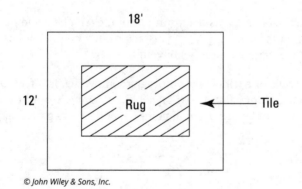

The rug costs $7.50 a square foot, and tile costs $9.00 a square foot. One rug they like is 16 feet by 10 feet, leaving just a little area around the rug for tiles. At the store, however, they see a nicer rug that is only 12 feet by 8 feet, leaving a larger area for tile. That rug costs $7.50 a square foot, too. Which floor treatment is less expensive?

(A) both are the same cost

(B) the larger rug

(C) the smaller rug without the paneling

(D) the smaller rug

24. Brad is a secret shopper for the Friendly Furniture store. His job is to go to competitive stores and price a series of items to make sure his employer can advertise that he has the best prices. His boss wants to start a new advertising campaign: "Friendly Furniture — always lower than the average price of our competitors." Brad's job is to shop several stores to make sure the claim is accurate. Brad's results are recorded in the following table:

Item	Store A	Store B	Store C	Store D	Friendly Furniture
Couch	$1,729	$1,749	$1,729	$1,699	$1,719
Dining room set	$4,999	$4,899	$5,019	$4,829	$4,899
Loveseat	$1,259	$1,199	$1,279	$1,149	$1,229
Coffee table	$459	$449	$479	$429	$449
Reclining chair	$759	$799	$739	$699	$739

Which item cannot be advertised as "lower than the average price"?

(A) couch

(B) dining room set

(C) loveseat

(D) coffee table

25. In a pistachio-shelling contest, Sarah shells 48 pistachios in 18 minutes. If she could maintain her rate of shelling pistachios, she could shell ⬚ pistachios in 2 hours. You may use numbers, a decimal point (.), and/or a negative sign (−) in your answer.

26. Kevin wants to paint the door and walls of a windowless storage room, which is 9 feet long, 8 feet wide, and 8 feet high with one coat of paint. He will need to buy enough paint to cover ⬚ square feet. You may use numbers, a decimal point (.), and/or a negative sign (−) in your answer.

27. Which of these shapes has 180 degrees?

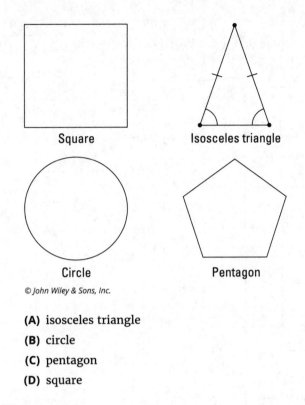

© John Wiley & Sons, Inc.

(A) isosceles triangle

(B) circle

(C) pentagon

(D) square

28. In a large company, the top four positions are organized as follows.

© John Wiley & Sons, Inc.

Each department has the following budget:

Department	Budget ($ Millions)
Operations	14.7
Human Resources	2.1
Marketing	5.6

What is the ratio of the largest budget to the smallest budget? [   ]

29. A company has doubled its sales from the first to the third quarters. Graph [＿＿＿＿] indicates this pattern.

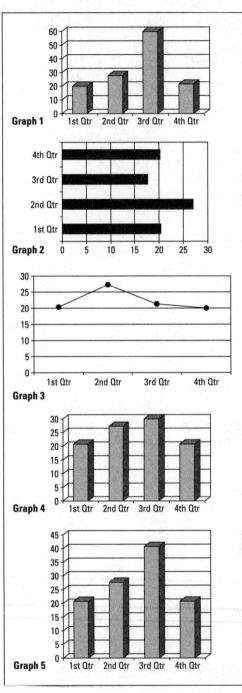

30. A tree casts a 15-foot shadow. A forester determines that the distance from the top of the shadow to the top of the tree is 25 feet. How many feet tall is the tree?

(A) 20

(B) 40

(C) $\sqrt{625}$

(D) $\sqrt{850}$

31. Laurie is trying to save money, so she opens a new savings account at the bank where she has her checking account. Each week for four weeks, she puts $24.00 from her paycheck into her savings account. However, the fourth week, she overdraws her checking account by $7.50, and the bank transfers the money from her savings account to cover it. For providing this service, the bank charges her savings account $10.00. Her savings account balance after the fourth week is [   ]. You may use numbers, a decimal point (.), and/or a negative sign (−) in your answer.

32. Sarah is shopping for a chair for her room. The original price for the chair she likes is $96.00. Store A offers her a third off. Store B offers her a discount of 30%. How much more money will Sarah save by taking the lower price instead of the higher price? You may use numbers, a decimal point (.), and/or a negative sign (−) in your answer. [   ]

Questions 33 and 34 are based on the following information and figure.

While a rock band is setting up for an outdoor concert, the audio engineer is calibrating the amplifiers used for the concert. He has an instrument that develops and displays a graph for each setting on the amplifier controls. The graph appears like this:

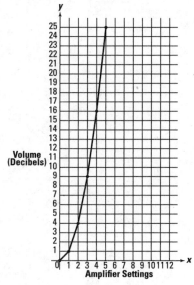

33. From the graph, calculate the volume in decibels for a setting of 10 on the amplifier.

(A) 20

(B) 30

(C) 50

(D) 100

34. The equation that produced this graph is $V = S^2$, where V is the volume in decibels and S is the volume setting. If the volume is 64 decibels, what is the volume setting on the amplifier?

(A) 4

(B) 6

(C) 8

(D) 10

35. In this particular location, the volume of sound decreases by 6 decibels for every 10 feet of distance from the stage a person sits. If the volume at the stage is 120 decibels, the volume in decibels for a person sitting 20 feet from the stage will be

(A) 84

(B) 108

(C) 114

(D) 132

36. Gary and Georgina George bought a new car and want to figure out the gas mileage. The new car travels 480 miles at a cost of $54.00. The price of gasoline is $2.70 per gallon. The new car gets [ ] miles per gallon. You may use numbers, a decimal point (.), and/or a negative sign (−) in your answer.

Question 37 is based on the following figures, which are reprinted from Physical Science: What the Technology Professional Needs to Know, *by C. Lon Enloe, Elizabeth Garnett, Jonathan Miles, and Stephen Swanson (John Wiley & Sons, Inc.).*

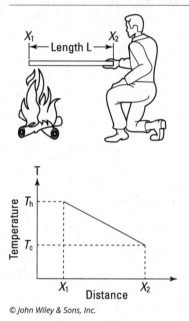

© John Wiley & Sons, Inc.

37. If the person pictured wants to walk but remain at a constant temperature, what geometrical shape should he follow as a path?

(A) ellipse

(B) line

(C) square

(D) circle

38. Igor is in charge of the swimming pool at the local recreation center. The pool is 120 feet long and 24 feet wide and holds 11,520 cubic feet of water. The average depth of the pool in feet is [ ]. You may use numbers, a decimal point (.), and/or a negative sign (−) in your answer.

Average Mileage and Annual Fuel Cost of Selected Vehicles

Vehicle	Mileage (Miles per Gallon) City	Mileage (Miles per Gallon) Highway	Annual Cost ($)*
A	23	28	840
B	21	29	875
C	19	25	1000
D	18	24	1050
E	17	22	1105
F	16	22	1167
G	15	21	1235
H	14	19	1314
I	13	18	1400
J	12	16	1,823

Annual cost includes 15,000 miles driven annually; 55% of the miles in the city and 45% on the highway; standard price of fuel

39. If you were in the market for a car, how much could you save, in dollars, over a three-year period, by buying the most fuel-efficient car over the least fuel-efficient car?

(A) 983

(B) 2,520

(C) 2,949

(D) 5,469

40. What is the average city MPG for these vehicles?

(A) 16.0

(B) 16.8

(C) 17

(D) 22.3

41. What is the difference between city and highway mileage for Vehicle A? [   ] You may use numbers, a decimal point (.), and/or a negative sign (−) in your answer.

42. To solve a problem in her mathematics class, Jan had to solve the following set of equations:

$$2x + 3y = 10$$
$$5x + 6y = 13$$

What is the correct value of y?

(A) −8

(B) −6

(C) 6

(D) 8

43. An international survey found the following information about participation in adult education:

Percent of Population over Age 21 Participating in Adult Education

Country	Total Participation Rate (%)
Denmark	62.3
Hungary	17.9
Norway	43.1
Portugal	15.5
United States	66.4

Compare the participation rates of the countries with the highest and lowest rates. Approximately how many times higher is the rate in the country with the highest participation rate than in the country with the lowest rate?

(A) 2 times as high

(B) 4 times as high

(C) 6 times as high

(D) 8 times as high

44. Gordon has the following six bills to pay this month:

Bill Payable To	Amount
Bedding by Vidalia	$23.00
Chargealot Credit Corp.	$31.00
Dink's Department Store	$48.00
Furniture Fit for a Princess Shoppe	$13.00
Highest Fidelity Sound Shop	$114.00
Overpriced Gas Corporation	$39.00

Each month, he allocates $250.00 to pay his bills. This month, his bills are over this budget. How much extra money must he find from other parts of his budget or savings to pay all his bills?

(A) $8.00

(B) $18.00

(C) $28.00

(D) $268.00

45. Georgette needs $200.00 to buy books for her science course, but she cannot afford to buy them, even though she needs them. Walking to class, she notices a sign offering to loan her $200.00 for one month for $20.00 interest. She calculates that if she can repay the money within the month by working extra hours, she will be able to afford the principal and the interest.

When Georgette applies for the loan, she reads the contract carefully and notices that after the initial one-month period, the interest rate climbs to 15% per month and includes the previous month's principal and interest. If she earns $11.00 per hour, how many extra hours (to the nearest hour) would she have to work to pay the additional second month's <u>interest</u>? You may use numbers, a decimal point (.), and/or a negative sign (–) in your answer. [   ]

46. Andrew just bought a small circular swimming pool for his children. The diameter of the pool is 12 feet, and Andrew can fill it safely to a depth of 9 inches. If a cubic foot of water weighs 62.42 pounds, how many pounds does the water in Andrew's pool weigh, rounded to the nearest hundred pounds?

(A) approximately 27,000

(B) approximately 5,300

(C) approximately 2,700

(D) approximately 1,300

47. If Giorgio borrows $100 for one year and three months and repays $108 including simple interest, what rate of interest was he charged?

(A) 8.0%

(B) 6.4%

(C) 4.6%

(D) 4.0%

48. Chico went shopping for some groceries for his family. His shopping list was as follows:

- 2 pounds of apples
- 5 bananas
- 1 container of milk
- 1 loaf of bread

If apples were $0.79 a pound, bananas $0.23 each, milk $1.27 a carton, and bread $0.98 a loaf, what is the approximate total cost of the groceries?

(A) $3.90

(B) $4.10

(C) $4.90

(D) $5.50

49. From the numbers listed, what number should go in the box?

SERIES, 4, 7, 12, 19, [   ], 38, ...

(A) 28

(B) 26

(C) 24

(D) 22

50. A rectangle 5 units long and 4 units high is represented on a graph. If three of the corners are placed at $(3,2)$, $(3,-2)$, and $(-2,2)$, where should the fourth corner be placed?

(A) $(-2,2)$

(B) $(2,-2)$

(C) $(-2,-2)$

(D) $(2,2)$

Chapter **26**

Answers for Practice Test 1, Mathematical Reasoning

This chapter provides you with answers and explanations for the Mathematical Reasoning practice test in Chapter 25. The answers tell you whether you answered the questions right or wrong, but the explanations are even more important. They explain why your answers were right or wrong and give you some hints about the areas that were tested. Reading the explanations and checking the areas where your answers were incorrect will help you identify where you should spend more time preparing for the test.

Answers and Explanations

1. **D. Sign D offers the worst deal.** This problem tests your understanding of numbers and their equivalents (integers, fractions, decimals, and percents) in a real-world situation. Signs A, B, and C give customers 50% off. Sign D gives them $45\% \left(9 \times 5\% \text{ sales tax}\right)$ off. Sign D offers the worst deal.

2. **A. *ab* must be perpendicular to *ad*.** This problem involves measurement and geometry and tests your understanding of perpendicular and parallel lines in a geometrical figure. Frames are rectangles. In a rectangle, opposite sides are parallel, and intersecting sides (*ab* and *ad*) are perpendicular.

3. **$2,160.** This problem tests your knowledge and mastery of number operations and number sense. Use a calculator, because several calculations are involved, including the following:

   Area of the deck is $18 \times 24 = 432$ square feet

   9 square feet = 1 square yard

   48 square yards $\dfrac{432}{9} = 48$

   One square yard of decking costs $45.00, so 48 square yards of decking costs $2,160 ($45 \times 48 = $2,160$).

4. **B. grommets.** This problem tests your data-analysis skills. You're asked to interpret and draw inferences from the bar graph and data from the presentation. The profit per unit is the same for grommets and gadgets but is less than the profit on widgets, which are twice as profitable. In this case, grommets seem to be less profitable than gadgets because grommets sold the lowest numbers. Therefore, grommets are recommended as the line to drop.

5. **0.27.** Quan's average is 94 $((97 + 98 + 99 + 87 + 97 + 94 + 86) / 7)$, while the class's average is 94.27. Therefore, the difference between the class's average and Quan's average is 0.27 $(94.27 - 94.00)$. This problem tests your skills in solving a problem in two steps. You're asked to use the data to calculate Quan's average grade. Then you use subtraction to compare his performance to the performance of his classmates.

6. **B. June.** Alice has converted her story into a graph, and you're being asked to interpret the line graph in conjunction with her story. Because her average daily time had been increasing until May, dropped in June, and recovered in July and August, you can assume that the twisted ankle slowed her down. It likely happened in June.

7. **D. 19:18.** A number of operations are involved in solving this problem. You're asked to calculate the average of a set of grades for each person and compare them by using a ratio. You can simplify this question, using a calculator.

   The total of Paula's marks is $80 + 64 + 76 + 72 + 88 = 380$.

   The total of Dominic's marks is $63 + 76 + 65 + 84 + 72 = 360$.

   Because you divide each total by 5 to get the average marks for Paula and Dominic, you can simply use the ratio of the totals to get the answer because it will equal the ratio of the averages. (Note that if one of the students had six grades and the other had five, for example, you'd have to use the ratio of the averages, not of the totals.)

   The ratio of Paula's marks to Dominic's marks is 380:360, which you can simplify by dividing each number by 20 to get 19:18.

8. **66.** This problem involves algebra, functions, and patterns. The numbers 4, 6, 10, and 18 form a pattern (also called a series). After looking carefully at the series, you see that the second term is formed by subtracting 1 from the first term and multiplying by 2. Try this on the third number: $(6-1)\times 2 = 10$. You've found your pattern. Continuing the series: 4, 6, 10, 18, 34, 66, ... The first term that is a multiple of 11 is 66.

You could also simply double the difference between the previous two numbers and add it to the second number to create the next one. For example, the difference between 4 and 6 is 2. Double that $(2+2=4)$ and add it to the 6 $(4+6=10)$ to get the next number. The difference between 6 and 10 is 4. Double that $(4+4=8)$ and add it to the 10 $(8+10=18)$ to get the next number. Continue with this pattern until you find the number you need.

9. **B. $16.13.** This problem involves data analysis and manipulation of numbers and is best done using a calculator. Most of the information in the table is irrelevant, except the price per share that Marta paid: $15.19. In addition to this price per share, Marta has to pay her broker 3% commission.

Therefore, her final price per share on September 24 is $15.19 + (0.03 \times \$15.19) = \$15.6457$. Because you're dealing with money, you have to round the number to two decimal places, making her final price per share $15.65. This is the amount that she paid for each share she bought.

If Marta decides to sell the shares at this price, $15.65, she has to pay her broker another 3% commission, or $0.03 \times \$15.65 = \$0.4695$. Rounded to two decimals, she has to pay a commission of $0.47 per share. She then receives the value of the shares, $15.65, minus the commission of $0.47, for a total of $15.18 per share — that is, for each share she sells, the broker pays her $15.18. Notice that this amount is less than the amount she paid for each share.

To break even, Marta has to receive $15.65 per share — after the commission. Set the equation up this way:

$1x - x(0.03) = 15.65$, where x is the selling price

$1x - 0.03x = 15.65$

$0.97x = 15.65$

Now divide both sides by 0.97 to get $x = 16.134$. Rounded to two decimal places, the answer is $16.13.

10. **C. –4.** This question involves algebra. You have to solve a linear equation, as follows:

$$22.4 = \frac{56a}{5a+10}$$

Cross-multiply and write this equation as $22.4(5a+10) = 56a$. Then, getting rid of the parentheses, the equation looks like this: $112a + 224 = 56a$. Next, bring all the a's to the left and the numbers to the right, so you have $112a - 56a = -224$. Then, combine the a's to get $56a = -224$. Finally, divide both sides by 56 to get one a on the left: $a = -4$.

11. **2/3 or 0.66.** This question tests your skills in measurement and geometry. You're asked to find the slope of a line that is drawn for you.

The x-axis runs horizontally across the grid. The y-axis runs vertically up and down the grid. The origin is where the two axes (that's the plural of axis) intersect. Points to the left of the y-axis have negative x-values. Points below the x-axis have negative y-values. The x-intercept of a line is the point where the line cuts the x-axis. The y-intercept of a line is the point where the line cuts the y-axis. All lines parallel to the x-axis have slopes of 0.

The slope of a line is the rise over the run. The rise is 4, and the run is 6. This means that the slope is 4/6 or 2/3 (divide by 2 to simplify), which can be expressed as 2/3 or 0.66.

12. $(-6, 0)$. This question tests your skills in measurement and geometry. You're asked to identify the x-intercept and the y-intercept and to draw a line with a slope of 2/3 on the graph.

If you draw a line through the point on the y-axis having the same slope, it crosses the x-axis at $(-6, 0)$. Simply count over 3 points to the left (the run), down 2 (the rise), and you're at $(-3, 2)$. But you're asked for the x-intercept, so repeat this process. Go over 3 more points to the left and down 2 more, and you're at $(-6, 0)$.

13. one extra-large pizza. You can use the formula for area of a circle to determine the amount of pizza you get with each size. The area of an extra-large pizza is 254.34 square inches ($\pi 9^2$) and of a medium pizza is 113.04 square inches ($\pi 6^2$). Because the special is for two medium pizzas, Janet will get around 226 square inches of pizza for $21. Therefore, an extra-large pizza, with 254 square inches of pizza for $20, is a better deal. Note that in this problem you don't have to calculate the cost per square inch because an extra-large pizza is already one dollar less than two mediums.

14. A. $2.19. Consider the price per square foot at each store.

Carnie's Carpets: $21.50 per square yard = $21.50 / 9 = $2.39 per square foot

Flora's Flooring: $2.45 per square foot

Dora's Deep Discount: The area of an 8×12-foot rug is $(8)(12) = 96$ square feet. The cost for 96 square feet is $210.24 or $210.24 / 96 = $2.19 per square foot.

Dora's Deep Discount is the lowest price, $2.19 per square foot.

15. C. 3rd quarter. In this question, you're asked to analyze graphs to identify patterns in a workplace situation.

In the 2020 graph, the largest area is for the 3rd quarter, over 50% of output. For 2021, the longest bar is also for the 3rd quarter, over 30% of production. Therefore, the correct answer is Choice (C).

16. 1,140. This problem involves measurement, specifically, area and money. Assuming that the estimate is accurate, the number of additional square feet that the owners can get for $18,000 is $18,000 / 15.80$ square feet $= 1,139.24$ square feet. Round this number to the nearest ten, 1,140.

17. (6,6)

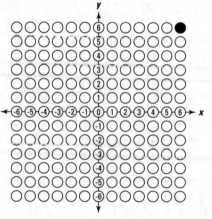

18. sedan. This problem is based on measurement, using uniform rates, and it asks you to make a decision based on factual information. To figure the cost of gasoline over five years, set up the problem this way:

$$18{,}000\,\text{miles} \times \frac{1\,\text{gallon}}{19.6\,\text{miles}} \times \frac{\$3.50}{\text{gallon}} \times 5\,\text{years}$$

To help you decide which car LeeAnne should buy, create a chart like the following:

Vehicle Type	Miles/Gallon	Total Gas Cost
2-door	19.6	$16,071.43
Sedan	19.5	$16,153.83

You can use the table to easily estimate that the difference over 5 years is less than $100, well under her target of $500, so she should get the sedan.

19. C. 1 hour and 45 minutes. This problem involves number operations. First you need to calculate the amount of time it will take Tom to drive to the test center: $50 / 40 = 1.25$, or 1 hour and 15 minutes. (Remember that 0.25 hours is ¼ hour, or 15 minutes.) When you add 30 minutes to that, you get 1 hour and 45 minutes. If you selected Choice (D), you confused 0.25 hour (15 minutes) with 25 minutes: $25 + 30 = 55$, which is incorrect.

20. D. 11. This question involves data analysis. You're given the average grade and asked to analyze the effect of changes in data on this measure. If Leonora's present average is 77.8% and she wants to get an average of 80%, she needs enough points to get an additional 2.2% $(80 - 77.8)$.

Because Leonora is taking five subjects, she requires 5 extra points for each percent increase. Thus, she requires $(2.2)(5) = 11$ additional points. The question says that English is her best subject, so she would need the 11 extra points in English.

21. A. 7 cups of soup and $7/8$ **cup of lentils.** This question tests your ability to figure out how a change in the amount of rice used results in changes to the amount of soup and lentils needed. Because each cup of rice requires 2 cups of soup, 3½ cups of rice require $3\frac{1}{2} \times 2 = 7$ cups of soup. Because each cup of rice requires ¼ cup of lentils, 3½ cups of rice require $3\frac{1}{2} \times \frac{1}{4} = \frac{7}{2} \times \frac{1}{4} = \frac{7}{8}$ cup of lentils.

TIP

Question 21 is a good example of when process of elimination can help you. Since you can easily calculate that 7 cups of soup are needed, you can immediately eliminate Choices (B) and (D). This strategy is particulary helpful if you are running out of time and want to guess. Without much calculating, you increased your odds of guessing to 50/50!

22. C. 1:46. This question is a test in probability. You're asked to figure out the probability of an event occurring. If you had an entire deck of 52 cards, the probability of drawing an ace of hearts would be 1:52. If you remove 6 cards and none of them is the ace of hearts, you may as well have a 46-card deck $(52 - 6)$. The probability of drawing the ace of hearts from a 46-card deck is 1:46.

23. B. the larger rug. This problem tests your measurement skills. You're asked to predict the impact of changes in the linear dimensions of the rug on its area and cost. Tile costs more per square foot than carpeting, so you know without doing any figuring that having more tile will result in higher costs. Choice (C) seems logical, but the question asks about the cost of the flooring only, so you can't consider the paneling in your answer.

Determining whether you can answer without calculating, as is the case with this question, can help you save time on the day of the test.

TIP

24. **C. loveseat.** This question is an exercise in data analysis. You're asked to compare sets of data based on the average prices of four other stores. You can summarize the average prices on a table like this one:

Item	Store A	Store B	Store C	Store D	Average Price	Friendly Furniture
Couch	$1,729.00	$1,749.00	$1,729.00	$1,699.00	$1,726.50	$1,719.00
Dining room set	$4,999.00	$4,899.00	$5,019.00	$4,829.00	$4,936.50	$4,899.00
Loveseat	$1,259.00	$1,199.00	$1,279.00	$1,149.00	$1,221.50	$1,229.00
Coffee table	$459.00	$449.00	$479.00	$429.00	$454.00	$449.00
Reclining chair	$759.00	$799.00	$739.00	$699.00	$749.00	$739.00

You can see that the only item Friendly Furniture sells for over the average price is the loveseat.

Questions with many calculations, such this one, take a lot of time. On the day of the test, you might flag this question to return to later, after you finish all the other items. Also, when you make the table, you only need to write the average price for each item of furniture, in order to save time.

TIP

25. **320.** This question tests your knowledge of number operations by asking you to solve a problem involving calculations. Sarah shelled 48/18 pistachios per minute. In 2 hours or 120 minutes, she could shell $120 \times \frac{48}{18} = 320$ pistachios, if she can maintain that rate for two hours. That's a lot of pistachios!

26. **272.** Because the storage room is 9 feet long, 8 feet wide, and 8 feet high, Kevin will need enough paint for two walls that are 9×8 feet and two walls that are 8×8 feet. To solve the problem, write or key into your calculator: $2(9 \times 8) + 2(8 \times 8)$. The correct answer is 272.

27. **A. triangle.** Only a triangle (Choice A) has 180 degrees. A circle (Choice B) and a square (Choice D) have 360 degrees. A pentagon (Choice C) has 540 degrees.

28. **7:1.** This question tests your data-analysis skills by asking you to interpret a chart and answer a question involving calculation.

The largest budget is the Operations budget, while the smallest budget is Human Resources. The ratio between these two budgets is 14.7 to 2.1 or 7:1 (dividing both sides by 2.1).

If you want to do this in your head to save time, notice that 14:2 (the approximate ratio between the Operations budget and the Human Resources budget) is double 7:1.

Question 28 is a good example of a time you need to ignore extraneous information: the organization chart does not contain information needed to answer the question, so you can safely ignore it.

TIP

29. **5.** This question tests your knowledge of patterns by asking you to compare information from different types of graphs to extract information. Graph 5 has the first and third quarters in the required ratio, and so 5 is the correct answer.

30. **A. 20.** This problem involves measurement and geometry, and it asks you to use the Pythagorean Theorem, which says $a^2 + b^2 = c^2$, where c is the measure of the hypotenuse, or long side, of a right triangle. Because you know the measure of the base of the triangle, and the hypotenuse (the distance from the top of the shadow to the top of the tree), you can set up the problem as $15^2 + b^2 = 25^2$, and solve for b. Because $15^2 = 225$ and $25^2 = 625$, $b^2 = 625 - 225$. Simplifying further, $b = \sqrt{400}$, or 20. This problem is a good illustration of how familiarity with this formula can help you solve a problem.

TIP

Remember, you can find the Pythagorean Theorem, as well as other important formulas, on the Formula Sheet. To access this valuable information during the real GED, just click the Formula button on the test screen.

31. **$78.50.** This question tests your knowledge of number operations by asking you to perform several operations to calculate an answer. After the fourth week, Laurie would've deposited $(4)(\$24.00) = \$96.00$. There would've been two withdrawals totaling $\$7.50 + \$10.00 = \$17.50$. Her balance after the fourth week would be $\$96.00 - \$17.50 = \$78.50$.

32. **$3.20.** This question tests your skills in using percentages and discounts. Store A offers Sarah 1/3 off or $96 / 3 = \$32.00$ off the original price. Store B offers her 30% off; 30% is 0.30, so she'll get $(96)(0.30) = \$28.80$ off the original price. By buying at Store A, she'd get the chair for $\$32.00 - \$28.80 = \$3.20$ less. Thus, she'd save $3.20.

33. **D. 100.** This question tests your skills by asking you to use information from a graph to solve a problem. From the graph, you can figure out that the volume in decibels is the square of the volume setting. For a volume setting of 4, the volume is 16 decibels. Therefore, for a setting of 10, the volume is 100 decibels (10^2).

34. **C. 8.** This question tests your skills in algebra by asking you to solve equations. The equation given is $V = S^2$. If $S^2 = 64$, the square root of 64 is 8. Thus, the correct answer is 8.

35. **B. 108.** If the volume decreases by 6 decibels for every 10 feet away from the stage you get, and the volume at the stage is 120 decibels, then a person sitting 20 feet from the stage would hear at a volume of 108 decibels: $120 - (6 \times 2) = 108$.

36. **24.** This question involves number operations. You're asked to calculate the average miles per gallon for a vehicle. Rather than being given the number of gallons used, you're given the cost of gasoline and the cost of the 480-mile trip. To calculate the amount of fuel used, you divide $\$54.00$ by $\$2.70$ to get 20 gallons. You can do this operation mentally or on the erasable tablet to speed things up. Next, you divide the miles, 480, by the fuel used, 20 gallons, to get the mileage, 24 miles per gallon $(480 / 20 = 24)$.

37. **D. circle.** This question tests your skills in measurement and geometry. To remain at a constant temperature, you have to remain at a constant distance from the fire.

The path of a point that travels a constant distance from another point is a circle.

38. **4.** This problem tests your ability to do calculations and use a formula: *Volume = length × width × depth*. Thus, $11,520$ cubic feet $= 120$ feet $\times 24$ feet $\times$ average depth. The average depth $= \dfrac{11,520}{(120 \times 24)} = 4$.

39. **C. 2,949.** This question tests your ability to make a decision based on data presented in a table and then to use that information to answer a question. The least economical car costs $\$1,823$ to drive for a year, while the most economical car costs $\$840$ for the same time under the same conditions. The difference in cost for one year is $\$1,823 - \$840 = \$983$. The cost for three years is $(\$983)(3) = \$2,949$.

You could also estimate an answer. The difference annually is just under $1,000. For three years, that's just under $3,000. So Choice (C) is the best answer.

40. B. 16.8. The average city mileage for all of the vehicles is the sum of the city mileages divided by 10 (the number of entries), which equals 16.8: $(23 + 21 + 19 + 18 + 17 + 16 + 15 + 14 + 13 + 12)/10 = 16.8$. Note that Choice (D) is the average highway MPG, which is a good reminder to read carefully and answer the exact question you are asked.

41. 5. This question tests your ability to analyze data.

For Vehicle A, the difference between the city and highway mileage is 5 miles per gallon $(28 - 23)$.

42. D. 8. This question tests your skill in algebra by asking you to solve a system of linear equations:

$$2x + 3y = 10$$
$$5x + 6y = 13$$

A linear equation is one in which the powers of the variables are all equal to 1. To solve this system, you have to eliminate x by multiplying each equation by a number that allows you to subtract one from the other and end up with just y's. Multiply the first equation by 5 and the second equation by 2:

$$5(2x + 3y = 10) = 10x + 15y = 50$$
$$2(5x + 6y = 13) = 10x + 12y = 26$$

Subtract the second equation from the first, and you get $3y = 24$; $y = 8$. (Note that you can also multiply the first equation by –2 and add the two equations together. Either way gets you the same answer.)

43. B. 4 times as many. This question asks you to analyze a situation presented in a table. The table tells you that the country with the highest participation rate is the United States, with a participation rate of 66.4. The country with the lowest participation rate is Portugal, with a participation rate of 15.5. Because you're asked for an approximation, you can say that the participation rate in the United States is 60 and in Portugal, it's 15, which means that 4 times as many adults participate in adult education in the United States as in Portugal: $60 \div 15 = 4$.

44. B. $18.00. This question involves number operations. The total amount of Gordon's bills is $23 + $31 + $48 + $13 + $114 + $39 = $268. (Note that you can leave off the zeroes to speed things up.) If Gordon allocates only $250 to pay these bills, he ends up $268 – $250 = $18 short. Be wary of Choice (D), which is a special trap for people who don't read the question carefully.

45. 3 hours. At the end of the first month, Georgette will owe $200 + $20 = $220. The second month's interest will be $($220$)($0.15$) = 33.00. At $11 an hour, Georgette would have to work an additional 3 hours to pay the second month's interest.

46. B. approximately 5,300. This question tests your knowledge of measurement and geometry by asking you to solve a problem involving volume and weight. You can answer this question using mental math and estimation, but I'll take you through the steps using calculations first.

The formula for volume of a cylinder (the cylinder is the circular inside of the pool to a height of 9 inches) is $\pi r^2 h$, where π = approximately 3.14, r = radius, and h = height. (You can find this formula in the GED Formula Sheet.) If the diameter is 12 feet, the radius is 6 feet. If the height is 9 inches, it's 9/12 feet, which can be simplified to 3/4 feet.

In a formula, don't forget that all units must be the same — that is, feet and feet or inches and inches.

The volume is $(3.14)\big[(6)(6)\big](3/4) = 84.78$ cubic feet. Remember that 3/4 foot is 0.75 foot.

Because 1 cubic foot weighs 62.42 pounds, the weight of 84.78 cubic feet is $(84.78)(62.42) = 5,291.96$ or 5,300 pounds rounded to the nearest hundred.

To estimate using mental math or the erasable tablet, multiply 6 by 6 to get 36. Multiply 36 by 3/4 to get 27, and multiply 27 by 3 to get 81. The approximate volume of the pool is 81 cubic feet, which isn't bad for an approximation. For your purposes, say the volume is 80 cubic feet, which is still close. The weight of a cubic foot of water is 62.42 pounds, so round it to 60 pounds. Now, multiply 80 by 60 to get 4,800, which is closest to Choice (B). You can go with that approximation because it's very close to one of the answer choices.

The erasable whiteboard (available only at a testing center) is a good tool to use when estimating. Just jot down the numbers and calculations.

TIP 47. **B. 6.4%.** This question tests your ability to evaluate an answer by using the formula for simple interest, which is in the GED Formula Sheet. This formula, $I = prt$, isn't in the format you want because you want to calculate the rate, which means solving for r. You can change the equation to $r = \dfrac{I}{p \times t}$, which allows you to calculate the rate from the information given. Substituting into this equation, you get $r = \dfrac{8}{100 \times 1.25}$.

(Remember that 1 year and 3 months is 1¼, or 1.25, years.)

Then $r = \dfrac{8}{125} = 0.064 = 6.4\%$.

Question 47 is a good example of when estimation and mental math can help you find the answer without any calculation. You can quickly eliminate Choice (A) because the annual interest rate has to be lower than 8%, since $8 is the amount of interest for a year and 3 months. Choice (D) is too low. The interest rate would not go down by half unless two years had gone by. Of the two remaining choices, (C) is also too low. That leaves Choice (B).

TIP

48. **C. $4.90.** This question involves number operations. You can estimate — in your head — the answer to the question.

To use mental math to solve this problem, round everything. Consider the apples at $0.80 a pound, bananas at $0.20 each, milk at $1.30, and a loaf of bread at $1.00. The total for this approximation is $(2)(\$0.80) + (5)(\$0.20) + \$1.30 + \$1.00 = \$4.90$. Looking at the answer choices, Choice (C) is the only one close to this approximation.

49. **A. 28.** This question tests your knowledge of patterns by asking you to figure out the next number in a series. By looking at the series, it looks like each number is the square of the placement of the number in the list, plus 3. That is, the first number is 1^2 plus 3, or 4. The second number is 2^2 plus 3, or 7. The third term is $3^2 (9)$ plus 3, or 12. The fifth term would be $5^2 (25)$ plus 3, which is 28.

50. **C.** $(-2, -2)$. This question tests your skills in geometry by asking you to visualize a graph of an object. Because the object is a rectangle, the opposite sides are equal in length and are parallel. The fourth corner will be 2 units to the left of the y-axis, giving it an x-coordinate of –2, and 2 units below the x-axis, giving it a y-coordinate of –2. Therefore, the point would be $(-2, -2)$.

The x-coordinate is the distance from the y-axis, and the y-coordinate is the distance from the x-axis.

Answer Key

1.	D	18.	sedan	35.	B
2.	A	19.	C	36.	24
3.	2,160	20.	D	37.	D
4.	B	21.	A	38.	4
5.	0.27	22.	C	39.	C
6.	B	23.	B	40.	B
7.	D	24.	C	41.	5
8.	66	25.	320	42.	D
9.	B	26.	272	43.	B
10.	C	27.	A	44.	B
11.	2/3, or 0.66	28.	7:1	45.	3 hours
12.	(–6,0)	29.	5	46.	B
13.	one extra-large pizza	30.	A	47.	B
14.	A	31.	$78.50	48.	C
15.	C	32.	$3.20	49.	A
16.	1,140	33.	D	50.	C
17.	(6,6)	34.	C		

7

Getting More Test Practice: GED Practice Test 2

IN THIS PART . . .

Continue building your skills and your confidence with another full-length GED practice test.

Score your answers quickly and compare your results from this practice test with Practice Test 1.

Check out detailed answer explanations for every question and sample scoring criteria for the Extended Response.

Chapter 27

Practice Test 2: Reasoning through Language Arts

Ready for more practice? You have 95 minutes to complete the question-and-answer section, followed by a ten-minute break, and then another 45 minutes to write the Extended Response (the essay). Remember, on the real GED test, you can't transfer unused time from one section to another. To keep track of time, use the timer on your mobile phone. If you run out of time, mark the last question you completed. Then finish the remaining times. This will show you how much faster you need to work on the real GED to answer all the questions.

The answers and explanations to this test's questions are in Chapter 28. Review the explanations to all the questions, not just the ones you didn't get. Going over the answers is a good review technique.

REMEMBER

Practice tests work best when you take them under the same conditions as the real test. Unless you require accommodations, you'll be taking the GED test on a computer. You'll see all the questions on a computer screen and use a keyboard or mouse to indicate your answers. I formatted the questions and answer choices in this book to make them appear as similar as possible to the real GED test. I had to retain A, B, C, and D choices for marking your answers, and I provide an answer sheet for you to do so. Also, to make it simpler for you to time yourself, I present the questions for Reading Comprehension and Grammar and Language together in one section rather than separately (as on the real GED), with the Extended Response at the end of the test. If possible, write the essay on a computer (with spell-check, grammar-check, and autocorrect turned off) to simulate conditions on test day. Have a sheet of paper or two to use to jot down notes and organize your ideas. Otherwise, use the lined paper I provide for you.

Answer Sheet for Practice Test 2, Reasoning through Language Arts

1. _____

2. _____

3. _____

4. _____

5. _____

6. _____

7. _____

8. _____

9. _____

10. _____

11. _____

12. _____

13. _____

14. _____

15. _____

16. _____

17. _____

18. _____

19. _____

20. _____

21. _____

22. _____

23. _____

24. _____

25. _____

26. _____

27. _____

28. _____

29. _____

30. _____

31. _____

32. _____

33. _____

34. _____

35. _____

36. _____

37. _____

38. _____

39. _____

40. _____

41. _____

42. _____

43. _____

44. _____

45. _____

46. _____

47. _____

48. _____

49. _____

50. _____

TIME: 95 minutes

ITEMS: 50

DIRECTIONS: You may answer the questions in this section in any order. Mark your answers on the answer sheet provided.

Questions 1–10 refer to the following passage.

[Select... ▼] the same. Many bottlers use the same municipal water that comes from your tap. They merely have [Select... ▼] do some additional filtration to enhance the taste. [Select... ▼] different. The mineral content of [Select... ▼] from spring to spring, producing water with a unique taste. Other bottled waters [Select... ▼] to the clean taste of water.

If you find mineral water whose taste you enjoy and don't mind the cost, enjoy. From our "Green" perspective, the plastic litter is a huge negative. Also, the effect on the environment of moving large quantities of potable water from one area to another make this an undesirable solution.

Many people enjoy [Select... ▼] taste. So how can you get the same clean taste without the waste? The [Select... ▼] expensive way is to use a jug with a charcoal filter cartridge. Filling that jug with clean tap water removes the chlorine and unpleasant tastes or odors. It also removes some of the lead found in the water pipes of older buildings. This is an [Select... ▼] inexpensive choice. Certainly our morning coffee and tea tastes better for this filtration.

A more advanced and expensive counter-top system is a distillation pot. This system boils water, collects the steam, and condenses it into absolutely pure water. But not everyone likes the taste of totally mineral-free water, and the electricity costs add up.

There are also more extensive systems available. If you get tired of changing cartridges or storing the [Select... ▼] can also have an under-the-counter system installed on your kitchen sink. In townhouses, you can add such a system on the main water pipe and provide the same filtration to the entire house. Some of these systems use carbon blocks and ceramic filters. The blocks are more effective than loose charcoal [Select... ▼] of pesticides and other chemical contaminants. Ceramic filters remove cloudiness and micro-particles, spores, and other microscopic matter. They deliver excellent drinking water. In either case, there is little waste other than the filters.

1. [Select... ▼] the same.

   (A) But not all brands of bottled water are

   (B) Not all brands of bottled water are

   (C) But, not all brands of bottled water are

   (D) Not all brands of bottled water is

2. They merely have [Select... ▼] do some additional filtration to enhance the taste.

   (A) to remove the chlorine completely,

   (B) to remove the chlorine completely and

   (C) to complete the removal of the chlorine and

   (D) a removal of the chlorine and

3. [Select... ▼] different.

   (A) Bottled spring waters are

   (B) Bottled, spring waters are

   (C) Bottled spring waters were

   (D) Bottled spring waters is

4. The mineral content of [Select... ▼] from spring to spring, producing water with a unique taste.

   (A) water are different

   (B) water differ

   (C) waters differs

   (D) waters differ

5. Other bottled waters [Select... ▼] to the clean taste of water.

   (A) are carbonated, either naturally or artificially in the bottling process, carbonation can add

   (B) are carbonated naturally or artificially in the bottling process, carbonation can add

   (C) are carbonated. Either naturally or artificially in the bottling process. Carbonation can add

   (D) are carbonated, either naturally or artificially in the bottling process. Carbonation can add

6. Many people enjoy [Select... ▼] taste.

   (A) there bottled water's

   (B) their bottled water's

   (C) they're bottled water's

   (D) their bottled waters

7. The [Select... ▼] expensive way is to use a jug with a charcoal filter cartridge.

   (A) less

   (B) least

   (C) lesser

   (D) lessor

8. This is an [Select... ▼] inexpensive choice.

   (A) effective, and

   (B) effective and

   (C) effective

   (D) effective; and

9. If you get tired of changing cartridges or storing the [Select... ▼] can also have an under-the-counter system installed on your kitchen sink.

   (A) plastic, jug in your fridge, you

   (B) plastic jug, in your fridge, you

   (C) plastic jug in your fridge you

   (D) plastic jug in your fridge, you

10. The blocks are more effective than loose charcoal [Select... ▼] of pesticides and other chemical contaminants.

    (A) filters also removing traces

    (B) filters. Also removing traces

    (C) filters; also removing traces

    (D) filters for removing traces

Questions 11–17 refer to the following business letter.

BEST Institute of Technology

75 Ingram Drive
Concord, MA 01742

To whom it may concern:

I am pleased to comment on the relationship of our organization to Jane Fairfax of the York Square [Select... ▼]. The BEST Institute of Technology [Select... ▼] with the York Square ERC in recruiting candidates for our Café Technician and Operator training programs since April 2010.

[Select... ▼] Ms. Fairfax provided many important services to our programs. Her duties included:

    Setting up information presentations and job readiness seminars

    Distributing print materials

    Counseling applicants

    Arranging five graduation ceremonies at York Square ERC

Ms. Fairfax [Select... ▼] a strong advocate for our program, which has trained more than 50 technicians and operators during the past 18 months. The fact that York Square has become our primary source of referrals [Select... ▼] a tribute to Ms. Fairfax's efforts. She has [Select... ▼]. On a personal level, it has been a joy to work with Ms. Fairfax, and I wish her the very [Select... ▼].

Dale Worth, PhD, Executive Director

11. I am pleased to comment on the relationship of our organization to Jane Fairfax of the York Square [Select... ▼].

    (A) employment resource Center

    (B) Employment resource Center

    (C) Employment Resource Center

    (D) Employment resource center

12. The BEST Institute of Technology [Select... ▼] with the York Square ERC in recruiting candidates for our Café Technician and Operator training programs since April 2010.

    (A) has partnered

    (B) partnered

    (C) partners

    (D) is partnering

 GO ON TO NEXT PAGE

13. [Select... ▼] Ms. Fairfax provided many important services to our programs.

    (A) In support, of the partnership,

    (B) In support of the partnership

    (C) In support of the partnership.

    (D) In support of the partnership,

14. Ms. Fairfax [Select... ▼] a strong advocate for our program, which has trained more than 50 technicians and operators during the past 18 months.

    (A) has always been

    (B) always is being

    (C) had been always

    (D) have always been

15. The fact that York Square has become our primary source of referrals [Select... ▼] a tribute to Ms. Fairfax's efforts.

    (A) are

    (B) is

    (C) were

    (D) was

16. She has [Select... ▼].

    (A) pursued her responsibilities with a high degree of professionalism

    (B) with a high degree of professionalism pursued her responsibilities

    (C) pursued with a high degree of professionalism her responsibilities

    (D) pursued with professionalism a high degree of responsibilities

17. On a personal level, it has been a joy to work with Ms. Fairfax, and I wish her the very [Select... ▼].

    (A) best in her future endeavors

    (B) best, in her future endeavors

    (C) best in her future, endeavors

    (D) best, in her future, endeavors

Questions 18–25 refer to the following excerpt from Customer Service For Dummies, *by Karen Leland and Keith Bailey (John Wiley & Sons, Inc.).*

The Care Token Coupon

A new copy shop [Select... ▼] near our office. Modern and full of new, streamlined, state-of-the-art [Select... ▼] store was just what I needed. [Select... ▼] I waited 45 minutes to get served because of a shortage of trained staff. They bounced back by apologizing, explaining the situation, [Select... ▼] a care token coupon that was worth 100 free copies. Okay, I thought, fair enough. They're new and getting their act together, so [Select... ▼] big deal. A week later, I went back for a second time. Right away, I [Select... ▼] it was a big mistake. I waited 30 minutes for service. [Select... ▼] apologized, explained the situation, and gave me a coupon for 100 free copies. This time I was [Select... ▼] little less understanding. Two weeks later, I went back and the same thing happened again. I didn't want another free coupon — they had bounced back just once too often. My opinion of their services were so soured that I began looking for another copy shop.

18. A new copy shop [Select... ▼] near our office.

    (A) recent opened

    (B) recently opened

    (C) opened recent

    (D) recently opening

19. Modern and full of new, streamlined, state-of-the-art [Select... ▼] store was just what I needed.

    (A) copiers. The

    (B) copiers, the

    (C) copiers; the

    (D) copiers and the

20. [Select... ▼] I waited 45 minutes to get served because of a shortage of trained staff.

    (A) Because to get served

    (B) When for the first time I went there,

    (C) To get served because

    (D) The first time I went there,

21. They bounced back by apologizing, explaining the situation, [Select... ▼] a care token coupon that was worth 100 free copies.

    (A) and given me

    (B) and giving myself

    (C) and giving me

    (D) and gave me

22. They're new and getting their act together, so [Select... ▼] big deal.

    (A) its no

    (B) it's no

    (C) it's know

    (D) its' no

23. Right away, I [Select... ▼] it was a big mistake.

    (A) known

    (B) news

    (C) new

    (D) knew

24. [Select... ▼] apologized, explained the situation, and gave me a coupon for 100 free copies.

    (A) But they

    (B) After they

    (C) They

    (D) When they

25. This time I was [Select... ▼] little less understanding.

    (A) a

    (B) too

    (C) to

    (D) an

Questions 26–31 refer to this excerpt from The Prince, *by Niccolò Machiavelli (Project Gutenberg;* www. gutenberg.org) *and the following short passage about* The Art of War, *an ancient Chinese military textbook.*

The Prince

A prince ought to have no other aim or thought, nor select anything else for his study, than war and its rules and discipline; for this is the sole art that belongs to him who rules, and it is of such force that it not only upholds those who are born princes, but it often enables men to rise from a private station to that rank. And, on the contrary, it is seen that when princes have thought more of ease than of arms they have lost their states. And the first cause of your losing it is to neglect this art; and what enables you to acquire a state is to be master of the art. Francesco Sforza, through being martial, from a private person became Duke of Milan; and the sons, through avoiding the hardships and troubles of arms, from dukes became private persons. For among other evils which being unarmed brings you, it causes you to be despised, and this is one of those ignominies against which a prince ought to guard himself, as is shown later on. Because there is nothing proportionate between the armed and the unarmed; and it is not reasonable that he who is armed should yield obedience willingly to him who is unarmed, or that the unarmed man should be secure among armed servants. Because, there being in the one disdain and in the other suspicion, it is not possible for them to work well together. And therefore a prince who does not understand the art of war, over and above the other misfortunes already mentioned, cannot be respected by his soldiers, nor can he rely on them. He ought never, therefore, to have out of his thoughts this subject of war, and in peace he should addict himself more to its exercise than in war; this he can do in two ways, the one by action, the other by study.

On *The Art of War*

The Art of War is an ancient text by a revered Chinese general, Sun Tzu. This book is considered to be one of the most insightful books on war ever written. One of the most important factors that contributes to military success, according to Sun Tzu, is leadership. On leadership, Sun Tzu said, "The commander of an army stands for these virtues: wisdom, sincerity, benevolence, courage, and strictness." Some of these characteristics seem obvious, but others are contradictory. A military leader clearly needs wisdom. And a good military leader needs sincerity in order to win the trust of subordinates and troops. And, of course, courage is a necessity in war. But what about benevolence and strictness? Obviously, balance is needed. Strictness is necessary to maintain discipline and order. But at the same time, a good leader cannot be harsh, unjust, or arbitrary. A good leader needs to consider each situation and make decisions that are fair and generous when warranted.

26. According to *The Prince*, why should a prince concentrate on the study of war?

    (A) It is the knowledge that preserves their position.

    (B) It allows the prince to lead a more comfortable life.

    (C) Not being focused on war makes you more beloved by the people.

    (D) Peaceful men are respected by their soldiers.

27. According to *The Prince*, why should a prince master the study of war and be armed?

   (A) Having a large army ensures lots of jobs.

   (B) People are suspicious of princes with large armies.

   (C) Slaves fear soldiers.

   (D) The armed do not readily yield authority to the unarmed.

28. How does Machiavelli think the population will react to a prince who is unarmed?

   (A) They will follow him.

   (B) They will respect him.

   (C) They will fear him.

   (D) They will despise him.

29. Which of these phrases best describes Machiavelli's attitude to the study of the art of war?

   (A) Study infrequently.

   (B) In times of peace, prepare for war.

   (C) Avoid war to gain the respect of your people.

   (D) Warriors respect only warriors.

30. According to "On *The Art of War*," what would a good general do if he found out that one of his top subordinates might be too sick to fight?

   (A) Make him fight anyway, even though he might die.

   (B) Send the subordinate to a hospital far from the front.

   (C) Harshly punish the subordinate in front of everyone.

   (D) Ask the subordinate what he needs in order to return quickly.

31. Which of these statements would Machiavelli and Sun Tzu agree on?

   (A) A strong leader crushes all opposition and dissent.

   (B) To maintain power, leaders only need superior strength.

   (C) To maintain power, leaders must master the art of war.

   (D) A ruler can delegate military affairs to his generals.

Questions 32–36 refer to the following passage from The Adventures of Tom Sawyer, *by Mark Twain (Project Gutenberg;* www.gutenberg.org). *The speaker is Tom Sawyer's guardian, his Aunt Polly.*

"Hang the boy, can't I never learn anything? Ain't he played me tricks enough like that for me to be looking out for him by this time? But old fools is the biggest fools there is. Can't learn an old dog new tricks, as the saying is. But my goodness, he never plays them alike, two days, and how is a body to know what's coming? He 'pears to know just how long he can torment me before I get my dander up, and he knows if he can make out to put me off for a minute or make me laugh, it's all down again and I can't hit him a lick. I ain't doing my duty by that boy, and that's the Lord's truth, goodness knows. Spare the rod and spile the child, as the Good Book says. I'm a laying up sin and suffering for us both, I know. He's full of the Old Scratch, but laws-a-me! he's my own dead sister's boy, poor thing, and I ain't got the heart to lash him, somehow. Every time I let him off, my conscience does hurt me so, and every time I hit him my old heart most breaks. Well-a-well, man that is born of woman is of few days and full of trouble, as the Scripture says, and I reckon it's so. He'll play hookey this evening*, and I'll just be obleeged to make him work, tomorrow, to punish him. It's mighty hard to make him work

Saturdays, when all the boys is having holiday, but he hates work more than he hates anything else, and I've GOT to do some of my duty by him, or I'll be the ruination of the child."

*Southwestern for "afternoon"

32. Why did Mark Twain write this dialogue in such an ungrammatical manner?

    (A) He did not know any better.

    (B) He assumed his readers spoke in a "folksy" dialect.

    (C) He wanted to reflect the character of the speaker.

    (D) Everyone spoke like that back then.

33. Which of these statements does Aunt Polly use to support punishing Tom?

    (A) Man that is born of woman is of few days and full of trouble.

    (B) Spare the rod and spile the child.

    (C) Old fools is the biggest fools there is.

    (D) Can't learn an old dog new tricks.

34. Why does the speaker believe she is committing a sin?

    (A) She can't make Tom go to church.

    (B) She occasionally hits Tom.

    (C) She is not strict enough with Tom.

    (D) She makes Tom work on Saturdays.

35. What evidence is there in the text to support the idea that the speaker considers herself a good, God-fearing woman?

    (A) She makes references to religion.

    (B) She worries about making Tom work on Sundays.

    (C) She gets mad at Tom Sawyer for the tricks he pulls.

    (D) She wants Tom Sawyer to go to school every day.

36. What does Tom Sawyer hate the most?

    (A) work

    (B) painting fences

    (C) playing hookey

    (D) annoying his aunt

Questions 37 and 38 refer to the following excerpt from the Central Intelligence Agency Careers website (www.cia.gov).

Instilling Inclusive Work Practices

In our organization, we are working to ensure every officer's views are heard and that their ideas and skills are given due consideration. This enables us to fully leverage our talented and dedicated workforce.

The Agency has a variety of employee resource groups comprised of employees [Select... ▾] a common affinity (gender, sexual orientation, disability, ethnic, and racial backgrounds) and their allies. The employee resource groups make the organization stronger by:

- increasing cultural awareness,

- providing insight, practical solutions, and best practices, and

- promoting engagement and collaboration.

[Select... ▼] mentoring, coaching, training, and recognition for collaborative and inclusive behaviors foster employee engagement, professional development, and career advancement.

37. The Agency has a variety of employee resource groups comprised of employees [Select... ▼] a common affinity (gender, sexual orientation, disability, ethnic, and racial backgrounds) and their allies.

(A) whom share

(B) who share

(C) whom shares

(D) who shares

38. [Select... ▼] mentoring, coaching, training, and recognition for collaborative and inclusive behaviors foster employee engagement, professional development, and career advancement.

(A) In addition,

(B) However,

(C) In contrast,

(D) In other words,

Questions 39–44 refer to the following passage.

Facilities for Access to Creative Enterprise (FACE)

Originally founded in 1982 to train unemployed youth in small "hand skill" craft workshops, this project provides occupational and entrepreneurial skills as an alternative to scarce traditional manufacturing jobs. Beginning with glass engraving and sign writing, FACE now offers training in more than 200 hand skill occupations, including antique restoration, clothing manufacturing, graphic design, masonry, sail making, specialist joinery, weaving, and wood turning. Funded through the Youth Training Program, FACE provides 800 internships under the premise that if young people can't secure employment, they can develop skills to create their own businesses.

Based on its experience, FACE has developed a Certificate in Small Business and Enterprise Skills. The aim of the certificate is "to develop the skills of enterprise management across a range of occupational sectors, within small business and in general employment and which are applicable in a wide range of personal and social contexts outside work." Competencies include self-evaluation, decision making, initiative taking, resource and time management, opportunism and self-motivation, problem solving, and learning-to-learn skills, as well as communication and number skills vital to personal effectiveness.

39. What is the overall purpose of the FACE project?

(A) to provide manufacturing jobs

(B) to engrave glass and make signs

(C) to train jobless young people

(D) to offer a training certificate

40. Which of the following are examples of hand-skill craft occupations? Write the letters in the box.

[   ]

- **(A)** weaving
- **(B)** wood turning
- **(C)** sail making
- **(D)** robotic assembly

41. How can young people best secure employment?

- **(A)** by getting factory jobs
- **(B)** by creating new enterprises of their own
- **(C)** by learning to make furniture
- **(D)** by obtaining a Certificate in Small Business

42. What is the difference between the training in hand-skill crafts and the Certificate in Small Business and Enterprise Skills?

- **(A)** The training is on specific crafts and the certificate develops general business anvd personal skills.
- **(B)** The training focuses on job-search skills and the certificate develops personal skills.
- **(C)** The training develops personal skills through training in a craft, and the certificate recognizes academic achievement.
- **(D)** The training is on traditional hand crafts and the certificate is on high-tech skills.

43. Which competency is included in each part of the program? Write the letters in the appropriate boxes.

Hand-Craft Training	Certificate in Small Business Skills

- **(A)** self-evaluation
- **(B)** anger management
- **(C)** graphic design
- **(D)** mobile phone repair

44. What wording in the passage suggests that FACE does not expect its graduates to find work with large industrial employers after completing their training?

- **(A)** develop occupational skills
- **(B)** an alternative to scarce traditional manufacturing jobs
- **(C)** competencies include self-evaluation and decision making
- **(D)** in general employment

TO: James Tiberius, President, ABLE Books, Inc.

FROM: Akira Hudson, Director, New Book Development

RE: Survival Math Book Proposal

We meet mathematical problems every day in our lives. How we handle them makes the difference between winning and losing. Many of our decisions require knowledge of "survival mathematics," the skills and concepts that help us survive in an increasingly complex world. Many students drop high-school mathematics as soon as they can. Few are willing or able to take in school the life skills courses that would help them later in life. As a result, they never learn some of the important math life skills. This book has a built-in target audience, the people who need "survival mathematics" to get ahead in this world.

The key life skills are the everyday arithmetic that helps one survive in the marketplace. We propose to help readers learn and practice the following skills:

- Different methods of earning a paycheck: A comparison of hourly wages, piecework, commission, and salary.

- Pay and deductions on pay slips: What comes off and why, and making sure your paycheck is correct.

- Budgeting: Making your money last from paycheck to paycheck, creating a household budget, and covering all your regular expenses.

- The deal: How to read ads. Just how good a deal is "the deal"? Do coupons really save money?

- Credit cards: How you pay, what you pay for, and the real cost of loyalty programs.

- Compound interest: The true cost of borrowing money. We show you how to compare interest rates on debt, ranging from bank loans to credit card debt, and how to work out just how expensive credit card debt is.

- Payday loans: Working out the true costs of these high-interest, short-term loans.

- Compound interest on savings: Earning money on money. We explain how you can reinvest to earn more, and the magic of time in accumulating wealth.

- Keeping more of what you earn: Some simple strategies to minimize taxes, from education and retirement savings to mortgage interest deductibility.

- Owning a car: Calculating the pros and cons. We compare used versus new, purchase versus lease, and examine the true cost of owning a car. Because a car is probably the second-biggest purchase most people will ever make, this is an important part of consumer knowledge. This unit is specially aimed at first-time car purchasers.

The application of basic arithmetic skills will help readers become better consumers and teach them how to deal with mathematical issues in everyday life.

45. Why does the writer of the email suggest that this new book is needed?

(A) Many students don't take enough math courses in high school.

(B) Many students want to take advanced math in college but lack the preparation.

(C) Many people make a lot of math mistakes in their checkbooks.

(D) Many people don't use coupons at the supermarket.

46. According to the email, what is the point of budgeting?

(A) to minimize taxes

(B) to avoid running out of money between paychecks

(C) to set aside some savings from each paycheck

(D) to allocate some money for donations to charity

47. What does *regular* mean in this excerpt from the passage?

Budgeting: Making your money last from paycheck to paycheck; creating a household budget; covering all your regular expenses.

(A) usual

(B) special

(C) extra

(D) favorite

48. Why are car purchases considered important enough to be given a heading of their own?

(A) Everyone needs a car.

(B) Students in particular want to buy cars.

(C) Car loans are more expensive than credit card debts.

(D) Cars are among the largest purchases most people ever make.

49. Which of the following would be a good additional topic for the book? Write the letters in the correct box.

In the Book	Not in the Book

(A) saving money by stopping routine maintenance on your car

(B) saving money on major purchases by "shopping around"

(C) taking full advantage of employer plans to save for retirement

(D) reducing costs by canceling anti-virus software on your computer

50. What is the primary purpose of this email?

(A) to convince people to study more math

(B) to inform readers of ways to save money

(C) to convince readers to buy the book

(D) to convince the company to publish the book

At this point, you may take a 10-minute break before beginning the Extended Response.

Extended Response

Article 1: Higher Education

(This article was extracted from the White House Support for Higher Education website: `www.whitehouse.gov`*.)*

Earning a post-secondary degree or credential is no longer just a pathway to opportunity for a talented few; rather, it is a prerequisite for the growing jobs of the new economy. Over this decade, employment in jobs requiring education beyond a high school diploma will grow more rapidly than employment in jobs that do not: of the 30 fastest-growing occupations, more than half require post-secondary education. With the average earnings of college graduates at a level that is twice as high as that of workers with only a high school diploma, higher education is now the clearest pathway into the middle class.

In higher education, the U.S. has been outpaced internationally. In 1990, the U.S. ranked first in the world in four-year degree attainment among 25–34 year olds; today, the U.S. ranks 12th. We also suffer from a college attainment gap, as high school graduates from the wealthiest families in our nation are almost certain to continue on to higher education, while just over half of our high school graduates in the poorest quarter of families attend college. And while more than half of college students graduate within six years, the completion rate for low-income students is around 25 percent.

Acknowledging these factors early in his Administration, President Obama challenged every American to commit to at least one year of higher education or post-secondary training. The President has also set a new goal for the country: that by 2020, America would once again have the highest proportion of college graduates in the world.

To achieve this bold goal for college completion, ensure that America's students and work-ers receive the education and training needed for the jobs of today and tomorrow, and provide greater security for the middle class, President Obama and his Administration are working to make college more accessible, affordable, and attainable for all American families.

America is home to the best colleges and universities in the world — and increasing college attainment has never been more important to our economic competitiveness — yet tuition and fees have skyrocketed over the past decade, making it more difficult for American families to invest in a higher education for their future. Today's college students borrow and rack up more debt than ever before. Student loan debt has now surpassed credit card debt for the first time ever.

Our nation's commitment to placing a good education within reach of all who are willing to work for it helped build a strong American middle class over the past several generations. In keeping this promise alive, President Obama has expanded federal support to help more stu-dents afford college, while calling for a shared responsibility in tackling rising college costs. President Obama's efforts of reform in higher education funding have produced the largest investment in student aid since the G.I. Bill, while resulting in a more efficient, reliable, and ef-fective system for students to help them afford college and manage debt.

The President is calling on Congress to advance new reforms to give more hard-working students a fair shot at pursuing higher education, because education is not a luxury: it is an economic imperative that every hard-working and responsible student should be able to afford. President Obama has emphasized that the federal government, states, colleges, and universities all have a role to play in making higher education more affordable, by reining in college costs, providing value for American families, and preparing students with a solid education to succeed in their careers.

In his State of the Union address, President Obama emphasized this shared responsibility of states and higher education institutions — working with the federal government — to promote access, affordability and attainment in higher education. It is not enough to increase federal student aid alone — state policymakers and individual colleges and universities bear a shared responsibility to take action against rising college tuition and costs.

Providing greater pathways for students to enter into and succeed in higher education is in the interest of all Americans, and is critical to developing a highly educated, highly skilled work-force that will attract business and lead to lower unemployment. The Administration has taken several steps and advanced several proposals to put higher education within reach for more Americans.

The President has placed a strong emphasis on making America's community colleges stronger, ensuring that they are gateways to economic prosperity and educational opportunities for millions of Americans each year. Each year, over 1,100 community colleges provide students and workers with critical skills to succeed in a 21st-century economy. To help reach the President's college attainment goal, the Obama Administration has called for an additional 5 million graduates from community colleges by 2020. Working in partnership with states and communities, community colleges are well suited to promote the dual goal of academic and on-the-job preparedness for the next generation of American workers.

Many community colleges are already working with businesses to develop programs and classes — ranging from degree-granting curricula to certified courses for retraining — that will enhance skills for workers.

President Obama has consistently strived to lead the most open, efficient and accountable government in history. Over the last two years, new initiatives have increased public participation in government, opened up new information to Americans on a variety of topics, and improved citizens' everyday lives. In the vein of transparency and accountability, the President tasked his Administration with giving students and families new tools and relevant information that will help them make sound financial decisions in pursuing their higher education goals.

Article 2: Higher Education Is Not For Everyone

(This opposing article was written by Murray Shukyn and Achim Krull.)

Not everyone needs a post-secondary education. Numerous pathways to successful employment work well and do not require years of college or university education. Whether it is apprenticeships in trades, training through the military, or entrepreneurial initiative, these approaches work. Moreover, people acquire skills and employment without the huge debts incurred in formal post-secondary education.

It is true that unemployment rates decrease with educational attainment. The rate for people with only a high-school diploma is about 25 percent higher than that of people with a completed university degree. After they start working, that scenario changes. The high-school graduate has been working for at least four years before the college graduate can start looking for work. The median income for a high-school graduate is about $35,000, while the university graduate's is $54,000. At a median income difference of about $20,000 a year, it will take the college graduate's total earnings at least seven years to catch up to the high-school graduate, just based on lost income alone. But then you need to consider the cost of going to college. In 2010–2011, private colleges and universities in the United States cost (including residence fees) an average of $36,000 annually, while public institutions cost about $13,000. In the meantime, fees have continued to increase. When you include the cost of education for those four years, it now would take the college graduate from public institutions another two years of employment to catch up to the high-school graduate. If the student went to a private college, it would take an additional seven years.

In effect, just based on median incomes and tuition fees, the college graduate will take between 10 and 15 years to catch up in total earnings. And we have not considered the costs of books and incidentals, which the Department of Education suggests will add approximately another $5,000 annually. That adds at least another year to the time it takes to catch up.

Forbes Magazine, which writes mainly for an audience of wealthy business people, argued in a 2013 article that few jobs require a university education. The article takes the position that most of what you learn at college or university has little relevance to what you end up doing on the job. The main benefit of a degree is that it shows prospective customers that you are smart.

And then there are the people who made it without even finishing high school. That list includes Dave Thomas, founder of Wendy's, John D. Rockefeller, and many others. A whole collection of wealthy entrepreneurs started with just a high-school diploma, like Richard Branson of Virgin Records, Virgin Atlantic airline, and now Virgin Galactic, a private space travel venture. We also know of many successful entrepreneurs who dropped out of university to start businesses, from Steve Jobs to Bill Gates and Mark Zuckerberg.

That does not mean degrees are useless; it does tell us that drive and ideas are more important than formal education.

Chapter 28

Answers for Practice Test 2, Reasoning through Language Arts

You've done the test. Now you need to check your answers. If you just want a quick look at what you got right or wrong, check out the abbreviated answer key with just the answers at the end of this chapter. The better approach is to read all the answers and explanations so you find out the reasoning behind the answers. You can discover just as much from your errors as from understanding why the right answers are correct.

Answers and Explanations

1. **B. Not all brands of bottled water are.** Choice (B) is an effective introduction to the paragraph and introduces no errors. Although starting a sentence with *and* or *but* isn't a grammar error, it's confusing to start this article with *but*. Therefore, Choices (A) and (C) are incorrect. Choice (C) also contains an unnecessary comma. Choice (D) introduces a subject-verb agreement error.

2. **B. to remove the chlorine completely and.** Choice (B) joins the two phrases correctly with *and*. Choice (A) is incorrect because it creates a comma splice. The other two options do not make sense.

3. **A. Bottled spring waters are.** Only Choice (A) uses correct subject-verb agreement and avoids other errors. Choice (B) has an unneeded comma. There is no reason to use the past tense (Choice C). Choice (D) has incorrect subject-verb agreement.

4. **C. waters differs.** Only Choice (C) has correct subject-verb agreement. The subject of the sentence is *content*, which is singular and requires a singular verb. So the correct form of the verb is *differs*. Using the word *waters* instead of *water* as in Choice (B) has no effect on the sentence and introduces a subject-verb agreement error with *differ*. The other choices merely introduce new errors or offer no change.

5. **D. are carbonated, either naturally or artificially in the bottling process. Carbonation can add.** Choice (D) is correct because inserting a period after *bottling process* creates two complete sentences. Choices (A) and (B) create comma splices. Choice (C) creates a fragment.

6. **B. their bottled water's.** In the case of *there/their/they're*, the correct choice is *their*. The word *there* refers to location, while *their* shows possession, and *they're* is the contraction of *they are*. Because the sentence is talking about someone's water, the possessive form is correct, which is Choice (B). Therefore, Choices (A) and (C) are incorrect. Choice (D) is incorrect because it omits a necessary apostrophe needed to show that the taste belongs to the water.

7. **B. least.** The expense of three or more things is being compared in this section of the passage, so the superlative *least* is the answer (Choice B). Therefore, Choices (A) and (C) are incorrect. Choice (D) is incorrect because *lessor* means "landlord." This is a good example of how an unusual homonym can cause confusion.

8. **B. effective and.** Choice (B) is correct because no punctuation is needed to join two adjectives (*effective* and *inexpensive*) with *and*. Therefore, Choices (A) and (D) are incorrect. It's possible to put two adjectives in a row without *and*, as in Choice (C), but a comma is needed between them, so that choice is incorrect.

9. **D. plastic jug in your fridge, you.** This item focuses on commas. Only Choice (D) uses a comma correctly to join a dependent clause to an independent clause. Choice (C) omits this necessary comma, while Choices (A) and (B) add unnecessary commas.

10. **D. filters for removing traces.** Choice (D) correctly joins the phrase beginning with *removing* to the main clause by adding the preposition *for*. Choice (A) doesn't make sense. Choices (B) and (C) create sentence fragments.

11. **C. Employment Resource Center.** In the letter, the York Square Employment Resource Center is a title; therefore, all words except prepositions and articles must be capitalized. The other choices, which do not capitalize all the necessary words, are therefore incorrect.

12. **A. has partnered.** You need the present perfect tense *has partnered* here rather than the simple past tense *partnered* because the action started in the past and is ongoing. Your clue to this tense is the phrase *since April 2010.* None of the other choices improve the sentence.

13. **D. In support of the partnership,** Choice (D) is correct because a comma is needed after this introductory phrase. Choices (B) and (C) are therefore incorrect. Choice (A) adds an extra comma.

14. **A. has always been.** The present perfect tense is required here because the action began in the past and is ongoing, and a singular verb, has is required, because the subject of the sentence, Ms. Fairfax, is singular. The tenses in Choices (B) and (C) do not make sense. Choice (D) is incorrect because the subject of the sentence is singular, and *have* is plural.

15. **B. is.** The subject of the sentence is *fact,* which is singular, so a singular verb is required. This question shows that the subject of a verb is not always the noun closest to it. Choice (A), *are,* agrees with the plural word referrals, which is just before it but not the subject of the sentence. The past tense does not make sense in this sentence, so Choices (C) and (D) are incorrect.

16. **A. pursued her responsibilities with a high degree of professionalism.** Choice (A) is the most straightforward ordering of the words. The other choices are awkward. Choice (D) changes the meaning of the sentence and does not make sense.

On the Grammar and Language Component of the GED, answer choices that change the meaning of the sentence are almost always incorrect.

TIP 17. **A. best in her future endeavors.** No commas are needed in this expression, so Choice (A) is correct. All the other choices add unnecessary commas.

18. **B. recently opened.** In this sentence, the adverb *recently* is needed to modify the verb *opened,* so Choice (B) is correct. Therefore, Choices (A) and (C) are incorrect. Choice (D) is incorrect because changing *opened* to *opening* results in a sentence fragment, since *opening* is not a complete verb.

19. **B. copiers, the.** Choice (B) is correct because it creates one complete sentence. The remaining choices are incorrect because they create sentence fragments.

20. **D. The first time I went there,** Choice (D) is a transitional phrase that shows the relationship among the actions in the story. The remaining choices are awkward or ungrammatical.

21. **C. and giving me.** Choice (C) puts the verbs in correct parallel structure: *apologizing, explaining,* and *giving.* Maintaining parallel structure in sentences is important and is frequently tested on the GED. Choices (A) and (D) have faulty parallel structure. There is no reason to change *me* to *myself* (Choice B).

22. **B. it's no.** Choice (B) uses the correct word *no* and the correct contraction for *it is, it's.* Therefore, Choice (C), which uses the incorrect homonym, the verb *know,* is incorrect. There is no reason to change *it's* to the possessive word *its* (Choice A). There is no such word as *its',* so Choice (D) is incorrect.

23. **D. knew.** The past tense of the verb *know, knew* (Choice D), is needed here, not its past participle, *known* (Choice A), or its homonym, *new* (Choice C). Choice (B) makes no sense.

24. **C. They.** Choice (C) is correct because his sentence has three verbs (*apologized, explained, gave*) with the same subject, *they.* Adding *after* (Choice B) or *when* (Choice D) makes the whole sentence a dependent clause, which cannot stand alone. Adding *but* (Choice A) does not make sense.

25. **A. a.** Choice (A) is the correct word to use in this expression. The phrase *too little less understanding* creates an awkward sentence with too many words modifying *understanding*, so Choice (B) is incorrect. Choice (C) does not make sense, and there is no reason to use *an* (Choice D), which is only used before vowel sounds.

26. **A. It is the knowledge that preserves their position.** The text clearly states that princes lose their states when they neglect this art. Although Choice (B) may be true, it has nothing to do with the question. Choices (C) and (D) are the opposite of what the text states.

27. **D. The armed do not readily yield authority to the unarmed.** Although Choices (A), (B), and (C) are all possible, they don't answer the question. However, further into the text, Machiavelli states that it's unreasonable for the armed to yield power to the unarmed.

28. **D. They will despise him.** This answer is stated directly in the passage.

29. **B. In times of peace, prepare for war.** The last sentence of the text makes it clear that Choice (B) is the best answer. Although Choice (D) may be partially correct, it's not the whole answer. Choices (A) and (C) are contradicted by the text.

30. **D. Ask the subordinate what he needs in order to return quickly.** Only Choice (D) follows the advice of balancing benevolence and strictness. Choices (A) and (C) are excessively cruel. Choice (B) is excessively kind.

31. **C. To maintain power, leaders must master the art of war.** Both writers believe that military mastery is important to staying in power. Sun Tzu would disagree with Choices (A) and (B). Machiavelli would disagree with Choice (D).

32. **C. He wanted to reflect the character of the speaker.** The speaker in this case is Aunt Polly. She's a simple country woman with little education. This pattern of speech reflects that. Choices (A) and (B) are certainly wrong because Mark Twain was a talented and capable writer. Choice (D) is simply wrong.

33. **B. Spare the rod and spile the child.** This statement is the only one that supports punishing Tom. Choice (A) shows that Aunt Polly feels conflicted about how she should raise Tom. Choices (C) and (D) are not related to child-rearing.

34. **C. She is not strict enough with Tom.** The correct answer refers to the quote, "spare the rod and spoil the child." The speaker, Aunt Polly, goes on to say, "I'm a laying up sin." She is a good woman who wants to do the right thing. Not being strict enough with Tom goes against Biblical rules as she understands them.

35. **A. She makes references to religion.** The key evidence about the speaker's religiosity consists of her frequent references to the Bible, religion, sin, and so on. The remaining choices are mentioned in the passage but do not demonstrate that she is religious.

36. **A. work.** Aunt Polly says, "He hates work more than he hates anything else." Therefore, the other choices are incorrect. He likes playing hookey (Choice C), which means, "missing school without permission." Tom certainly annoys his aunt, but the passage makes no mention of his feelings about it, so Choice (D) is incorrect. If you selected Choice (B), keep in mind that you need to answer based only on the information in the passage. While painting the fence is one of the most famous episodes in this book, it's not mentioned in the passage.

37. **B. who share.** Choice (B) is correct because the subject pronoun *who*, not the object pronoun *whom*, is needed. The correct verb form is *share* because its subject, *who*, refers to a plural noun, *groups*. The other options use the wrong pronoun or have a verb agreement error, or both.

38. **A. In addition,** Choice (A) is correct because the sentence adds an idea to the information that comes before. Only this transitional phrase shows this relationship. Therefore, the remaining choices are incorrect.

39. **C. to train jobless young people.** The overall purpose of the FACE project is to train unemployed youth. Manufacturing jobs are in short supply, resulting in the need for entrepreneurial skills, so Choice (A) is incorrect. Glass engraving and sign writing (Choice B) are the first skills FACE began to teach. Choice (D) is a later offering of the program, not its main purpose.

40. **A, B, C.** These choices are all mentioned in the passage as hand-craft skills that participants can learn in the program. Robotic assembly (Choice D) is a high-tech computer-assisted approach to manufacturing, not a hand-craft skill, and is not mentioned in the passage.

41. **B. by creating new enterprises of their own.** The best way for youth to secure employment is to "create their own businesses," as the passage states. Jobs are being lost in traditional manufacturing, so Choice (A) is incorrect. Furniture making (Choice C) and obtaining a business certificate (Choice D), don't refer directly to securing employment.

42. **A. The training is on specific crafts and the certificate develops general business and personal skills.** Only Choice (A) accurately states the purpose of each offering. The remaining choices partially state or misstate the purposes of the offerings.

43. **Hand-Craft Training: C. Certificate: A.** Anger management (Choice B) and mobile phone repair (Choice D) aren't mentioned in the passage.

44. **B. an alternative to scarce traditional manufacturing jobs.** Choice (B) is the most clear and direct statement in the text that the FACE program doesn't expect graduates to find traditional jobs in industry but instead is preparing them for some alternative form of employment. Choices (A) and (D) could apply to any form of employment, so they're wrong. Choice (C) mentions skills developed in the certificate, but that are not linked to a specific kind of employment.

45. **A. Many students don't take enough math courses in high school.** According to the introduction to the text, students both drop mathematics courses and are unwilling or unable to take life skills courses, so Choice (A) is correct. The other choices are not mentioned in the passage.

46. **B. to avoid running out of money between paychecks.** The item about budgets specifically mentions making the money last between paychecks, so Choice (B) is correct. Choices (C) and (D) are also reasons to budget but are not mentioned in the passage. Choice (A) is not a reason to budget.

As shown in both Questions 45 and 46, it's important to remember that your answers need to be based on information in the passage and not on your own background knowledge.

REMEMBER

47. **A. usual.** Only Choice (A) indicates a recurring expense. Choices (B) and (C) have the opposite meaning. Choice (D) does not make sense.

48. **D. Cars are among the largest purchases most people ever make.** As the proposal states, cars are the second-largest purchase most people will ever make. Although Choices (A) and (B) are partially correct, they don't answer the question. Choice (C) is not mentioned in the passage and is, in any event, not true.

49. **In the Book: B, C. Not in the Book: A, D.** The book focuses on ways to use math to make prudent decisions. Both Choices (B) and (C) are these kinds of decisions. While Choices (A) and (D) might save money, they can both result in harm in the future, and so do not belong in the book.

50. **D. to convince the company to publish the book.** The letter gives reasons why this book is needed and is directed to the president of the company. Therefore, Choice (D) is correct. The letter is not directed to people outside the company, so the remaining choices are incorrect.

Sample Extended Response

Here's an example of an essay in response to the articles about higher education. Your essay will look different, but this example can help you compare your response to a well-structured essay. Your essay could raise many of the same points that this essay does, perhaps organized differently, but above all, it should be well organized with a clear introduction, conclusion, and supporting evidence.

Compare the following sample to the response you wrote, and then compare it to the criteria the GED Testing Service uses to evaluate your writing (review Chapter 8 for more details on the scoring criteria):

» Creation of an argument and use of evidence

» Development and organizational structure

» Clarity and command of standard English conventions

Higher education should be accessible for all, but the reality is that it is not. Both articles point out the problems in attaining that education. The first article discusses plans for promoting higher education and opening doors for people to attain that education. The second article discusses the expense involved in obtaining a post-secondary education. However, neither article offers any real answers to the issue of accessibility to post-secondary education. In terms of argument, the second article certainly provides far greater specific detail on the issues and thus makes a stronger case.

The first article, the White House statement, clearly states that more jobs will require more education, and that at least half of the fastest-growing areas of employment will require post-secondary education. It also points out that the United States is falling behind the rest of the world in terms of the percentage of the population attaining such higher education. It goes on to make a number of statements about how the administration is working toward improving access. Yet these statements are vague and general, offering no concrete answers.

It then goes on to state that the administration wishes to help make college and university affordable, so that everyone has a "fair shot at pursuing higher education." However, that section of the article is also woefully weak in terms of actual specifics on how this is to be done.

The second article, on the other hand, is full of very specific details. It explains the financial challenges facing individuals trying to obtain a post-secondary education. It presents statistics about average income of high-school graduates, comparing it to that of university graduates. It then presents details about the cost of a post-secondary education and the debt loads students acquire. For example, the article states that the average high-school graduate currently earns about $35,000 annually, nearly $20,000 less than a university graduate. It shows that the average college or university student's debt load will take that student anywhere from 10 to 15 years of full employment to catch up with the earnings of the average high-school graduate, providing that both fall into the average income bracket for their education level.

There are problems with both articles. The first article is indeed quite vague. It talks about how the president has tasked the administration to give "students and families new tools and relevant information that will help them make sound financial decisions in pursuing their higher education goals." Nowhere does it state any specifics. Earlier, the article talks about the president's emphasis on strengthening the community college system to ensure that there are gateways to economic prosperity. While it states the goal is to provide an additional 5 million graduates, nothing is said about how this will be achieved.

There are similar weaknesses within the second article. After demonstrating how expensive a post-secondary education can be, it goes on to talk about individuals who have obtained amazing careers, all without or with very limited post-secondary education. The weakness of this argument is that the article only presents five or six examples, while we are talking about a potential post-secondary population in the hundreds of thousands. The article says post-secondary education is not for everyone, but most people are not going to have the careers of a Dave Thomas or John D. Rockefeller, not without assistance. Undeniably, for the average person, post-secondary education still opens doors that will remain closed for most without that education.

Both articles have problems. The first article talks about the desirability of a post-secondary education and many possible solutions to the problem of obtaining that education. However, it is woefully weak on specifics. The second article basically says forget about a post-secondary education, by presenting in great detail the financial issues, but also offers no concrete answers on how to get ahead. In the context of supporting their arguments, the second article is the stronger.

Answer Key

1.	B	19.	B	37.	B
2.	B	20.	D	38.	A
3.	A	21.	C	39.	C
4.	C	22.	B	40.	A, B, C
5.	D	23.	D	41.	B
6.	B	24.	C	42.	A
7.	B	25.	A	43.	Hand Craft Training: C. Certificate: A.
8.	B	26.	A		
9.	D	27.	D	44.	B
10.	D	28.	D	45.	A
11.	C	29.	B	46.	B
12.	A	30.	D	47.	A
13.	D	31.	C	48.	D
14.	A	32.	C	49.	In the Book: B, C. Not in the Book: A, D.
15.	B	33.	B		
16.	A	34.	C	50.	D
17.	A	35.	A		
18.	B	36.	A		

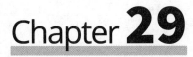

Chapter **29**

Practice Test 2: Social Studies

'm a firm believer that practice makes better, if not perfect. So here's another Social Studies practice test. Give yourself 70 minutes to complete the question-and-answer test to best simulate the real test-taking experience. Remember, on the real test you can use the onscreen calculator (or your own calculator if you take the test at a testing center). The answers and explanations to this test's questions are in Chapter 30.

Answer Sheet for Practice Test 2, Social Studies

1. _____

2. _____

3. _____

4. _____

5. _____

6. _____

7. _____

8. _____

9. _____

10. _____

11. _____

12. _____

13. _____

14. _____

15. _____

16. _____

17. _____

18. _____

19. _____

20. _____

21. _____

22. _____

23. _____

24. _____

25. _____

26. _____

27. _____

28. _____

29. _____

30. _____

31. _____

32. _____

33. _____

34. _____

35. _____

36. _____

37. _____

38. _____

39. _____

40. _____

41. _____

42. _____

43. _____

44. _____

45. _____

46. _____

47. _____

48. _____

49. _____

50. _____

TIME: 70 minutes

QUESTIONS: 50

DIRECTIONS: Mark your answers on the answer sheet provided.

Questions 1–4 refer to the following passage, which is excerpted from Cliffs Quick Review U.S. History I, *by P. Soifer and A. Hoffman (John Wiley & Sons, Inc.).*

The First Inhabitants of the Western Hemisphere

In telling the history of the United States and also of the nations of the Western Hemisphere in general, historians have wrestled with the problem of what to call the hemisphere's first inhabitants. Under the mistaken impression he had reached the "Indies," explorer Christopher Columbus called the people he met "Indians." This was an error in identification that has persisted for more than five hundred years, for the inhabitants of North and South America had no collective name by which they called themselves.

Historians, anthropologists, and political activists have offered various names, none fully satisfactory. Anthropologists have used "aborigine," but the term suggests a primitive level of existence inconsistent with the cultural level of many tribes. Another term, "Amerindian," which combines Columbus's error with the name of another Italian explorer, Amerigo Vespucci (whose name was the source of "America"), lacks any historical context. Since the 1960s, "Native American" has come into popular favor, though some activists prefer "American Indian." In the absence of a truly representative term, descriptive references such as "native peoples" or "indigenous peoples," though vague, avoid European influence. In recent years, some argument has developed over whether to refer to tribes in the singular or plural — Apache or Apaches — with supporters on both sides demanding political correctness.

1. What name has been favored since 1960?

   (A) Amerindian

   (B) Native American

   (C) native peoples

   (D) indigenous peoples

2. Why did Columbus call the native inhabitants "Indians"?

   (A) They were in the Western Hemisphere.

   (B) He thought he'd reached the Indies.

   (C) North and South America had not been discovered.

   (D) They were the hemisphere's first inhabitants.

3. Who used the term *aborigine,* according to the passage?

   (A) historians

   (B) political activists

   (C) Columbus

   (D) anthropologists

4. How was America named?

   (A) after an Italian explorer

   (B) after its first inhabitants

   (C) after its discoverer

   (D) after Columbus

The Voyages of Christopher Columbus

Christopher Columbus, a Genoese sailor, believed that sailing west across the Atlantic Ocean was the shortest sea route to Asia. Ignorant of the fact that the Western Hemisphere lay between Europe and Asia and assuming the earth's circumference to be a third less than it actually is, he was convinced that Japan would appear on the horizon just three thousand miles to the west. Like other seafarers of his day, Columbus was untroubled by political allegiances; he was ready to sail for whatever country would pay for his voyage. Either because of his arrogance (he wanted ships and crews to be provided at no expense to himself) or ambition (he insisted on governing the lands he discovered), he found it difficult to find a patron. The Portuguese rejected his plan twice, and the rulers of England and France were not interested. With influential supporters at court, Columbus convinced King Ferdinand and Queen Isabella of Spain to partially underwrite his expedition. In 1492, Granada, the last Muslim stronghold on the Iberian Peninsula, had fallen to the forces of the Spanish monarchs. With the Reconquista complete and Spain a unified country, Ferdinand and Isabella could turn their attention to overseas exploration.

5. Why was Columbus's estimate of the time required to reach Japan wrong?

   (A) He thought Japan was much farther away.

   (B) He thought Japan was much closer.

   (C) He was just taking a blind guess.

   (D) He was using Vespucci's maps.

6. Why did the Spanish Crown sponsor Columbus's exploration?

   (A) The royals were competing with the British for new colonies.

   (B) Queen Isabella admired Columbus.

   (C) The war with the Muslims was over, and they could focus on other things.

   (D) The Crown worried Columbus would be sponsored by a competing nation.

7. Columbus sailed in what direction to reach Asia?

   (A) east

   (B) south

   (C) north

   (D) west

8. What about Columbus made finding sponsors for his voyage difficult?

   Write the correct letter(s) in the box. [   ].

   (A) He was arrogant.

   (B) His demands were out of line.

   (C) He was a shrewd politician.

   (D) He refused to learn Spanish.

9. How much funding did Columbus finally receive?

   (A) complete funding

   (B) partial funding

   (C) a small percentage

   (D) a commission on whatever he discovered

Questions 10–12 refer to the following graph.

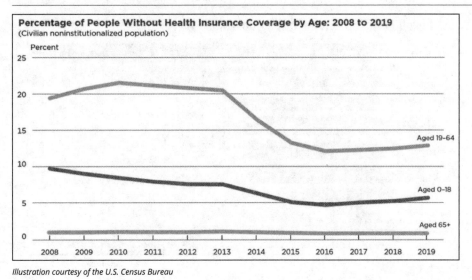

Percentage of People Without Health Insurance Coverage by Age: 2008 to 2019
(Civilian noninstitutionalized population)

Illustration courtesy of the U.S. Census Bureau

10. Which age group has the fewest people without healthcare insurance overall? [   ]

11. Among adults aged 19 to 64, what happened to the uninsured rate between 2013 and 2016?

(A) It decreased.

(B) It increased.

(C) It stayed the same.

(D) It showed no pattern.

12. In which year was the uninsured rate highest for adults aged 19 to 64?

(A) 2009

(B) 2010

(C) 2011

(D) 2012

Questions 13–15 refer to this graph.

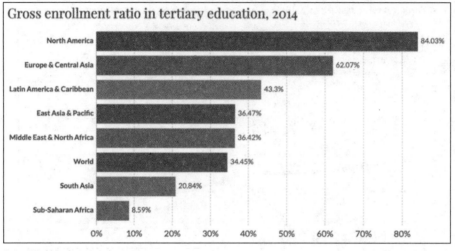

Source: World Bank

13. Which region of the world has the highest level of enrollment in higher education?

(A) Latin America and the Caribbean

(B) Europe and Central Asia

(C) East Asia and the Pacific

(D) North America

14. What is the difference between the enrollment ratios for Europe/Central Asia and East Asia/Pacific?

(A) 47.56%

(B) 25.6%

(C) 21.96%

(D) 18.77%

15. Which of the following individuals would be counted in the graph?

(A) A woman who graduated from high school ten years ago and recently started college.

(B) A grandmother who got her GED last month and started college right away.

(C) A learner taking GED classes at a community college.

(D) A teacher who graduated from college five years ago and recently started a master's degree.

Questions 16–20 refer to the following passage, which is excerpted from The Declaration of Independence, 1776.

Declaration of Independence

We hold these truths to be self-evident: that all men are created equal; that they are endowed by their Creator with certain inalienable rights; that among these are life, liberty, and the pursuit of happiness. That to secure these rights, governments are instituted among men, deriving their just powers from the consent of the governed; that whenever any form of government becomes destructive of these ends it is the right of the people to alter or to abolish it, and to institute a new government, laying its foundation on such principles, and organizing its powers in such form, as to them shall seem most likely to effect their safety and happiness. Prudence, indeed, will dictate that governments long established should not be changed for light and transient causes; and accordingly, all experience hath shown, that mankind are more disposed to suffer, while evils are sufferable, than to right themselves by abolishing the forms to which they are accustomed. But when a long train of abuses and usurpations, pursuing invariably the same object, evinces a design to reduce them under absolute despotism, it is their right, it is their duty, to throw off such government, and to provide new guards for their future security. Such has been the patient sufferance of these colonies; and such is now the necessity which constrains them to alter their former system of government. The history of the present king of Great Britain is a history of repeated injuries and usurpations, all having in direct object the establishment of an absolute tyranny over these states. To prove this, let facts be submitted to a candid world.

16. What truths were self-evident?
    (A) that all men are not created equal
    (B) that men don't have rights
    (C) that men are suffering
    (D) that men have certain rights

17. From where do governments get their power?
    (A) from the people
    (B) from the Creator
    (C) among men
    (D) from a new foundation

18. According to the Declaration of Independence, the people should overthrow their government when it does which of the following?

    Write the letter(s). [_____]
    (A) when government prevents abuse
    (B) when government abuses and usurps people's rights
    (C) when government resorts to absolute despotism
    (D) when government increases taxes

19. How does the Declaration of Independence describe the king of Great Britain?
    (A) He caused injuries.
    (B) He was a kindly ruler.
    (C) He was an absolute tyrant.
    (D) He was a friend of the people.

20. Why should a new government be instituted in this case, according to the passage?
    (A) There were light and transient reasons.
    (B) It was long established.
    (C) The people were suffering.
    (D) They needed to abolish the accustomed forms.

"DUE PROCESS OF LAW."

Cartoon by Samuel D. Ehrhart, Puck, December 23, 1903.

21. What is the social issue being depicted in this editorial cartoon?

(A) The legal system has sentenced innocent people to death.

(B) The legal system is biased.

(C) The legal system is slow and has many obstacles.

(D) The legal system is expensive.

22. What does the building at the top of the hill represent?

(A) a courthouse

(B) the Capitol Building

(C) the White House

(D) the National Archives Building

23. Which of the following statements is closest in meaning to the main idea of the cartoon?

(A) The administration of justice is the firmest pillar of government (George Washington).

(B) Justice is blind (legal saying).

(C) I think the first duty of society is justice (Alexander Hamilton).

(D) Justice delayed is justice denied (legal saying).

Resistance to Slavery

Resistance to slavery took several forms. Slaves would pretend to be ill, refuse to work, do their jobs poorly, destroy farm equipment, set fire to buildings, and steal food. These were all individual acts rather than part of an organized plan for revolt, but the objective was to upset the routine of the plantation in any way possible. On some plantations, slaves could bring grievances about harsh treatment from an overseer to their master and hope that he would intercede on their behalf. Although many slaves tried to run away, few succeeded for more than a few days, and they often returned on their own. Such escapes were more a protest — a demonstration that it could be done — than a dash for freedom. As advertisements in southern newspapers seeking the return of runaway slaves made clear, the goal of most runaways was to find their wives or children who had been sold to another planter. The fabled Underground Railroad, a series of safe houses for runaways organized by abolitionists and run by former slaves like Harriet Tubman, actually helped only about a thousand slaves reach the North.

24. Why did enslaved people refuse to work?

   (A) They were ill.

   (B) They did their jobs poorly.

   (C) They destroyed farm equipment.

   (D) They were resisting enslavement.

25. According to the text, the Underground Railroad helped only about 1,000 enslaved people escape. Why is the Underground Railroad still considered "fabled"?

   (A) It offered hope of permanent escape to all enslaved people.

   (B) It was the most successful option for escaping slavery.

   (C) It supported rebellions of enslaved people.

   (D) It is only a story or fable.

26. Who organized the Underground Railroad?

   (A) Harriet Tubman

   (B) railroad companies

   (C) abolitionists

   (D) runaways

Questions 27–30 refer to the following report.

Weather and Traffic Report

Good morning and welcome to America's weather and traffic on WAWT, the voice of the world in the ear of the nation. Today is going to be hot. That's H-O-T, and we all know what that means. The big "P" is coming back for a visit. We are going to have pollution today for sure. With our record heat today on each coast, there is a problem. If you think that it's hot here, it's even hotter up higher. And that means unhealthy air leading to unhealthy people. I can hear the coughs and sneezes coast to coast. I think I hear a whole series of gasps from our nation's capital, good ol' Washington, D.C., and it's not Congress that is producing all that hot air. And out in western California, it's just as bad. Just the other day, I looked up "poor air quality" in the dictionary, and it said "see California." Lots of luck breathing out there.

This morning, once again, there's a layer of hot air just above ground level. That's where we live — ground level. This air acts like a closed gate, and it keeps the surface air from going up and mixing.

Of course, we are all going to drive our cars all day in heavy traffic, and some of us will go to work in factories. And, surprise — by afternoon, all those pollutants from the cars mix with the emissions from the factories and get trapped by the layer of hot air, and it's try-to-catch-your-breath time. Unhealthy air is here again. Tomorrow and every day after, we'll probably have more of the same until we learn to take care of our environment.

Well, I'll see you tomorrow, if the air's not too thick to see through.

27. When is the worst time for pollution?

   (A) in the morning

   (B) in the afternoon

   (C) late at night

   (D) before breakfast

28. What are the main sources of pollution?

   (A) record heat

   (B) air rising and mixing

   (C) exhausts and emissions

   (D) warmer air aloft

29. According to the report, what is causing the pollution?

   Write the letter(s) of the appropriate factors. ☐

   (A) hot air trapping emissions

   (B) car exhaust

   (C) Congress

   (D) California

30. What is the best way to prevent pollution?

   (A) Change the temperature.

   (B) Reduce emissions.

   (C) Get rid of the hot air layer.

   (D) Prevent air from rising.

Questions 31–33 refer to the following passage.

The End of the Soviet Union

The repudiation of the Brezhnev Doctrine, which had sanctioned the intervention of the Soviet Union in other Communist countries, marked the beginning of the collapse of the Soviet Union. The Soviet Union's defeat in the war in Afghanistan made Soviet leaders realize that the Doctrine was not sustainable. However, this left the other Communist states free to pursue their own political reforms, because they no longer had to fear reprisals from Moscow. Soon, various Communist countries, as well as several Soviet republics, began to move toward reform or independence. Inside the Soviet Union, new policies of Mikhail Gorbachev, perestroika and glasnost, opened new fissures in Soviet society and government. Eventually, the Communist governments in Eastern Europe collapsed. The Berlin Wall fell in November, 1989, and a divided Germany reunited. Finally, the Soviet Union broke up. An agreement among the leaders of the Soviet republics, held in Almaty, Kazakhstan, on December 21, 1991, formalized the end of the Soviet Union. Gorbachev resigned on December 25, 1991. The republics that had comprised the Soviet Union became sovereign states. The Soviet Union had ended.

31. Which of the following started the process that led to the collapse of the Soviet Union?

(A) repudiation of the Brezhnev Doctrine

(B) fall of the Berlin Wall

(C) perestroika and glasnost

(D) independence of the former Soviet republics

32. Put the events in chronological order. Write the letters in order. [   ]

(A) The Berlin Wall fell.

(B) The Brezhnev Doctrine was repudiated.

(C) Gorbachev resigned.

(D) Leaders of the Soviet republics formalized the end of the Soviet Union.

33. What happened to the republics of the Soviet Union?

(A) They remained Communist.

(B) They joined the Russian Federation.

(C) They joined together in a new country.

(D) They became sovereign states.

Questions 34–38 refer to the following passage, which is excerpted from Cliffs Quick Review U.S. History I, *by P. Soifer and A. Hoffman (John Wiley & Sons, Inc.)*

The Panic of 1873

During his second term, President Grant was still unable to curb the graft in his administration, Secretary of War William Belknap was impeached by the House, and he resigned in disgrace for taking bribes from dishonest Indian agents. The president's personal secretary was involved with the Whiskey Ring, a group of distillers who evaded paying internal revenue taxes. A much more pressing concern though was the state of the economy.

In 1873, over-speculation in railroad stocks led to a major economic panic. The failure of Jay Cooke's investment bank was followed by the collapse of the stock market and the bankruptcy of thousands of businesses; crop prices plummeted and unemployment soared. Much of the problem was related to the use of greenbacks for currency. Hard-money advocates insisted that paper money had to be backed by gold to curb inflation and level price fluctuations, but farmers and manufacturers, who needed easy credit, wanted even more greenbacks put in circulation, a policy that Grant ultimately opposed. He recommended and the Congress enacted legislation in 1875 providing for the redemption of greenbacks in gold. Because the Treasury needed time to build up its gold reserves, redemption did not go into effect for another four years, by which time the longest depression in American history had come to an end.

34. Which of the following was a problem President Grant had in his second term in office?

(A) corruption

(B) whiskey

(C) tax debts

(D) personal bankruptcy

35. What type of money was used for investment at this time?

(A) British pounds

(B) silver

(C) gold

(D) greenbacks

36. What was the cause of the Panic of 1873?

    (A) crop failures

    (B) bankruptcy

    (C) over-speculation

    (D) tax evasion

37. What followed the failure of Jay Cooke's bank?

    (A) collapse of the stock market

    (B) increase in market value

    (C) business profitability

    (D) rising crop prices

38. How did Congress end the depression?

    (A) It provided easy credit.

    (B) It leveled prices.

    (C) It built up gold reserves.

    (D) It hoarded greenbacks.

Questions 39–41 refer to the following tables.

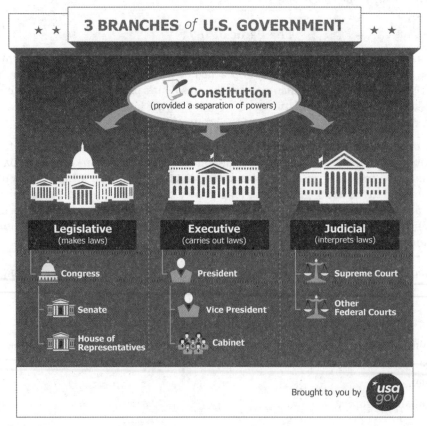

Source: usa.gov

39. Which branch of government includes the cabinet? [　　　]

40. The legislative branch is composed of which two bodies? Write the letters. [　　　]

(A) House of Representatives

(B) Supreme Court

(C) vice-president

(D) Senate

41. What is the purpose of having three branches of government? [　　　]

Questions 42 and 43 refer to the following graph.

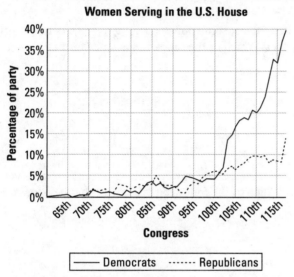

Women Serving in the U.S. House

42. The 19th Amendment to the Constitution, which gave all American women the right to vote, was passed in 1920, during the 66th Congress. Which of the following explains the presence of women serving in Congress prior to then? Choose the letter or letters. [　　　]

(A) There was no federal law against women serving in Congress.

(B) People began to ignore the laws that stopped women from voting.

(C) Some states already allowed women to vote.

(D) Women began to organize to vote long before they were able to vote.

43. Which party has had a higher proportion of women in Congress in recent years? [　　　]

Questions 44 and 45 refer to the following passage.

The 19th Amendment to the Constitution says, "The right of citizens of the United States to vote shall not be denied or abridged by the United States or by any State on account of sex. Congress shall have power to enforce this article by appropriate legislation." The amendment was approved by the House in May 1919 and by the Senate in June 1919. It was ratified by 36 of the 48 states, the number needed to approve it, by August 18, 1920. However, several states refused to ratify it, and the last of the 48 states to ratify it did so only in 1984.

44. Which of the following can be concluded about the 19th Amendment?

    (A) It had strong, widespread support.

    (B) It was not considered important.

    (C) It was controversial.

    (D) It was considered unnecessary in states where women could already vote.

45. Why does the 19th Amendment give Congress the right to pass laws to enforce it?

    (A) Congress needed to be forced to implement the amendment.

    (B) The amendment was not clear.

    (C) States or local governments might continue to prevent women from voting.

    (D) To prevent the amendment from being repealed.

46. Under the Constitution of the United States, some powers belong to the federal government and some powers belong to the states. Which of the following is a power that belongs to <u>state</u> governments?

    (A) to declare war

    (B) to print money

    (C) to make treaties

    (D) to provide education

47. Under the Constitution of the United States, some powers belong to the federal government and some powers belong to the states. Which of the following is a power that belongs to the <u>federal</u> government?

    (A) to create an army

    (B) to set up local governments

    (C) to issue driver's licenses

    (D) to implement assistance programs

Questions 48–50 refer to the following information.

Each branch of the federal government has powers that limit the powers of other branches. Write the letter of the power next to the branch of government.

    (A) Can declare a law unconstitutional

    (B) Can veto legislation

    (C) Can override a veto

48. Executive branch ☐

49. Legislative branch ☐

50. Judicial branch ☐

Chapter 30

Answers for Practice Test 2, Social Studies

This chapter has the answers and explanations for the Social Studies practice test in Chapter 29. I provide detailed answer explanations to help you review areas where you may need to do more work. Reading the explanations, even for the questions you got right, will help you understand how these question-and-answer items are set up. If you're short on time and just want to check your answers, you can skip directly to the abbreviated answer key at the end of the chapter.

Answers and Explanations

1. **B. Native American.** In the 1960s, after much debate, *Native American* was chosen as the name for the indigenous peoples. Other terms, such as *Indian, Amerindian*, and *indigenous peoples*, were discarded.

2. **B. He thought he'd reached the Indies.** Columbus thought he had reached the Indies when he landed in North America, so he called the natives "Indians." The other answers — the natives' being in the Western Hemisphere, the fact that the Americas hadn't been discovered yet, or the natives' being the hemisphere's first inhabitants — just don't make sense.

3. **D. anthropologists.** This information is stated directly in the passage.

4. **A. after an Italian explorer.** According to the passage, America was named after Italian explorer Amerigo Vespucci. Choice (C) is incorrect because the European explorers who first reached the Americas did not "discover" it. These lands were already inhabited by millions of native peoples.

5. **B. He thought Japan was much closer.** Columbus thought the earth's circumference was a third less than it really was. As a result, he thought Japan was much closer than it turned out to be. The other answers are incorrect, according to the passage.

6. **C. The war with the Muslims was over, and they could focus on other things.** Spain had been at war, trying to recapture the Iberian Peninsula from Muslim conquerors. That done, the king and queen now had time and resources to focus on other ideas. The options of approaching France or England are wrong, based on the passage, and nothing in the passage indicates that the Spanish Crown was worried about competition from other countries.

7. **D. west.** According to the passage, Columbus sailed west to cross the Atlantic Ocean in search of Asia.

8. **A, B. He was arrogant; His demands were out of line.** Columbus was regarded as arrogant. He demanded the patrons cover all costs and award him the governorship of whatever colonies he established. Nothing in the text talks about learning Spanish, and Columbus's behavior is certainly not that of a shrewd politician.

9. **B. partial funding.** Columbus convinced Ferdinand and Isabella to partially fund the voyage. They certainly did not provide complete funding nor offer a commission on whatever he found.

10. **Age 65+.** The line for this age group is consistently the lowest for all years covered by the graph. The likely reason is that these older adults are covered by Medicare if they do not have their own insurance.

11. **A. It decreased.** The line on the graph for this age group shows a clear, consistent decrease for the years between 2013 and 2016.

12. **B. 2010.** The highest point on the line for this age group is in 2010.

13. **D. North America.** The longest bar on the bar chart corresponds to North America, so Choice (D) is correct.

14. **B. 25.6%.** The difference between the two ratios is $62.07 - 36.47 = 25.6$, or 25.6%. The other choices show the differences between different combinations of geographic regions. This item is an example of where the calculator can help you.

15. **B. A grandmother who got her GED last month and started college right away.** According to the information in the graph, the data covers students who graduated from high school in the last five years. The only person who qualifies is the grandmother in Choice (B). The others graduated from high school too long ago (Choices A and D) or have not graduated yet (Choice C). Remember, your GED score can indicate college-readiness or college credit, so do your best to get your GED, start college, and get included in the next edition of this graph!

16. **D. that men have certain rights.** The passage lists two self-evident truths: that all men are created equal and that the Creator endowed men with certain rights. (*Self-evident* means "evident without need of explanation or proof.")

17. **A. from the people.** According to the passage, governments were to get their power from the people. Getting power from the Creator (Choice B), among men (Choice C), and from a new foundation (Choice D) are incorrect answers, according to the passage.

18. **B, C. when government abuses and usurps people's rights; when government resorts to absolute despotism.** These two choices are correct. Choice (A) is not a reason to overthrow a government. Choice (D) doesn't qualify as "destructive" enough to warrant revolution.

19. **C. He was an absolute tyrant.** George III had become an absolute tyrant. He was neither a kindly ruler nor a friend of the people. Causing injuries isn't the best choice because, although it is partially true, the text clearly goes further to paint the picture of King George as a tyrant.

20. **C. The people were suffering.** The people were suffering because of the evils of the old government, which was the main reason why they sought a new government. The other answers may have some truth to them, but they aren't the main reasons, according to the passage.

21. **C. The legal system is slow and has many obstacles.** The female figure representing justice is riding a snail on a path strewn with rocks and boulders. This indicates that the legal system is slow and full of obstacles. The other choices may be true but are not related to the main idea of this cartoon.

22. **A. a courthouse.** The only building in the answer choices that is related to the legal system is a courthouse, so Choice (A) is correct.

23. **D. Justice delayed is justice denied (legal saying).** This common saying is closest in meaning to the cartoon, and so is correct. Choice (B) is tempting because the image that represents justice is wearing a blindfold, which suggests that the legal system is impartial. However, that is not the main idea of this cartoon.

24. **D. They were resisting enslavement.** Refusing to work was the main way enslaved people showed resistance to enslavement. Illness (Choice A), poorly done jobs (Choice B), and destroyed equipment (Choice C) were other ways they showed resistance.

25. **A. It offered hope of permanent escape to all enslaved people.** The Underground Railroad actually succeeded in getting enslaved people to Canada, a permanent safe haven and a new life. The text doesn't support the idea that it was the most successful escape method (Choice B) nor that it supported rebellions (Choice C). And there's no question that it actually existed (Choice D).

26. **C. abolitionists.** The Underground Railroad was organized by abolitionists. Other possible players, such as Harriet Tubman and runaways, may have been involved, but, according to the passage, they weren't the organizers. The Underground Railroad was metaphorical, so Choice (B) is incorrect.

27. **B. in the afternoon.** Pollution tends to be at its worst in the afternoon when exhausts and emissions are trapped. According to the passage, other times of day don't have as much pollution.

28. **C. exhausts and emissions.** Exhausts and emissions are the main sources of pollution. Other answers, such as record heat, air rising, and warmer air, are factors, but they aren't the most important ones.

29. **A, B. hot air trapping emissions; car exhaust.** Pollution tends to be caused by emissions. In this case, the only available choice is cars. It is then made worse by the effect of hot air trapping the air pollution close to the ground. Although Congress (Choice C) may be a source of hot air, it plays no role in this case. And California (Choice D) is just there to trip you up because it's mentioned in the passage as a place with poor air quality.

30. **B. Reduce emissions.** Pollution can best be prevented by reducing emissions. The other choices (changing the temperature, eliminating the hot air layer, and preventing air from rising) may contribute, but they aren't the best answers.

31. **A. repudiation of the Brezhnev Doctrine.** The process of dissolution began when the Soviet Union stopped controlling its satellites directly. This started reform or independence movements, which spread into the Soviet Union itself. The other events are related to the collapse of the Soviet Union, but none of them started the movement toward dissolution.

32. **The correct order is B, A, D, C. The Brezhnev Doctrine was repudiated; The Berlin Wall fell; Leaders of the Soviet republics formalized the end of the Soviet Union; Gorbachev resigned.** Although other events happened in between, this is the order of the events in the question.

33. **D. They became sovereign states.** The former Soviet republics became sovereign states. The other choices are not supported by information in the passage.

34. **A. corruption.** The main problems President Grant faced involved graft in his administration, which meant that members of his administration faced all sorts of problems and left their jobs under pressure. The other answers are incorrect, based on the passage.

35. **D. greenbacks.** Greenbacks — not British pounds, gold, or silver — were used as a source of investment capital.

36. **C. over-speculation.** Over-speculation (Choice C) in railroad stocks led to the Panic of 1873. The factors in the other choices, such as crop failures (Choice A), bankruptcy (Choice B), and tax evasion (Choice D), may have also occurred, but they didn't directly cause the Panic of 1873.

37. **A. collapse of the stock market.** The failure of Cooke's bank was followed by a collapse of the stock market. The other answers are the opposite of what happened, according to the passage.

38. **C. It built up gold reserves.** The main way Congress ended the depression was to build up its gold reserves. Credit, prices, and greenbacks didn't have as much to do with the end of the depression.

39. **executive.** The graphic shows the cabinet under the executive branch. The role of the cabinet members is to lead various government departments and agencies. Members of the cabinet also advise the president.

40. **A, D. House of Representatives; Senate.** These two bodies together form the U.S. Congress. The Supreme Court (Choice B) is in the judicial branch. The vice-president (Choice C) is in the executive branch and is also president of the Senate. However, this does not make this official one of the two legislative bodies in Congress.

41. **provide a separation of powers.** The purpose of the three branches is to provide checks and balances through the separation of powers.

42. **A, C. There was no federal law against women serving in Congress; Some states already allowed women to vote.** Choice (A) is correct because there was no federal law that barred women from serving in Congress. Choice (C) is correct because at the time of the amendment, women could vote in Wyoming, Utah, Colorado, Idaho, Washington, California, Oregon, Montana, Arizona, Kansas, Alaska, Illinois, North Dakota, Indiana, Nebraska, Michigan, Arkansas, New York, South Dakota, and Oklahoma. There is no support in the passage for Choice (B). Choice (D) would not explain the presence of women in Congress before the passage of the amendment.

43. **Democratic Party.** Starting from approximately the 102nd Congress, there has been a higher proportion of women in Congress from the Democratic Party than from the Republican Party. The line for the Democratic Party is consistently higher than the line for the Republican Party in this part of the graph.

44. **C. It was controversial.** While the rapid passage might suggest the 19th Amendment had strong support, the fact that only 36 states ratified it, and that some waited until as late as 1984, showed that Americans were not of one mind about the amendment. In fact, passage of the amendment was a hard-won battle over many years.

45. **C. States or local governments might continue to prevent women from voting.** Because the law was controversial, the government needed the power to enforce it, especially in places where equal voting rights were controversial. The remaining choices do not make sense.

46. **D. to provide education.** Providing education (Choice D) is a power reserved by the states. The federal government has the power to declare war (Choice A), to print money (Choice B), and to make treaties (Choice C).

47. **A. to create an army.** Only the federal government can raise an army (Choice A). The powers in the other choices are reserved by the states.

48. **B. Can veto legislation.** The executive branch (the president) can veto bills made by the legislative branch if they do not agree that the bill should become a law.

49. **C. Can override a veto.** The legislative branch can override a president's veto with a two-thirds majority in both the House and the Senate. This way, a bill can become law over the president's objection.

50. **A. Can declare a law unconstitutional.** The courts can declare a law (or a provision of a law) unconstitutional if they believe it does not follow the Constitution. A majority of the judges on the Supreme Court must agree in order to declare a law unconstitutional. Usually, this number is five.

Answer Key

1.	B	18.	B, C	35.	D
2.	B	19.	C	36.	C
3.	D	20.	C	37.	A
4.	A	21.	C	38.	C
5.	B	22.	A	39.	executive
6.	C	23.	D	40.	A, D
7.	D	24.	D	41.	provides a separa-tion of powers
8.	A, B	25.	A		
9.	B	26.	C	42.	A, C
10.	Age 65+	27.	B	43.	Democratic Party
11.	A	28.	C	44.	C
12.	B	29.	A, B	45.	C
13.	D	30.	B	46.	D
14.	B	31.	A	47.	A
15.	B	32.	B, A, D, C	48.	B
16.	D	33.	D	49.	C
17.	A	34.	A	50.	A

Chapter 31

Practice Test 2: Science

The Science test includes multiple-choice, fill-in-the-blank, drop-down, and drag-and-drop questions. They measure your reading comprehension of passages and visuals. You have 90 minutes to complete all the questions in this practice test. Do the easiest questions first, and remember to use process of elimination on multiple-choice questions if you can't find the answer.

Don't forget, you are allowed to use a calculator on the GED Science test.

The answers and explanations for this practice test are in Chapter 32. Be sure to review the explanations for all the questions, even for the ones you got right. The explanations are a good review of the techniques I discuss throughout the book.

REMEMBER

On the real GED, you'll take the test on a computer. Instead of marking your answers on an answer sheet, like you do for the practice tests in this book, you'll use the keyboard and mouse to indicate your answers. I formatted the questions and answer choices in this book to make them appear as similar as possible to what you'll see on the computer screen, but I had to retain some A, B, C, D choices for marking your answers, and I provide an answer sheet for you to do so.

You have 90 minutes to answer the 50 questions on this practice test. Use the timer on your phone to keep track of time. If you run out of time, mark the last question you answered. Then answer the rest of the questions. This will help you figure out how much more quickly you will have to work to complete the entire test in the time allotted.

Answer Sheet for Practice Test 2, Science

1. _____

2. _____

3. _____

4. _____

5. _____

6. _____

7. _____

8. _____

9. _____

10. _____

11. _____

12. _____

13. _____

14. _____

15. _____

16. _____

17. _____

18. _____

19. _____

20. _____

21. _____

22. _____

23. _____

24. _____

25. _____

26. _____

27. _____

28. _____

29. _____

30. _____

31. _____

32. _____

33. _____

34. _____

35. _____

36. _____

37. _____

38. _____

39. _____

40. _____

41. _____

42. _____

43. _____

44. _____

45. _____

46. _____

47. _____

48. _____

49. _____

50. _____

Questions 1 and 2 refer to the following passage.

We have many perennial plants in our gardens. Plants such as roses and irises grow and flower year after year. They become dormant through the winter and then come back to life in the spring. Tulips are beautiful flowers that are among the earliest to come up every spring. They are fragile in appearance but manage to survive the uncertain weather of spring, and then bloom in a rainbow of colors. Tulips have a distinctive fragrance.

Tulips grow from bulbs. As the plant grows in summer, it develops two bulbs that store moisture and food. When the weather turns, the plant becomes dormant. The roots and leaves dry out and fall off, but the bulbs develop a tough outer skin to protect themselves. However, the bulbs do not reliably regrow. Depending on conditions, the bulbs may regrow or simply remain in the ground. Conversely, bulbs may remain in the ground for several years and then suddenly regrow. Gardeners report that sometimes old tulip beds that were replanted with grass or other plants have tulips emerge unexpectedly years later. Tulips really depend on cultivation by humans to survive. This is why most gardeners say that tulips act more like annuals than perennials. The only way to ensure that you have tulips in the spring is to plant new bulbs in the fall. The bulbs develop roots in early fall and then emerge in spring.

1. Write *annual* or *perennial* on the correct line. Though considered a/an [   ], the tulip acts more like a/an [   ].

2. What is the lifecycle of a tulip? Write the letters in the correct order on the line. [   ]

   (A) The plant becomes dormant.

   (B) A gardener plants a tulip bulb in fall.

   (C) The tulip grows and blossoms once.

   (D) The plant develops two new bulbs.

   (E) The bulb grows roots.

Question 3 refers to the following passage.

Cells are the basic unit of all living things in the universe. Not only are flowers, weeds, and trees composed of cells, but you, your dog, and all other living things are also composed of cells. However, cells are different from organism to organism. That is why some plants produce roses and others produce dandelions, and why some cells are in people and others in fish.

3. Which of the following is supported by information in the passage?

   (A) Some organisms are unicellular.

   (B) Cells contain genetic information.

   (C) Cells are differentiated.

   (D) Cells can reproduce.

Engaging in regular physical activity is one of the most important things that people of all ages can do to improve their health. Physical activity strengthens bones and muscles, reduces stress and depression, and makes it easier to maintain a healthy body weight or to reduce weight if overweight or obese. Even people who do not lose weight get substantial benefits from regular physical activity, including lower rates of high blood pressure, diabetes, and cancer. Healthy physical activity includes aerobic activity, muscle-strengthening activities, and activities to increase balance and flexibility. As described by the Physical Activity Guidelines for Americans, adults should engage in at least 150 minutes of moderate-intensity activity each week, and children and teenagers should engage in at least one hour of activity each day.

4. According to the passage, how much time should be spent on exercise?

   (A) 2 hours per week for adults and 1 hour per week for children

   (B) 120 minutes per week for adults and 150 minutes per week for children

   (C) 180 minutes per week for adults and 60 minutes per week for children

   (D) 2½ hours per week for adults and 1 hour per day for children

5. Based on the information in the passage, which two of the following statements are true? Write the letters. [ ] [ ]

   (A) Exercise can lower the blood pressure of people suffering from high blood pressure.

   (B) Exercise provides psychological benefits as well as physical ones.

   (C) Elderly people will derive little benefit from exercise.

   (D) People who have achieved their ideal weight no longer need to exercise daily.

Questions 6 and 7 refer to the following passage.

Have you ever wondered how a rocket ship moves? Perhaps you have seen science-fiction movies in which a captain uses a blast of the rocket engines to save the ship and its crew from crashing into the surface of a distant planet.

Usually, a fuel, such as the gasoline in a car, needs an oxidizer, such as the oxygen in the air, to create combustion, which powers the engine. In space, there is no air and, thus, no oxidizer. The rocket ship, having a clever design, carries its own oxidizer. The fuel used may be a liquid or a solid, but the rocket ship always has fuel and an oxidizer to mix together. When the two are mixed and combustion takes place, a rapid expansion is directed out the back of the engine. The force pushing backward moves the rocket ship forward. In space, with no air, the rocket ship experiences no resistance to the movement. The rocket ship moves forward, avoids the crash, or does whatever the crew wants it to do.

6. Why is the rocket engine the perfect propulsion method for space travel?

   (A) It extracts the oxygen from space for combustion.

   (B) It can operate without an external oxidizer.

   (C) It carries a lot of fuel.

   (D) It produces a forward thrust.

7. Fuel on a rocket ship may be in the form of [ ].

Questions 8–15 refer to the following passage.

Where Does All the Garbage Go?

When we finish using something, we throw it away, but where is "away"? In our modern cities, "away" is frequently an unsightly landfill site, full of all those things that we no longer want. A modern American city generates solid waste at an alarming rate. Every day, New York City produces 14,000 tons of trash. On average, an American produces nearly five pounds of solid waste per day. In spite of all the efforts to increase recycling, we go on our merry way producing garbage without thinking about where it goes.

In any landfill, gone is not forgotten by nature. By compacting the garbage to reduce its volume, we slow the rate of decomposition, which makes our garbage last longer. In a modern landfill, the process produces a garbage lasagna. There's a layer of compacted garbage covered by a layer of dirt, covered by a layer of compacted garbage, and so on. By saving space for more garbage, we cut off the air and water bacteria need to decompose the garbage and, thus, preserve it for future generations. If you could dig far enough, you might still be able to read 40-year-old newspapers. The paper may be preserved, but the news is history.

One of the answers to this problem is recycling. Any object that can be reused in one form or another is an object that shouldn't be found in a landfill. Most of us gladly recycle our paper, which saves energy and resources. Recycled paper can be used again and even turned into other products. Old, recycled newspapers are not as valuable as hidden treasure, but when the cost of landfills and the environmental impact of producing more and more newsprint are considered, it can be a bargain. If plastic shopping bags can be recycled into a cloth-like substance that can be used to make reusable shopping bags, maybe American ingenuity can find ways to reduce all that garbage being stored in landfills before the landfills overtake the space for cities.

8. Why are the disposal methods used in modern landfills as much a part of the problem as a part of the solution?

   (A) They look very ugly.

   (B) They take up a lot of valuable land.

   (C) The bacteria that aid decomposition do not thrive.

   (D) Newspapers are readable after 50 years.

9. Why is recycling paper important?

   (A) Recycling increases the greenhouse effect.

   (B) Recycling reduces the need for new landfill sites.

   (C) Newspaper is not biodegradable.

   (D) Recycling increases logging.

10. Why is solid waste compacted in a modern landfill?

   (A) to reduce the odor

   (B) to help the bacteria decompose the waste

   (C) to make the landfill look better

   (D) to reduce the amount of space it occupies

11. What is the modern landfill compared to?

    (A) an efficient way of ridding cities of solid waste

    (B) a garbage lasagna

    (C) a place for bacteria to decompose solid waste

    (D) a huge compost bin

12. Why is it important for cities to establish recycling programs?

    (A) Recycling makes people feel good about their garbage.

    (B) Recycling centers are more attractive than landfills.

    (C) Recycling lets someone else look after your problem.

    (D) Recycling is more sustainable than using landfills.

13. What can individual Americans do to reduce the amount of waste that is going into landfills?

    (A) Eat less.

    (B) Reuse and recycle as much as possible.

    (C) Stop using paper.

    (D) Import more nitrogen.

14. What is the role of bacteria in a landfill?

    (A) They help get rid of rodents.

    (B) They prepare the garbage for recycling.

    (C) They are part of the inorganic cycle.

    (D) They help decompose waste.

15. If municipalities lose money recycling paper, why do they continue?

    (A) The politicians don't know they are losing money.

    (B) Municipalities don't have to make money.

    (C) The public likes to recycle paper.

    (D) The cost is less than acquiring more landfill sites.

Question 16 refers to the following passage based on information on the NASA website (www.nasa.gov).

The seasons on Earth are caused by the tilt of the Earth as it rotates on its axis and revolves around the Sun. The 23.5-degree tilt of the Earth's axis results in changes of the angle of incident sunlight. A common misconception is that the seasons are caused by the distance between the Earth and Sun. In fact, summer in the Northern Hemisphere occurs at aphelion, the farthest distance between the Earth and Sun, and follows summer solstice when incident sunlight is most concentrated along the Tropic of Cancer, 23 degrees 26 minutes 22 seconds.

16. The point at which the Earth and Sun are farthest apart is called the

    (A) solstice.

    (B) aphelion.

    (C) axis.

    (D) Tropic of Cancer.

Questions 17 and 18 refer to the following passage.

Airbags

All new cars are equipped with airbags. In a crash, the airbags quickly deploy, protecting the driver and front-seat passenger by inflating to prevent them from moving around and being injured by the steering wheel or front dash. When used together with seatbelts, airbags save lives. A person in the front seat of a modern car equipped with airbags who also wears a seat-belt stands a much better chance of surviving a crash than an unbelted person. The two safety devices work together to save lives but must be used properly. For example, an infant car seat should be placed in the back seat. The success of front-seat airbags has prompted other airbags to be added to cars. Some cars now boast side airbags in case of a side-impact accident and knee airbags to prevent injury to lower extremities in a frontal collision. Some new cars now have five or more airbags installed.

17. In a front-end collision, the [   ] prevents the front-seat occupants from injury.

18. Where is the safest place for an infant in a car seat in a car equipped with airbags?

(A) in the right rear passenger seat

(B) in the front passenger seat

(C) in the left rear passenger seat

(D) in the middle rear passenger seat

Questions 19 and 20 refer to the following diagram, which is excerpted from The Sciences: An Integrated Approach, *3rd Edition, by James Trefil and Robert M. Hazen (John Wiley & Sons, Inc.).*

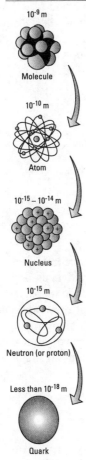

10^{-9} m
Molecule

10^{-10} m
Atom

$10^{-15} - 10^{-14}$ m
Nucleus

10^{-15} m
Neutron (or proton)

Less than 10^{-18} m
Quark

© John Wiley & Sons, Inc.

 GO ON TO NEXT PAGE

19. According to this diagram, what is the building block upon which the other particles are made?

(A) atom

(B) molecule

(C) neutron

(D) quark

20. According to this diagram, how many times larger is a molecule than a quark?

(A) 100

(B) 1,000

(C) 1,000,000

(D) 1,000,000,000

21. The seat you are sitting on seems solid, but in reality, it is composed of atoms. Each of the atoms is composed of a nucleus, which is composed of neutrons and protons, but much of the space occupied by an atom is just empty space. This means that the chair you are sitting on is mostly empty space. It follows that when you stand on the floor of a building, you are ultimately being supported by ⬚.

*Question 22 refers to the following passage from the U.S. Department of Energy/Pacific Northwest National Laboratory website (*www.pnni.gov*).*

Proteins found in nature form the molecular machines that make life possible. Peptoids are highly stable, protein-like molecules developed by scientists to mimic natural proteins. They are cheap, versatile, and customizable and can be designed to have specific forms and functions. Molecular self-assembly is key in biology to building well-defined protein materials. The researchers were able to achieve a controllable self-assembly of peptoids on a flat surface by manipulating molecular-level interactions through advanced chemistry and microscopy techniques.

22. How have scientist been able to mimic natural proteins?

(A) They have built molecular machines.

(B) They have developed peptoids.

(C) They have assembled cheap, versatile chemical elements.

(D) They have cloned molecular interactions.

Questions 23 and 24 refer to the following passage.

The Surface of the Moon

The Moon, a hostile, barren landscape, has no atmosphere, great variance in temperature, and only 17 percent of Earth's gravity. On the surface, astronauts found boulders as large as houses in huge fields of dust and rock. Although the astronauts and scientists had maps and photos of the Moon's surface, the astronauts were not 100 percent sure of what they would encounter until they landed. The astronauts survived, thanks in part to careful planning and extensive training for the mission. Part of their preparation included training in northern Iceland, where the geography was thought to resemble the Moon's. Thirty-two astronauts trained in Iceland, including 9 of the 12 astronauts who walked on the Moon.

23. Which of the following is another detail that would support the idea that landing on the Moon was dangerous?

    (A) Solar radiation is much stronger on the Moon than on Earth.

    (B) The Moon only receives light from the Sun on one side.

    (C) The Moon rotates on its axis.

    (D) The same side of the Moon always faces Earth.

24. Why did astronauts train in Iceland?

    (A) The low temperatures resembled those of the Moon.

    (B) The land resembled the Moon in certain ways.

    (C) Iceland has huge boulders.

    (D) Iceland's small population made it safe to make a test landing there.

Questions 25 and 26 refer to the following passage.

Pushing Aside the Water

If you fill a glass right to the brim with water, you have to drink it at its present temperature. If you decide that you want to add ice, the water spills over the brim. The ice has displaced an amount of water equal to the volume of the ice.

When you lower yourself into a luxurious bubble bath in your tub, the water rises. If you could measure the volume of that rise, you could figure out the volume of your body. Because you would displace a volume of water in the tub equal to the volume of your body, the new combined volume of you plus the water, minus the original volume of the water, equals the volume of your body. Next time you sink slowly into that hot bathwater, make sure that you leave room for the water to rise, or make sure that you are prepared to mop the floor.

25. When you sink into a tub of water, you displace

    (A) your weight in water.

    (B) your weight plus the weight of the water left in the tub.

    (C) the volume of your body plus the volume of the bubbles.

    (D) a volume equal to the volume of your body.

26. If you wanted to find the volume of a small, irregularly shaped rock, how could you do it?

    (A) Immerse the rock in a pre-measured volume of water and measure the increase.

    (B) Measure the rock and calculate the volume.

    (C) Determine the rock's mass and calculate the volume.

    (D) Put the rock in a bubble bath.

Questions 27-29 refer to the following passage.

Newton's First Law of Motion

In 1687, Isaac Newton proposed three laws of motion. These laws are not the types of laws that we are familiar with; they are statements of a truth in the field of physics. Newton's first law of motion states that a body at rest prefers to remain at rest, and a body in motion prefers to stay in motion unless acted upon by an external force. One example you may be familiar with is the game of billiards. Each of the balls will remain in its position unless hit by the cue ball. Once hit, the ball will continue to roll until the friction of the table's surface or an external force stops it. Inertia is the tendency of any object to maintain a uniform motion or remain at rest.

GO ON TO NEXT PAGE

27. If your car becomes stuck in a snowbank, what must you do to free it?

  (A) Apply a force downward to increase the traction of the wheels.

  (B) Leave it at rest until it wants to move.

  (C) Apply a force in the direction you want it to move.

  (D) Sit on the hood to increase the weight on the front tires.

28. Which of the following is a result of inertia?

  (A) A skateboard hits a large crack in the sidewalk and the skateboarder flies off their skateboard.

  (B) A baseball player swings at a pitch and hits a grand-slam home run.

  (C) A golfer tees off and makes a hole in one.

  (D) A volleyball player returns a serve.

29. When you are driving at a steady speed on the highway, it takes great effort to stop suddenly because

  (A) the weight of the car is too light.

  (B) it takes too much power to start driving again.

  (C) brakes have an unlimited stopping potential.

  (D) your car tends to continue at the same rate.

Question 30 refers to the following passage.

Newton's Second Law of Motion

Newton's second law of motion states that when a body changes its velocity because an external force is applied to it, that change in velocity is directly proportional to the force and inversely proportional to the mass of the body. That is, the faster you want to stop your car, the harder you must brake. The brakes apply an external force that reduces the velocity of the car. The faster you want to accelerate the car, the more force you must apply. Increasing the horsepower of an engine allows it to apply greater force in accelerating. That is why drag-racing cars seem to be all engine.

30. If you want a car that accelerates quickly, which attributes give you the best acceleration?

  (A) light weight and two doors

  (B) automatic transmission

  (C) automatic transmission and two doors

  (D) light weight and high horsepower

Question 31 refers to the following passage.

Newton's Third Law of Motion

Newton's third law of motion states that for every action there is an equal and opposite reaction. If you stand on the floor, gravity pulls your body down with a certain force. The floor must exert an equal and opposite force upward on your feet, or you would fall through the floor.

31. A boxer is punching a punching bag. What is the punching bag doing to the boxer?

(A) bouncing away from the boxer.

(B) reacting with a force equal and opposite to the force of their punch.

(C) swinging back an angle perpendicular to that of the punch.

(D) swinging back with a force greater than that of the punch.

Questions 32–34 refer to the following passage.

Why Don't Polar Bears Freeze?

Watching a polar bear lumber through the frigid Arctic wilderness, you may wonder why it doesn't freeze. If you were there, you would likely freeze. In fact, you may feel cold just looking at photographs of polar bears.

So why don't polar bears freeze? Polar bears have black skin. Because black absorbs light energy, this means that, in effect, polar bears have a huge solar heat collector covering their bodies. Covering this black skin are hollow hairs. These hairs are clear but look white. Because these hairs are clear, they allow sunlight to reach the skin, where it is absorbed, while also acting as insulation.

32. The most important element in retaining the polar bear's body heat is its [   ].

33. What is the polar bear's solar heat collector?

(A) caves

(B) ice

(C) its furry coat

(D) its skin

34. Which of these additional details is relevant to the passage?

(A) Arctic explorers wear bright colors (usually red) for safety reasons.

(B) The polar bear's white appearance provides it with effective camouflage.

(C) A layer of fat under the bear's skin provides additional insulation.

(D) Polar bears' habitat is shrinking because of global warming.

Questions 35 and 36 refer to the following diagram, which is excerpted from The Sciences: An Integrated Approach, *3rd Edition, by James Trefil and Robert M. Hazen (John Wiley & Sons, Inc.).*

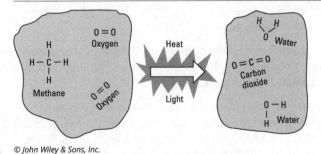

35. When methane (natural gas) burns, it produces light, heat, carbon dioxide, and water. Why would natural gas be a good choice for keeping your house warm in winter?

(A) The chemical reaction produces carbon dioxide.

(B) The chemical reaction produces light.

(C) The chemical reaction produces water.

(D) The chemical reaction produces heat.

36. If firefighters were faced with a methane fire, what would they want to eliminate to put out the fire?

(A) light

(B) water

(C) carbon dioxide

(D) oxygen

Questions 37 and 38 refer to the following passage.

DNA Testing

DNA has become part of everyone's vocabulary, and several crime shows on television use it as a key plot element. DNA has put criminals in jail and freed the innocent. It is used as proof in trials and is an important dramatic tool on many television dramas and talk shows. Because a child inherits the DNA of their parents, DNA testing can be used to prove paternity. Nowadays, many people use DNA tests to find out more information about their ancestry and ethnic heritage.

37. Paternity tests compare DNA to determine whether an individual is a child's ⬚.

38. Because every person's DNA is unique (except for identical twins), what forensic tool can DNA testing replace?

(A) eyewitness accounts

(B) shoe prints

(C) fingerprints

(D) sketch artist renderings

Questions 39–44 refer to the following passage. Some information in the passage is adapted from the NASA website (www.nasa.gov).

Space Stuff

Each space flight carries items authorized by NASA, but the quirky little items astronauts have carried onboard their spacecraft frequently catch the interest of collectors. Auction sales have been brisk for material carried aboard various space flights.

On the second crewed Mercury flight, Gus Grissom carried two rolls of dimes. He was planning to give these to the children of his friends after he returned to Earth. If you carried two rolls of dimes worth ten dollars around Earth, they would still add up to ten dollars. When Gus Grissom returned to Earth, however, these dimes became space mementos, each worth many times its face value. Though seemingly innocuous, sometimes unauthorized objects cause hazards. A sandwich smuggled aboard a NASA Gemini flight created crumbs that floated around the inside of the space capsule. That event triggered a Congressional hearing.

Although NASA has authorized astronauts to carry small personal items into space, it does not allow astronauts to sell these items as souvenirs. Nevertheless, many items have found their way to market. The astronauts who flew on Apollo 15 were disciplined for selling stamped envelopes they had carried with them to the moon.

As you might expect, living in space is very different from living on Earth. In space, astronauts' bodies change. Because they spend a lot of time in a weightless environment, their leg muscles and lower backs begin to lose strength. Their bones also begin to get thin. The heart and blood change, too. When we stand up on Earth, blood goes to our legs. Without gravity, the blood moves to the upper body and head. When the astronauts return to Earth, they often look puffy and feel weak. Thus, Grissom's dimes became an even bigger hazard. In fact, an incident with the spacecraft's hatch made Grissom's return to earth more challenging. A later investigation examined whether the added weight of the dimes had contributed to the difficulties.

39. On which crewed Mercury mission did Gus Grissom carry rolls of dimes?

(A) first

(B) second

(C) third

(D) fourth

40. What is the most likely reason the sandwich crumbs posed a safety hazard?

(A) They could get into the spacecraft's gauges and switches.

(B) They could attract insects and pests.

(C) They could trigger a Congressional hearing.

(D) They could block the spacecraft's windshield.

41. Which of the following is a safety hazard posed by Grissom's dimes?

(A) They could become radioactive because of increased radiation in space.

(B) They could damage his space suit.

(C) They could become the subject of an investigation.

(D) They could weigh him down after returning to earth.

42. What might be a helpful piece of exercise equipment onboard the International Space Station?

(A) a trampoline

(B) a hot tub

(C) a jump rope

(D) a treadmill

43. Which of the following is a reason that astronauts would have trouble walking upon their return to earth?

(A) They are no longer used to earth's gravity.

(B) Their bones begin to get thin.

(C) They have gained weight.

(D) They are happy to be back on earth.

44. Why were the Apollo 15 astronauts punished?

(A) The souvenirs were fake.

(B) The souvenirs caused an accident in space.

(C) Astronauts are not allowed to profit by selling souvenirs from space.

(D) Astronauts are not allowed to bring personal items into space.

Questions 45 and 46 refer to the following passage.

Work

When we think of work, we think of people sitting at desks operating computers or building homes or making some other effort to earn money. When a physicist thinks of work, they probably think of a formula — force exerted over a distance. If you don't expend any energy — resulting in a force of zero — or if your force produces no movement, then no work has been done. If you pick up your gigantic super-ordinary two-pound hamburger and lift it to your mouth to take a bite, you do work. If you want to resist temptation and just stare at your hamburger, you do no work. If your friend gets tired of you playing around and lifts your hamburger to feed you, you still do no work, but your friend does. In scientific terms, two elements are necessary for work to be done:

A force must be exerted and the object to which the force has been exerted must move.

45. If the formula for work is Work = Force × Distance, how much more work would you do in pushing a 40-pound box 3 feet instead of 2 feet?

(A) half as much

(B) three times as much

(C) a third as much

(D) one-and-one-half times as much

46. Although you may see that you do work in climbing a flight of stairs, why do you also do work when you descend a flight of stairs?

(A) It is hard to descend stairs.

(B) You have traveled a distance down the stairs.

(C) You feel tired after descending stairs.

(D) You have exerted a force over a distance.

Questions 47 and 48 refer to the following figure and passages, which are excerpted from Physical Science: What the Technology Professional Needs to Know, *by C. Lon Enloe, Elizabeth Garnett, Jonathan Miles, and Stephen Swanson (John Wiley & Sons, Inc.).*

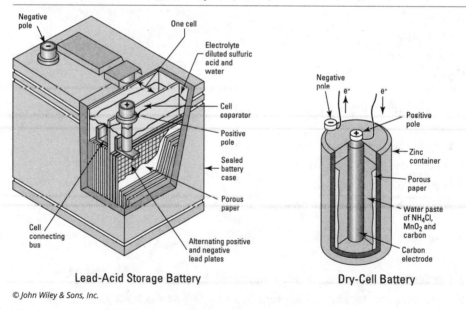

Lead-Acid Storage Battery

Dry-Cell Battery

The Lead-Acid Storage Battery

One battery you rely on is the 12-volt lead-acid storage battery used in gas-powered cars and trucks. This battery is composed of six separate cells, each developing about 2 volts. By connecting the six cells in series, the overall voltage becomes the sum, or 12 volts.

The Dry-Cell Battery

The traditional dry-cell or flashlight battery is a zinc-carbon battery. It derives its name from the fact that the liquid portion has been replaced by a moist paste of ammonium chloride, manganese dioxide, and carbon. These components are the anode portion of the cell, and the zinc container serves as the cathode.

47. If you wanted a 48-volt lead-acid battery, how many cells would it need?

(A) 24

(B) 26

(C) 28

(D) 36

48. What replaces the liquid-acid portion of the lead-acid battery in a dry-cell battery?

(A) a moist paste

(B) a powder

(C) dry acid

(D) carbon and zinc

Questions 49 and 50 refer to the following passage.

The Cell and Heredity

Each cell in a living organism consists of a membrane surrounding a cytoplasm. The cytoplasm is like jelly and has a nucleus in its center. Chromosomes are part of the nucleus. They are important because they store DNA. Most DNA molecules are made up of two strands that are coiled around each other in a double helix formation. The strands are made up of four chemical bases: adenine, guanine, cytosine, and thymine. DNA carries the genetic code that is the basis of heredity.

49. What determines what traits that you inherit from your parents?

(A) the cell

(B) the atom

(C) the nucleus

(D) DNA

50. What makes up the DNA molecule?

(A) membrane

(B) cytoplasm

(C) jelly

(D) four chemical bases

Chapter 32

Answers for Practice Test 2, Science

In this chapter, you find the answers and explanations for the Science practice test in Chapter 31. Review the answer explanation for all the questions, even for the ones you got right, and keep track of areas where you need some additional studying. If you just want a quick look at the answers, check out the abbreviated answer key at the end of this chapter. Once you review your answers and finish any additional studying, you are ready for the online practice test.

Answers and Explanations

1. **perennial, annual.** These answers are correct because even though plants develop new bulbs, they do not reliably regrow. The plants depend on humans to cultivate them.

2. **B, E, C, D, A.** This order correctly restates the lifecycle, the description of which is spread throughout the passage.

3. **C. Cells are differentiated.** Although all of the choices are true, only Choice (C) is supported by information in the passage.

4. **D. 2½ hours per week for adults and 1 hour per day for children.** The passage states that adults should exercise for 150 minutes (2½ hours) per week, and children should exercise for 60 minutes (1 hour) daily. This item is a good example of why you should pay attention to how numbers are labeled — in this case, hours or minutes.

5. **A, B.** According to the passage, exercise can lower the blood pressure of people suffering from high blood pressure, and exercise provides psychological benefits as well as physical ones. The other choices are contradicted by the information in the passage.

6. **B. It can operate without an external oxidizer.** In space, there's no oxidizer to take part in the chemical reaction needed for combustion. A rocket ship carries its own oxidizer and, thus, can travel through airless space (which doesn't contain oxygen). Because the passage specifically discusses oxidizers, Choice (B) is the best answer.

7. **a liquid or a solid.** The passage states in the second paragraph that "the fuel used may be a liquid or a solid."

8. **C. The bacteria that aid decomposition do not thrive.** The passage states that with the methodology used for burying solid waste in a modern landfill, the bacteria needed for decomposition can't do their work. The reason for using landfills is that they require less space — not that they promote decomposition. Thus, the landfill and the processes used within it are as much a part of the problem as they are a part of the solution. The other choices may be partially correct, but the key point in the text concerns the decomposition of wastes.

9. **B. Recycling reduces the need for new landfill sites.** Recycling newspapers, or many other items that would go to the landfill, reduces the need for new landfill sites.

10. **D. to reduce the amount of space it occupies.** Solid waste is compacted to reduce the amount of space it occupies, which also happens to make the landfill last longer. The waste is compacted in spite of the fact that doing so slows down decomposition and lengthens the life of the garbage.

11. **B. a garbage lasagna.** A modern landfill is compared to garbage lasagna because it's made up of alternating layers of compacted garbage and dirt. This method prevents timely decomposition.

12. **D. Recycling is more sustainable than using landfills.** Landfills are costly and allow solid waste to accumulate without decomposing. Recycling will solve this and other issues associated with landfills. Therefore, Choice (D) is correct.

13. **B. Reuse and recycle as much as possible.** As long as you dispose of waste by taking it to the curb or the dump, there will be an excess amount of waste being disposed of. Every piece of waste that you can reuse or recycle lives on to be useful again and, thus, eliminates some of the waste in America.

14. **D. They help decompose waste.** The passage states that bacteria decompose waste. Therefore, Choice (B) is incorrect. Choice (A) is not discussed in the passage. Decomposition is part of the organic cycle, so Choice (C) is incorrect.

15. **D. The cost is less than acquiring more landfill sites.** Landfill sites are more expensive to acquire than the cost of recycling. In most cities, people hope to find new uses for recycled materials, which could increase the value of garbage.

16. **B. aphelion.** The passage states, "summer in the Northern Hemisphere occurs at aphelion, the farthest distance between the Earth and Sun. . ." Even though this is a dense paragraph, you don't have to spend a lot of time reading it as long as you read the question first. You just need to scan quickly for the definition given in the question.

17. **airbag.** The purpose of the airbag, according to the passage, is to absorb some of the forces in a front-end crash and prevent injury to the passenger.

18. **D. in the middle rear passenger seat.** According to the passage, the infant car seat should be placed in the rear seat. You can infer that the safest place in the rear seat would be in the middle seat, in case of a side collision.

19. **D. quark.** The diagram (going from bottom to top) indicates the process of building up a molecule. The quark is the smallest particle, and the molecule is the largest. Sometimes you have to read a diagram in an unfamiliar way to answer the question.

20. **D. 1,000,000,000.** According to the diagram, a quark is 10^{-18} meters across and a molecule is 10^{-9} meters across. The molecule would be $10^{-9}/10^{-18} = 1/10^{-9}$ or 1,000,000,000 times the size of a quark.

    A number with a negative exponent, like 10^{-9}, equals 1/10 to the positive power of the negative exponent (for example, $10^{-9} = 1/10^9$).

21. **atoms.** The passage states that everything is composed of atoms. As a result, the floor must be composed of atoms.

22. **B. They have developed peptoids.** This is another dense science reading where you need to read carefully and pay attention to the answer choices. Many of the incorrect answers use language from the passage; however similar the words may be, the other choices don't answer the question. According to the second sentence of the passage, the only correct answer is Choice (B).

23. **A. Solar radiation is much stronger on the Moon than on Earth.** Only this statement presents a hazard to astronauts or their vehicle.

24. **B. The land resembled the Moon in certain ways.** This information is stated directly in the passage. The other choices are not supported by information in the passage.

25. **D. a volume equal to the volume of your body.** The passage tells you that you would displace a volume equal to your own volume.

26. **A. Immerse the rock in a pre-measured volume of water and measure the increase.** An object displaces a volume of water equal to its volume. Thus, putting an irregularly shaped object in a pre-measured volume of water is one way to measure the volume of that object. The other methods would not work. Choice (C) would only work if you knew the density of the rock, which you do not. Though bubble baths are mentioned in the passage, Choice (D) would not help you determine the volume of the rock.

27. **C. Apply a force in the direction you want it to move.** According to Newton, a force must be applied to move an object at rest. Newton, who never drove a car, said that you have to apply an external force on the object at rest (the car in this question) in the direction you want it to move. If you want your car to move deeper into the snow, you push it down. If you have a crane or a helicopter, which the passage doesn't mention, you apply a force upward to lift it out of the snow. Choice (C) is the best answer.

28. **A. A skateboard hits a large crack in the sidewalk and the skateboarder flies off their skateboard.** Choice (A) is correct because when the skateboard hits a crack, the skateboarder flies off the skateboard in the same direction they were traveling in. All the other choices are examples of a body being acted upon by another force, either changing the velocity and/or direction, or putting it in motion.

29. **D. your car tends to continue at the same rate.** When driving at a uniform rate of speed, the car resists changes in speed. The car wants to continue to travel at the same speed. To change that speed suddenly, you must apply great effort to your brakes. While the weight, or mass, of the car plays a role in changing speed, that is only a partial answer.

30. **D. light weight and high horsepower.** Newton's second law of motion states that when a body changes its velocity because an external force is applied to it, that change in velocity is directly proportional to the force and inversely proportional to the mass of the body. If you decrease the weight of the body and increase the size of the external force, the acceleration increases.

31. **B. reacting with a force equal and opposite to the force of their punch.** Newton's third law of motion states that for every action there's an equal and opposite reaction. If the boxer is exerting a force on the punching bag, the bag is exerting an equal and opposite force on the boxer.

32. **hair** or **fur.** The passage states that the hair acts as insulation, retaining the polar bear's body heat.

33. **D. its skin.** The passage states that the polar bear's dark skin collects heat from the sun.

34. **C. A layer of fat under the bear's skin provides additional insulation.** The passage is primarily about how polar bears stay warm and avoid freezing. Only Choice (C) supports this main idea. The other choices are not relevant.

35. **D. The chemical reaction produces heat.** In cold weather, you need a source of heat to warm your house, and methane produces heat in the chemical reaction. The other answers are incorrect.

36. **D. oxygen.** Methane requires oxygen to produce light and heat. If there's no oxygen, the methane can't burn.

37. **father.** A paternity test can determine whether an individual is the biological father of a child.

38. **C. fingerprints.** Although identical twins have the same DNA but different fingerprints, DNA evidence is often easier for crime lab specialists to find than intact fingerprints. Eyewitness accounts, shoe prints, and artist sketches aren't as reliable as DNA or fingerprints.

39. **B. second.** According to the passage, Grissom carried the dimes on the second crewed Mercury voyage.

40. **A. They could get into the spacecraft's gauges and switches.** The crumbs could float anywhere in the weightless environment and cause problems with the gauges and switches, which would affect safety. The other choices do not make sense.

41. **D. They could weigh him down after returning to Earth.** Of the choices, only this one is a likely safety hazard, and so is the correct answer.

42. **D. a treadmill.** Because the astronauts lose muscle mass in their legs, having a treadmill onboard would help them exercise their lower extremities. NASA's treadmills are especially designed for use in space. They include special bungee ropes to hold the astronauts to the machine. Astronauts report that it's a fun, bouncy way to exercise. None of the other choices would work in space. A hot tub (Choice B) does not provide exercise.

43. **A. They are no longer used to Earth's gravity.** Only this choice explains why the astronauts would have trouble walking. The other choices do not make sense.

44. **C. Astronauts are not allowed to profit by selling souvenirs from space.** According to the passage, NASA forbids the sale of items carried into space. Therefore, Choice (C) is correct. The souvenirs were authentic space items, so Choice (A) is incorrect. Choice (B) is not supported by information in the passage. Choice (D) is contradicted by the passage; NASA can authorize astronauts to bring personal items with them. However, the astronauts are not allowed to sell them.

45. **D. One-and-one-half times as much.** Because the force remains constant, the work done is proportional to the distance traveled, which means you would do 3/2 or $1\frac{1}{2}$ times as much work.

46. **D. You have exerted a force over a distance.** Walking down the stairs, you have to exert a force for a distance (the definition of work in physics). In real life, it seems easier to walk down a flight of stairs than to walk up it, but, in both cases, work is being done.

47. **A. 24.** If you want a 48-volt lead-acid battery, and each cell produces 2 volts, you need 24 cells ($48 \div 2 = 24$).

48. **A. a moist paste.** The moist paste replaces the acid in the battery.

49. **D. DNA.** DNA stores the genetic code, which determines heredity, and you get your DNA from your parents.

50. **D. four chemical bases.** According to the passage, DNA is a double helix molecule made up of adenine, guanine, cytosine, and thymine, which are all chemical bases.

Answer Key

1.	perennial, annual	18.	D	35.	D
2.	B, E, C, D, A	19.	D	36.	D
3.	C	20.	D	37.	father
4.	D	21.	atoms	38.	C
5.	A, B	22.	B	39.	B
6.	B	23.	A	40.	A
7.	a liquid or a solid	24.	B	41.	D
8.	C	25.	D	42.	D
9.	B	26.	A	43.	A
10.	D	27.	C	44.	C
11.	B	28.	A	45.	D
12.	D	29.	D	46.	D
13.	B	30.	D	47.	A
14.	D	31.	B	48.	A
15.	D	32.	hair or fur	49.	D
16.	B	33.	D	50.	D
17.	airbag	34.	C		

Chapter **33**

Practice Test 2: Mathematical Reasoning

In 115 minutes, you have to solve a series of questions involving general mathematical skills and problem solving. These questions may be based on short passages, graphs, charts, or figures. You must do the first five questions without a calculator, but after that, you can use a calculator for the rest of the test. For now, the calculator on your phone is fine, but eventually you will want to become familiar with the TI-30XS calculator that you will use during the real test. You will also have an online whiteboard or an erasable tablet (only at a test center) to help you visualize problems, jot down equations, or write notes. For now, have a couple of sheets of scratch paper handy.

You also have at your fingertips a list of formulas to help you with some of the questions. Remember that the calculator and list of formulas aren't a magic solution. You have to know how to use them. The GED formula sheet is on the page before the first test question. Only some of the questions require you to use a formula, and you may not need all the formulas given.

TIP

If you have time before the test, memorize the most commonly tested formulas: area of a square or rectangle, area and circumference of a circle, and the Pythagorean Theorem. Questions using these formulas appear frequently on the GED test.

REMEMBER

On the real GED, you'll take test on a computer, where you use the mouse and the keyboard to indicate your answers. The questions and answer choices are formatted in this book to make them appear as similar as possible to what you'll see on the computer screen, but I had to retain some A, B, C, and D choices and provide an answer sheet for you to mark your answers. When you're ready for the included online practice test, you will be able to see and try the actual question types as they appear on the test.

Use the timer on your phone to keep track of time. If you run out of time, mark the last question you answered. Then answer the rest of the questions. This will help you figure out how much more quickly you have to work to complete the entire test in the time allowed.

Answer Sheet for Practice Test 2, Mathematical Reasoning

1. _____

2. _____

3. _____

4. _____

5. _____

6. _____

7. _____

8. _____

9. _____

10. _____

11. _____

12. _____

13. _____

14. _____

15. _____

16. _____

17. _____

18. _____

19. _____

20. _____

21. _____

22. _____

23. _____

24. _____

25. _____

26. _____

27. _____

28. _____

29. _____

30. _____

31. _____

32. _____

33. _____

34. _____

35. _____

36. _____

37. _____

38. _____

39. _____

40. _____

41. _____

42. _____

43. _____

44. _____

45. _____

46. _____

47. _____

48. _____

49. _____

50. _____

Mathematics Formula Explanations

This displays formulas relating to geometric measurement and certain algebra concepts and is available on the GED® test — Mathematical Reasoning.

Area of a:

square	$A = s^2$
rectangle	$A = lw$
parallelogram	$A = bh$
triangle	$A = \frac{1}{2} bh$
trapezoid	$A = \frac{1}{2} h(b_1 + b_2)$
circle	$A = \pi r^2$

Perimeter of a:

square	$P = 4s$
rectangle	$P = 2l + 2w$
triangle	$P = s_1 + s_2 + s_3$
Circumference of a circle	$C = 2\pi r$ OR $C = \pi d$; $\pi \approx 3.14$

Surface area and volume of a:

rectangular prism	$SA = 2lw + 2lh + 2wh$	$V = lwh$
right prism	$SA = ph + 2B$	$V = Bh$
cylinder	$SA = 2\pi rh + 2\pi r^2$	$V = \pi r^2 h$
pyramid	$SA = \frac{1}{2} ps + B$	$V = \frac{1}{3} Bh$
cone	$SA = \pi rs + \pi r^2$	$V = \frac{1}{3} \pi r^2 h$
sphere	$SA = 4\pi r^2$	$V = \frac{4}{3} \pi r^3$

(p = perimeter of base with area B; $\pi \approx 3.14$)

Data

mean	mean is equal to the total of the values of a data set, divided by the number of elements in the data set
median	median is the middle value in an odd number of ordered values of a data set, or the mean of the two middle values in an even number of ordered values in a data set

Algebra

slope of a line	$m = \dfrac{y_2 - y_1}{x_2 - x_1}$
slope-intercept form of the equation of a line	$y = mx + b$
point-slope form of the equation of a line	$y - y_1 = m(x - x_1)$
standard form of a quadratic equation	$y = ax^2 + bx + c$
quadratic formula	$x = \dfrac{-b \pm \sqrt{b^2 - 4ac}}{2a}$
Pythagorean theorem	$a^2 + b^2 = c^2$
simple interest	$I = Prt$
	(I = interest, P = principal, r = rate, t = time)
distance formula	$d = rt$
total cost	total cost = (number of units) x (price per unit)

Æ Symbol Tool Explanation

The GED® test on computer contains a tool known as the "Æ Symbol Tool." Use this guide to learn about entering special mathematical symbols into fill-in-the-blank item types.

Symbol	Explanation	Symbol	Explanation	Symbol	Explanation
π	pi	$\mid$	absolute value	−	minus or negative
f	function	×	multiplication	(	open or left parenthesis
≥	greater than or equal to	÷	division	)	close or right parenthesis
≤	less than or equal to	±	positive or negative	>	greater than
≠	not equal to	∞	infinity	<	less than
2	2 exponent ("squared")	√	square root	=	equals
3	3 exponent ("cubed")	+	plus or positive		

TIME: 115 minutes

ITEMS: 50

DIRECTIONS: Mark your answers on the answer sheet provided.

1. Yvonne is studying a map. Her destination is 4 miles due north of her current location, but to avoid a small lake, the road goes 3 miles due west to an intersection and then goes northeast to her destination. Approximately how much extra must she drive because of the way the road goes?

   (A) 4 miles

   (B) 5 miles

   (C) 7 miles

   (D) 8 miles

2. After asking for directions to a restaurant, Sarah was told it was 1,000 yards ahead, but her car's odometer reads distances in miles and tenths of miles. How many miles (to the nearest tenth) does she have to drive to find the restaurant? (There are 1,760 yards in a mile.) You may use numbers, a decimal point (.), and/or a negative sign (−) in your answer. [   ] miles

3. Arthur is making a circular wall hanging, using small pieces of cloth glued onto a backing that is attached to a frame. If he wants a wall hanging that is 7 feet 8 inches across, including a 2-inch fringe all around the backing, how many square feet of backing does he need to cover, rounded to one decimal place?

   (A) 42.2

   (B) 43.0

   (C) 45.7

   (D) 46.1

4. The vertices of a triangle are A(−6,4), B(−8,−6), and C (8,7). Mark the verticies on the coordinate plane. What is the longest side of the triangle? [   ]

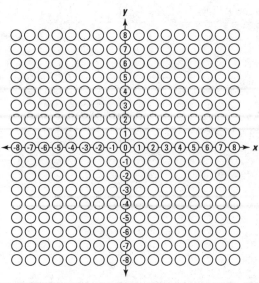

© John Wiley & Sons, Inc.

Question 5 refers to the following graph.

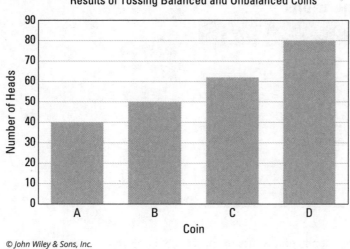

Results of Tossing Balanced and Unbalanced Coins

5. As an experiment, students in a statistics class toss four coins 100 times each and chart the results. Three coins are not fairly balanced. From the chart, which coin is closest to being fairly balanced?

   (A) coin A

   (B) coin B

   (C) coin C

   (D) coin D

6. Donna is a very dedicated runner. To improve her breathing, she has started inhaling for two steps and then exhaling for two steps. Her average step is 27 inches long. How many times does she inhale in 1000 yards of her daily 1-mile run?

   (A) 111

   (B) 333

   (C) 589

   (D) 5,332

7. Sam and Arnold were eating ice-cream cones. Arnold wondered what volume of ice cream his cone would hold if filled to the top. Sam measured the cone and found it to be 2-1/2 inches across the top and 5-1/2 inches high. The cone would hold ⬚ cubic inches of ice cream, rounded to one decimal place, if it were filled to the top. You may use numbers, a decimal point (.), and/or a negative sign (−) in your answer.

Room Level Dimensions

Room	Measurement (In Feet)
Dining room	10×8
Living room	20×13
Kitchen	14×8
Solarium	19×8
Bedroom	14×13
Office	12×8

8. Singh has bought a new condo and wants to carpet the living room, dining room, and bedroom. A nearby store has carpet that he likes for $35.00 per square yard plus free installation. How much will the new carpet cost without tax? You may use numbers, a decimal point (.), and/or a negative sign (−) in your answer. [   ]

Questions 9 and 10 refer to the following information.

Carlos wants to buy a used car. He has been told that a car loses 4.3 cents from its book value for every mile over 100,000 that it has traveled. He sees just the car he wants, but it has 137,046 miles on the odometer. The book value of the car is $13,500.

9. Which is the best estimate of the realistic value of the car to the nearest $10, according to the information Carlos was told?

    (A) $10,910

    (B) $11,000

    (C) $12,020

    (D) $14,980

10. According to the information Carlos was told, the realistic actual value of the car to the nearest dollar is [   ].

11. Elena wants to paint a mural on the wall of her house. The wall is 9 feet high and 17 feet long. To plan the mural, she draws a scale drawing of the area for the mural on a piece of paper 11 inches long. How high, in inches, should the drawing be to maintain scale?

    (A) 6.2

    (B) 5.8

    (C) 8.5

    (D) 9.0

12. If the slope of a line is 0.75, and $y_2 = 36$, $y_1 = 24$, and $x_1 = 12$, what is the value of x_2?

(A) 28

(B) 14

(C) –14

(D) –28

Questions 13 and 14 refer to the following table.

Literacy Rates in Selected Countries

Country	Literacy Rate (%)
China	90.9
Cuba	99.8
Ethiopia	35.9
Haiti	54.8
India	61.0
Israel	97.1
Russia	99.4
South Africa	82.4
United States	99.0

13. If the literacy rates of China, the United States, and Russia were compared, the highest literacy rate would be how many times larger than the lowest?

(A) 1.0

(B) 1.1

(C) 1.2

(D) 1.3

14. How many countries have a literacy rate higher than the United States?

(A) 1

(B) 2

(C) 3

(D) 4

15. The dimensions of a cube are 7 inches on all sides. Which expression shows the volume of the cube?

(A) 7^1

(B) 7^2

(C) 7^3

(D) 3^7

Peter's grades are 81, 76, 92, 87, 79, and 83.

16. To renew his scholarship, Peter's average grade must be above the average grade for the school, which is 82. By how many points is he above or below that standard?

    (A) 2

    (B) 1

    (C) −1

    (D) −2

17. If Peter's goal is to get an average grade of 90 percent, by how many total points is he failing to achieve his goal?

    (A) 42

    (B) 43

    (C) 44

    (D) 45

18. Workers at Olga's Cookie Shop store molasses in a cylindrical tank that measures 4.8 feet tall and 2.1 feet in diameter. How many cubic feet of molasses can workers store in the tank? You may use numbers, a decimal point (.), and/or a negative sign (−) in your answer. [   ]

19. Amy's son received $1,574 in gifts when he graduated from middle school. If she lets her son spend $74, and she invests the rest of the money in a certificate of deposit paying 1.4 percent simple interest for the four years until he starts college, how much money will be in the certificate of deposit? You may use numbers, a decimal point (.), and/or a negative sign (−) in your answer. [   ]

20. Consider the equation $E = mc^2$. If the value of m triples and the value of c remains constant, the effect on E would be how many times larger?

    (A) the same

    (B) 3 times larger

    (C) 9 times larger

    (D) 27 times larger

21. Tyrone recently got permission to telework from home, so he is setting up his home office. He wants to put a chair mat under his desk. In front of the chair mat, he wants to put a small area rug. According to their labels, the chair mat measures 36 inches by 48 inches and the rug measures 3 feet by 4 feet. How much total surface area will be covered by the chair mat and the rug in square feet?

    (A) 12

    (B) 24

    (C) 1,728

    (D) 3,456

22. Vladimir wants to install a small cylindrical water tank to store rain water for his garden. He wants a tank with a 6-foot diameter. He can buy a tank that is 4 feet tall or 6 feet tall. How many more cubic feet of water can the larger tank hold?

(A) 57

(B) 113

(C) 170

(D) 283

23. Forty tenth-grade social studies students are on a field trip, but many of the students don't feel well. Ten students are healthy, but each of the remaining thirty has a sore throat, a cold, or both. If 15 students have sore throats and 25 have colds, how many students have both?

(A) 25

(B) 20

(C) 15

(D) 10

24. Graph the point $(-3,4)$ on the coordinate plane.

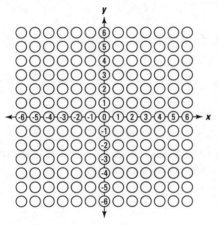

© John Wiley & Sons, Inc.

25. A local hospital offers a 4-week parenting course for new parents. The cost is $40 per person, but 75% of the cost is paid for by a government grant. The hospital absorbs the rest of the cost, so the classes are free to the parents. If 11 parents take the course this month, how much will the hospital absorb? $\boxed{}$ You may use numbers, a decimal point (.), and/or a negative sign (−) in your answer.

26. Jerry has started a business selling computers. He can buy a good used computer for $299 and sell it for $449. The only question he has is whether he will make money. If his overhead (rent, light, heating, and cooling) amounts to $48 per unit and his taxes amount to $2 per unit, how many computers will he have to sell to make $700 profit per week?

(A) 6

(B) 7

(C) 8

(D) 9

27. Jerry also repairs customers' computers. The minimum charge is $45 for one hour. Each additional hour is $30. This week, he repaired 3 computers in under an hour. It took him 3 hours to repair a fourth computer. How much did he make this week repairing computers? [   ] You may use numbers, a decimal point (.), and/or a negative sign (−) in your answer.

Question 28 and 29 refer to this table.

Top Installed Geothermal-Electric Capacity, by Country, in 2019

Country	Installed Capacity (Gigawatts)
United States	3.7
Indonesia	2.1
Philippines	1.9
Turkey	1.5
New Zealand	1.0

28. Which country has the highest installed geothermal–electric capacity?

(A) Indonesia

(B) Philippines

(C) Turkey

(D) New Zealand

29. Iceland has an installed geothermal–electric capacity of 0.8 gigawatts. What is the difference between Iceland's installed capacity and the next highest on the list?

(A) 0.2 gigawatts

(B) 0.7 gigawatts

(C) 1.3 gigawatts

(D) 2.9 gigawatts

30. Elayne wants to buy a new fuel-efficient car. She notices that a new car is advertised as getting 100 miles per gallon in city driving and 70 miles per gallon on the highway. After a week of record keeping, she produces the following table for her old car.

Day	City Driving (Miles)	Highway Driving (Miles)
Monday	30	5
Tuesday	35	25
Wednesday	25	10
Thursday	30	20
Friday	20	5
Saturday	5	70
Sunday	5	75

If Elayne's old car gets 18 miles per gallon in the city and 12 miles per gallon on the highway, and gas costs $2.70 a gallon, how much would she save in a week by buying this new fuel-efficient car?

(A) $12.15

(B) $22.50

(C) $47.25

(D) $57.60

Question 31 refers to the following table.

Interest Rates Offered by Different Car Dealerships

Dealer	Interest Rate Offered
A	Prime + 2%
B	7.5%
C	1/2 of prime + 5%
D	Prime + 20% of prime for administrative costs

31. Donald is looking for a new car, but each dealership offers him a different interest rate. If the prime lending rate is 6 percent, which dealer is offering Donald the best terms to finance his car?

(A) Dealer A

(B) Dealer B

(C) Dealer C

(D) Dealer D

32. Henry wanted to find out how many people watched *Four's a Mob*, the newest sitcom, this week. He did a survey of 12 of his friends and found that 9 of them had seen the last episode. What percentage of his friends watched the sitcom this week? You may use numbers, a decimal point (.), and/or a negative sign (−) in your answer. ☐.

Questions 33 and 34 refer to the following information.

33. The Corner Bookstore is going to mail 3 GED books to an adult school. The books are 1¾ inches thick. How deep should the box be in order to hold all the books with room for ¼ inch of packing material above and below the books?

(A) 2 inches

(B) 2¼ inches

(C) 5¼ inches

(D) 5¾ inches

34. In September, Ken and Ben decided to lose some weight by the following July. They figured that by supporting each other, eating a balanced diet with reduced calories, and exercising, they could lose 0.5 pound per week. If Ken and Ben stick to their plans, approximately how much weight could they each lose between the beginning of September and the end of June, assuming there are about 4 weeks in a month?

(A) 20 pounds

(B) 30 pounds

(C) 36 pounds

(D) 48 pounds

35. Mary and Samantha are planning a 900-mile trip. Mary says that she can drive at an average speed of 45 miles per hour. Samantha says that she will fly, but it takes her 45 minutes to get to the airport and 1 hour and 15 minutes to get from the airport to her destination after she lands. If she has to be at the airport 3 hours before take-off and the airplane travels an average of 300 miles per hour, how many hours longer is Mary's travel time compared to Samantha's (not counting time for rest or sleeping)?

(A) 8

(B) 9

(C) 12

(D) 16

Question 36 refers to the following information and graph.

The Queenly Hat Company of Lansing, Michigan, produces designer hats for women who feel that a hat completes an outfit. Their sales vary from quarter to quarter and factory to factory. The following chart reflects their sales for one year.

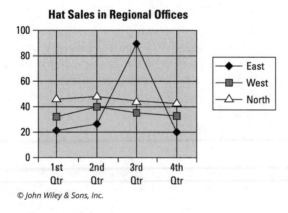

© John Wiley & Sons, Inc.

36. Of the three factories, which factories and in which quarter are sales figures approximately in the ratio of 2:1?

(A) east and west in 2nd quarter

(B) west and north in 3rd quarter

(C) east and north in 3rd quarter

(D) west and east in 1st quarter

Life Expectancy in the United States, by Current Age

Age (In Years)	Males	Females
10	66.6	71.5
20	56.9	61.6
30	47.7	52.0
40	38.6	42.5
50	29.7	33.2
60	21.6	24.6
70	14.93	16.54

37. Trent and Tina are unidentical twin brother and sister. From the data presented in the table, which of these possible predictions is most likely if they are currently 30 years old?

(A) Trent will likely live longer than his sister Tina.

(B) Tina will likely live longer than her brother Trent.

(C) They are identical twins, and so will likely live to the same age.

(D) The average life expectancy for Tina is 47.7 years.

38. On average, what age will a 20-year-old female reach?

(A) 56.9

(B) 61.6

(C) 76.9

(D) 81.6

39. The cost of a finished item of a certain product is equal to 2 times the production cost, plus 120 percent of the overhead costs at the retail level, plus profit. If three stores, A, B, and C, each sell the product, and Store B has a 50-percent raise in rent, how will this affect the selling price for the item?

(A) The selling price will go down.

(B) The selling price will remain the same.

(C) The selling price will go up.

(D) Customers can get a discount with a coupon.

40. Sol wants to write the population of the United States in scientific notation for a project he is working on. If the population of the United States is estimated at 328,000,000 and he writes it out as 3.28×10^x, the value for x is ⬚ .

41. Harry and Karry are preparing for the big race. They have been keeping track of their times in the following table.

Comparative Times

Harry's Times (In Seconds)	Karry's Times (In Seconds)
15.6	15.9
14.9	16.1
16.0	15.8
15.8	16.2
16.1	14.8

What conclusion can you reach from comparing their mean times?

(A) Karry is slightly faster.

(B) Harry is slightly slower.

(C) They are about even.

(D) Karry has a higher average time.

42. The total floor area of Maria's new apartment is 1,400 square feet. If the ceilings are 9 feet high and her air system withdraws and replaces 63 cubic feet of air each minute, how long, in minutes, does it take to withdraw and replace all the air in her apartment?

(A) 180

(B) 200

(C) 220

(D) 240

43. Peter is emptying his swimming pool. He can pump 9 cubic feet of water per minute. If his pool measures 45 feet by 12 feet with an average depth of 4 feet, when will his pool be empty if he starts pumping at noon on Tuesday?

(A) 4 a.m. on Wednesday

(B) 6 p.m. on Tuesday

(C) 2 p.m. on Tuesday

(D) 4 p.m. on Tuesday

44. Mohammed works in sales. He has earned an average of $420 per week for the last four weeks. If he earned $480 the first week, $400 the third week, and $550 the final week, how much did he earn the second week of the month?

(A) $190

(B) $250

(C) $280

(D) $340

45. Georgia took her children shopping for school clothes. She started shopping with a $500 gift card and a credit card in her purse. When she returned home after shopping, $126 remained on the gift card and she had $83 in credit card receipts. How much did she spend shopping? You may use numbers, a decimal point (.), and/or a negative sign (−) in your answer. [_____]

46. If you cut almost all the way around the top and bottom of an empty vegetable can and then open it flat along the seam, what shape would you end up with?

   (A) two circles

   (B) a rectangle with a circle on each side

   (C) a rectangle

   (D) a rectangle with a circle on each end

47. Sonya's car uses gasoline in direct proportion to her speed. If she increases her average speed by 10 miles per hour to save time, the consequence is that

   (A) she would save money.

   (B) she would spend more money on fuel.

   (C) she would spend the same amount as before.

   (D) she would use up her savings paying speeding tickets.

48. A circle is drawn with its center at the origin and a diameter of 8 units. Where will the circumference intersect the negative y-axis? Circle this point on the graph.

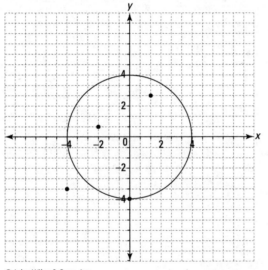

49. A fuel gauge reads 1/8 full. If the fuel tank holds 24 gallons, how many gallons of fuel will fill it?

   (A) 18

   (B) 19

   (C) 20

   (D) 21

50. As part of a mathematics test, Ying was given the following equations to solve:

$4x + 2y = 20$

$2x + 6y = 35$

What is the value of y?

   (A) 4

   (B) 5

   (C) 6

   (D) 7

Chapter **34**

Answers for Practice Test 2, Mathematical Reasoning

This chapter gives you the answers and explanations for the Mathematical Reasoning practice test in Chapter 33. The first question you may ask yourself is why you should bother with the explanations if you got the answers right. The simple answer is: The explanation walks you the steps you follow to answer the question. This reinforces your understanding in preparation for the real test. If you made an error, the explanation can save you from a lot of frustration. By followig the steps, you can discover why and where you went wrong and figure out a way not to repeat the error on similar questions on the real test. After you finish reviewing your answers, you may want to review relevant chapters in this book. Then, when you are ready, you can take the full-length online practice test.

Answers and Explanations

1. **A. 4 miles.** This problem is a test of your knowledge of how to use the Pythagorean Theorem. Sketch out a map for this question: Her destination is 4 miles due north of her current location. To get to her destination she has to drive due west and then northeast. Due north and due west are at right angles. So Yvonne's journey is a triangle, with the last part being the hypotenuse. Pythagoras (the guy who, as you may expect, is credited with discovering the Pythagorean Theorem) said that the square of the hypotenuse of a right triangle is equal to the sum of the squares of the other two sides $\left(a^2 + b^2 = c^2\right)$. Thus, the square of the last leg of Yvonne's journey equals $16 + 9 = 25$. The square root of 25 is 5. However, the question asks how much further Yvonne must travel: She ended up driving $5 + 3 = 8$ miles but was originally only 4 miles from her destination. Therefore, she traveled $8 - 4 = 4$ miles extra.

2. **0.6.** To convert yards into miles, you have to divide the number of yards you want to convert into miles by 1,760 (because 1 mile equals 1,760 yards). One thousand yards is about 0.57 mile $\left(1,000 / 1,760 = 0.568181818\right)$. Odometers usually read to one decimal point, so Sarah should drive about 0.6 mile, rounded up because the second decimal place is larger than 5, which would be just past the restaurant.

3. **A. 42.2.** The wall hanging has a diameter of 7 feet 8 inches, and it has a 2-inch fringe all the way around it. To calculate the diameter that will be covered by the backing, you have to subtract the width of the fringe (which you get by multiplying 2 inches by 2 because the fringe adds 2 inches to both sides of the circle): 7 feet 8 inches $-$ 4 inches = 7 feet 4 inches

   Because the units must be the same to calculate the area, you need to convert the diameter into inches: 7 feet 4 inches $= 7 \times 12 + 4 = 88$ inches. The diameter is twice the radius, so the radius of the backing is $88 / 2 = 44$ inches.

   Now you can use the formula for the area of a circle given on the formula page, $A = \pi r^2$, where π is approximately 3.14. Thus, the area is $3.14 \times 44 \times 44 = 6,079.04$ square inches.

   Because the question asks for an answer in square feet, you have to convert square inches to square feet by dividing by 144 $\left(12 \text{ inches} = 1 \text{ foot}; 12^2 = 144\right)$: $6,079.04 / 144 = 42.215555$ or 42.2, rounded to one decimal place.

4. **BC.** Calculating the length of each side requires many steps. Luckily, all you have to do is mark the vertices on the coordinate plane and then determine the longest side.

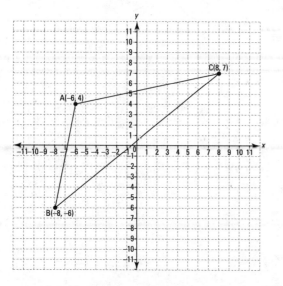

From the drawing, you can determine that the longest side is *BC*.

5. **B. coin B.** This question asks you to draw an inference from a graph. Looking carefully at the graph, Coin B in the first set comes closest to 50 percent, which is the theoretical chance of a heads or tails landing when the coin is balanced.

6. **B. 333.** Here, you're asked to solve a problem using basic operations. If Donna inhales for two steps and exhales for two steps, and each step is 27 inches long, then she inhales once for each 108 inches she covers: $27 \times 4 = 108$. In 1,000 yards (which equal 36,000 inches because there are 36 inches in a yard), she takes $36,000 / 108 = 333.3$ breaths, which rounds to 333.

7. **9.** The shape of an ice-cream cone is a cone, and the formula for determining the volume of a cone is $\frac{1}{3} \times \pi \times \text{radius}^2 \times \text{height}$, where π is approximately equal to 3.14. (This formula appears on the formula sheet.)

   To make the calculations simpler using the calculator, change the fractions to decimals:

   $2\frac{1}{2} = 2.5, 5\frac{1}{2} = 5.5$, and $\frac{1}{3} = 0.3333333$

   Now you have to insert the values from the question into the formula (remember that you find the radius by dividing the diameter by 2): Volume $= 0.3333333 \times 3.14 \times (2.5 / 2)^2 \times 5.5 = 8.9947896$, or 9.0 cubic inches, rounded to one decimal place.

8. **$2,030.** In this question, you're given more information than you need. You're given the dimensions of every room in the condo, but Singh doesn't want to carpet all of them. Because you can use the calculator in this part of the test, you can calculate an accurate answer. The first thing to do is to calculate the area of each of the rooms Singh wants to carpet with the formula for area: *Area = length × width*. (This formula is in the formula sheet.)

   Substituting the numbers from the table for each room, here are the areas you come up with:

   Living room: $20 \times 13 = 260$

   Dining room: $10 \times 8 = 80$

   Bedroom: $14 \times 13 = 182$

   Next, add the areas of the three rooms: $260 + 180 + 82 = 522$.

   Because the lengths and widths are in feet, the answer is in square feet, but the cost of the carpet is in square yards. To convert square feet into square yards, you divide by 9: $522 / 9 = 58$, which is the area in square yards.

   The carpet costs $35.00 a square yard, so you have to multiply the total area Singh wants to carpet by the cost per square yard: $58 \times \$35.00 = \$2,030$.

9. **C. $12,020.** If you want to use approximate values in this problem, you can say that the car depreciates about 4 cents, or $0.04, a mile over 100,000 miles. This car is about 37,000 miles over that milestone, which means it's depreciated about $0.04 \times 37,000 = \$1480$. You can then subtract this value from the book value$13,500 - \$1,480 = \$12,020$.

10. **$11,907.** Using the same calculation you use in Question 9 but with exact values, you get $13,500 - (0.043 \times 37,046) = 11,907.02$ or $11,907, when rounded to the nearest dollar.

11. **B. 5.8.** This problem tests your skills in geometry and involves similarity of geometrical figures. To draw a scale drawing, the lengths and widths must be reduced in the same ratio. Use a simple proportion. With x as the drawing height, 11 as the drawing length, 9 as the actual height, and 17 as the actual length, you can write $\frac{x}{11} = \frac{9}{17}$.

    By cross-multiplying, you get $17x = 9(11)$. This simplifies to 5.8 when rounded.

12. A. 28. This question tests your skills in algebra by asking you to evaluate a term in an equation. The equation for the slope, m, of a line is $m = \dfrac{y_2 - y_1}{x_2 - x_1}$

Substituting the values into the equation, you get $0.75 = \dfrac{36 - 24}{x_2 - 12}$

Then, because 0.75 is the same as 3/4, you can say the following: $\dfrac{3}{4} = \dfrac{12}{x_2 - 12}$

Cross-multiplying, you get the following: $x_2 = \dfrac{84}{3} = 28$

13. B. 1.1. From the table, you can see that of the three countries, the highest literacy rate is Russia at 99.4 percent, and the lowest is China at 90.9 percent.

If you divide the literacy rate for Russia by that for China, you get $99.4 / 90.9 = 1.093509351$ or 1.1, rounded to one decimal place, which is Choice (B).

14. B. 2. According to the table, the literacy rate of the United States is 99.0. Only two countries have literacy rates higher than that, Russia (99.4) and Cuba (99.8). As you examine these statistics, keep in mind that literacy is difficult to measure and other sources might calculate them differently.

15. C. 7^3. The volume of a cube is determined by the formula $\text{length} \times \text{width} \times \text{height}$. For this cube, the formula becomes $7 \times 7 \times 7$, which can be simplified to 7^3 (pronounced "seven cubed").

16. B. 1. Peter's average grade is $(81 + 76 + 92 + 87 + 79 + 83) / 6 = 83$. Because Peter's average grade is 83, it is one point higher than the school's, so the answer is Choice (B), 1.

17. A. 42. This question is a test of your skills in data analysis. You already determined that his average grade is 83. He's failing to meet his goal by 7 percent. Each percent is equivalent to one point per subject, or $7 \times 6 = 42$ points.

18. 16.6. This question tests your skills in measurement involving volume of a cylinder. The volume of a cylinder is calculated using the formula, $V_{\text{cylinder}} = \pi \times \text{radius}^2 \times \text{height}$. Substitute the numbers from the question into the formula:

$$\text{Volume of cylinder} = 3.14 \times \left(2.1\frac{1}{2}\right)^2 \times 4.8 = 16.61688 \text{ or } 16.6$$

19. $1,584. Using the formula for simple interest given on the formula sheet, you can calculate the simple interest over 4 years, and then add the principal amount. The principal amount is $1,500 because she lets her son spend $74 of the money right away. The total interest for 4 years, using the formula, would be $1500 \times 0.014 \times 4 = \$84$. The interest added to the principal would total $1,584 ($1,500 + $84 = $1,584$).

20. B. 3 times larger. This question tests your knowledge of equations by asking you to analyze how a change in one quantity in an exponential equation, $E = mc^2$, results in a change in another quantity. The variation between E and m in this function is linear and direct, which means that whatever happens to m also happens to E. If m is 3 times larger, so is E.

21. B. 24. This question tests your ability to figure out the areas of two different objects and combine them. The answer should be expressed in square feet, but the dimensions of the chair mat are in inches. When you convert the dimensions of the chair mat into feet, you quickly realize that the rug and the chair mat are the same size: 36 inches by 48 inches = 3 feet by 4 feet. Then, calculating the dimensions of the two is easy: $2(3 \times 4) = 24$. Choice A is the area of only one of the items. Choice (C) is the area of one of the items in square inches. Choice (D) is the area of both items expressed in square inches. Always make sure you express the answer in the unit of measure that the question specifies. In this case, the unit of measure is square feet.

22. **A. 57.** Using the formula for the volume of a cylinder, you can figure out the volume of each tank and then subtract the volume of the smaller tank from the volume of the larger tank. The volume of the smaller tank is $\pi \times 3^2 \times 4 = 113.04$. The volume of the larger tank is $\pi \times 3^2 \times 6 = 169.56$. Rounding to the nearest cubic foot and then subtracting the volume of the smaller tank from that of the larger tank, you get $170 - 113 = 57$.

23. **D. 10.** This question tests your knowledge of equations. Create an equation in which x is the number of people with both a sore throat and a cold. Thus $(15 - x)$ is the number of students with a sore throat only and $(25 - x)$ is the number of students with a cold only. The total number of students with a sore throat only, with a cold only, and with both is equal to 30. So $(15 - x) + (25 - x) + x = 30$. Solve for x: $x = 10$.

24. **(–3,4)**

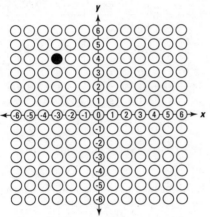

25. **110.** This question tests your knowledge of math basics. This item is a good one to calculate quickly using mental math. You know that the grant will cover 75% of the cost of the course, so the hospital will absorb 25 percent, which is one-fourth. The course costs $40 per person, and one-fourth of $40 is $10. The information says that 11 parents will take the course, so the total amount that the hospital will absorb is 10×11, or $110.

26. **B. 7.** To calculate the total cost of the computer, you have to add the purchase cost plus the overhead $(299 + 48 + 2 = 349)$. Because each computer costs Jerry $349 and he sells it for $449, he has a net profit of $100 $(\$449 - \$349 = \$100)$ per computer.

   To calculate the number of computers Jerry would have to sell to make $700 a week, divide the amount of profit he wants to make ($700) by the profit on each computer ($100): $\frac{700}{100} = 7$

27. **$240.** The minimum charge for repairing a computer is $45 and each additional hour costs $30. Jerry repaired 4 computers and had 2 additional hours. You can solve this problem by writing the equation $4(\$45) + 2(\$30) = \$240$.

28. **A. Indonesia.** The country with the largest installed capacity is Indonesia, with 2.1 gigawatts. The remaining countries have smaller installed capacities.

29. **A. 0.2 gigawatts.** The next country in the list is New Zealand, with an installed capacity of 1.0. The difference between the two countries' installed capacity is $1.0 - 0.8 = 0.2$.

30. D. $57.60. You can answer this question by figuring out the costs of the old car per week and the costs of the new car per week, by dividing the miles driven by the mileage and multiplying by the cost per gallon. For example, that week, Elayne drove 150 miles in the city, so she spent 150 miles / 18 mpg × $2.70 = $22.50 on gas for her old car. You can make a chart like this one:

Day	City Driving	Cost for Old Car	Cost for New Car	Highway Driving	Cost for Old Car	Cost for New Car
Monday	30			5		
Tuesday	35			25		
Wednesday	25			10		
Thursday	30			20		
Friday	20			5		
Saturday	5			70		
Sunday	5			75		
TOTAL	150	$22.50	$4.05	210	$47.25	$8.10

The savings are the difference between the old car's costs and the new car's costs:

$$\left(\$22.50 + \$47.25\right) - \left(\$4.05 + \$8.10\right) = \$57.60$$

Because this item requires a lot of calculations, it might be one to flag and return to later, to avoid spending too much time on it.

TIP

31. D. Dealer D. This question tests your ability to use number operations. If you adapt the table, it looks like this:

	Interest Rate Offered	Equivalent Rate
A	Prime + 2%	$8\%\left(6\% + 2\%\right)$
B	7.5%	7.5%
C	1/2 of prime + 5%	$8\%\left(\left[\frac{1}{2} \text{ of } 6\%\right] + 5\% = 3\% + 5\%\right)$
D	Prime + 20% of prime for administrative costs	$7.2\%\left(6\% + \left[20\% \text{ of } 6\%\right] = 6\% + 1.2\%\right)$

Dealer D is offering the best terms for financing the car.

32. 75%. The question tells you that 9 of 12 people that Harry asked had watched the sitcom. Therefore, to calculate, divide 9 by 12: $9 \div 12 = 0.75$. Then, convert that number to a percentage by moving the decimal point two places to the left and adding a percentage sign: 75%. Always be careful to include the correct numbers and symbols when answering questions like this one.

33. D. 5 ¾ inches. You can solve the problem by multiplying fractions, but for this problem, it's probably easier to convert the fractions to decimals ($1\frac{3}{4} = 1.75$) and use your calculator. To do this, multiply the dimension of the books by 3 and multiply the dimension of the packaging by two, and add the two numbers: $\left(1.75 \times 3\right) + 2(0.25) = 5.75$.

34. **A. 20 pounds.** This question tests your skills in using estimation to solve a problem involving number operations. If there are about 40 weeks in the 10 months from September to June, then each of them could lose about 20 pounds (40×0.5).

35. **C. 12.** This question tests your skills in measurement to solve a problem involving uniform rates. If Mary can drive at an average speed of 45 miles per hour, it will take her $900 / 45 = 20$ hours to drive the 900 miles. Samantha, on the other hand, will travel at 300 miles per hour on a plane for a flying time of $900 / 300 = 3$ hours, but she will add
$45 + 75$ (1 hour and 15 minutes is 75 minutes) $+ 180$ (that's 3 hours in minutes) $= 300$ minutes, which is 5 hours $(300/60)$. Her total trip would be 3 hours $+ 5$ hours $= 8$ hours in duration, or 12 hours shorter than Mary's trip, not counting time for breaks or sleep.

36. **C. east and north in 3rd quarter.** Looking at the graph, in the third quarter, the east plant seems to have produced twice (ratio of 2:1) as many hats as the north plant.

37. **B. Tina will likely live longer than her brother Trent.** This question tests your ability to interpret data presented in a table. The table shows that for people of age 30, women will live longer than men, which is Choice (B). Choice (C) is not possible because the question states that they are unidentical twins. Option (D) gives Trent's life expectancy, and so is incorrect.

Read the answers as carefully as you read the questions. Women may have a greater life expectancy, but that doesn't necessarily mean that they age better or worse than men. That's a topic for another question.

38. **D. 81.6.** This question asks you to find the age a 20-year-old woman will live to on average. Given that the table shows life expectancy for 20-year-old females to be 61.6 years, the average woman will live to be $20 + 61.6 = 81.6$ years old. Choices (A) and (B) show the number of years a male and female would have to live at age 20. Choice (C) gives the age a male of 20 would likely live to. Always read each question carefully to make sure you answer that question, and not a different one.

39. **C. The selling price will go up.** This question tests your skills in analysis by asking you to explain how a change in one quantity affects another quantity. The price of the article is set by a linear function involving the overhead (the costs of doing business that don't change with how many products you sell — things like rent, utility bills, salaries, and so on), the cost of acquiring the item, and the profit. If any of these numbers go up, the selling price goes up, too, which is why the correct answer is Choice (C).

40. **8.** This question tests your skills in number operations by asking you to write a large number in scientific notation. To write 328,000,000 in scientific notation starting with 3.28×10, you count the number of places to the left that the decimal point needs to move. That number is 8: 3.28×10^8.

41. **D. Karry has a higher average time.** This question tests your skills in statistics by asking you to compare averages. Harry's average time is $(15.6 + 14.9 + 16.0 + 15.8 + 16.1)/5 = 15.68$. Karry's average time is $(15.9 + 16.1 + 15.8 + 16.2 + 14.8)/5 = 15.76$. Karry has a higher average time (which means that Harry is slightly faster).

42. **B. 200.** This question tests your skills in measurement by asking you to solve a problem involving volume. If the total floor area is 1,400 square feet and the ceilings are 9 feet high, the volume of the apartment is $1,400 \times 9 = 12,600$ cubic feet. If the air system can replace 63 cubic feet per minute, it requires $12,600 / 63 = 200$ minutes to withdraw and replace all the air, which is Choice (B). The other answer choices are wrong, but Choices (A) and (C) are close enough that if you tried to do the question using approximations, you might select the wrong answer choice.

When some of the answer choices are close in value, it's usually a good idea to do the calculations instead of estimating.

43. **D. 4 p.m. on Tuesday.** This question tests your skills in measurement and geometry. You have to solve a problem involving uniform rates. Peter's swimming pool holds $45 \times 12 \times 4 = 2,160$ cubic feet of water. He can pump 9 cubic feet per minute. It would take him $2,160 / 9 = 240$ minutes to empty the pool. To get from hours to minutes, divide by 60 (because every hour has 60 minutes). So it would take Peter $240 / 60 = 4$ hours to empty his pool. If he started pumping at noon on Tuesday, Peter would finish four hours later, which is at 4 p.m. on Tuesday.

44. **B. $250.** This question tests your skills in algebra by asking you to use an average number to calculate a missing value. If Mohammed earned an average of $420 for four weeks, he earned a total of $420 \times 4 = \$1,680$ for the four-week period. In the other three weeks, he earned $\$480 + \$400 + \$550 = \$1,430$. In the missing week, he earned $\$1,680 - \$1,430 = \$250$.

45. **$457.** This question tests your skills in number operations. Georgia spent $\$500 - \$126 = \$374$ using the gift card, plus $83.00 in credit card purchases, so she spent $\$374.00 + \$83.00 = \$457.00$.

46. **B. a rectangle with a circle on each side.** This question tests your skills in geometry and spatial visualization. If you cut open and almost remove the ends of the can, open the can along the seam, and then lay it flat, you'd have a rectangle and two circles, one on each side of the rectangle. Questions of this type require the use of imagination. Imagine opening a can, cutting the seam, and making it lay flat.

47. **B. she would spend more money on fuel.** This question tests your skills by asking you to read carefully to answer a question. If Sonya's car uses gasoline in direct proportion to her speed, then the faster she goes, the more gas she uses. The more gas she uses, the more it costs her to drive, which is an economic consequence — so she would spend more money on fuel.

48. $(0, -4)$. If the center is at the origin and the diameter (which is twice the radius) is 8 units, the circle will intersect each of the axes (that's the plural of axis) at a distance of 4 units from the center. Therefore, it intersects the negative y-axis at $(0, -4)$.

49. **D. 21.** If the gauge reads 1/8 full, it has $24 / 8 = 3$ gallons of fuel left in it. Because it holds 24 gallons, it needs $24 - 3 = 21$ gallons to fill it.

50. **B. 5.** To solve these equations, you need to subtract one from the other and end up with just the ys. To get rid of one of the variables using this method, you need to have the same coefficient in front of the variable you're planning to eliminate. (The coefficient is a fancy word for the number in front of a variable. In the expression $4x$, the coefficient is 4.) You can multiply each term of an equation by a number and still maintain the equation. Here's how.

Multiply the second equation by 2 and leave the first equation as it is:

$$\left(4x + 2y = 20\right) = 4x + 2y = 20$$
$$2\left(2x + 6y = 35\right) = 4x + 12y = 70$$

Subtract, and you get $10y = 50$; $y = 5$.

Note that you can also multiply the second equation by –2 and add the two equations together. Either way gets you the same answer.

Answer Key

1.	A	18.	16.6	35.	C
2.	0.6	19.	A	36.	C
3.	A	20.	B	37.	B
4.	*BC*	21.	B	38.	D
5.	B	22.	A	39.	C
6.	B	23.	D	40.	8
7.	9	24.	(–3,4)	41.	D
8.	$2,030	25.	110	42.	B
9.	C	26.	B	43.	D
10.	$11,907	27.	$240	44.	B
11.	B	28.	B	45.	$457
12.	A	29.	A	46.	B
13.	B	30.	D	47.	B
14.	B	31.	D	48.	(0,–4)
15.	C	32.	75%	49.	D
16.	B	33.	D	50.	B
17.	A	34.	A		

8

The Part of Tens

IN THIS PART . . .

Check out ten tips for preparing for the GED test in the weeks, days, and hours leading up to the test.

Plan your path to surviving on the day of the test and maximizing your scores.

Discover all the things you can do with your GED diploma after you pass all the sections of the GED test, including using it as decoration in your home or office.

Chapter **35**

Ten Surefire Ways to Prepare for the GED Test

Of course you want to do well on the GED test — otherwise, you wouldn't be reading this book. But you also know that your time is limited, so this chapter gives you ten ideas and tips for preparing for the test, from selecting the right test-taking time to working through practice tests and getting familiar with the computer format, so you can do your very best on test day. These tips are all part of preparing for the big day. You want to be able to arrive at the test site with the least amount of worry and stress. Removing as many sources of stress as possible before that day will make everything go much smoother.

Strategizing Where and When You Will Test

An important decision you need to make is whether to take the test at home or at a testing center. Although testing at home is convenient, your home has to meet a number of requirements. At the same time, with the online-proctored test, you have to use the onscreen calculator and whiteboard. If you want to use the erasable whiteboard and your own TI-30XS calculator, you have to test at a testing center. Many test-takers find having those tools helpful, especially for the writing and the math tests. Remember, you can take some of the tests at home and others at a testing center. For example, you might take the math test at a testing center so you can bring your handheld calculator, and take the others at home. For complete criteria on selecting where to test, see Chapter 1.

Once you know how you will test, you need to figure out when. Why take time to prepare for the GED test when you have a million other things to do? Sure, you probably live a busy life all the time, but do your best to find a period in your busy schedule when you can concentrate on preparing for and passing the test. You can take all the tests in one day if you want. If you do so in a testing center, you will only have 10 minutes between each test. Most people spread the tests over several days, weeks, or even months, and schedule them as they feel ready. You can make your own decision depending on where you live, the time you have available, your readiness for each test, and other factors.

No matter when or where you test, you schedule your tests on the GED Testing Service's website, ged.com. If you decide to take the online-proctored test, you must take and pass the GED Ready Official Practice Test in order to sign up. Even if you test at a testing center, taking the GED Ready test is a good idea, because if you pass it, you will probably pass the actual test. Choose the test date wisely. If you have enough time to prepare, you'll do well. It's just that simple. Select dates that give you enough time to prepare, but not so far in the future that you'll retire before you take the test. If you need accommodations for special needs, make sure you address them when you sign up. Check out Chapter 1 for more information on scheduling the test.

Taking Practice Tests

Taking practice tests before you take the actual test will help you get familiar with the test format, the types of questions you'll be asked, and what subject areas you may need to work on. Take as many practice tests as you can before test day, and take them under the same conditions as the actual test (and be sure to practice with the time limits, too).

You can find two complete practice tests for each section of the GED in this book (check out Parts 6 and 7), as well as a complete online test. Still want more practice? The GED Testing Service also provides some free practice tests at www.gedtestingservice.com/educators/freepracticetest. Before you schedule your test, you should definitely take the GED Ready Practice Test on the GED Testing Service's website. It will tell you if you are ready to test or you need more preparation. It will give you an estimated score and a rating of red (not likely to pass), yellow (too close to call), and green (likely to pass), along with detailed feedback on skills to review. If you have to repeat a test, you will also get detailed feedback on areas for improvement.

Studying Subject-Matter Books

If you've taken all the practice tests in this book and reviewed the answer explanations (see Parts 6 and 7) and completed the online practice test, you may have identified key areas in which you're lacking skills. Although those practice tests can't help you predict your score on the real GED test, they can help prepare you for the actual test and give you a general idea of your strengths and weaknesses. If you didn't get at least 70 percent correct on any of the sample test sections, then you need to work on your test-taking skills and the subject matter.

TIP

Visit your local bookstore or library (so you don't end up spending all your hard-earned money) for the many *For Dummies* books that are meant just for students. For example, consider the following fun, interesting, and easy-to-read books (all published by John Wiley & Sons, Inc.) that can either improve your skills or simply make you more familiar with (and, therefore, more comfortable with) certain subjects:

>> *Algebra I For Dummies,* 2nd Edition, by Mary Jane Sterling

>> *Algebra II For Dummies,* 2nd Edition, by Mary Jane Sterling

>> *Anatomy and Physiology For Dummies,* 3rd Edition, by Erin Odya and Maggie A. Norris

>> *Astronomy For Dummies,* 4th Edition, by Stephen P. Maran

>> *Biology For Dummies,* 3rd Edition, by René Fester Kratz

>> *The Civil War For Dummies,* by Keith D. Dickson

- *Congress For Dummies,* by David Silverberg
- *English Grammar For Dummies,* 3rd Edition, by Geraldine Woods
- *Everyday Math For Dummies,* by Charles Seiter
- *Geometry For Dummies,* 3rd Edition, by Mark Ryan
- *Politics For Dummies,* 3rd Edition, by Ann M. DeLaney
- *U.S. History For Dummies,* 4th Edition, by Steve Wiegand
- *World History For Dummies,* 2nd Edition, by Peter Haugen

To find other helpful *For Dummies* books, check out www.dummies.com.

In many ways, the GED is primarily a reading test. Strong reading skills will help you raise your score, so consider ramping up your reading. Choose content you will enjoy and that is related to the test. Try reading a few short stories or even a novel of interest to you. Read as many nonfiction articles in magazines, newspapers, or online as you can. Try to vary the content of your reading. Choose articles on current events, history, politics, and science.

Enrolling in a GED Test Preparation Class

If you like to interact with other people and prefer a teacher to guide you through your preparation, consider taking a *GED test preparation class* — a class designed to prepare you to take and pass the GED test. Costs for these classes vary widely, and many are offered free of charge. Consider whether you learn better on your own or in a group, and whether you have the time to take a class, and make your decision accordingly.

To find a class in your location, create an account at the GED Testing Service website, ged.com. It will help you find adult education programs in your area where you can prepare for free. You can also ask around. Talk to people you know who have taken the GED test, or people at your local GED testing center. You may also be able to take online courses (where you do your assignments on your own and contact your instructor via the Internet), which may be a good choice for you.

You may also find that some subject areas, like math, require more help. Many people take a class for math and writing, and prepare for the other tests on their own.

After deciding on a few potential classes, visit the class or instructor, if possible. Make sure that their teaching style matches your learning style. The preparation class will be a big investment of your time, so shop around wisely.

After finding a preparation class, consider joining or forming a study group with other GED test-takers. You can help each other study and ask each other questions about different aspects of the test. Be wary before committing to a group, though: If the other group members' idea of studying is to party for three hours to get ready for five minutes of study, and you want to study for three hours and then spend five minutes on social activity, you won't be happy. Talk to the other members of the study group and find out what their goals are for the group. If you can find a suitable group, make a commitment and enjoy your new friends.

Setting a Time and a Place to Study

Whether you study on your own, with a group, or with an instructor, find a regular place to study, and set up a study schedule. If possible, set up an area on a desk or table in your home and keep all your study materials there. That way, you don't have to hunt for them every time you want to study. If you can't do that, keep all your study materials together in a box or bag. If you decide to study at the public library, you might invest in an inexpensive backpack to store and carry your materials.

Next, make a schedule. Keep your work schedule and other responsibilities in mind. The best time for you to study may be early in the morning, or at night after your kids go to bed. Whatever you decide, stick to your schedule as if your grade depends on it (and, by the way, it does!). Study regularly by doing the following:

1. **Take practice tests to find out in which subject area(s) you struggle.**

   Check each answer on the practice tests, and read all the answer explanations. Make sure you understand your mistakes.

2. **Focus your studies on the subject area(s) you're weakest in.**

3. **Take more practice tests.**

Getting Familiar with the Computer and Calculator

On the real GED test, you'll be typing on a keyboard, using a mouse to select or drag items, and reading and digesting information on the screen. You'll also be using an onscreen or real scientific calculator. The day of the test isn't the time to get familiar with these tools. Be sure to get familiar with them before the test. You can get started by reading the information in the Appendix. If you don't have a computer, most public libraries offer computer access. Also consider taking a basic keyboarding class or computer literacy class at a local library, adult education center, or community center. These classes are usually free, and they're useful if you're a novice.

Make sure you are familiar with the layout of the screens on the test. Luckily, the screen layout is the same whether you test at home or at a testing center. (Check out Chapter 2 for information on screen layout of each test.) Then use the free test at www.gedtestingservice.com/educators/freepracticetest. Finally, the GED Ready Practice Test will let you know for sure whether you have the computer skills you need to succeed.

Get familiar with the TI-30XS MultiView calculator, too — the handheld or onscreen version, whichever you will be using. It's a scientific calculator with a lot of functions, not all of which you will use on the test. The GED Testing Service's website, ged.com, has a number of calculator resources, including a reference sheet that shows you all the features you need to know and an actual onscreen emulator you can practice with. If you test at a testing center, you can use the onscreen version or bring your own TI-30XS MultiView calculator. If you test at home, you have to use the onscreen version. Prepare with the calculator you will actually use — the onscreen or the real one. You don't want to be fumbling on test day.

Preparing for the Test in Your Mind

To make yourself less anxious about the GED test, visualize yourself taking the test on test day. In your mind, see yourself enter the room, sit down at the computer, and reach out to the keyboard. Go through this routine in your mind until it begins to feel familiar. Then see yourself starting the test and scrolling through questions (questions that are likely familiar to you because you've taken many practice tests). See yourself noting the easy questions and beginning to answer them. By repeating this visual sequence over and over again in your mind, it becomes familiar — and what's familiar isn't nearly as stressful as what's unfamiliar. (This process, by the way, is called *visualization* and really works at putting your mind at ease for the test.) And if you are taking the test at home, you can set up your test area and practice this routine for real!

Getting Good Rest the Week before the Test

As part of your plan for preparation, include some social time, some down time, and plenty of rest time because everyone performs better when well rested. In fact, your memory and ability to solve problems improve remarkably when you're properly rested.

REMEMBER

Whatever you do, don't panic about your upcoming test and stay up all night (or every night for a week) right before the test. Last-minute cramming rarely works. Instead, plan your last week before the test so you get plenty of sleep and are mentally and physically prepared for the test.

Making Sure You Have Proper Identification

To take the GED test, you need an acceptable picture ID. Because what's *acceptable* may vary from state to state, check with your state GED office or your local testing center (or check the information they send you after you register) before the test.

REMEMBER

The picture ID required is usually a driver's license, state ID card, passport, or other government-issued ID (including a *matricula consular* issued by a Mexican consulate in the United States); at any rate, it's usually something common and easy to get. Just check in advance for what's required, and make sure you have it ready and with you on test day.

Setting Up Your Test Area or Getting to the Test Site

On certain days and occasions, you just don't want to be late, get lost, or have a problem. These days include your wedding day, an important interview, and the day you're taking the GED test. So be prepared, whether you are taking the online-proctored test or testing at a test center.

If you are taking the test at home, both your computer and the room you test in have to meet special requirements. Don't leave this to the last minute. Check the latest requirements on the ged.com website and the email you receive when you sign up for the test. The week before the test, make sure you can meet all the requirements. Check again the night before the test, too. You can view all the requirements at app.ged.com/portal/aboutOnVueTest.

If you are going to a testing center to take the test, make sure you are prepared. Make sure you plan a route from your home or job, or wherever you'll be commuting from, to the testing site. Map it out and practice getting to the test center. Prepare everything you will need, including your ID, your TI-30XS calculator, and your glasses if you need them for the test. If you're driving to the test center, make sure you know where to park. Arrive early enough that you can be sure to find a spot. Remember, you can't leave your car in the middle of the street if you expect to drive it home, too!

TIP

Leave extra time for surprises. You never know when your street could be declared the site for an elephant crossing or when a herd of oxen decides to meander across your road. The crowd, oxen, and elephants could make you late for the tests unless you allow yourself some extra time.

Chapter **36**

Ten Tips for Surviving Test Day

B esides all those hours of studying, to succeed on the GED test, you also need to know what to do on the day of the test and how to stay focused through each test section. In this chapter, I give you ten quick and easy ways to help you survive the GED test.

Wear Comfortable Clothes

Consider the following situation. You're about to sit in front of a computer screen for at least 70 minutes (both the Mathematical Reasoning and Reasoning through Language Arts tests are longer). You'll be sitting on what will probably be an uncomfortable chair. The room may be too warm or too cold.

Choosing from the following answers, what's the appropriate dress for the GED test?

(A) formal dress because this is an important occasion

(B) a parka over a bathing suit because one can never predict the weather

(C) something very comfortable so you can concentrate on the test

(D) your best clothes because you need to impress others

If you picked Choice (C), you have the right idea. Dress comfortably and in layers. All your concentration should be on the test, not on your clothes, not on the people around you, and not on the conditions in the room.

Arrive at the Test Site Early

Consider the following two characters, Paula Prepared and Peter Procrastinator. Both have prepared to take the GED test, but they have their own personalities and individual quirks. On the day of the test:

>> Peter drives up to the test center 5 minutes before the beginning of the test and feels nothing but panic. He can't find legal parking and barely enters the testing center in time to begin the test. He's so distracted that he takes 15 minutes to calm down, and by then, the test is well underway.

>> Paula arrives 40 minutes early. She has time to get a drink of water, use the restroom, and relax before the test. Sitting calmly at the computer, Paula gets comfortable, arranges the keyboard and mouse, and begins the test in a relaxed manner.

Who would you rather be?

Here's something else to consider: If you're late to the test site, you may not be allowed to enter, you'll likely have to reschedule the test for another time, and you'll probably have to pay again for the test. Who needs all this grief? All you have to do to prevent this tragedy is to arrive early for the test, which, contrary to popular belief, isn't as difficult as it may seem. You can plan ahead by checking out some route maps to the test site on the Internet. Or look into the schedules for your local public transportation services. If you decide to drive yourself, check the availability of parking and even practice your route to the test site (see Chapter 35). Do your research, leave extra time for unforeseen situations, and arrive early and ready for the test.

It pays to be early if you test at home, too. You can check in for the test as early as 30 minutes before the time of your appointment. Once you check in, you will be placed in a queue for the first available proctor.

TIP

It pays to have everything organized the night before — your ID, the clothes you will wear, the directions to the test center, your TI-30XS calculator (if you are testing at a test center), a nutritious snack to eat before the test or during a break, your glasses (if you wear them), and so on. If you test at home, you can prepare the room, too. You don't want to be rushing the day of the test.

Keep Conversations Light and Short

A little bit of stress is normal when you walk into a test. So the last thing you want to do is increase your stress level by getting into a conversation and losing your focus.

Although it may seem antisocial, keep conversations to a minimum just before the test. If you want to exchange pleasantries about the weather, go ahead. If you want to arrange to go for coffee after the test, plan away. If you want to get into a serious conversation about how everything you've done to this point will only guarantee failure, run away as fast as you can and don't talk to anyone! If you've prepared, you're ready. Listen to the voice in your head that says you're ready, and don't let anyone at the testing center stress you out. If someone tries to corner you with conversation about how hard the test is or how they had to take out a mortgage to pay for repeated failures, pretend you only speak a rare dialect of Klingon, go to the restroom, or start coughing. Nobody wants to start up a conversation with a Klingon-speaking, contagious person with a weak bladder. Or you may want to try some more plausible excuses, but whatever you do, escape!

Arrange Your Work Area

You're going to be sitting in front of a computer screen for at least 70 minutes. Before starting the test, be sure to adjust the screen, the keyboard, the mouse, and the chair to comfortable positions. The last person to use that computer may have been 6 feet 10 inches with arms like a gorilla. What was comfortable for him likely won't do for you. If you are left-handed, you may need to rearrange your keyboard and mouse. If you notice any problems, let someone know right away. You want to get rid of any and all distractions, so taking a minute to adjust the computer station to suit you is well worth the effort. After you start the test, you won't have the time to fuss around. There is one adjustment you can't make until the test starts: you can enlarge the size of the font. That can help some people a lot!

Relax and Breathe

Feeling a bit of stress before taking the GED test is normal. Psychologists even say that a little bit of stress can help you function better. But it's a balancing act; you don't want to become so stressed that you can't think.

Here are some techniques that may help you relax before you take the GED test, or anytime you're feeling a bit stressed:

>> **Think positively.** Instead of listing all the negative things that may happen, think about the positive things that can come of this situation. You *can* pass the GED test. You *can* go on to college. You *can* get a great job. You *can* receive a surprise inheritance — well, maybe that's going too far. Don't be greedy. Just be positive!

>> **Breathe deeply.** The first thing to remember during a stressful situation is to breathe. The second thing is to breathe deeply. Follow these steps:

- **Find your diaphragm.**

  No, not a *diagram* — although you could use a diagram to find your diaphragm. Your *diaphragm* is that flat muscle under your ribcage that fills your lungs with air. It's above your navel.

- **Breathe in and make your diaphragm rise as much as you can.**

- **Exhale slowly.**

- **Repeat, making your diaphragm rise higher each time.**

  After you see how this process relaxes you, try it just before each test section.

>> **Count backward from ten (in your head).** You can do this before any test, not just the math one. Start to count backward from ten with no thoughts in your mind. If a thought, even a teeny one, enters your mind, you have to start over. See how many times it takes to count from ten to one without a single thought entering your mind.

  Don't do this *during* the test, only *before* to help relax you. This exercise could eat up precious time if you tried it during one of the tests.

>> **Clench and unclench your fists.** This simple relaxation technique involves your hands and reminds you to relax:

- **Sit with your hands in front of you.**

- **Inhale deeply as you slowly clench your fists.**

- **After your fists are clenched, slowly exhale as you unclench them.**

You may have to repeat this process several times, but within a couple of repetitions, you'll begin to feel relaxed.

>> **Stare out a window.** Stare out a window, far into the distance. Try to see a point beyond the horizon. As you do, feel your eyes relax. Let your eyes relax until the feeling spreads to every part of your body. Enjoy the feeling long enough to let go of all the stress that has built up. When you're calm and full of energy, return to the test.

If your testing room doesn't have a window, stare at a blank wall and envision your favorite relaxing scene. Don't close your eyes, though. If you're the least bit tired or stressed, you may fall asleep and not wake up until the test is over.

>> **Talk to yourself silently in the third person.** Tell yourself that you are prepared and can relax and do well. The third person allows you to detach your stress from yourself.

Stay Focused on the Task at Hand

An archer who wants to hit the bull's-eye keeps all their mental faculties focused on the goal at hand. Nobody ever hit the center of the target daydreaming about the next social gathering. For this reason, put your mind on a leash; don't let it wander during the test. Letting your mind wander back to the greatest vacation you ever had can be very relaxing, but letting it wander during a test can be a disaster. You want your mind sharp, keen, and focused before and during the test, so concentrate on the task at hand — doing your best and passing the GED test.

TIP

Be sure to get plenty of sleep in the nights and weeks before the test. If you're well rested, you'll have an easier time focusing on each item and answering it correctly. Also, if you're planning to take the test in the morning, then in the week before the test, set your alarm to awaken you at the same time you'll need on exam day.

Look at Only Your Test

If there were a Biggest Mistake Award for test takers, it'd go to someone who looks at their neighbor's computer screen during the test. This action is called cheating and is a very serious matter. Not only will you be asked to leave the testing center, but you may have to wait for several months to a year before you're allowed to schedule another test. So keep your eyes on your own test. More than likely, your neighbor will have a different test anyway.

If you take the online-proctored test, follow all the instructions carefully. In particular, make sure that preparation materials are put away and small electronics are out of reach.

WARNING

Don't even give the slightest hint that you may be looking at someone else's work. The test proctor probably won't care about what you were actually doing; what they'll see is you looking in the general direction of another person's computer, which is considered cheating.

Start with the Easy Questions

As you begin the test, start with the easy questions — the ones you know you can do. As soon as the test questions come up on the computer screen, scroll through them quickly, identify the easy ones, and do those items first. Then you'll be ready to tackle the other questions in a relaxed, confident mood. Use the Flag feature and Review Screen to help you. Flag answers that you are unsure about and skip items that are hard or time-consuming. The Review Screen will let you quickly return to these items when you are ready to tackle them.

Write Clearly and Carefully

Following a few tips can make writing the essay easier. Take time to prepare your ideas using the onscreen whiteboard or the erasable tablet provided at the testing center. Your responses will be evaluated on clarity as well as accuracy, so organize your ideas before you write. As you write, use complete sentences, but don't worry too much about small mistakes. Go back and review your spelling and grammar after you finish writing. And, finally, make sure you stay on topic; anything else will count against you.

Do Your Best, No Matter What

Not everyone passes the GED test the first time. If you've taken the test before and didn't pass, don't automatically think you're a failure — instead, see the situation as a learning experience. Use your last test as motivation to discover your academic weaknesses. Sometimes you can gain more from not succeeding than from succeeding. Whether you're taking the test for the first time or the third, focus on doing your best. You can find out how to sign up for a retake at ged.com.

TIP

After the test, give yourself a small reward. Whether it's an ice cream cone, a run in the park, or dinner with a loved one, do something nice for yourself. You deserve it! Remember to thank all the people who supported you along the way, too.

Chapter 37

Ten Ways to Use Your GED After You Pass the Test

Passing the GED test makes life more rewarding because it opens doors that you may not have even known were closed. You've probably already figured out why you want your GED; if not, this chapter shares ten great advantages the GED can give you.

Getting a Job

Many employers want to see a high-school diploma or its equivalent before they even consider giving you a job. In fact, a high-school diploma is often used as a screening tool for interviews. A GED allows you to jump this hurdle. It shows potential employers that you've mastered skills equal to most high-school graduates. It also shows determination and dedication — skills all employers look for. This accomplishment can help you get an interview, and, when the interviewer sees how brilliant you are, it can help you get a job. And to make that process easier for you, the GED Testing Service will automatically link your results to your transcript. After you send your results to an employer or college, it can link to a complete transcript and description of your achievements.

REMEMBER

The U.S. government, the country's largest employer, accepts a GED as equivalent to a high-school diploma. Who's going to argue with Uncle Sam?

Getting a Promotion

If you're already working, you want to show your supervisor that you're ready for a promotion. The GED says, "I worked hard for this diploma and achieved something special!" Passing the GED test helps you show your employer that you're ready to do the same — that is, work hard — on the job. It also shows that you've taken responsibility for your life and are ready to take on additional responsibility at work. Earning a GED gives you certification that shows you've mastered skills and are ready to master some more.

Updating Your Resume

Whether you've updated your resume lately or not, now is a great time to do so. In addition to adding your GED, you likely have more new skills and experiences that you can add, such as computer skills and calculator skills.

Whether your resume needs just a few tweaks or a complete overhaul, *Resumes For Dummies,* by Laura DeCarlo (John Wiley & Sons, Inc.), is a great resource.

TIP

When you update your resume or talk to employers about your GED, find ways to show how your new skills will make you a strong, effective employee. For example, your new writing skills can help you compose effective emails. Your new math skills can help you with reports. And your new critical thinking skills can help you solve complex problems.

Showing Others What You Can Achieve

When you earn your GED, you show the world what you accomplished — on your own. You show that you're an independent learner. You caught up with all your old high-school friends, and you did it on your own. All you needed was a bit of help and direction. Be as proud of your accomplishment as those high-school friends are proud of their achievement. Having completed your GED, now is the perfect time to visit old teachers and go to reunions to show your past acquaintances what you've accomplished. Sometimes I even think you should get to wear a badge that says, "GED — I Did It!" After all, being able to show others that you've accomplished something major, thanks to your own hard work and determination, is important — in both your personal and professional life.

Proving You're Ready for Further Education

After you master the skills required to earn your GED, you're ready to go on to the next step: a community college or a four-year college. Over 98 percent of colleges and universities in the United States accept the GED for admission, and over 60 percent of GED graduates go on to further education within three years of passing. If you score high enough, you can even qualify for college credit at many institutions. Not all schools require interviews for admissions, but if yours does, remind the interviewer that you're a mature student who has worked hard to get where you are. Emphasize the skills you've mastered by working in the real world, and explain how those skills make you a great candidate for college. To request a copy of your transcript to be sent to a college admissions office, go to the GED Testing Service's website, ged.com.

Setting an Example for Your Kids

If you're like most people, you want your kids (or grandkids) to be better educated and more successful than you were. As soon as you pass the GED test, you set the bar a little higher for them. Your accomplishment also reminds your kids that education is important — for you and, by your example, for them.

Enhancing Your Wall Décor and Social Media

You may already have interesting mementos of your life hanging on your wall, but what could be more exciting than your very own framed GED diploma? A diploma looks great on your wall because it represents all the hard work you put in to passing the test — not to mention your accomplishment in doing so. Soon after you pass, your state will send you an online or printed GED diploma. Procedures vary by state and change periodically, so check the GED Testing Service's website for details on your state. If you don't hang your certificate on your wall, keep it in a safe place. You never know when you will need it!

If you are big into social media, or even a social media influencer, you should check out the GED Testing Service's digital badges. You can place them on your accounts so that everyone can see!

TIP

If you plan to frame your GED certificate, make a few copies for prospective employers and colleges before you do so. Make copies of the transcript of your test results as well. That way, you're ready to include these copies with your job and college applications.

Making You Feel like Part of a Select Group

Earning your GED means that you've outperformed 40 percent of high-school seniors, which in itself is impressive. It also places you among great company. Judge Greg Mathis, Michael J. Fox, Christian Slater, and the late founder of Wendy's, Dave Thomas, are GED graduates. So are Chris Rock, D.L. Hughley, Angelina Jolie, and Waylon Jennings. Although no one can promise that passing the GED test will make you a show-business star or help you start a fast-food chain, it will make you feel very special. Who knows when you'll become famous enough to be listed in this section of a future edition?

Motivating Yourself

One thing about taking challenging tests is that you have to face the challenges they throw at you on your own. You can use the fact that you overcame those challenges, thanks to your hard work and determination, to motivate yourself in your future endeavors. If you successfully passed the GED test through rigid preparation and planning, nothing can stop you. After all, you've accomplished something not everyone can do. Enjoy the feeling you get from passing the GED test, and use it as you go on to bigger and better pursuits.

Improving Your Self-Esteem

When you pass the GED test, you're essentially a high-school graduate and can prove it (thanks to the handy diploma and transcript you receive upon passing the test). But the piece of paper is only concrete proof of your accomplishment. The real results are in your brain and in your own feelings about yourself. You need to remember that you passed the test by yourself — with a little help from preparation texts, perhaps — but the real work was yours. Remember the steps you took toward this accomplishment, and use that same approach to help you reach other goals. Remember that you were both the teacher and the learner. You deserve double credit for this major accomplishment. Let this accomplishment motivate you to your next challenge.

Appendix A

Practicing Basic Computer Skills for the GED Test

Whether you take the online-proctored GED test at home or the computer-based test at a testing center, you will take the GED test on a computer. You use the mouse to select the correct answer, you use the keyboard to type up your Extended Response essays, and you use the calculator and built-in formula sheet on-screen for the math and some science and social studies questions. Best of all, you get your results and a detailed breakdown of how you did within hours of completing the test.

Don't worry: Even if you're not familiar with using a computer, the test doesn't require you to be either an expert typist or an expert computer user. The GED Testing Service assures that even amateur users of computers won't be at any disadvantage in taking the test. However, it's to your advantage to practice your computer skills before test day so your unfamiliarity with the keyboard or mouse doesn't slow you down or frazzle you.

In this appendix, I walk you through the basic computer skills you need to know to take the computerized GED test. That includes using the mouse to click on the appropriate answer choice, to drag and drop items, or to manipulate text; getting familiar with the layout of the keyboard and some special keys you may need for typing in the basic word processor included on the test; and figuring out how to use the calculator, formulas menu, and symbols menu on-screen in the Mathematical Reasoning and Science test sections.

If you're unsure about how to do any of these skills, my advice is to practice, practice, practice. Working with any word processor on any computer will allow you to practice these skills. If you don't have a computer, check your local library, community college, or community center. These places often have computers available for public use, free of charge. They may even offer basic instructions. And if you find you need more computer keyboard practice, install one of the free or inexpensive typing tutors on your computer.

TIP

The GED Testing Service (ged.com) offers a free quarter-length test, which isn't scored, at https://ged.com/study/free_online_ged_test/. When you feel ready for the actual GED test, you can take the GED Ready Official Practice Test for a fee. It's required if you want to take the online-proctored test, and recommended for everyone else. It allows you to practice doing an online test under conditions similar to what you'll experience when taking the real test. It's worthwhile just to get familiar with the computer format alone.

Using a Mouse

The mouse skills you need to know when taking the GED test on a computer are pretty basic, and, no, they don't include figuring out how to put a tiny piece of cheese in a mousetrap without getting snapped yourself! We cover the basics of using a *computer* mouse in the following sections.

Making selections

The most basic skill for using a computer mouse is just knowing how to select the correct answer. On the GED test, you do so in one of two ways: point and click or drag and drop.

Point and click

In Figure A-1, you have a traditional multiple-choice question with four possible answers. To select an answer in this situation, you simply need to click on the correct choice. That means you need to move the mouse cursor (the pointer) over the spot for the correct answer and then click the left mouse button. If you change your mind, simply click on another answer choice to override your first selection. You can click on the different answer choices as often as you want; just make sure the one you want is selected before you move on to the next question.

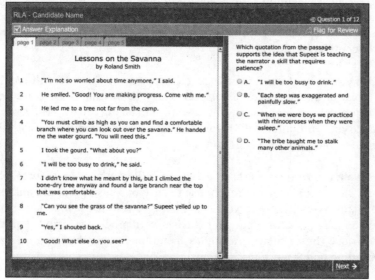

FIGURE A-1: Standard split-screen multiple-choice item.

© 2014 GED Testing Service LLC

Math and science hot-spot questions also require you to use your mouse to select an answer. In these questions, the computer screen has a series of virtual "hot spots" or areas representing the correct answer. When you click on one of these hot spots with your mouse, it registers your answer. The remainder of the screen is wrong, so be sure of your answer when you click and where. In the example hot-spot question in Figure A-2, you simply click above the number on the plot line for the point to appear. Hot-spot items are not on every test, so don't worry about these items too much.

Drag and drop

When you encounter a question that tells you to "drag and drop," you simply pick up an object with your mouse (by clicking on the object and holding the left mouse button down), drag it to where you want it, and then drop it (release the mouse button) in that new location. See Figure A-3 for the drag-and-drop feature the GED test employs.

Moving around the page

The sample screen in Figure A-4 includes several tabs at the top of the text side of the screen. These tabs indicate that the text you're expected to read covers more than one screen page. Recognizing these tabs and what they represent is important because you need to read all the material before you answer the question.

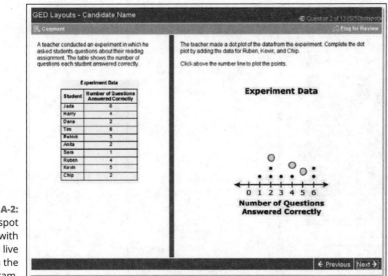

FIGURE A-2: Hot-spot item with virtual live spots on the diagram.

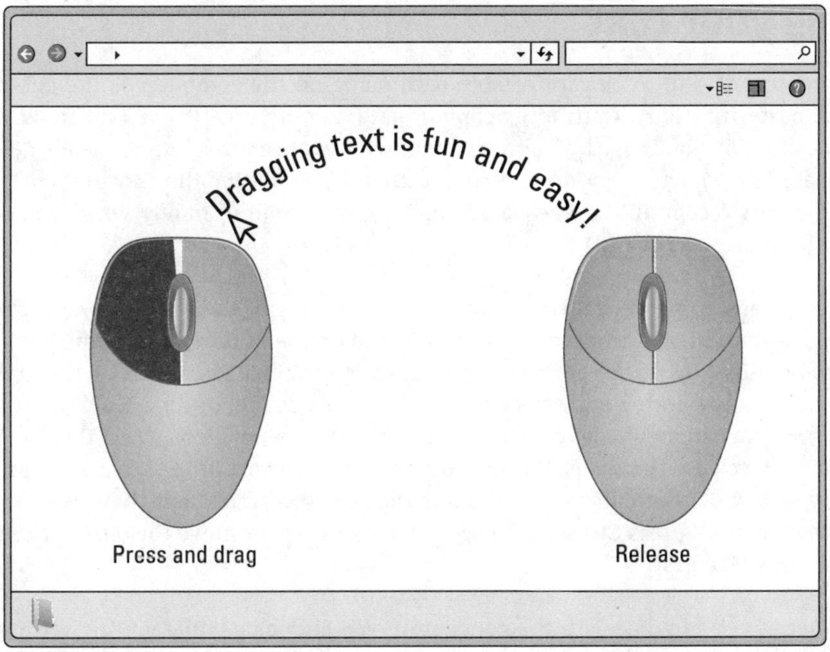

FIGURE A-3: Drag and drop objects by clicking and holding the left mouse button, moving it by dragging your cursor, and then letting go of the mouse button to release it in the desired location.

Dragging text is fun and easy!

Press and drag

Release

The second thing to note in Figure A-4 is a scroll bar on the right edge. It's the bar that runs up and down the right-hand side, with an arrow on either end and a darker section somewhere along its length. That bar tells you that you need to scroll up or down for more text (where there isn't enough content to create a new page or tab). To use your mouse to move the scroll bar up and down and make the screen move so you can see the additional text, simply click on the top or bottom of the bar. Alternatively, you can drag the light portion of the bar up or down for the same effect or use the scroll wheel on your mouse. When you're finished with the item, click on the Previous or Next buttons on the bottom right of the screen to go to a new or previous question.

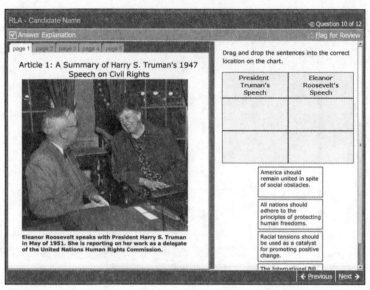

☑ Answer Explanation   ⚑ Flag for Review

page 1 | page 2 | page 3 | page 4 | page 5

Article 1: A Summary of Harry S. Truman's 1947 Speech on Civil Rights

Eleanor Roosevelt speaks with President Harry S. Truman in May of 1951. She is reporting on her work as a delegate of the United Nations Human Rights Commission.

Drag and drop the sentences into the correct location on the chart.

President Truman's Speech	Eleanor Roosevelt's Speech

America should remain united in spite of social obstacles.

All nations should adhere to the principles of protecting human freedoms.

Racial tensions should be used as a catalyst for promoting positive change.

The International Bill

← Previous | Next →

FIGURE A-4:
The tabs at the top left of the screen tell you that there's more text to read.

Editing your text

Another important skill to be comfortable with using on the computer is the cut-and-paste or copy-and-paste functions. Cutting or copying and pasting means you can move some text to another position on your page by highlighting it with your mouse. *Cutting* means deleting it from the original position, while *copying* means exactly that: You leave the text in its original location as well as insert a copy into a new location. That can come in handy when you're writing an Extended Response on the GED test.

To cut or copy and paste, move the cursor to the beginning of the text you want, click on it with the left mouse button, and then continue holding down the button as you drag the mouse across the text to highlight the entire portion you want to copy or cut. Then click on the highlighted text with the right mouse button and select *cut,* which means delete, or *copy.* Holding the right mouse button down, you can move the text in its entirety to a new position. When the text is where you want it, simply release the mouse button. For you expert word processors, you can also use the customary keyboard shortcuts. You highlight the text you want, and then use the keyboard to activate the function: press Ctrl + C for copy, Ctrl + X to cut, or move the cursor to a new location and press Ctrl + V to paste.

You also need to be familiar with the concept of *redo* and *undo* while you're writing and editing text. If you've used a word processor before, you know that those two little curved arrows at the top of the screen allow you to reverse an action. Those arrows are the Redo and Undo buttons. You have the option to use these buttons on the Extended Response sections and on the fill-in questions on the test.

Using the calculator

When you need a calculator to answer questions on the Mathematical Reasoning, Science, and Social Studies tests, a digital image of a calculator appears on screen, or you can bring a handheld TI-30XS Multiview Scientific Calculator if you test at a testing center. When the on-screen calculator is available, you will see a calculator button in the upper-left corner of your screen. You interact with the onscreen calculator the same way you would with one in your hand. The only difference is that you push the buttons with the mouse by moving the cursor over the appropriate buttons and then clicking. If you're unsure how to use that calculator, the test offers a cheat sheet with instructions. However, to save yourself precious time while taking the exam, get some practice beforehand; the test uses a Texas Instrument 30XS calculator (see Figure A-5). You can try out the on-screen calculator by logging into your account on ged.com. If you can afford it, you can buy the real thing for less than $20.

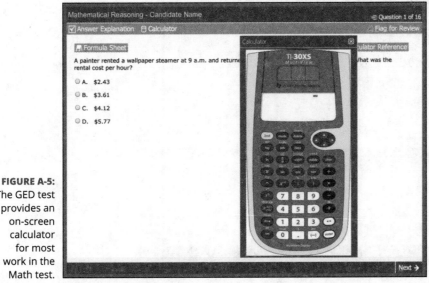

FIGURE A-5:
The GED test provides an on-screen calculator for most work in the Math test.

Finding math formulas and symbols

In the Mathematical Reasoning, Science, and Social Studies tests, you use formulas, and some questions require special symbols or signs. Don't worry — you don't need to memorize pages of formulas; the computerized GED test provides all the formulas you need in a handy, easy-to-access window (see Figure A-6). To access, click the Formula Sheet button in the upper left corner of your screen.

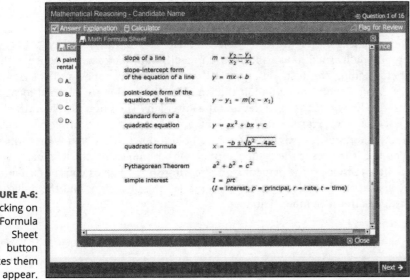

FIGURE A-6:
Clicking on the Formula Sheet button makes them appear.

You can also find the special symbols that aren't shown on your keyboard in the Symbols window by clicking the Symbol button at the top of the screen, as you can see in Figure A-7, clicking the symbol you want, and then clicking the Insert button.

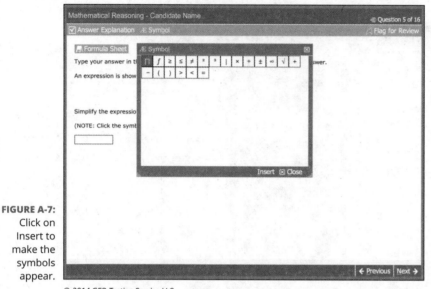

FIGURE A-7: Click on Insert to make the symbols appear.

Practicing Your Typing on a Keyboard

If you're more at home with a tablet or a mobile phone or you still remember (or use) your old typewriter fondly, you'll want to sit down at a computer and practice typing on a keyboard before you take the GED test. You don't need to become a typing master; as long as you can type with reasonable speed, you'll be fine. The only time when you need to do more than simply click with the mouse is on the Extended Response and fill-in questions, where you have to write either a short essay or a a few words or numbers.

Not being able to type may slow you down, so you should at least have a familiarity of where individual letters, punctuation, and numbers are located on the keyboard. For an example of a standard computer keyboard, check out Figure A-8. (*Note:* Standard North American keyboards aren't standard everywhere. If you learned to use a keyboard in a different language, practice with this form of keyboard before doing the test. Doing so will help you avoid typos and wasting time searching for letters, symbols, and punctuation that may not be in the accustomed locations.) Two keys you also need to know are the Shift key and the Enter key. The Enter key, identified with the word *Enter* or a hooked arrow, starts a new paragraph or line of text. The Shift key is identified with the word *Shift* or sometimes just an up arrow. You hold it down when you want to insert a capital letter, and you use it to access the symbols found with numbers on the keyboard. So, for example, pressing Shift + 5 produces the percent sign. Pressing Shift + 1 gives you the exclamation mark. The Shift key also accesses various punctuation marks, the plus sign, and the dollar sign. (The multiplication sign is in the Symbols window.)

FIGURE A-8:
Standard
North
American
keyboard,
like what
you'll see on
the comput-
erized GED
test.

© John Wiley & Sons, Inc.

Reading and writing on a computer screen is very different from reading and writing on paper. Studies have shown that people tend not to read as deeply when reading from a screen and aren't able to organize their thoughts as easily when writing on-screen. However, you'll have an eras-able tablet to jot down and organize ideas for your essay. Practice reading and writing on-screen before you take the GED test, especially if you're not accustomed to working that way. It, too, is a skill that improves with practice.

Index

About the Author

For over 25 years, **Tim Collins, PhD,** has specialized in materials development for the GED, and his books and media publications have helped countless learners pass this life-changing test.

Altogether, he has worked in the field of education for over 40 years, and he has taught learners of all ages and backgrounds from early childhood to adult. He began his career as a high school teacher in Morocco, where, as part of a school-wide improvement program, he helped his school reduce the number of drop-outs while aiding school-leavers pass the required graduation test. As a result of this community-wide effort, the graduation rate increased from one of the lowest in in the country to one of the highest. Since then, he has taught young children in Spain, university students in China, Spain, and the United States, and adult learners in the United States. Beginning in 1987, he began to specialize in materials development and worked for several major publishers.

Tim knows the challenges of pursuing education as an adult. While working full time, he completed his PhD at the University of Texas at Austin. After that, he worked as a professor at a major U.S. college of education for 15 years, where he helped prepare teachers to meet the challenges of today's elementary, middle school, and high school classrooms. Tim currently manages international education programs while continuing to develop materials that give adult learners the skills they need to succeed.

Dedication

This book is dedicated to adult learners everywhere. *You can do it!*

Author's Acknowledgments

Any book is always the result of the efforts of many. In this case, special thanks go to the authors of the prior editions of this book, Murray Shukyn, Dale Shuttleworth, and Akim Krull, whose original vision for this book has stood the test of time as the GED has gone through multiple revisions to become the challenging online exam we know today. Many people played key roles in the development of this newest edition, which has been thoroughly updated to reflect the latest changes to the GED test. I owe a debt of gratitude to several people at Wiley, including development editor Tim Gallan and acquisitions editor Greg Tubach. The eagle eye of copy editor Marylouise Wiack made every page better. Paul Buckley, a gifted high school math teacher, provided invaluable assistance by preparing the math online test. His math questions are thought-provoking and instructive. I'd also like to thank my agent, Grace Freedson, for her constant support. Finally, no acknowledgement would be complete without thanking Mary Jane Maples, who got me started in educational publishing so many years ago.

Publisher's Acknowledgments

Acquisitions Editor: Greg Tubach

Development Editor: Tim Gallan

Copy Editor: Marylouise Wiack

Technical Editor: Amy Nicklin

Production Editor: Mohammed Zafar Ali

Cover Image: © dusanpetkovic/Getty Images